Equal Opportunity in Education

A reader in social class and educational opportunity

edited by HAROLD SILVER

Methuen & Co Ltd
London

First published in 1973
by Methuen & Co Ltd
11 New Fetter Lane, London EC4
© *1973 by Harold Silver*
Printed in Great Britain by
Cox & Wyman Ltd
Fakenham, Norfolk

SBN (hardbound) 416 78530 1
SBN (paperback) 416 78540 9

Distributed in the USA by
HARPER & ROW PUBLISHERS INC.
BARNES & NOBLE IMPORT DIVISION

Contents

CONTENTS   vii

Editor's acknowledgements

My main debt in preparing this book has been to Judith Ryder, who has helped both in clarifying the issues and in making my attempted explanations more coherent. David Harris and Rob Walker have made valuable comments, and Pamela and Claire Silver have helped me to eliminate some of the wilder obscurities and errors.

Acknowledgements

The editor and publishers wish to thank the following for permission to reproduce material from the publications listed below:

George Allen & Unwin for 'Ability and opportunity in English education' by J. L. Gray and Pearl Moshinsky (in *Political Arithmetic* ed. Lancelot Hogben) and *Equality* by R. H. Tawney; the *Atlantic Monthly* and the author for 'Inequality: do schools make a difference?' by Godfrey Hodgson; Ed. J. Burrow & Co. Ltd for *Mass Education in England* by J. H. Garrett; the Critical Quarterly Society and the author for 'Comprehensives and equality: the quest for the unattainable' by Richard Lynn (in *Black Paper Two* ed. C. B. Cox and A. E. Dyson); Faber & Faber Ltd for *Education in an Industrial Society* by G. H. Bantock; the *Guardian* and the author for 'Expansion and equality' by A. H. Halsey (in the *Guardian* (25 April 1963)); Harper & Row Inc. for *Who Shall be Educated?* by W. Lloyd Warner, Robert J. Havighurst and Martin B. Loeb; Heinemann Educational Books Ltd for *Social Class and Educational Opportunity* by J. E. Floud (ed.), A. H. Halsey and F. M. Martin; HMSO for *The Education of the Adolescent* (Hadow Report), *Curriculum and Examinations in Secondary Schools* (Norwood

Report), *The New Secondary Education* by the Ministry of Education, *Early Leaving* by the Central Advisory Council for Education, *Circular 10/65* by the Department of Education and Science, *Children and their Primary Schools* (Plowden Report) and *Educational Priority* by A. H. Halsey; Hutchinson & Co. Ltd for 'Educational systems and selected consequences of patterns of mobility and non-mobility in industrial societies: a theoretical discussion' by Earl Hopper (in *Readings in the Theory of Educational Systems* ed. Earl Hopper); the Labour Party for *Secondary Education for All* by R. H. Tawney; Lawrence & Wishart Ltd, for 'Intelligence testing and the comprehensive school' in *Intelligence, Psychology and Education: a Marxist critique* by Brian Simon; Longman Group Ltd and Humanities Press Inc. for *Born and Bred Unequal* by George Taylor and N. Ayres and *From Birth to Seven* by Ronald Davie, Neville Butler and Harvey Goldstein; MacGibbon & Kee for *The Home and the School* by J. W. B. Douglas; Brian Simon for *Three Schools or One?* by Lady Simon of Wythenshawe; National Foundation for Educational Research and the National Children's Bureau for *A Pattern of Disadvantage* by David Donnison (ed.); Routledge and Kegan Paul Ltd for *Social Progress and Educational Waste* by Kenneth Lindsay and *Education and the Working Class* by Brian Jackson and Dennis Marsden; Routledge and Kegan Paul Ltd and Humanities Press Inc. for *Social Class and the Comprehensive School* by Julienne Ford and 'Social status and secondary education since the 1944 Act: some data for London' by H. T. Himmelweit (in *Social Mobility in Britain* ed. D. V. Glass); SPCK for *Education and Social Change* by F. Clarke; the author for *Social Class and Educational Adaptation* by D. F. Swift; Tavistock Ltd for 'An approach to the study of curricula as socially organized knowledge' by Michael F. D. Young (in *Knowledge, Education and Cultural Change* ed. Richard Brown): C. A. Watts & Co. Ltd for *Eleven-Plus and All That* by Flann Campbell, John Wiley & Sons Inc. for 'The Case of Sweden' (in *Educational Research and Educational Change* by Torsten Husén and Gunnar Boalt).

Editor's introduction

The discussion of education and social class has been the most prolonged educational issue of twentieth-century Britain. In its early
phases, particularly in the 1930s and 1940s, it was related closely to
psychological views of intelligence. From the 1950s it was the central
concern of the rapidly growing sociology of education. Philosophers
have been engaged in the discussion of the concepts, and the arguments in favour of wider opportunity have sometimes been conducted
in economic terms. Given the political repercussions of the discussion,
some of the most interesting recent literature has been produced by
political scientists. The record of the discussion is of major importance to the historian. Although the readings in this book lead into all
of these areas, our main interests here are the historical conditions in
which the issues have evolved, and the nature of the concepts under
discussion.

For most of this century the discussion of education in relation to
such concepts as 'equality', 'equality of opportunity', 'democracy' or
'social justice' has focused on the *structure* of the educational system,
and *access* by children from different social groups to its different
component parts. As early as the 1890s, in the context of two distinct
educational systems – elementary for working-class and secondary for
middle-class children – there were pressures within the labour movement for the adoption of the principle of equality of opportunity in
education. At the 1896 TUC, for example, a motion was put forward
urging 'that our education system should be completely remodelled
on such a basis as to secure the democratic principle of equality of
opportunity'. Although this was amended to read that the system
'should be reorganized upon a broader and more democratic basis',

the concept of equality of opportunity continued to be present in resolutions to future congresses.[1] It was not until after the First World War, however, that concern for social justice found major expression in educational terms, coupled with programmes for educational action and structural reforms to secure 'secondary education for all'.

The effective starting point for this movement is the beginning of the 1920s. The crucial figure in establishing and sustaining a new consciousness of the relationship between social injustice and the existing educational system was R. H. Tawney. Tawney wrote *Secondary Education for All* for the Labour Party in 1922, served on the epoch-making Hadow Committee which produced *The Education of the Adolescent* in 1926, and published his famous *Equality* in 1931. The discussion of equal opportunity in education began not in research but in socialist politics, in demands for an end to nine-teenth-century class assumptions. 'The hereditary curse upon English education is its organization upon lines of social class,' wrote Tawney in one of the angriest passages of *Equality*. Public opinion, he continued, was 'saturated with the influence of a long tradition of educational inequality'. The individual needs of children were not met because of 'the barbarous association of differences of educational opportunity with distinctions of wealth and social position'.[2] It is with the concepts of equality and equal opportunity, anger at social injustice and social waste, and attempts to demonstrate the relation-ship between educational underprivilege and social underprivilege that the earlier contributions (illustrated in section I) are mainly concerned. The aims being pursued were, in general, wider access for working-class children to grammar schools, and the creation of a new kind of secondary school (called senior or modern schools) for those who did not go to grammar schools. Under the Hadow scheme these aims were beginning to be implemented in some areas in the years up to the Second World War. What Tawney and the Labour Party were mainly anxious to achieve was 'the improvement of primary educa-tion and the development of public secondary education to such a point that all normal children, irrespective of the income, class, or

---

[1] Jack Schofield, 'The labour movement and educational policy 1900–1931' (Manchester M Ed thesis, 1964), I, pp. 58–9.
[2] R. H. Tawney, *Equality* (London, 1931), pp. 142–4. See pp. 51–4 below.

occupation of their parents, may be transferred at the age of eleven + from the primary or preparatory school to one type or another of secondary school, and remain in the latter till sixteen'.[3]

For a quarter of a century from the outbreak of the Second World War the contributors to the discussion were involved in investigating and explaining the precise nature of injustice in the educational and social structure, and in advocating alternative approaches. The primary concern of contributions such as most of those collected in section II was to undermine what had so far seemed to be psychological and sociological certainties. They presented a detailed analysis of the failure of British society to confront inequality in access to secondary and higher education, in spite of the reorganization that had occurred after the 1944 Education Act. The central target of attention was social bias in selection for secondary education. Floud, Halsey and Martin, in their *Social Class and Educational Opportunity* (1956) made the most influential of all the analyses of the continued social class differential in access to grammar schools, on the basis of a study of the relationship between entry to grammar schools by working-class and middle-class children in south-west Hertfordshire and Middlesborough. Basil Bernstein in the late 1950s and 1960s provided an influential theory of working-class and middle-class language codes to explain the poor performance of working-class children within the terms of reference laid down by the schools. The socially conditioned educational disabilities of working-class children became dominant features of educational debate and radical programmes. Early in this period, in a pioneer book which argued the case for comprehensive (or 'omnibus') schools, Lady Simon of Wythenshawe asked:

How can we best carry out the new duty to provide secondary education for *all* children over 12, according to their age, ability and aptitude? How can we combine this with ensuring real equality of educational opportunity? There are also some of us who are wondering how to organize the schools so as to bring about a more democratic state of society than now exists.[4]

[3] R. H. Tawney (ed.), *Secondary Education for All* (London, [1922]), p. 7.
[4] Lady Simon of Wythenshawe, *Three Schools or One?* (London, 1948), p. 7.

Eighteen years later, summarizing some of the findings of the period,
D. F. Swift began a research article:

> The basic facts of social class performance in school are so well
> known as hardly to need repeating. As all teachers know, the
> children who do the best work, are easiest to control and stimulate,
> make the best prefects, stay at school longest, take part in extra-
> curricular activities, finish school with the best qualifications
> and references and get into the best jobs, tend to come from the
> middle class. The relationship exists in the Junior School, manifests
> itself in the 11+ and seriously affects secondary education.

He had himself found 'that the children of middle class parents had
six times as good a chance of selection at 11+ as working class
children'.[5] In the two decades separating these statements the comprehensive school was the focal point of the programmes and reforms
which grew out of the increasingly sharp demonstration of how the
machinery of educational injustice worked. Parallel with, and partly
the result of, the kind of contributions included in section II were
sharp political and public controversies about comprehensive and
segregated secondary schools. At the same time there were attempts
(outstandingly by Robin Pedley)[6] to collate information about the
comprehensive schools that had been created in some areas after the
war.

This pattern of sociological and political analysis and debate was
not unique to Britain: extracts from United States and Swedish
material written in this period are included to indicate some of the
international dimensions of the discussion. In spite of the difficulties
of comparing the concepts, situations and data of different countries,
a sense of this dimension is important for two reasons. First, the
protagonists on both sides in Britain as elsewhere reached out for
support to experience wherever they could find it. Second, the basic
discussion abut injustice, élites and separate or common schooling
points towards social, philosophical and political positions that were

[5] D. F. Swift, 'Social class and achievement motivation', *Educational Research*, VIII (1965–6), p. 83.
[6] Pedley published an 'interim survey' of the *Comprehensive Schools To-day*
in 1954, and *Comprehensive Education: a new approach* in 1956. Halsey
reviewed Pedley's *The Comprehensive School*, published in 1963. See pp.
205–8 below.

to assume a real international momentum in radical movements in the 1960s.

By the mid-1960s the broad lines of the sociologists' investigations were familiar and influential. Political parties were responding, though to different extents, to the now long-standing demands, and to the research, experiments and models. The responses were different in different parts of the country. At the end of the 1960s three major developments emerged in research and discussion – and are illustrated in section III.

First, the interest in social class in broad terms began to be replaced by an emphasis on more detailed aspects of social structure, mainly the family. The work of the fifties and early sixties had considered the relationship between the family's economic and social status and educational opportunity. The family was investigated in this way mainly as the unit of social class differentiation. The Ministry of Education's *Early Leaving* report of 1954, for example, recognized and discussed the influence of the home environment on children at different ages. It stressed that this 'had not yet received adequate attention and urgently needs prolonged and thorough investigation' – research which the advisory council that produced the report considered beyond its means.[7] Elizabeth Fraser in 1959 produced one of the first important studies of *Home Environment and the School*, which aimed 'to determine to what extent the school progress of a child is related to factors in his home environment, and to compare this relationship with that existing between home environment and intelligence'; it indicated that the home environment was 'more clearly correlated with school progress than with intelligence'.[8] J. W. B. Douglas's *The Home and the School* in 1964 examined relationships between the family and children's attitudes and performance. It ended, however, with a plea for more research, so as 'to measure more fully the impact of the family on the early processes of learning and on the acquisition of incentives before children reach

[7] Ministry of Education, *Early Leaving* (London, 1954), p. 56. Floud, Halsey and Martin in 1956 also called for urgent investigation of 'the precise nature of the hindrances placed by their home background in the way of educating working-class children in grammar schools' (*Social Class and Educational Opportunity*, p. 148).

[8] Elizabeth Fraser, *Home Environment and the School* (London, 1959), p. 75.

xvi   EDITOR'S INTRODUCTION

school'[9] (a challenge which was taken up – for example by D. F. Swift). The Plowden Report on *Children and their Primary Schools* (1967) urged a more detailed concern with parental attitudes. Davie, Butler and Goldstein, in *From Birth to Seven* (1972), reported investigations into reading backwardness in relation to an intricate network of factors, including social class but also detailed aspects of family size, the position of children in the family, mother's health and sex differences. Work of this kind began from the broad concept of social class (what Swift called 'analytical abstractions from reality')[10] and moved on to new areas of detail.

Second, questions of inter- and intra-regional underprivilege were the subject of heightened interest. The concept of educational priority areas developed by the Plowden Committee was an important stimulus to this interest. So also were other schemes of aid to poor urban areas, the problems of concentrated immigrant populations arriving in the mid-1960s, and research into the difficulties and potential of the different economic planning regions. The Northern Economic Planning Council, covering areas with a long history of economic and educational backwardness, reported on education in this region in 1970 and stated bluntly that 'education is, in fact, the chief and most readily available catalyst of much-needed change in the region. But to carry out this task, it needs to be "geared up" in the same way as road construction has been.'[11] Educational expansion in the 1960s had failed to overcome problems left by decades of economic underprivilege. There was now increasing concern about the educational effects of differences in regional environments, regional spending, regional provision.

Third, under the influence of radical social and political theories, the attention of some sociologists began to focus on the failure of existing policies and programmes for structural reforms to achieve any fundamental change in relation to working-class children. Suspicions had been increasingly voiced about the ability of comprehensive schools to avoid using machinery (notably streaming) which

[9] J. W. B. Douglas, *The Home and the School* (London, 1964), p. 128.
[10] D. F. Swift, 'Social class and educational adaptation', in H. J. Butcher (ed.), *Educational Research in Britain* (London, 1968), p. 290. See p. 266 below.
[11] Northern Economic Planning Council, Report on Education. Part I: *Education up to 18 years of age* (Newcastle upon Tyne, 1970), p. 1.

replicated *within* schools the socially conditioned inequalities pre-viously existing *between* schools. The very sociological assumptions on which analyses and programmes had previously rested, it began to be argued, were inadequate – and this explained the inevitable failure of attempts to provide structural answers to problems which were really more fundamental and needed to be presented differently. The discussion, it was suggested, should move into the fields of the sociology of knowledge, the organization of knowledge in school curricula, and social control through the ordering of ideas. 'Without a theory of knowledge', said one such contributor, 'it is difficult to know what the stratification debate is about.'[12] Basil Bernstein opened one of the most important contributions to the new area of discussion with the statement:

> How a society selects, classifies, distributes, transmits, and evaluates the educational knowledge it considers to be public reflects both the distribution of power and the principles of social control. . . . British sociologists have fought shy of this question. As a result, the sociology of education has been reduced to a series of input-output problems; the school has been transformed into a complex organization or people-processing institution; the study of socialization has been trivialized.[13]

Implicit in the criticisms of the earlier concern with educational opportunity was a sense of problems that lay beyond its terms of reference. The critics were aware of social and cultural processes which helped to strengthen existing social class identities. This 'British perspective', says Ioan Davies, for example,

> is primarily concerned with who gets into the system. It stresses class factors, income factors and other elements of stratification. The system is examined – and conclusions drawn – largely from this perspective: if input suggests an unbalanced selection, then either the selection procedure must be changed (abolish 11 +) or else the institutions must be enlarged or made more 'open' (as with comprehensives). . . . In many respects this type of research

---

12 Ioan Davies, 'The management of knowledge', in Michael F. D. Young, *Knowledge and Control* (London, 1971), p. 268.
13 Basil Bernstein, 'On the classification and framing of educational know-ledge', in ibid., p. 47.

has been very important for collecting data, but again one may wonder whether it has done much more than improve our knowledge of social stratification and raise uncomfortable questions about the consequences of political policy.[14]

A theoretical framework was now being sought to replace what was considered the narrowly pragmatic or politically reformist sociology involved in earlier contributions on the subject of educational opportunity.

The readings in this book illustrate some of these differences of emphasis within and between periods. It will be easier to put these into perspective if we look first in more detail at the nineteenth century.

The outstanding feature of nineteenth-century educational history in Britain was the conscious establishment of two separate educational systems. The creation of an elementary school system for the children of the poor was an attempt to meet a new situation brought about by industrialization – the disruption of a traditional, rural-based social order. Cheap mass schooling ('monitorial' for the first half of the nineteenth century) was designed to provide basic literacy and to inculcate 'necessary' social and moral virtues. The 1870 Elementary Education Act, which supplemented the existing voluntary schools with rate-supported board schools, did not alter the elementary system's explicit identification with the children of the poor. In this situation those old endowed grammar schools which had been providing some 'elementary' schooling for local children began to shed this lower-level work and to aim at the higher standards of the more successful, more completely classical schools. The grammar schools were reformed, most notably by the Endowed Schools Act of 1869, in such a way as to ensure their efficiency as *secondary* schools – providing for the middle and upper echelons of the community. Gradations of quality and social composition in these and most of the public schools did not alter the fact of their identification with middle-class children. Victorian England knew that elementary education was for working-class children, and that the grammar schools were for middle-class children. This was as salient a fact of nineteenth-century England and Wales (the same would not be as

[14] Davies, 'The management of knowledge', p. 272.

true for Scotland) as the fact of class consciousness itself. Although most radical and working-class movements of the nineteenth century expressed educational ideals and criticized aspects of the voluntary and board schools, it was not the class basis of the two systems that they attacked. Their educational views and efforts were generally seen as part of a popular struggle to replace the whole social and political structure. Movements such as Owenite co-operation and Chartism were engaged in attempts to provide their own forms of education, for children and adults, as part of their vision of an 'alternative' society which would bypass, reform or overthrow industrial capitalism. Education was also seen in most working-class programmes, and in the activities of self-educated working men and working-class radicals, as the point of access to aspects of culture otherwise denied them – for example, Shakespeare, economic and political ideas, phrenology, history or nature study. Universal, free and compulsory elementary education became the main working-class demand up to and beyond the 1870 Education Act. Only rarely, at least in the first three-quarters of the nineteenth century, was there any working-class or radical discussion of reforms which would enable poor children in large numbers to gain access to grammar school and university education. The very concept of secondary education as a *stage* beyond elementary education was only beginning to take shape in the last quarter of the century.

The situation in which educational opportunity appeared on the agenda in a new sense was created by the school boards and by international industrial competition. Some of the school boards began to confront the problem of the needs of the older and abler elementary school children, and evolved *within the elementary system* forms of para-secondary education – senior classes, senior tops, higher-grade schools and evening classes. Although these still confirmed the separateness of working-class education, they presented a challenge to the grammar schools, and were seen as undermining the traditional classical and academic emphases of 'genuine' secondary education. At the same time, industrial competition from countries such as Germany, whose progress was demonstrably based on a better system of elementary and technical education, led to public finance becoming available in Britain from the end of the 1890s. These and other resources in the hands of the new

county and county borough authorities led to the first important
development of a scholarship system for poor, able children from the
elementary schools. The scholarship 'ladder' or bridge was erected,
and the 'free place' system of 1907 followed. The 1902 Education
Act had given responsibility for both elementary and secondary
education to the councils, and under the 1907 arrangements secondary schools in receipt of public funds had to provide not less than a
quarter of their places free of charge to children from elementary
schools.

The equality of opportunity that the TUC had discussed in the
1890s could now be, and was, discussed in a different setting. A
small fraction of working-class children was now reaching the
grammar school, and manifestly *unequal* opportunity was being
sharply demonstrated. The existence of a scholarship ladder also
began to attract more middle-class children into the elementary
schools, resulting in a problem of greater class differentiation *within*
the contingent of children going from elementary to grammar
schools. We shall trace these developments further at appropriate
points in future sections. One final indication of the scale of the
developments in the early twentieth century can be made here. The
Board of Education estimated that even in 1907 children from public
elementary schools constituted 'rather more than half the pupils in
the (grammar) schools, those of them who paid fees and those who
did not being about equal in number. But while some schools consisted almost entirely of such children, others had few or none of
them, and their incursion on a large scale was dreaded.' In 1930 a
committee reviewing the position set alongside this estimate the
fact that in 1927–8

> nearly 72 per cent of the pupils admitted had been in public
> elementary schools, and the great majority of them took up free
> places. No less than 42 per cent of all the places in recognized
> secondary schools were free of fees. ... To-day about 64,000
> pupils proceed annually from elementary to secondary schools,
> about 38,000 of them as the result of competitive examination.

The committee went on to quote from the Manchester education
officer, who had written in 1924 'that at no period since 1902 has
the provision for further education kept pace with the demand for it,

and at the present time, in spite of the greatly increased provision of the last ten years, there are probably more suitable pupils demanding further education and failing to get it than at any time since the State assumed responsibility for education'.[15] It is against this background of gradually increasing opportunity for elementary school children to obtain a grammar school education (or 'secondary', 'further' or 'higher' education – the words were interchangeable), and awareness of the large numbers who were failing to get it, that the discussion illustrated in this book begins. The demand was increasing, and the total number of children transferring at eleven also contained a growing number of middle-class children following this route. A national figure of 64,000 children in 1930, 38,000 of them via competitive examination, indicates overall the very modest number of working-class children able to reach secondary education at this point.

The two nineteenth-century systems were no longer totally separate, but the 'ladder' between them had not altered their basic configuration. In *Secondary Education for All* Tawney describes this situation as 'educationally unsound and socially obnoxious'.[16]

(ii)

'Equality' unqualified by an 'of . . .' is perhaps a meaningless term in the discussion of education. In its broad political and philosophical contexts it has value. Equality before the law, equal pay for equal work, racial equality – concepts such as these can be both precise ideals and practical politics. The removal or diminution of inequality is an accessible concept in various areas of human experience. Equality is a useful concept in education only in qualified forms. Equality of treatment by the educational system could have various limited meanings – including the equal right to attend school (though this immediately raises further problems about differences between schools, and the purposes to which attendance is put). A

[15] Joint Advisory Committee of the Association of Education Committees and the National Union of Teachers, *Examinations in Public Elementary Schools* (London, [1930]), pp. 22–3. The quotations are from Board of Education pamphlet No. 50, *Recent Development of Secondary Schools in England and Wales*, and Spurley Hey, *Central Schools*.
[16] Tawney, *Secondary Education for All*, p. 11.

discussion of 'equal education' – equal in the sense of 'identical' in both quality and quantity – is difficult to envisage in any total sense. Even 'equality of', notably of opportunity, is attacked by critics as a muddled concept which produces educational institutions aiming to do the wrong things for the wrong people. 'We can't,' says Professor Bantock, 'perpetually live in an *Alice of Wonderland* world where all the creatures are to have a prize.'[17]

The concept of equality of opportunity is a more restricted one than that of equality. It implies open access, but raises the further question – access to what? In the past half century or so educationists and politicians have framed two different answers with regard to secondary education. First, they have postulated access to different kinds of secondary school, parallel in status, and 'appropriate' to the children entering them. Tawney, the labour movement generally, *Secondary Education for All* and the Hadow Committee firmly held this view in the 1920s. Most local authorities interpreted the 1944 Act and its provision for secondary education for all children according to their 'ages, aptitudes and abilities' to mean this. Ellen Wilkinson and George Tomlinson, Labour's education ministers in the post-war Labour government, believed this, and this view was strongly held in the Labour Party until the 1960s. It was increasingly accepted in the Conservative Party, in response to the comprehensive policies evolving on the political Left. Only slowly were the difficulties of achieving parallel status for grammar and secondary modern schools, and social inequalities inherent in selection for 'appropriate' schools, seen to be weaknesses in this interpretation of equal opportunity. Second, and most strongly in the 1950s and early 1960s, educationists and politicians have postulated equality of access not to an appropriate school, but to an appropriate education within a common, comprehensive school (though they at first paid little attention to the implications of different approaches to the internal organization of such schools).

For reluctant egalitarians a midway position appeared tenable, with a 'mixed' system – selective grammar schools alongside non-selective comprehensive schools – a situation which became increasingly common in the 1960s. This view gained ground in the

[17] G. H. Bantock, *Education in an Industrial Society* (London, 1963), p. 186. See p. 216 below.

early 1960s, in response to mounting pressure within the Labour Party for commitment to a completely comprehensive programme. In the Labour Party it was an effort at compromise; in the Conservative Party it was an attempt to balance the principle of equal opportunity against the concepts of 'freedom' and 'democracy'. There is an interesting similarity between the two situations. Those who held this 'mixed' view were willing, in the final analysis, to abandon the concept of equal opportunity altogether, as being incompatible with British educational traditions and ideals of democracy. The upholders of the second, 'comprehensive', view of equal opportunity – and this became true of the Labour government in office from 1964 to 1970 – considered that a full system of comprehensive schools, with the abolition of the grammar schools and of selection, matched in practice the principle of equal opportunity, offering by definition equal access to an appropriate education.

From the late 1960s, however, a third interpretation of the concept became current in Britain, largely under the stimulus of the Plowden Report. As early as 1963 A. H. Halsey was expressing the view that equality as a slogan of reform had failed. In 1972 he wrote in *Educational Priority* that 'the essential fact of twentieth-century educational history is that egalitarian policies have failed'.[18] A more radical interpretation of equal opportunity was being sought. In an unequal society, it was argued, equality of opportunity could only have meaning if those who began with unequal chances had *unequal* support from the educational system. The underprivileged, insisted the Plowden Report, needed *more* money spent on their education, *better* primary schools, a *larger* number of teachers and helpers than did other children. The concept of educational priority areas and schools was the central feature of the Plowden recommendations. The Plowden phrase 'positive discrimination' passed into the current language of education. The paradox within the concept of equality of opportunity was demonstrated – it was shown that opportunity meant no more than access, and that equal access was not as egalitarian a principle as its proponents had intended. Equality of opportunity, it was explained, meant equality of access *plus* positive discrimination.

[18] 'Expansion and Equality', the *Guardian* (25 April 1963); *Educational Priority*, I. *E.P.A. Problems and Policies* (London, 1972), p. 6. See pp. 205 and 346 below.

The focus of attention in the discussion was now moving, therefore, from secondary school structures to the primary school and to pre-school experience.

The interpretations, research and policies of the 1950s and 1960s raise the question of how far education can at all 'compensate' for social handicap. American experience of early and pre-schooling experiments in the 1960s proved disappointing. The concepts involved in these projects and in British thinking were attacked by Basil Bernstein in 1970:

> The concept, 'compensatory education', serves to direct attention away from the internal organisation and the educational context of the school, and focus our attention on the families and children. 'Compensatory education' implies that something is lacking in the family, and so in the child. ... It follows, then, that the school has to 'compensate' for the something which is missing in the family, and the children are looked at as deficit systems. If only the parents were interested in the goodies we offer, if only they were like middle-class parents, then we could do our job. Once the problem is seen even implicitly in this way, then it becomes appropriate to coin the terms 'cultural deprivation', 'linguistic deprivation', and so on. ... If children are labelled 'culturally deprived', then it follows that the parents are inadequate ...[19]

Bernstein was directing attention to questions of values, knowledge and assumptions that had been inadequately examined in the 1950s and 1960s. The work of these decades which marshalled data of unequal opportunity rested on simple, sometimes unspoken beliefs that the revealed data could and would be followed by social action to remedy the inequalities.

The sociologists, and even the politicians, concerned expressed in only vague terms their view of the society in which reform was possible and to which it would contribute. C. A. R. Crosland, one of the Labour Party's main spokesmen on education in this period, wrote in 1956 about the comprehensive school that 'all schools will more and more be socially mixed; all will provide routes to the

---

[19] Basil Bernstein, 'Education cannot compensate for society', *New Society* (26 February 1970), p. 344. The American experience is discussed in Halsey, *Educational Priority*, chapter 2.

Universities and to every type of occupation, from the highest to the lowest. ... Then, very slowly, Britain may cease to be the most class-ridden country in the world.'[20] Raymond Williams, a leading figure in the new Left during the same period, postulated in 1961 'a public education designed to express and create the values of an educational democracy and a common culture'.[21] Jackson and Marsden's *Education and the Working Class*, in 1962, after pressing for 'open' schools through the abandonment of selection at eleven and acceptance of the comprehensive principle, concluded: 'Of course this would not solve everything. Social inheritance and deprivation would not be abolished with the abolition of selection and rejection. ... But a huge amount would be achieved by shared schooling in a "national society", and the way to richer progress at last opened.'[22] There are major differences between some of these expressed ideals, and between the levels of optimism of, say, Crosland on the one hand and Jackson and Marsden on the other. The most prevalent view among the sociologists was that the recognition of selection as a mechanism of educational injustice would enable a 'national society' to be at least more nearly achieved. Not all the proponents retained a firm confidence in the ability of the comprehensive schools to act as an effective weapon of greater social equality. In 1963 A. H. Halsey, one of the central figures involved, was significantly using the past tense when discussing Robin Pedley's egalitarian views on the comprehensive school: 'I used to think that the comprehensive school was a major instrument of egalitarian reform in education.'[23] Bernstein was doubting in 1958 how big a role the schools could play in the reordering of society, but his discussion indicates a view of that society: 'the integration of the lower-working class into the wider society raises critical problems of the nature of society and the extent to which the school, by itself, can accelerate the process of assimilation.'[24] 'Educational democracy',

[20] Quoted from Julienne Ford, *Social Class and the Comprehensive School* (London, 1969), p. 123.
[21] Raymond Williams, *The Long Revolution* (London, 1961), p. 155.
[22] Brian Jackson and Dennis Marsden, *Education and the Working Class* (London, 1962), pp. 224–5.
[23] Halsey, 'Expansion and equality'. See p. 205 below.
[24] Basil Bernstein, 'Social class and linguistic development: a theory of social learning', in A. H. Halsey, Jean Floud and C. Arnold Anderson (eds.), *Education, Economy, and Society* (New York, 1961), p. 310.

'common culture', 'national society', 'integration of the lower-working class into the wider society' – such are some of the declared ideals or objectives. Sociologists in the late 1950s and early 1960s did not feel the need to spell out the relationship between education and such concepts in any detail, because these went together with another set of concepts which were more publicly acceptable – those relating to economic policy.

The discussion of injustice was easily translated into terms of economic inefficiency. Injustice, as Kenneth Lindsay and others had pointed out in the 1920s and 1930s, resulted in 'educational waste'. A study of the experience of national service recruits in the Crowther Report on *15 to 18* (1959) offered detailed evidence of the amount of untapped ability in the lower strata of the social scale. Douglas took up this theme of waste in *The Home and the School* and attacked the notion that there was a limited national 'pool of talent' available. In 1963 both the Robbins Report on *Higher Education* and the Newsom Report on the education of children of average and less than average ability, *Half our Future*, expressed the same view: 'there is very little doubt that among our children there are reserves of ability which can be tapped, if the country wills the means . . . in the national economic interest we cannot afford to go on waiting.'[25] In an introduction to Douglas's book David Glass wrote:

> Modifying and postponing selection in this way would make it possible to offer to a much larger fraction of the new generations the kind of education which should help them to face an inevitably more complex technology and to meet with greater competence the responsibilities of citizenship. Of course the cost would be great. But if we are an affluent society, what better use could be made of part of our affluence – as well as part of our extended expectation of life – than in applying the foundations for a more instructed citizenship.[26]

The sociological studies of the 1950s were rooted in the work on social mobility being conducted at the London School of Economics under Professor Glass, who edited *Social Mobility in Britain* in

[25] Ministry of Education, *Half Our Future* (London, 1963), pp. 6–7.
[26] Douglas, *The Home and the School*, pp. xxiii–xxiv.

1954. Floud, Halsey and Martin were all associated with this research, and their crucial book *Social Class and Educational Opportunity* was announced in Glass's 1954 volume as in preparation under the title of *Secondary Education and Social Mobility*.[27]

Much of the subsequent work in this field bears the imprint of the early demographic and economic context of the research. Jean Floud concluded her contribution to the 1954 book (a description of the educational experience of the adult population of England and Wales as sampled in 1949) by emphasizing that 'the 1944 Act . . . provides a framework of reform. It constitutes a promise of change in the nature and distribution of educational opportunity which, if it materializes, will almost certainly be accompanied by considerable changes both in the social hierarchy of occupations and in the degree of mobility within and between occupations.'[28] At a European conference on 'ability and educational opportunity' in 1961 she read a paper on 'Social class factors in educational achievement'. The problem facing the conference, in her view, was, 'given that in a modern economy the quality and efficiency of the working population very largely depend on the educational system, how can we secure a qualified, fluid and economically distributed labour force?' The educational system of most European countries, she pointed out, had 'grown up in the image of out-moded social class systems', but now 'the social role of the secondary schools as agents of interchange between the classes (social mobility) has become of considerable importance'. Her argument concluded:

> A modern economy depends on maximizing the educational output of every individual, which is to say that the aim of policy must be to maximize the supply of and the demand for educational facilities . . . social investigators could profitably and economically devote themselves to more complex and intensive research into the workings of the processes of social selection and differentiation through education which largely determine its efficiency in relation to the economy and policy of a modern industrial society.[29]

This explanation of what social investigators could profitably do, and

[27] David Glass (ed.), *Social Mobility in Britain* (London, 1954), p. 160n.
[28] ibid., p. 123.
[29] A. H. Halsey (ed.), *Ability and Educational Opportunity* (OECD, 1961), pp. 91, 95, 108–9.

the linking of selection purely with economic efficiency, are not un-typical. Views about mobility and economic efficiency, it is clear, were easier to explain, and could be more immediately influential, than views about an egalitarian society. Other European contributors to this discussion made it clear that the twin argument appealed to them also: a Swedish paper on 'Reserves of ability', for example, began by saying that

> the interest in higher education in modern society springs from two sources. One is of ethical origin and is related to the growing belief that every individual, regardless of his social status and origin, should be given equal opportunity for education up to the highest level. The other is economic and has its origin in the recognition that qualified manpower is a fundamental factor of production.[30]

The argument from two premises meant that the politically more difficult part of it was conducted publicly in terms of the easier part. Equal opportunity as an ideal related to a more just society could easily be narrowed into a search for politically acceptable arguments for the improvement of scientific, technological and technical man-power. Halsey has since written:

> What, then, are the sought ends in the politics of education in modern Britain? The dominant slogans are combinations of efficiency and equality. Efficiency for modernity. Equality for efficiency and justice. But both the meaning of these combined ends and the means postulated as adequate to their attainment remain dubious and confused. Thus the combination of equality of educational opportunity with the goal of national efficiency has led to policies designed to create and maintain a meritocracy – a principle which by no means commands universal acceptance.[31]

The importance of all these interpretations of the concept of equality of opportunity is that they were based on the rational pur-suit of data which would explain inequality – and which, like the work of social investigators in Britain from the late nineteenth century,

---

[30] P. de Wolff and K. Härnqvist, 'Reserves of ability: size and distribution', in ibid., p. 137.
[31] Halsey, *Educational Priority*, p. 6. See p. 346 below.

would demonstrate reality to a society that was oblivious of it. If the work was pragmatic and conducted within narrow theoretical frames of reference, it had one overriding merit. The American sociologist, C. Wright Mills, in a discussion of another difficult, and related, concept – that of democracy – pointed to the fact that neither the United States nor any other society was 'altogether democratic'. By using reason, however, 'we are trying to act in a democratic manner in a society that is not altogether democratic. But we are acting as if we were in a fully democratic society, and by doing so, we are attempting to remove the "as if".' He maintained that 'the problem of the social sciences as a prime carrier of reason in human affairs is in fact a major problem of democracy today'.[32] Even if the aims of the sociologists in the 1950s and 1960s were 'dubious and confused' they were also, it can be argued, the 'prime carriers' of reason, attempting at an important moment in social and educational change to remove the 'as if'.

(III)

T. H. Marshall, in a discussion of 'citizenship and social class' in 1949 described the concentration of social mobility into the early years of schooling, in connection with selective processes:

> The right of the citizen in this process of selection and mobility is the right to equality of opportunity. Its aim is to eliminate hereditary privilege. .... Equality of opportunity is offered to all children entering the primary schools, but at an early age they are usually divided into three streams – the best, the average and the backward. Already opportunity is becoming unequal, and the children's range of chances limited. About the age of eleven they are tested again. .... Classification follows for distribution into the three types of secondary school. Opportunity becomes still more unequal, and the chance of further education has already been limited to a select few. Some of these, after being tested again, will go on to receive it.[33]

[32] C. Wright Mills, *The Sociological Imagination* (New York, 1959; 1967 edition), pp. 189–90.
[33] T. H. Marshall, *Sociology at the Crossroads and other essays* (London, 1963), p. 114.

In spite of its sceptical tone, this passage assumes – as did most people in the 1940s – that these stages of selection, whatever other disadvantage they might have, had the advantage of 'the elimination of hereditary privilege'. What Marshall missed in his description of the 'meritocratic' process at work was the built-in situation of social class handicap, the continued operation of inequalities not of individual *talent* but of social class. The educational handicaps which resulted from continued social inequalities were to receive close attention in the following decades. So was the very notion of an intellectual élite, a 'meritocracy'. This concept was satirized by Michael Young in *The Rise of the Meritocracy* in 1958, when he described, as from the middle of the twenty-first century, the fundamental change which appeared to have begun by the 1960s: 'intelligence has been redistributed between the classes, and the nature of the classes changed. The talented have been given the opportunity to rise to the level which accords with their capacities, and the lower classes consequently reserved for those who are also lower in ability.'[34]

Some of the underlying assumptions and surrounding difficulties in defining and manipulating the term 'social class' emerge in these documents. The concept is interpreted in so many ways that it is frequently suggested that it no longer has a meaning or a place in social analysis; it is equally frequently retrieved for discussion as a concept and an explanation of social reality. The extraordinary divergences in structuring a picture of that reality can be judged from two passages which, only five years apart, attempt to discuss something like the same social phenomenon. In 1966, in a book on *The New Classes*, Robert Millar wrote:

> The British class system is in a process of radical change. No longer is it simply a matter of a small minority drifting slowly from one recognized class to another. The changes at work are transforming the traditional system into something qualitatively different . . . the old class lines are not crumbling as much as becoming irrelevant. In the socially-fluid society of the Sixties new lines are being drawn which owe little to the old criteria of

[34] Michael Young, *The Rise of the Meritocracy 1870–2033* (London, 1958; 1961 edition), p. 14.

accent, social behaviour and family background. There is forming at all levels of society an aristocracy of achievement which has little in common with the hereditary hierarchy ... [but] we are still in a state of transition from a social stratification based on birth to one based on money and achievement.[35]

Alongside this vision of a socially fluid, meritocratic society in which old class lines are becoming irrelevant, we can place a passage from Barbara Wootton's *Contemporary Britain*:

> Today a miner's son can not only hold exalted political office, but can also rank as a distinguished historian and move in highly cultivated circles in the upper strata of British society, as Roy Jenkins has done; but this does not mean that the men who are still working at the coal face and the members of the intellectual élite normally entertain one another at dinner, still less that they habitually intermarry or have equal opportunities of professional advancement. A rigid class structure is not incompatible with a considerable measure of individual mobility.[36]

This juxtaposition, and the prolonged and detailed debate it reflects, is important in arriving at judgements about the social reality, and about the observers' personal construction of pictures of that reality. The class relationships of the nineteenth century were vividly clear to the participants. The class relationships of the twentieth century have become blurred because new occupations have not fitted snugly into old definitions; new wage, housing and other hierarchies have taken shape. In a multiracial society questions of class have also become enmeshed with those of race. Within marxism, and between marxism and its critics, controversy has waxed and waned, and attempts have been made to redefine or sharpen some of the economic and sociological concepts used. The discussion of social class has been carried into subtler analyses of social stratification in a variety of forms. To most of the contributors to the discussion in this book the concept of class has, however, been acceptable in one guise or another. Most of the research has explicitly accepted the concept, and would agree with Barbara Wootton that 'a rigid class structure

---

[35] Robert Millar, *The New Classes* (London, 1966), pp. 18–19.
[36] Barbara Wootton, *Contemporary Britain* (London, 1971), pp. 20–1.

is not incompatible with a considerable measure of individual mobility'. D. F. Swift, for example, wrote in a research article that education could be seen

> as one of the methods by which the social class system perpetuates itself whilst providing for some social mobility. That is, to the extent that the values and skills of one social class are represented in the normative and behavioural requirements of the school system, children from that social class will be at an advantage. In this way social mobility is checked.[37]

The definitions of class rest in some cases on occupational or other structures, in others on consciousness; the determinants of class are differently assessed; the boundaries are differently established. For most of the sociologists who have analysed the mechanisms of inequality or social control through education, the concept of class has remained an essential instrument even when they have felt the need to qualify previously accepted usages of the term. A quotation used in Swift's article in section III explains how central this concept is to the discussion illustrated in this book:

> social class has proved to be so useful a concept because it refers to more than simply educational level, or occupation, or any of the large number of correlated variables. It is so useful because it captures the reality that the intricate interplay of all these variables creates different basic conditions of life at different levels of the social order. Members of different social classes, by virtue of enjoying (or suffering) different conditions of life, come to see the world differently – to develop different conceptions of social reality, different aspirations and hopes and fears, different conceptions of the desirable.[38]

The collection of readings which follows is concerned, then, with the workings of the public system of education, and with views of the operation of the machinery of attribution of working-class children to positions within the system. It examines roughly three phases of

---

[37] D. F. Swift, 'Meritocratic and social class selection at age eleven', *Educational Research*, VIII (1965–6), p. 66.
[38] Swift, 'Social class and educational adaptation', p. 290. See p. 266 below.

the discussion: the first is from 1920 to the end of the Second World War, the second takes in mainly the 1950s and early 1960s, the third covers the period from 1964. The discussion represented here does not embrace the question of the independent schools. Although there have been two attempts by official committees to establish a relationship between the public schools and the state system (by the McNair Committee on the public schools in 1944 and the Public Schools Commission which reported in 1968), the independent schools have remained to all intents and purposes inaccessible to working-class children; although this is an 'inequality of opportunity' it is of a different order from the one mainly discussed in this book, and raises a complex of issues of a different kind.

The documents included represent different types and levels of contribution to the discussion. Some are based on detailed programmes of original research; others were not seminal at the time, but indicate clearly the focus of attention at that point; some are reports and surveys which use familiar data and extend the argument; others illustrate the background of polemic. Not all the data used in these extracts have the same status of validity, and one of the problems in debates of this kind is to assess the reliability of information and judge the purposes which underlie comment. The methodology and assumptions behind evidence produced need to be examined – including for example the validity of researchers' assumptions about family background or behaviour, about what is 'normal' and what is 'deviant'. If a historical sequence of other people's evidence and angles of vision makes it easy for us to enjoy the luxury of hindsight, it does not make it less necessary for us to scrutinize the evidence and be conscious of our own angle of vision.

NOTE ON THE EXTRACTS

All omissions within extracts are indicated by marks of omission. Footnotes and references have not been reproduced unless their presence is necessary for an understanding of the text. For full bibliographical references, readers should consult the original texts – publication details of which are indicated in all cases.

CHRONOLOGY

1918   Education Act (Fisher Act)
1926   *The Education of the Adolescent* (Hadow Report)
1931   *The Primary School* (second Hadow Report)
1932   Replacement of 'free place' by 'special place' system
1933   *Infant and Nursery Schools* (third Hadow Report)
1936   Education Act
1938   *Secondary Education with Special Reference to Grammar Schools and Technical High Schools* (Spens Report)
1943   *Curriculum and Examinations in Secondary Schools* (Norwood Report)
1944   Education Act (Butler Act)
       The Public Schools and the General Educational System (Fleming Report)
       Teachers and Youth Leaders (McNair Report)
1947   School leaving age raised to fifteen
1954   *Early Leaving* Report
1959   *15 to 18* (Crowther Report)
1960   *Secondary School Examinations other than the GCE* (Beloe Report)
1963   *Half Our Future* (Newsom Report)
       Higher Education (Robbins Report)
1965   *The Organisation of Secondary Education* (circular 10/65)
1967   *Children and their Primary Schools* (Plowden Report)
1968   Public Schools Commission, *First Report*
1970   Public Schools Commission, *Second Report* (on independent day schools and direct grant schools)
       The Organisation of Secondary Education (circular 10/70)
1972   School leaving age raised to sixteen
       Teacher Education and Training (James Report)
       Education: A Framework for Expansion (government white paper)

I

Secondary education for all? 1922-47

I

I

Secondary education for all?   1922-47

Although the 1902 Education Act and the free place regulations of
1907 increased the numbers of elementary school children able to
obtain a grammar school education, the situation was not dramatically
changed. More middle-class as well as working-class children benefited from the expansion of secondary education by local authorities
under the 1902 Act. It was common for working-class children to be
unable to take up free places because maintenance grants were not
sufficient, because children needed to go out to work and contribute
as soon as possible to the family budget, or because the middle-class
image of the grammar schools was unattractive to working-class
parents. The rate of early leaving among working-class children in
grammar schools was high. Pressures from working-class organizations were directed towards an increase in the number of secondary
school places and better maintenance awards, the raising of the
school-leaving age nationally, and provisions for continued part-time
education for young employees. The 1918 Act raised the leaving age
to fourteen, and provided for a system of part-time education to
sixteen and later to eighteen – though this plan for continuation
schools was not implemented.

By the time the Hadow Committee reported on *The Education of
the Adolescent* in 1926 public opinion was awakening to injustices
and wastefulness in the existing system, whereby only a small proportion of children made the transition to secondary education. The
state of public opinion in 1925 can be judged from an official report
on the training of elementary school teachers published in that year:

> Elementary schools have long ceased to constitute the whole field
> included in the national system. The tendency is rather to regard
> the system of national education as expressing the effort made

by the community to fulfil what is recognized to be the social
duty of providing adequate opportunities for the fullest possible
development of those who have not yet begun to render service to
the community in their capacity as individual members of society.
For such an outlook national education is one problem with one
aim, and its divisions correspond rather with stages of the individual's development than with kinds of schools as they exist. ...
As they are organized at present Elementary and Secondary
Schools overlap.[1]

The ideal of making the public system of education correspond to
these 'stages of the individual's development' was to dominate educational discussion and efforts until after the Second World War. It
had become the policy of the labour movement generally, expressed
most eloquently by R. H. Tawney. It was embodied in the Hadow
Report, and was accepted by psychologists, social investigators and
official committees. As J. H. Garrett's view of the Hadow Committee shows, however, the aim of extending educational opportunity
was not – and never has been – expressed without strong opposition.

The fundamental Hadow proposal to remodel elementary and
secondary education into a single, end-on system of primary and
secondary schools began to be acted on in many parts of the country
during the late 1920s and 1930s, with some encouragement from the
Board of Education. Financial obstacles, and difficulties in involving
the voluntary schools in such reorganization, resulted in slow progress
being made: by 1938 some 63 per cent of children over the age of
eleven were in 'reorganized' schools. The concept of 'stages' of
development in children and schooling, however, raised the problem
of selection for secondary schools. Working-class and educational
bodies had in general accepted the need for different kinds of secondary school, and the process of selecting children for grammar school
places became increasingly important. The distinctions between
types of secondary school were reinforced by psychologists who, from
the beginning of the century, had been asserting with growing confidence that it was possible to measure intelligence scientifically and
therefore to allocate children to the right kind of secondary school.
In the 1930s intelligence testing gradually became accepted as a key

[1] Board of Education, *Report of the Departmental Committee on the Training
of Teachers for Public Elementary Schools* (London, 1925), pp. 152-3.

element in the selection process. The Spens Report on *Secondary Education* (1938) based its analysis of secondary education on the view that 'intellectual development during childhood appears to progress as if it were governed by a single central factor, usually known as "general intelligence", which may be broadly described as innate all-round intellectual ability. . . . Our psychological witnesses assured us that it can be measured approximately by means of intelligence tests.'[2] Since more specific, environmentally influenced aptitudes – the psychologists affirmed – became prominent after the age of eleven, the existing system of transfer at eleven was obviously justified. The Norwood Report on *Curriculum and Examinations in Secondary Schools* (1943) distinguished unhesitatingly between different 'varieties of capacity' in children: there were pupils who were 'interested in learning for its own sake', those 'whose interests and abilities lie markedly in the field of applied science or applied art' and those who deal 'more easily with concrete things than with ideas'. It therefore strongly supported the existing division of secondary schools into grammar, technical and modern schools.

From a number of quarters, however, doubts about the division of secondary education, processes of selection, and the justice of the new organizational basis were beginning to be expressed. Research workers like Gray and Moshinsky began to point to the unequal *social* distribution of children from different classes in the different kinds of secondary school. Within the labour movement views were being expressed about the inadequacy of the demand of 'secondary education for all', and about the fairness of selection at eleven. Leah Manning, a Labour MP, said in the House of Commons in 1931 that 'there are no means of telling at that early and tender age what a child is going to be'. In 1937 another Labour MP, Lees-Smith, pointed out that 'we talk of class distinctions and how to get rid of them, but a new class distinction is arising, namely, the distinction between those who pass an academic examination at the age of eleven and those who do not pass it'.[3] Support for the idea of 'common' secondary schooling increased during the war.

[2] Board of Education, *Report of the Consultative Committee on Secondary Education* (London, 1938), p. 123.

[3] The quotations are from D. W. Dean, 'The political parties and the development of their attitude to educational problems from 1918 to 1942' (London, M Phil thesis, 1968), p. 139.

The 1944 Education Act enshrined the doctrine of phases of education, with secondary education for all according to age, aptitude and ability. Most local authorities interpreted this to mean the tripartite system of different types of school, and the post-war Labour Ministers of Education did the same. Ellen Wilkinson defended the publication by the Ministry of Education in 1945 of *The Nation's Schools*, which justified the tripartite system; a revised version, *The New Secondary Education*, did the same in 1947. The whole subject was now a source of controversy within the Labour Party. Moves away from the assumption that secondary education for all necessarily meant different schools were being made in other quarters. The London County Council, under its Labour majority, in 1947 issued its plans for the reorganization of London schools, starting from the concept of equal opportunity:

> ... it is evident that it is now the duty of authorities to establish equality of opportunity for all children – a phrase that implies the provision for every pupil of a 'place' in a school where his spiritual, physical, social and mental development can be properly nurtured. Mere equality of opportunity, however, will not meet the case unless that opportunity is at the appropriate high level, and the requirement therefore involves the setting up of a standard not only of equality but of quality in educational opportunity which is high enough to satisfy national needs.

The LCC had decided (as early as 1944) that the tripartite system did not match up to this philosophy, and 'that the plan should aim at establishing a system of Comprehensive High Schools, throughout the Administrative County of London, providing for all pupils equal opportunity for physical, intellectual, social and spiritual development'.[4] Some other areas also adopted the comprehensive school principle, among other reasons to avoid the necessity of selection at eleven. By the end of this period the certainties about 'secondary education for all' voiced at the beginning of it were being disturbed by the view that a divided secondary school system was not adequate to the ideals that had sustained it. Some of the argument was based on social justice, some of it on educational need. In the latter category, H. C. Dent, for example, wrote in 1949:

[4] London County Council, *London School Plan* (London, 1947), pp. 7, 230.

Everyone agrees ... at least in theory, that secondary education
for all does not mean merely modifying or watering down the
grammar school curriculum to make it digestible by children of
somewhat lower intellectual ability and rather different aptitudes
and interests. But what hardly anyone appears to be prepared to
face is the hard fact that to provide suitable secondary education for all children is so utterly different a problem from providing a special kind of secondary education for a few selected
children as to constitute an entirely new problem. ... To realize
what secondary education for all means we shall have to perform
the almost superhuman feat of thinking outside the categories of
thought in which practically all our educational thinking has
hitherto been done. ... [5]

Dent was not offering a programme: he was expressing a dilemma.
Hadow and the 1944 Act had been crude instruments: there were
curricular and other implications that had not yet been seriously
considered.

The period covered by this section, therefore, was one which began with a clearcut ideal and ended with an achievement, but one
which revealed some of the ambiguities concealed in the ideal. Out
of attempts to reformulate the ideal, as well as wartime experience,
American experience, and new political and educational initiatives,
different directions were later to emerge more clearly in the discussion of equal opportunity.

[5] H. C. Dent, *Secondary Education for All: Origins and development in
England* (London, 1949), p. 114.

R. H. TAWNEY (1922)

Secondary education for all*

(1)

Primary and secondary education have grown up in England as two separate systems, between which, since 1902, partly as a result of the Education Act of that year, partly through the development of the free place system, partly through the wise insistence of the Board of Education that intending teachers should spend four years in a secondary school, an increasing, if sadly inadequate, number of bridges have been cast. The time has now come for a radical reconstruction of the relations between them. . . .

What we require is to recognize boldly that nothing less than general secondary education will either stand the criticism of the educationalists, or satisfy the demands of a working class that has tasted of the tree of knowledge and does not intend that its children should be fobbed off with the educational shoddy which was foisted upon itself. In place, in short, of 'elementary' education for nine-tenths of the children and 'secondary' education for the exceptionally fortunate or the exceptionally able, we need to envisage education as two stages in a single course which will embrace the whole development of childhood and adolescence up to sixteen, and obliterate the vulgar irrelevances of class inequality and economic pressure in a new educational synthesis.

It is not suggested, of course, that the practical application of such principles can be other than gradual. Educational reforms are limited – to mention no other conditions – by the supply of teachers and of school accommodation. Neither can be improvised. When we speak of 'general secondary education' as the goal of educational policy, we do not in the least ignore these well-worn truisms. If the direction is agreed upon, the precise speed at which different stages on the road are to be reached is a question which must be solved in

* Reprinted from *Secondary Education for All : a policy for Labour* (London, Allen and Unwin and the Labour Party, 1922).

the light of the varying circumstances of different authorities. All, we
may take it, will begin by increasing the provision of secondary
school accommodation sufficiently to make up the gross and admitted shortage which exists at present. All will reject the odious and
short-sighted policy of making secondary education scarce and dear
by raising fees. All will free it, as soon as practicable, in the schools
provided by them, and will greatly develop their system of maintenance allowances. But naturally the scale on which they provide
facilities will depend on the extent and growth of the local demand.
In some places accommodation at the rate of 15–20 per 1,000 will
meet it for the time being; in others something more will be required almost immediately. In each case they will proceed, therefore,
experimentally. What they will *not* do is acquiesce – as in the past –
in the idea that the normal and inevitable thing is for only a small
fraction of the children leaving the primary schools to pass to any
kind whatever of secondary school. They will accept, as the object
to be aimed at, the establishment of a system under which the
majority of children will receive a secondary education from eleven-
plus to sixteen, and will plan their immediate developments with a
view to attaining it at the earliest moment that circumstances allow.

Such a policy is idealistic but it is not visionary. It is no part of
the purpose of this book to attempt, even in outline, to summarize
the recent history of secondary education in England. But it is permissible to emphasize that our proposals, so far from involving a
leap in the dark, are the natural culmination of the main developments which have taken place in the world of public education during
the last twenty years. The number both of pupils and school places
in 1922 is, as we show below, all too small. But, inadequate as they
are, they represent something like an educational revolution compared with the almost complete absence of public provision which
existed prior to 1902. When in 1895 the Royal Commission, of which
Lord Bryce was chairman, investigated secondary education, it found
that the pupils in secondary schools did not exceed 2·5 per 1,000 of
the population – in Lancashire they actually amounted only to 1·1
per 1,000 – as against the figure of 8·7 per 1,000 in the year 1918–19.
When, in 1897, the Education Department took a census of secondary schools, it found that of 6,209 schools, attended by 158,502
boys and 133,402 girls, more than two-thirds were conducted by

private enterprise, that more than a quarter were endowed schools, embracing every variety of foundation from the wealthy boarding school to the local grammar school with an income from its endowments of a few pounds a year, and that actually less than 2 per cent were owned and controlled by public authorities. Apart from the activities of the Charity Commissioners, the intervention of the State in secondary education was represented mainly by the Science and Art Department. In so far as school boards and County Councils had entered the field, they had done so piecemeal and almost furtively, sometimes by straining their powers and almost always in such a way as to compete with each other. Of any conception of the meaning of secondary education, of any central unifying purpose, of any philosophy of its function in society and of its relation to other parts of the educational system, in spite of the teaching of distinguished theorists, there was hardly a trace. The full comedy of the situation was revealed in 1900, when, nearly a century after France and Germany had laid the foundations of a public system of secondary education, the Court of Appeal virtually decided that there was no public authority in England with legal powers to establish and maintain secondary schools.

Of all the medley of schools which could be regarded as giving secondary education twenty years ago, there is probably only one group which can be said today to stand approximately where it did. The institutions conventionally described by the comically inappropriate name of public schools, and the private schools which prepare boys for them, have doubtless improved their methods and curriculum. Further – an important development – it is probable that the majority of the former are now open to inspection by the Board. But in their dominant characteristics – the classes they serve and the objects at which they aim – they are still much what they were in 1897. In the main, except in the matter of inspection, they stand by their own choice apart from the general system of public secondary education, and need not be taken into account in considering how that system can be improved and extended.

While, however, the great boarding schools, though educationally more efficient, remain in their general purpose and character much what they were, a new system of public secondary education has been brought into existence in the course of the present generation, if not out of nothing, at least out of chaos. It has been built up partly by the entry into a national system of schools already in existence, partly by the establishment of new schools by local education authorities. The intellectual foundations of it were laid by the Royal Commission of 1895. In 1901 the newly established Board of Education began the system of paying grants to such schools as would comply with its regulations, and 'recognizing as efficient' those which, without accepting grants, submitted to inspection. In 1902 elementary and secondary education were united in the hands of the county and county borough councils. The most obvious quantitative measurement of the movement is the increase in the number of schools on the grant list of the Board of Education. In 1902–3 there were only 31 schools in receipt of grants, and the Board still grouped schools of science and secondary schools together under the general name of higher education. In 1904–5, 482 schools, with 63,782 pupils, were receiving grants; in 1907–8, 742 schools, with 124,110 pupils; by 1914–15, 929 schools, with 180,507 pupils. The war naturally arrested the building of new schools. But in 1919–20 the number of grant-aided secondary schools in England and Wales had risen to 1,140, and the number of pupils to 307,759, or, in England alone to 282,005.

It is true, of course, that this increase in schools and in the school population must not be interpreted as representing anything like an equivalent net increase in the educational resources of the country, or in the number of children profiting by them, since a large proportion of the schools had been in existence before they became eligible for grants from the Board. The variety of institutions included in the system is one of its merits. It is an amalgam of schools old and new, endowed and proprietary, established by public authorities and taken over by them from other bodies. Even so, however, the development, though only the beginning of the provision which requires to be made, is impressive. It is noticeable that, apart from the endowed and other schools which have entered the public system by complying with the Board's regulations and receiving grants, municipal and county authorities have created in the last twenty years a fabric of secondary education which owes nothing to pre-existing institutions. In 1897 less than 2 per cent of the secondary schools of the country belonged to local authorities. In 1904 municipal and county schools numbered 61. By 1912 local authorities had established 329 secondary schools and taken over 53. In 1919–20, 487 out of 1,021 grant-aided secondary schools in England were controlled by local authorities. In fifteen years, therefore, the schools owned and managed by them had been multiplied approximately eight times. As secondary education develops, it is these schools which will more and more be the dominant and typical element in the system. Apart from them, the schools which in a more general sense are public secondary schools, because they comply with the regulations of the Board and receive grants from it, increased twentyfold between 1902 and 1914. The number of children educated in them today is considerably larger than the number educated in secondary schools of all kinds a generation ago.

Since 1902, therefore, we have nationalized the greater part of secondary education, though the service which we provide is still on a scale quite incommensurate both with the effective demand and – still more – with the educational needs of the community. Not only so, we have begun to communalize it. England has not yet imitated the example set by America and by most of the British Dominions in making public secondary education free. But since 1907 it has been the law of the land that all grant-aided secondary schools, in the absence of special permission by the Board of Education, must admit one-quarter of their entrants without payment of fees. As far as some 73,000 children are concerned – nearly one-third of all the pupils in public secondary schools – secondary education is already, like primary education, free. Certain authorities have gone further and abolished fees altogether in the secondary schools provided by them, and certain others propose to do so in the near future. . . .

It is still true that, as far as more than 90 per cent of the children are concerned, the primary school is like the rope which the Indian juggler throws into the air to end in vacancy; that while in the United States some 28 per cent of the children entering the primary schools pass to high schools, in England the percentage passing from elementary to secondary schools is less than 10, and that of those who do, the majority have hitherto left at, or soon after, their fifteenth birthday and after a school course of less than three years.

Nor can it be said that there is at present any clear conviction in England as to the part which secondary education should play in the life of the community or as to the lines upon which it should develop in the future. There are some signs, indeed, as we point out below, that the policy advocated in this pamphlet has commended itself to certain of the more progressive local education authorities, several of whom – we need mention only the West Riding and Durham among the counties, and Darlington and West Ham among the county boroughs – appear to envisage as their goal the development of full-time secondary education to such a point that the majority of children may be transferred to a secondary school at eleven, and remain in it to the age of sixteen. But the earlier tradition, which subordinated educational to social and economic considerations, dies hard. Apart from the children of the well-to-do, who receive secondary education almost as a matter of course, and whose parents appear usually, though quite mistakenly, to believe that they pay the whole cost of it, secondary education is still commonly regarded as a 'privilege' to be conceded only to the exceptionally brilliant or fortunate. It is still possible for an association of manufacturers to protest against any wide extension of it for the rank and file of children on the ground that it is likely to be 'unsuitable for the employment which they eventually enter'.[1] It is still possible for the largest education authority in the country to propose to erect inequality of educational opportunity into a principle of public policy by solemnly suggesting, with much parade of philosophical arguments, that the interests of the community require that the children of well-to-do parents, who pay fees, should be admitted to public secondary schools on easier intellectual terms than the children of poor parents who can enter them only with free places, and that the children who are so contemptible as to be unable to afford secondary education without assistance in the form of maintenance allowances shall not be admitted unless they reach a higher intellectual standard still!

These survivals from the doctrines of 1870 have their significance.

[1] Federation of British Industries Memorandum on Education (January 1918), p. 4:

At the same time they would very strongly advise that in selecting children for higher education care should be taken to avoid creating, as was done, for example, in India, a large class of persons whose education is unsuitable for the employment they eventually enter.

But they need not disturb us overmuch. It would be a grave injustice to employers to assume that the pronouncement of the Federation of British Industries represents the views of a majority even of its own members: as a matter of fact, indeed, it was immediately repudiated by a considerable proportion of them. Against the special pleading of the London County Council can be set the declarations of directors of education and of educational theorists, the policy of twenty other local education authorities, the policy of Parliament itself. For, whatever the shortcomings of the Education Act of 1918, it did two things of capital importance. For the first time in English history it imposed on local education authorities the *duty* of organizing higher education; for the first time it declared that no child capable of profiting by higher education should be prevented from obtaining it by inability to pay fees. But in effect this last provision concedes in principle the very demand for universal secondary education which is urged by the educationalists and which has been for a generation the policy of the Labour movement. For what the most recent expert inquiry tells us is that 75 per cent of the children in the primary schools are intellectually capable of profiting by full-time education up to sixteen. If secondary education is to be so organized that three-quarters of the children are to pass from the primary school to one type or another of secondary school, then clearly the old conception both of 'elementary' and of secondary education vanishes for good and all. The latter becomes the education of *all* normal children during the years of adolescence from eleven to sixteen; the former the preparatory education of children of whom three out of four will continue it in a secondary school. The doctrine of the parallel systems with links between them disappears. The doctrine of the single system, with two stages embracing various types of institution, takes its place.

It is such a system which it is the policy of the Labour movement to establish and of this book to commend. In doing so, we would emphasize the word 'various'. There must be local initiative and experiment. There is no probability that what suits Lancashire or the West Riding will appeal equally to London or Gloucestershire or Cornwall, and if education is to be an inspiration, not a machine, it must reflect the varying social traditions, and moral atmospheres, and economic conditions of different localities. And within the secondary system of each there must be more than one type of school. Like most of our educational terminology, the phrase 'secondary education' is not free from ambiguity. No statutory definition of it, so far as we are aware, has ever been given. But, for our purpose, it is sufficient to adopt the extremely catholic definition of a secondary school given by the Board as 'a school which provides a progressive course of general education suitable for pupils of an age range at least as wide as from twelve to seventeen'. Defined by the stage of life for which it provides, it is the education of the adolescent. . . .

(II)

The principal views which have been taken of the place of the secondary school in the educational system are three. They may be called respectively the doctrine of the two systems or of separation, the doctrine of selection or of the educational ladder, and the doctrine of the single system. From the time when in 1839 the Committee of the Privy Council expressed the wish that elementary instruction should be kept in close touch with 'the condition of workmen and servants' down almost to the end of the nineteenth century, public education in England developed as a class institution. 'Elementary' education was the education of 'the independent poor', established for them by the governing classes for religious, economic and humanitarian reasons. Secondary education was the education of the well-to-do. The most obvious fact about the systems was that the division between them was based, not on educational, but on social and economic considerations. Educational differentiation began not after the primary school, but before it, and was related not to the future of the children but to the position of the parents. Secondary education was not built upon primary education, but was parallel to it. They were, in short, not different stages in a single system, but different systems of education designed for classes whose capacities, needs and social functions were supposed to be necessarily so different as to make a unified system at once impracticable and disastrous.

This conception of secondary education has long been abandoned by such educationalists (if any) as ever held it, and has ceased for nearly a generation to be the dominant force in public policy. But, in spite of the progress made in the last twenty years, its evil legacy is not yet exhausted. When after 1902 the nation began to set in earnest about the creation of a system of public secondary education, the character of 'elementary' education was already fixed. It was to last till thirteen or fourteen. It was to be the education of children the vast majority of whom would receive no further education after they had ended it. It was, in short, not preparatory education, but working-class education.

Into these facts and the ideas on which they were based the new secondary education had to be, or at any rate in fact was, fitted. It was not considered whether, once a public system of secondary education were established, it would not be desirable to modify primary education in such a way as to make it preparatory to adolescent education beginning between eleven and twelve. It was not asked whether, if secondary education was good for some children, it would not be good for all. It was not attempted, in short, to make secondary and primary education successive stages instead of parallel systems. Nor, had such ideas been mooted, is it probable that they would have met with anything but derision, or that, had they commanded support, it would have been possible in the circumstances of the time to give effect to them. What was actually done was to establish an empirical compromise between the traditional conception of 'elementary' education as the education of a class and the new demand that opportunities of full-time secondary education should be given to some of the more intelligent of the children attending the primary schools. The practical form which that compromise assumed was a system of selection. The existing assumptions and organization of 'elementary' education were retained intact. But, by means of scholarships, free places and maintenance allowances, bridges were thrown ... between it and the newly organized system of public secondary education.

Selection for higher education by means of scholarships has been for the last twenty years the accepted policy of English education. The number of children passing by means of them from primary to secondary schools, though still small, has steadily increased, and if the schemes prepared by local education authorities under the Act of 1918 are carried out, it will increase more rapidly in the future. But the policy of selection may obviously be given two opposite interpretations. If, as is hinted might be the case by the Departmental Committee on Scholarships and Free Places, the effect of it were that 75 per cent of the children in primary schools passed to secondary schools, then selection would be hardly distinguishable from universal provision. When it results, as in certain areas today, in the pupils in the secondary schools amounting to less than 2 per 1,000 of the population, selection is hardly distinguishable from no provision at all.

One may, in fact, proceed either by inclusion or by exclusion, either by endeavouring to ensure that all children other than the obviously subnormal shall pass at adolescence to some form of secondary school, or by treating full-time secondary education as an exceptional privilege to be reserved for children of exceptional capacity. The plan of development suggested in the schemes of West Ham and of Gloucestershire would lead in the first direction. The scheme of the London County Council, or the views expressed in the scheme of the education authority of Salford that a 'secondary school is intended for those who will prepare for some of the more responsible positions in after life', or the opposition of the Federation of British Industries to a wide diffusion of higher education on the ground that it would 'unfit children for the employments they eventually enter', or the proposal of the Select Committee on Educational Expenditure to restrict the access to secondary schools by raising their fees, would lead to the second.

On the one view, primary and secondary education are stages in a single process through which all normal children ought to pass, because all, though in different degrees, will respond to them; the measure of the success of both is the heightened human capacity which they evoke. On the other view, the primary and secondary school represent, not stages of education, but systems of education. There must be facilities for passing from the one to the other, for the brighter children of the working classes are needed to supply the educated *personnel* – the 'intellectual proletariat' – which modern industry, in its higher ranges, requires. But equality of educational provision up to sixteen is impossible of attainment and mischievous could it be attained. Industry needs cannon fodder as well as staff officers, and it is not desirable that the minds of the rank and file, even if capable of development (which the Federation of British Industries doubt), should be unduly developed. When the cream of intelligence has been skimmed off by scholarships, the mass of children must pass at fourteen to the factory with such part-time continued education (if any) as the exigencies of industry may permit.

The choice between these two views is the most momentous issue of educational policy before the nation. As far as the workers of the country are concerned, their decision has already been made. They demand neither central schools, nor part-time continuation schools nor any other of the makeshifts by which it is sought to mitigate in detail the evil results of that organization on lines of class which is the tragedy of English education, while maintaining it in principle and in substance. They demand full-time secondary education for all normal children up to the age of sixteen.

CONSULTATIVE COMMITTEE
OF THE BOARD OF EDUCATION (1926)

The education of the adolescent
(Hadow Report)*

(I) POST-PRIMARY EDUCATION IN ENGLAND AND WALES

The Elementary Education Act, 1870, marks a most important stage in the development of the national system of elementary education. The Act mapped out the country into school districts, each of which might have a school board separately chargeable with the duty of providing elementary education within its own borders, which were to be boroughs or parishes or groups of parishes, London being constituted a district by itself. Section 5 of the Act enacted that 'there shall be provided for every school district a sufficient amount of accommodation in public elementary schools as hereinafter defined, available for all the children resident in such district for whose

* Reprinted from *The Education of the Adolescent* (London, HMSO, 1926).

elementary education efficient and suitable provision is not otherwise made'.

Section 74 empowered school boards to frame by-laws making attendance at school compulsory for children between the ages of five and thirteen. This provision, however, was only permissive, and the by-laws, if made, were subject to numerous exemptions. . . .

The provisions in the Education Acts of 1876 and 1880 in regard to attendance by-laws, and the like, had the indirect effect of producing a very considerable increase in the number of children who remained at school up to and beyond the age of thirteen. To meet the needs of these pupils a seventh standard was added in 1882 by the Education Department to the previously existing six standards.

It was found, however, that a number of children remained at school after passing the seventh standard. Ex-standard classes were accordingly formed for these, and after a time it was found convenient to draft off children from these schools into one central school. Sometimes a building was erected for the purpose and sometimes a previously existing school was set apart for the work, but in either case the school chosen became what was called in the last two decades of the nineteenth century a 'higher grade school'. By far the greater number of these higher grade schools had an upper portion arranged as an 'organized science course or school' under the Science and Art Department, though some school boards retained a few ex-standard scholars in their schools in 'science classes' under the Science and Art Department. A number of school boards, especially those in large urban areas, devoted much attention to the development of these 'higher grade' schools. . . .

As soon as it came to be understood that these schools were institutions at which education could be continued for a year or two longer than at the ordinary elementary schools a large number of parents who intended to keep their children at school after the age of thirteen began to send them to the 'higher grade' school as early as possible in their school life. Furthermore, the fact that the pupils in these schools were to have a two years' course beyond the ordinary standards reacted on the education given in the standards, with the result that in many schools it became the practice to begin the teaching of elementary mathematics and languages at the fifth or sixth standard. Many of the higher grade schools had preparatory, junior or elementary sections. . . .

The Welsh Intermediate Education Act of 1889 facilitated the development of an adequate system of secondary schools in the principality, but in England the public provision of secondary schools was retarded during the last two decades of the nineteenth century by the absence of larger local authorities vested with educational powers. On the other hand, much attention was devoted by many public men and members of school boards to what they regarded as the urgent need of the day, viz., more fully developed elementary education, particularly for children in the higher standards.

A further stage in the development is marked by the appointment in 1894 of the Royal Commission on Secondary Education, which reported in 1895, *inter alia*, in favour of a State system of secondary schools, including arrangements for transferring to them the more intelligent pupils from elementary schools, who desired to continue their education. . . . Higher grade schools, which were adduced as an example of the type required, were held to be an absolute necessity in any efficient system of secondary education. Properly organized they would become the crown of the elementary school system. . . .

The Royal Commission of 1895 had recommended that one central education authority should be established. This was effected by the Board of Education Act, 1899, which merged the powers of the Education Department, the Science and Art Department and the Charity Commission (in respect of educational trusts and endowments) in the newly constituted Board of Education, which was at the same time authorized to inspect secondary schools. The control of the board over secondary education was increased by the Education Act, 1902, which empowered the newly created Part II local education authorities to aid higher education and provide new secondary schools. Even before the passing of the Act of 1902, the position of the higher grade schools had been seriously affected by the decision of the Court of Queen's Bench (1901) against the London School Board (upheld by the Court of Appeal) on the point raised by Mr Cockerton, the Auditor of the Local Government Board, that the school board had spent the rates illegally on educating children on lines not provided for in the Code. . . .

After the passing of the Education Act, 1902, many of the 'higher grade' schools and pupil teacher centres were being converted into council secondary schools. The merging of this important type of higher primary education, which had slowly developed since 1870, into secondary education marks a very important stage in the history of secondary education in England and Wales; for these new municipal secondary schools, influenced by the tradition of the higher grade schools, attached more weight on the whole to scientific and modern studies than the older types of secondary school, especially for girls.

The development of higher elementary schools and post-primary education generally after the passing of the Education Act, 1902, was much influenced by the policy of the Board in regard to secondary schools, which were defined in the Secondary School Regulations for 1905–6 as being schools which 'offered to each of their scholars up to and beyond the age of sixteen, a general education, physical, mental and moral, given through a complete graded course of instruction of wider scope and more advanced degree than that given in Elementary Schools'. . . .

In 1913 the Board issued regulations for a new category of junior full-time schools to be known as junior technical schools. These were day schools, providing courses for boys and girls during two or three years after leaving the public elementary schools, in which a continued general education was to be combined with a definite preparation for some industrial employment at the age of fifteen or sixteen. . . .

Section 2 (I) (a) of the Education Act, 1918, which came into operation on 1 August 1919, gave a new direction to post-primary education by providing that it should be the duty of the local education authority responsible for elementary education so to exercise its powers in regard to elementary education as to make, or otherwise to secure, adequate and suitable provision by means of central schools, central or special classes, or otherwise:

(i) for including in the curriculum of public elementary schools, at appropriate stages, practical instruction suitable to the ages, abilities, and requirements of the children; and

(ii) for organizing in public elementary schools courses of advanced instruction for the older or more intelligent children in attendance at such schools, including children who stay at such schools beyond the age of fourteen. . . .

It will be seen from this historical survey that at every stage of the development it has been the general tendency of the national system of elementary education to throw up experiments in post-primary education. Though such experiments have again and again been curtailed or rendered difficult by legislative or administrative action, they have persistently reappeared in various forms. This fact in itself seems to indicate the half-conscious striving of a highly industrialized society to evolve a type of school analogous to and yet distinct from the secondary school, and providing an education designed to fit boys and girls to enter the various branches of industry, commerce and agriculture at the age of fifteen.

(II) THE FACTS OF THE PRESENT SITUATION

The rising interest in the problem presented by children between eleven and fifteen or sixteen can be traced in the literature, official and unofficial, on educational subjects for many years before 1918. It was due in the main to two different, but closely connected, considerations. The first, directed to the individual demoralization and social wastage too often following on the completion of the elementary school life, was emphasized in the Report by this Committee, on *Attendance Compulsory or Otherwise at Continuation Schools*, which appeared in 1909, as well as in the Majority and Minority Reports of the Poor Law Commission of the same year, the Report of the Departmental Committee on *Juvenile Education in Relation to Employment after the War*, issued in 1917, and the Report of the Ministry of Reconstruction on *Juvenile Employment* published in 1918. The questions raised by these Reports, all of which made educational recommendations of far-reaching importance, are partly outside our purview, and for an account of the social and economic conditions of the children concerned – 'the educational and industrial chaos' described by the Departmental Committee of 1917 – we must refer our readers to the relevant passages in the documents mentioned. But the problems which they described had also, as was emphasized in the Reports, an educational reference. For school and industry are different facets of a single society, and the habit of mind which isolates them from each other is a habit to be overcome. Education fails in part of its aim, if it does not prepare children for a life of active labour and of social co-operation; industry fails no less, if it does not use and strengthen the qualities of mind and character which have been cultivated by education. It is to a clearer realization of the dangers to which many boys and girls are exposed at a critical period of their lives that the increased public interest in the education of children between eleven and fifteen years of age is in great measure due. In considering the difficult questions connected with it – the curriculum best suited to develop their powers, the age up to which full-time attendance at school is desirable, the school as a training ground of character – the educationalist, unless he would build his castles in the air, is bound at every turn to take into account the probable future of the children and the nature of the industrial society into which, when their formal education has ceased, the majority of them will enter.

If one consideration which has concentrated attention on the years between eleven and sixteen has been a growing sensitiveness to the social problem which they present, a second and not less significant has been the progress of education itself. The remarkable advance made in the period since 1902 has had the effect both of raising new questions and of restating old questions with a heightened emphasis. The improvement in the quality of primary education has raised the general level of attainment among the older pupils in the elementary schools, has thus strengthened the foundations upon which further education can be built, and, for an increasing number of children, has turned attendance at school from a tiresome obligation, from which escape is to be sought at the earliest possible moment, into an interest and a pleasure, which, if opportunity is forthcoming, and if the financial circumstances of the family permit, both they and their parents desire to be continued. The raising of the age of compulsory school attendance to the end of the term in which the fourteenth birthday is reached, which was completed by the final abolition of partial exemption in 1921, and has been followed by an increase in the number of children remaining at school beyond the age when the legal obligation to do so ceases, has emphasized the importance of ensuring that the fullest advantage is taken of the time thus gained, and has made it at once more urgent and more feasible to plan the education of children over the age of eleven-plus as a progressive course, with a unity and character of its own. . . .

The progress of elementary education which has prepared the way for that development has been reinforced by equally important changes in other parts of the educational system. The expansion of public secondary education, which has resulted in the number of pupils attending grant-aided secondary schools being increased from 138,443 in 1907–8 to 354,165 in 1922–3, the improvement in its quality, and the development of central and similar schools which began about 1910, and has already proceeded far in certain areas, have had profound reactions both upon the other parts of the educational system, and upon the public attitude towards the value of post-primary education. On the one hand, thanks largely to the bridges thrown by the Free Place system from the elementary to the secondary school, many thousands of parents, who twenty years ago did not think of education other than elementary as a possibility open to their children, have been familiarized with the conception of primary education as a preparatory stage which should lead naturally to some form or another of more advanced work; and a public demand for post-primary education has been created which the existing secondary schools, with the resources at present at their disposal, are not always easily able to satisfy. On the other hand, the growth of secondary and of central schools has revealed a wealth of ability among children attending the elementary schools, the existence of which is a ground both for confidence and for anxiety – confidence in the natural endowments of our fellow countrymen and anxiety lest, at the age at which the powers of the rising generation are most susceptible of cultivation and sensitive to neglect, the nation should fail to turn to the best account so precious a heritage. The precise proportion of children 'capable of profiting' by post-primary education continuing to the age of fifteen-plus is not susceptible of exact statistical expression. Any attempt to estimate the proportion must depend partly on the interpretation assigned to the word 'profit', and partly also, in as much as children who show little response to one type of education may nevertheless derive much benefit from another, on the range and character of the facilities which are offered. So long, however, as the proportion of children for whose post-primary education special provision is made – whether by 'higher tops' and analogous arrangements within the elementary schools, or by central schools, or by secondary schools – is not larger than it appears to be today, the problem of determining exactly the proportion of children capable of profiting is not, perhaps, of very great or immediate practical moment, since by general consent it is considerably greater in all parts of the country than the proportion for which facilities at present exist.

(III) THE LINES OF ADVANCE

In our preceding chapters we have traced the steps taken to make special provision for the education of children between the ages of eleven-plus and fifteen-plus, and have endeavoured to indicate the dimensions of the problem which awaits solution. As our survey shows, that problem has behind it a history extending back almost to the beginning of public education in England, and it has given rise, particularly in recent years, to much fruitful educational activity. It is on the basis of the experience thus obtained that further progress will now be made. The question is not one of erecting a structure on a novel and untried pattern, but of following to their logical conclusions precedents already set, and of building on foundations which have long been laid. The initiative of enlightened education authorities and the progress of educational science have revealed both the possibilities of post-primary education and the practical steps by which those possibilities may be made a living reality. What is now required is to act upon the lines suggested by the results of the efforts already made, to secure for all normal children the opportunities which have hitherto been confined to a small, though growing, number among them, and to extend as widely as possible, though with due regard for difference of local circumstances and needs, methods of organization that have proved their value in the limited field in which they have hitherto been applied. We proceed accordingly to set out shortly our conclusions regarding the principles upon which the further development of the education of children of the age mentioned in our terms of reference ought, as it seems to us, to be based.

The first main conclusion which we have reached is concerned with the successive stages in education and with the relations which should exist between them. It is as follows: *Primary education should be regarded as ending at about the age of eleven-plus. At that age a second stage, which for the moment may be given the colourless name 'post-primary' should begin; and this stage which, for many pupils would end at sixteen-plus, for some at eighteen or nineteen, but for the majority at fourteen-plus or fifteen-plus, should be envisaged so far as possible as a single whole, within which there will be a variety in the types of education supplied, but which will be marked by the common characteristic that its aim is to provide for the needs of children who are entering and passing through the stage of adolescence.*

Such a conception of the relations between primary and post-primary education obviously presents some points of contrast with the arrangement which has hitherto obtained in England, under which, until recent years, approximately 90 per cent of children have received elementary education up to the age of thirteen or fourteen, and a small minority have been transferred to secondary education, or to that given in central schools, at about the age of eleven; and we discuss later the administrative problems to which, if generally accepted as the basis of educational organization, it would give rise. It appears, however, to correspond to the views held by a large and influential section of educational opinion, and it has already received partial recognition both in administrative action taken by the Board and in a recent resolution on educational policy of the House of Commons. There was, indeed, something like unanimity among our witnesses as to the desirability of treating the age of eleven to twelve as the beginning of a new phase in education, presenting distinctive problems of its own, and requiring a fresh departure in educational methods and organization in order to solve them.

Thus – to quote only a few of the opinions submitted to us by witnesses of widely varying types of experience – Professor T. Percy Nunn informed us that he had 'long been strongly in favour of a "clean cut" across our public educational system at the age of eleven-plus', that he wished 'to see the present parallel arrangement of elementary and secondary schools replaced definitely by an "end-on" arrangement, based upon the principle that education falls naturally into two divisions or phases (i) primary education, the education of childhood, and (ii) post-primary education, the education of adolescence', and that 'it is vital to regard all types of post-primary education as attempts to solve, by means appropriate to the differing cases, what is essentially a single problem, namely the education of adolescent boys and girls'. . . . Practical administrators spoke with equal emphasis to the same effect. The Association of Directors and Secretaries of Education, for example, dwelt on the importance of regarding education as 'a single organic whole', and urged that post-primary education, while embracing various types of institution, should 'include all education of the second stage, including what is now termed "secondary education"'. . . .

As far as we can judge, those views are endorsed by the bodies which represent the experience of professional teachers. The representatives of the National Union of Teachers, while emphasizing its demand that 'as soon as it is possible, secondary education shall be provided for all children capable of benefiting from it', submitted proposals intended to 'result in the provision of education which might be called secondary in character for those children who are not attending "secondary schools" in the narrower sense of the words'. The evidence given on behalf of the Association of Head Mistresses stated that 'the break in school life for children attending primary schools should come at eleven-plus, the age at which the free place scholar will pass into the secondary school. All the children, at the age of eleven-plus, should pass either into secondary schools, or into schools, which for want of a better name, we will call Central Schools.' The representatives of the Association of Assistant Mistresses urged that 'children who remained at school till the age of fifteen-plus should follow a continuous course from eleven-plus, at which age they should be transferred to a different school', which 'should approximate closely to the existing secondary school in regard to accommodation and staffing'. Recent expressions of opinion by organizations representing the layman rather than the expert suggest that a similar conception is being increasingly accepted outside the ranks of professional educationalists. The witnesses who came before us on behalf of the General Council of the Trade Union Congress stated that in their view 'all children about the age of eleven-plus should be transferred from elementary schools to some form of secondary school or "central" school', and on 8 April 1925, the House of Commons carried a resolution in favour of the provision of secondary or some form of full-time post-primary education up to the age of sixteen.

KENNETH LINDSAY (1926)

Social progress and educational waste*

(1)

The problem examined in these pages is how far the 'educational ladder' is effective; whether in fact it is, as it has been described, a greasy pole; and what are the main difficulties that beset the path of the child, the parent, the teacher and the local education authority. ... Studies of particular areas have served to throw light, in greater or less detail, on different aspects of the problem, such as the methods and age of selection, maintenance, and entry to a trade or occupation, while an attempt has been made to estimate the extent of vertical mobility in society.

Perhaps two figures will give perspective to the whole problem and point to the heart of the matter. First, of the 550,000 children who leave elementary schools each year, 9·5 per cent of an age-group proceed to secondary schools, one-third exempt from fees and two-thirds fee-paying, while 1 per 1,000 reach the university. Secondly, of 2,800,000 adolescents in England and Wales, 80 per cent are not in full-time attendance at any school. In conjunction with these important figures two more should at this stage be stated. First, from the evidence of these pages, at least 50 per cent of the pupils in elementary schools can profit by some form of post-primary education up to the age of sixteen; second, something under 10 per cent

* Reprinted from *Social Progress and Educational Waste : being a study of the 'free-place' and scholarship system* (London, Routledge, 1926).

of the jobs done by ex-elementary school leavers can be described as skilled work. At the same time *registered* juvenile unemployment is about 65,000, a figure admittedly an underestimate, which takes account neither of casual employment, changing employment nor under-employment. Finally, it has been conclusively proved that success in winning scholarships varies with almost monotonous regularity according to the quality of the social and economic environment. London, Bradford, Liverpool and the countryside bear this out in the minutest detail.

One school in Lewisham wins as many scholarships as the whole of Bermondsey put together, seven poor London boroughs have an average of 1·3 scholars per 1,000 children in average attendance, as against 5·3 in seven better-placed London boroughs. In Oxfordshire only 40 schools out of a total of 212 appear as sending scholars or free-placers to secondary schools in 1924; the remaining 172 are mainly poor and remote schools. At Bradford 75 per cent of the children qualified in a school situated in a well-to-do district, while 34 per cent qualified in a poor district. Out of 321 departments at Liverpool, from which free-placers and scholars might have come, 78 failed to nominate a single one, 208 did not win a scholarship, and 115 did not win a free place. If the thirty-nine wards of the city are analysed, it appears that eight, with an average attendance of 37,133 children, sent 1,224 scholars and free-placers, and that the thirty-one other wards with 81,422 children had only 850 places distributed among them.

It is proposed to quote from two public men who have ventured opinions on this subject, in order to show the confusion of the public mind. The first was volunteered by Lord Birkenhead: 'There is now a complete ladder from the elementary school to the university, and the number of scholarships from the elementary to the secondary school is not limited, awards being made to all children who show capacity to profit.' The second, made by Alderman Conway, an ex-President of the National Union of Teachers, and an experienced educational administrator, runs as follows: 'The restrictive, ineffective scholarship system in vogue for the vast majority of children coincides with a commonly held view that secondary education is something to be doled out with a sparing hand to the bright child of impecunious origin.' Someone else has remarked that the elementary school blames the secondary, the secondary the university, the university both; all blame the local education authority, who blame the Board of Education, who blame the people. The distribution of praise or blame might be spared if more light could be shed; minor differences might be dispelled, and a larger view obtained. Mr Middleton Murry more wisely suggests that equality of opportunity is a happy conjunction of the man and the moment which no amount of preparation can assure, but that it is an injustice, and a remediable one, that a child, who is not yet fit to battle with circumstances, should be deprived of the opportunity to become the best man he is capable of becoming. However, the literature of speculation on this subject is endless, and few living publicists have failed to deliver themselves in varying accents. It may be that the working mother with three or four children is an even wiser judge, both of the benefits and drawbacks of our scholarship system. Nor can the protagonists of separate views afford to forget the conclusive evidence of 'marking time' in the top standards of some elementary schools and of 'wasting time' in and out of industry between fourteen to sixteen years.

In this connection the Insurance Gaps, with the exception of Widows' Pensions (recently made law), Trade Board Rates of Wages and the absence of apprenticeship, except in unusual cases, before the age of sixteen, must all be remembered. Each of these social arrangements is calculated to provide cheap labour between the ages of fourteen and sixteen.

The two official declarations governing and determining the scope of this inquiry are the definition of a 'free-place' originally given by Mr McKenna in 1907, subsequently elaborated in the same sense by the Board of Education and the amplification made in the Education Act of 1918, which provides that no child capable of profiting shall be debarred from receiving the benefits of any form of higher education through inability to pay fees. Although shortage of accommodation, a defect admitted on all sides, necessarily converts a qualifying examination into a competitive one, it is impossible to estimate anything until every child in the locality has been reviewed.

It must be more than a coincidence that Bradford and Wallasey, the two districts with the highest secondary school population, one industrial and one residential, have made the most searching and careful annual review of their children. Without such care and comprehensiveness, backed up by publicity and parental co-operation, we are in the region of nebulous guesswork. This is true of London itself. All the evidence collected about London goes to prove that *at least* another 1,500, and probably many more, might with advantage be awarded scholarships and free places, but until some such review, as at Bradford, is undertaken, there is no definite statistical proof. Again, in Oxfordshire and the countryside generally, until a similar and more thorough canvassing of all children is put in hand, it is impossible to give an accurate estimate. In Banbury, the largest single district of Oxfordshire, it is computed that at least as many again could have taken up scholarships, with benefit to themselves and the community, were there a sufficient number available. What seems quite clear is that the gap between primary and secondary education cannot be bridged by a limited number of scholarships or free places. The compulsory percentage of 25 may, at the discretion of the local authority, be raised to 40, and in forty-two schools all entrance fees are abolished.

Even where fees have been abolished altogether, and where secondary education is free, the number of refusals of free places exceeds the number of acceptances, as the figures from Bradford testify. This is all the more serious because among the refusals are 50 per cent of the first 200 on the list, and – a statement which is true also of Manchester – a number of the abler children prefer the shorter course at the central school to the full secondary school course. Thirdly, the Director of Education in Manchester informs us that, even were all their schools free, 60 per cent of the children would not be able to afford a full course of secondary education. London has chosen another way out of the difficulty, if, indeed, it should not be described as an evasion of it. Although the total population of maintained secondary schools has doubled in the last ten years, the percentage of free places to fee-payers has actually diminished. An alternative, however, in the shape of sixty central schools has been provided, and each year some 5,000 children are drafted into these schools from the public elementary schools. We are inevitably led on to the conclusion that the two stumbling-blocks are:

1 Shortage of accommodation.
2 Poverty of parents.

Owing to the different methods adopted by local authorities the table below is made out differently for each district, but the main facts are identical in each case, and are explained in detail later. . . .

TABLE I

District	Age-group (10–11) years)	Number of scholar-ships and free places	Central schools	Fee-players	Numbers remain-ing un-selected	or	Per-centage of age-group (10–11)
London	70 000	2 146[a]	5 000	2 500	60 354	or	86·2
Oxfordshire	1 890	84	—	166	1 640	or	81·4
Warrington	1 400	25	—	50	1 325	or	94·6

	Numbers examined (1)	Qualified (2)	Percent-age of (2) to (1) (3)	Number of free entrants (4)	Percent-age of (4) to (2) (5)
Bradford	5 202	2 950	56·7	1 189	40

	Passed eliminating examination	Qualified for scholarship	Admitted	Remained after quali-fication	or	Per-centage of those quali-fied
Middlesex	4 243	2 947	1 362	1 585	or	53·4

	Numbers over 80 per cent marks	Refused another examination by parents	Total for second examina-tion	Percentage remaining after quali-fication
Manchester	7 611	3 842	4 130	33

	Examined	Passed	Remaining after second-ary and central schools filled	or	Per-centage of those passed
Wallasey	1 124	778	300	or	38·5

	Examined	Qualified	Free further education	Remaining	or	Per-centage of those quali-fied
East Ham	1 150	806	437	314	or	38·8

[a] Includes 600 trust and charity scholarships, but not 1,000 supplementary and trade scholarships awarded at age of thirteen.

The latest available year is given in each case: fee-payers are excluded, except where stated, though they form an average of two-thirds of secondary school entrants, except at Bradford, where all municipal secondary schools are free.

The important but subsidiary questions, such as age and method of selection, the variety of post-primary curricula, the relation between curricula and after-careers, all vitally affect the two outstanding difficulties and cannot be separated from them. Mention has already been made of the economic character of the districts from which scholars come, but there is also the kindred question of occupational classes and the extent to which recruitment is from one class to another. We will deal with each point in turn.

The conclusions that emerge, particularly from a study of Bradford and Wallasey, but also from an examination of other areas, are in the main alike. Between the ages of ten and twelve, say at eleven-plus, a change of school, teacher and atmosphere is good for the average child; at that age there is a rich variety of capacity among children, and the various forms and tendencies of post-primary education should correspond to the varying capacities of the children. At present the main types of post-primary education are represented by secondary, central, technical, trade and continuation schools, higher tops and intermediate schools, and in addition a network of evening classes. There is general agreement that a period of four years is the least possible time during which an ample groundwork can be laid. Counter-arguments may be advanced by rate-payers or by industry, but not by educationists. The method of selection is bound to vary, but the broad principle of testing capacity and general ability and of estimating the school record has found common acceptance. Intelligence tests, such as have been used in London, Northumberland and other areas, have, on the whole, confirmed the other evidence and sometimes corrected errors, but their significance cannot yet be stated with scientific precision. The establishment of impartial examiners, the elimination of the personal factor, the coordinating of marking, have all been treated with enormous care and imagination by certain areas, as the pages on Bradford and Wallasey suggest. The very fact of tightening up these arrangements has stimulated public interest in education, and in both the above-mentioned areas about 80 per cent of all possible children are reviewed.

Wallasey has conducted a searching inquiry into the personal circumstances of the remaining 20 per cent, and has tabulated the causes of backwardness. Bradford is about to inquire into the reasons for refusal of scholarships and free places. Sifting and selection are, then, vital, but if any real meaning is to be given to the selection, the post-primary years must be followed up on that basis. Selection by differentiation must replace selection by elimination. For the one conclusion that emerges from a study of secondary school talent and after-careers, illustrated scientifically by Dr Burt, the psychologist to the London County Council, is the large number of children of average ability (described by the headmaster of a London secondary school as 'ordinary good stuff') with peaks at either end. And yet it is true to say that at present the peaks are lost in the clouds, particularly the peaks of high ability.

Parents' occupations and after-careers of scholars are given in a summary and estimate below.

TABLE 2. *Parents' occupations (secondary school pupils)*

	Boys (%)		Girls (%)	
	1913	*1921*	*1913*	*1921*
Ministers	2·1	1·4	2·0	1·5
Teachers	3·9	3·1	4·2	3·4
Other professions	*12·9*	*12·1*	*13·0*	*11·9*
Farmers	5·5	5·4	5·0	5·5
Wholesale traders (managers and proprietors)	*10·0*	*9·0*	*9·6*	*8·5*
Retail traders (managers and pro-prietors)	*19·2*	*17·8*	*18·7*	*16·9*
Trade assistants	1·2	0·8	1·0	0·8
Contractors	2·3	2·2	2·3	2·3
Minor officials	4·9	4·8	4·7	4·8
Clerks, commercial travellers and agents	*13·9*	*14·0*	*13·2*	*13·1*
Post, police and soldiers	2·2	3·8	2·3	3·9
Domestic and other servants	1·9	1·8	2·0	1·9
Skilled workmen	*16·3*	*19·7*	*17·0*	*20·5*
Unskilled workmen	2·4	2·8	2·6	3·2
No occupations	1·6	1·3	2·4	1·8

TABLE 3. *After-occupations (secondary school pupils)*

		1911 (%)	1921 (%)
To proportions going on to further education			
Schools on grant list		3·5	4·9
Schools on efficient list		0·7	0·9
Schools not on efficient list		4·3	3·9
Universities under 17		0·3	0·3
Universities over 17		2·3	3·9
Other institutions		6·4	8·2
Pupil teachers, or training college uncertified and supplementary		10·9	9·8
	Totals	28·4	31·9
Abroad		2·2	3·3
To professional, clerical and commercial			
Under 15		7·9	4·9
15 and under 16		11·5	8·0
16 and under 17		8·7	8·9
17 and over		4·5	4·9
	Totals	32·6	26·7
To industrial and manual			
Under 15		3·3	2·9
15 and under 16		3·4	3·9
16 and over		2·2	3·1
	Totals	8·9	9·9
To agricultural and rural			
Under 15		1·2	1·4
15 and under 16		1·2	1·3
16 and over		0·8	1·2
	Totals	3·2	3·9
Residue (half girls at home)		23·6	25·4
	Totals	100·0	100·0

Tables 2 and 3 illustrate the main facts of parents' occupations and after-occupations of *all* secondary school pupils at periods before and after the war.

Table 4 reveals that, as between girls and boys, occupations taken up show considerable variation.

TABLE 4

	Boys (%) 1921	Girls (%) 1921
Full further education	20·0	14·4
Teachers	3·5	16·5
Professional, commercial and clerical	36·6	16·2
Industrial and manual	16·4	2·9
Agricultural	7·0	0·5
Abroad	2·0	2·3
Residue	14·5	37·2 (23·2 at home)

It may be assumed with some confidence that no great changes have come over secondary education in this particular respect during the years since 1921. Roughly two-thirds of the parents of pupils are engaged in the professions, trade, commerce or skilled work. Only about 13 per cent enter industrial, manual or agricultural pursuits.

Before making further comment, some particulars of free places and scholars from areas examined will be given. But each must be tabulated in its own form because of local variations. The second column, after-occupations, relates to the same year, not to the same pupils, as the first column. In each case the latest available year is taken.

TABLE 5

London

Parents' occupations (scholars at secondary schools)		After-occupations (scholars from secondary schools)	(%)
Skilled workers	672	Clerical and commercial	70
Dealers, shops, warehouse and minor officials	290	Engineering and trade	15
Clerks, agents, travellers	200	Professions	15
Proprietors, managers and senior officials	160		
Labour, attendants, porters	130		
Widows and pensions	80		
Teachers	54		
	1 586		

Bradford

Parents' occupations	(%)	After-occupations	(%)
Skilled workmen	38·1	Teachers	4·8
Unskilled workmen	10·0	Professions	4·9
Clerks, agents and commercial travellers	14·6	Clerical and commerical	33·8
		Industrial and manual	21·2
Retail traders (proprietors and managers)	10·8	Further education	14·9
		Rural occupations	0·3
Wholesale traders (proprietors and managers)	7·5	Abroad	1·5
		Unknown	18·6
Traders' assistants	5·4		
Professional	4·4		
Contractors and minor officials	3·5		
Others (post, police, soldiers, etc.)	5·7		

Oxfordshire (80 free places and scholars)

Parents' occupations		After-occupations	
Trade, salesmen and clerical	29	Clerks	33
Skilled workers	20	Teaching	35
Small holders	7	Apprentice and trade	20
Post and police	6	Further education	9
Widows	6	Unknown	3
Labourers	7		
Butlers and gardeners	5		

Warrington (32 free places)

Parents' occupations		After-occupations	
Trade or clerical	7	Clerks and civil service	30·8
Skilled workers	18	Teachers	32·3
Post and police	2	Apprentices	10·7
Labourers	5	At home	7·7
		Further education	18·5

The most significant revelation comes from Bradford, and can be seen from the figures below.

TABLE 6. *Parents' occupations*

	Grammar schools	Free municipal schools	All Bradford	County boroughs	All country
Traders' assistants	1·2	5·4	4·7	0·9	0·8
Skilled workmen	8·9	38·1	33·5	20·8	20·1
Unskilled workmen	—	10·0	8·4	2·9	3·0
Totals	10·1	53·5	46·6	24·6	23·9

Over 50 per cent of the children in Bradford municipal schools come from the homes of skilled workers, shop assistants and unskilled workers. The number of children of unskilled workers is 7 per cent higher than the average for the country. Not only is this true, but the number who go back to industrial or manual work is 21·2 per cent, or 11·3 per cent above the average for the country. In London 50 per cent of the free-placers and scholars come from homes which may be described as above – skilled and unskilled workers and widows – but there free-placers and scholars form only one-third of the total entrants. In Warrington a large percentage of children come from manual workers' homes, but the bulk of them pass to clerical and teaching posts; similarly in Oxfordshire. Again, in both these cases the free-placers and scholars form only one-third of the total entrants, and the number of total entrants to secondary schools is very much smaller relatively than at Bradford. It may be said, therefore, with some accuracy that the 'ladder' as it operates in London, Warrington and Oxfordshire succeeds in lifting a small number each year from manual to clerical and other occupations, while at Bradford free secondary education enables a larger number of children from manual workers' homes to receive the benefits of secondary education, while nearly 25 per cent of that number carry on manual and industrial occupations afterwards. Warrington is a diversified industrial community, and might do the same thing, were there sufficient opportunity. Rural communities, like Oxfordshire, would need to reorganize their main local industry – namely, agriculture – if they are to achieve a result even faintly resembling that of Bradford. London is more difficult because, apart from engineering, a very small number of secondary school pupils return to manual or industrial employment. The remaining skilled trades are recruited almost entirely by a non-secondary school population, while technical and continuation schools are gradually assuming a more important place.

Genius flourishes in a free soil, as Mill warned us during the last century. Fifty years of public education have told us that the soil must be fertile as well as free. Slums in London, Warrington and Bradford, remoteness and lack of community in Oxfordshire, reveal untilled ground in the shape of physical and social evils which are beyond the immediate influence of the educational system. Even

here an occasional genius emerges, as the after-careers of distinguished London scholars show. No scientist or educationist can set
the bounds of genius. Even physique eludes the well-worn rules.
For, though the Metropolitan Police are largely recruited from the
countryside, environment has condemned others from the same
districts to a life of physical poverty. A champion boxer is discovered
among a family of over ten in a Bermondsey slum, and from a neighbouring street a boy is raised to win the blue ribbon of scholarship at
Oxford. Nurture can and does drive nature out with a pitchfork:
character and tradition can serve mediocre ability with surprising
results.

Those are the only conclusions that spring from a study of parents'
occupations and after-careers. Warrington, Bradford, Oxfordshire,
London, all show that the unskilled and lowly paid worker, the farm
worker and the casual labourer, are as yet not really touched by the
scholarship system. Individuals undoubtedly are, but the mass
remains unaffected.

With the growth of repetitive processes and the ease and facility
with which such processes can be worked by young people between fourteen and eighteen, the solution of this problem becomes
all the more urgent. It is beside the point to say that our secondary
schools produce clerks instead of manual workers. In actual fact,
where the net is thrown most widely, the extent and care of testing
is most efficient, and where the free secondary school population is
largest, as at Bradford, the greatest number return to industrial
occupations. But if education is to serve industry, then it must give
industry what it most needs. ... A reorientation of view is now
necessary, because a new class in the community is knocking at
the doors of secondary schools. The artisan and skilled worker is the
largest single group from whom free-place winners come, and the
record of free-place winners, as is shown in different areas by headmaster after headmaster, is entirely creditable. In many cases the
educational process would reveal no vertical mobility at all, were
there no free-place system. This is best shown in Warrington. The
local grammar school takes the sons of manufacturers and professional men, and redistributes them among the same class. But the
effect of free places, though only a few in number, and still more of
the local maintained school, is to lift each year some sons of skilled

workers and of a few unskilled workers on to a new plane of understanding, and to give a chance to the boy or girl of exceptional gifts
to rise to the high places of knowledge.

All through society the biggest job-finding agency is the parent
and the friends and relations of the parent. This is as true of coal-
porters in the London docks as of farmers in Oxfordshire, merchants
in Bradford or skilled workers in Warrington. Secondary schools are
made up of three classes – the free-placer, the fee-payer from elementary schools and the fee-payer from private schools; each
represents roughly one-third of the annual entrance. . . . The
non-public secondary schools command a virtual monopoly of
certain better-paid jobs, and this is true to a lesser extent for the
sons of the more wealthy fee-payers at public secondary schools
(where fees form only one-third of the annual maintenance, the rest
being paid by rate-payers and charities). On the other hand, fee-
payers from elementary schools, unless they win an internal scholarship at the secondary school, tend to leave early owing to financial
circumstances. For them it is even more difficult to enter professions
where premiums are necessary, because the presumption is that they
are less able than the scholarship winner. The effect of scholarships
in polytechnics and technical colleges may be clearly observed by a
study of the after-career of the winners. By sheer merit and technical qualifications they are able to take their places in higher posts in
trade and industry. But nothing more than a beginning has been
made in this particular direction, in order to counteract the hereditary or moneyed qualifications for entering the vocations.

The writer therefore concludes that proved ability to the extent of
at least 40 per cent of the nation's children is at present being denied
expression, that the full extent of unproved ability is not yet known,
only because a sufficiently comprehensive test has not been applied,
and that if a very conservative estimate of 20 per cent may be described as below average ability, social environment, in many cases
remediable, is the main contributing cause. Furthermore, that the
effect of scholarships, limited though they are, has been to break
down the irrelevant but formidable barriers of caste, influence and
privilege, for the mutual benefit of the young and the nation as a
whole. Finally, the contention that financial considerations bar the
way for much greater progress can only be put forward by one half-

hearted in the belief that the right place for children under sixteen years of age is in a school of some kind, with its corporate life and membership of a spiritual community. . . . If finance is the key to the solution, no less important is a change in the social arrangements and way of life outside the school, in order to make maintenance a practicable and possible solution. The removal from the educational vocabulary of the 'ladder idea' does not therefore mean decrease of effort, but a higher minimum of general education and a prospect of indefinite expansion and growth along a variety of paths for the majority instead of a minority of young people.

(II)

It was stated in the earlier part of this book that having made primary education compulsory, it was found that many children were uneducable owing to neglect, disease and other causes. It may be said of secondary education that, with its rapid growth, particularly since the war, many children either cannot take advantage of it owing to inability to afford the money, or cannot continue it, having entered the schools, for the same reason. These pages reveal the fact that it is impossible to dissociate the free-place system from the maintenance system, or, to state the same thing in a different way, maintenance is affected by the fees prevalent in secondary schools. It is true that Bradford is faced with the same problem as other places, but the basis of judgement is easier where all pupils are on the same footing in regard to fees. At present fees vary between nothing at all and 27 guineas a year; there are twenty of the latter, all foundation schools. But the average fee is between 4 and 10 guineas a year. Again, while 25 per cent of the previous year's admission is the normal percentage of free places, eighty-nine foundation schools receive 10 or 12½ per cent, and thirty no free places at all.

Certain conclusions have already emerged from the study of particular districts. In 1919 we spent £250,000 on maintenance, just under 40 per cent of free entrants to secondary schools received some form of assistance, and about 10 per cent of all children in secondary schools. On the other hand, the income from fees amounted to about £3,000,000. Unless a most unlikely advance is made in real wages, it is safe to conclude that more and more maintenance will be

required. It is common knowledge that the chief difficulty in raising
the school-leaving age is the difficulty of the parents in forgoing their
children's earnings. In any working-class district the suggestion of
raising the school-leaving age to fifteen is greeted with disapproval,
unless liberal maintenance is also assured. But there is another side
to this question which was faintly suggested by Sir Michael Sadler in
1904. The households consisting of a husband, non-earning wife and
three dependent children number 56 out of every 1,000 skilled
workers, and 52 per 1,000 in the case of unskilled workers. These
households, containing a large percentage of the child population,
receive the same wage as a childless couple or a bachelor. The only
method of keeping head above water is for the mother to go out to
work, and the elder children to take what is often the first and most
unsatisfactory job at fourteen-plus. Many a free-placer is being kept
at a secondary school by the long hours of a sacrificing mother, a
fact which again and again came to my notice. Sir Michael Sadler
suggested a maintenance fund, and, if equitable treatment is to be
given to all children, it seems that nothing short of special provision
can supply the need. It is true that a certain section of the community
do not *need* assistance, and that fees can be easily afforded by a small
minority, but it has been shown that a new section of the community
is asking for secondary and continued education today, for whom
fees and lack of maintenance are the great difficulties, and, in not a
few cases, the only obstacles.

J. H. GARRETT (1928)

Mass education in England*

CRITICAL NOTES ARISING OUT OF THE CONSULTATIVE COM-
MITTEE'S REPORT ON THE EDUCATION OF THE ADOLESCENT
AND OTHERWISE

The 'Summary of the principal conclusions and recommendations'
of this Report very fairly indicate the contents of the Report itself.
Where a specific answer in close detail was required for practical
application, the Committee only reply in generalities, and avoid the
points of difficulty. They exceed their scope by including the whole
system of school education within the ambit of their inquiry, and
evolve a proposition that all children, that are effective for any
education, shall remain at school for an additional year, and that the
mode of education throughout the schools shall be fundamentally
altered to bring in a new system, divided into 'primary' and 'post-
primary' education, the latter of a new sort, and in a new place, by a
new type of teacher. They in no degree meet or assist in those
problems that have been found so difficult of solution – that fitting of
education to after-occupation, and to educational ability.

The same Consultative Committee, with some slight difference in
its *personnel*, had had referred to it, but a short time previously, the
question of 'Psychological Tests of Educable Capacity', which had
provided its members with an insight into all the facts of that subject.
They must, therefore, have been aware of the impossibility of the
proposition that the whole mass of the populace, as represented in its
children, does, or can, receive 'a good general education', but they
did not show sufficient regard for the great importance of this truth
being generally admitted, and so missed the opportunity of doing a
required service by publishing it.

To acknowledge the variations in the educable material of the
elementary schools is necessary to make the best of it, and to make

* Reprinted from *Mass Education in England : a critical examination of problem and possibility* (Ed. J. Burrow, 1928).

the best of it sums up the whole possibility of mass education. The references to the 'slower' children in the Report are only few and brief. They say their numbers 'only experience can decide'. Surely their numbers have already been decided; a great deal of experience has been gained in this matter. They further add that 'it may be hoped that with the improvement in the conditions in the primary school, and in the home, their number will diminish'. There is, nevertheless, the acknowledgement that their scheme will require either the establishment of several types of 'post-primary' school or, in the alternative, a 'system of parallel forms' to accommodate children of different educable capacity.

Although in all this there is no suggestion of how the whole business is to be performed, there is the discovery of so great a complication, and addition of labour and expense, as to invite the most careful examination of the new system before its adoption. Clearly, the cost, the result and the whole system itself, are most indeterminate. A calm consideration of the project will show it to be an expensive experiment that is really only fitted for a selected portion of the children of the masses, that portion not being in excess of the portion for which it is not fitted.

The system that is already at work, so far as it is a selective system admitting to the extra-standard VII, central schools and secondary schools, is a success, as far as the educable capacity of the children allows it to be so. In this connection it has already been discovered, in a most practical way, that the numbers of children suitable for entry into selective central and secondary schools are quite limited, the outcry having been soon raised that unsuitable children were being sent up, and there is a large mass of scholars, contributing about half the attendance of the elementary schools, who are bound to occupy a lower place, not being up to central-school form, much less to secondary school form. The division of the education into 'primary' and 'post-primary' parts can in no way increase the educable capacity of the scholars, and the degree of failure must be about the same under the one system as under the other. The fallacy and waste of spending undue effort and money on this less educable half are too glaring to be avoided. The argument that the children who form it would derive much by association with their mental betters is not of sufficient weight to counterbalance the added cost and waste of time incurred by allowing them all to pass through an equal course. In the case of those who are above the middle line it must be admitted that something further is possible, and the further development of higher grade senior classes, central, and secondary schools and technical classes, would give ample outlet for any talent that could be displayed, and provide the means for acquisition of such aids as school education can bring to members of all social grades. Even among the select, however, the children in the central schools who show themselves possessed of exceptional talent are but few, the success, for the main part, being only moderate and not up to the pretence of the advertisement of the Speech Days and Prize-Givings, where the glory and renown of a finger-count of exceptional pupils reflect their radiance over the rather ordinary rest of the attendance. Nevertheless, by continuing the education of selected children to fifteen or sixteen years of age, the effect of their school education is likely to be enhanced in a large proportion of the children on account of their superior age-maturity and consequent more certain and rapid powers for learning. Habits of study are likely to be engendered in some of them, and these will be able to apply themselves the better thereafter to their own education. But this is not an argument for the similar treatment of the non-selected, and from any advantage gained by the selected the deduction must be made of the loss of another kind of learning which another kind of employment would have brought them during the same period of time.

It is the case at any school that, ordinarily, you have not to wait longer than the twelfth year of age for learning capacity to make itself evident, or fail to do so and, where it is a matter of failure, experience teaches that further information to modify the first estimate is likely to be waited for in vain. Marked mental intelligence, and many fundamental traits of character, usually make themselves evident from a very early age indeed. The school, even, affords the best place for making an estimate of the ability and character of the adult, the mental characteristics from youth to age being so permanent; in this sense the child being truly father of the man.

In the body of their Report, the Committee, dealing with the 'lines of advance', try to give the impression that they are advocating an equal advance of all. They express the opinion, however, that many

more pupils than at present should enter the highest type of school –
their 'grammar school' – by free places, but, as this indicates that
many more will be successful in the competitive examination that
determines the selection, the number possessed of best ability must
be increased by some extraordinary means or other, which is not
demonstrated, or inferior pupils be admitted. They advocate the
retention of both selective and non-selective central schools – their
'modern schools' – but whether the non-selective are to be reserved
for children of lower grade of intelligence, or to be merely schools for
pupils up to fourteen years of age of mixed grade of intelligence, is
not made clear, the whole subject of the effect of difference of mental
intelligence in their system being left in an unsettled state. The
difference between a non-selective central school and an ordinary
school appears to be only one in name. For the best of the scholars
there must, of course, be the bifurcation that will lead some into the
'grammar schools' and some into the 'modern schools', but they
seem to think that more is required, so that the whole of the children
shall be caused to advance equally. The varying characters and
abilities of the children could but suggest to them the necessity of
the lines of advance being multiple, and they grow apologetic to the
advocates of 'equality of opportunity' and in face of the impossibility
of any such thing as equality of opportunity for all school children,
irrespective of their several natural powers for learning, they offer
the solution 'that all will go forward though along different paths,
selection by differentiation taking the place of selection by elimination'. You may have an advance in education by different routes as
well as by end-on progress, no doubt, but the euphemism is palp-
able when they omit to add 'for those capable of advancing'. These
multiple lines of advance would require many teachers, and more
than a few schools. The Committee recommends that time and
opportunity be allowed to the present teachers of the old schools for
improving themselves up to the required standard of teaching in the
schools that are to come into being. Here it seems to be forgotten
that the teachers are past their student age, many, in fact, having
passed middle life, and it should not be expected that they will
become students again. At the insistence of pedants who are brim-
ming over with their own several estimates of what school education
should mean and what, in fact, it may mean to them in the schools

they manage, they would push elementary school childen forward independently of their show of educable ability, and with no thought whatever of the incongruity of the education aimed at and the after-life occupation of the juvenile. If this recommendation were accepted, there would be great danger, indeed, that the secondary schools would become encumbered and hampered by an influx of unsuitable and unwanted pupils. It is supposed that there must be a gain for any and every child to continue to attend school, and the longer they attend, particularly in schools of the 'grammar school' type, even up to the age of eighteen or nineteen years, the greater the individual and national advantage, and there is no acknowledged loss to set against the gain; but want of acknowledgement does not obliterate the loss due to the using up of so long a part of life in formal school education. There are probably many people to whom their view will not be acceptable. There are two powerful opposing reasons against it. (1) The too low educability of many of the children. (2) The compulsory nature of the after-lives of the scholars as seen in the occupational census. No theoretical schemes for equal education of all the children can get away from these basic and fixed conditions. They are both bound to cause a separation of scholars which, it is true, can conveniently take place in the twelfth year of age, when those who are sufficiently reactive to an advanced and new type of education can go to the central schools, or to the secondary schools, and in view of the after-life and the numbers that must be engaged in one kind of work and another, it is the central school to which the greater number should proceed. For the remaining half it is quite sufficient for their school education to proceed to a less ambitious end, to direct it along numerous divergent lines as is proposed being impracticable and unprofitable. The only vital subjects required in the syllabus for their teaching are those pertaining to their native language and arithmetic, three-fourths of the subjects contained in the proposed whole curriculum being of no vital importance to them at all. By concentrating upon the three Rs, reading, (w)riting and (a)rithmetic, some of these children, at least, may acquire a useful facility in these leading subjects. Schoolmasters must be well aware of the best means to advance these subjects, which are of ancient knowledge and practice, being the methods found of most service and effect. If it should turn out thereafter that some of the backward pupils might, after all, have been advanced to the central school (and that is likely to be the case), the consequence to the child will not be great. Such children will be able to take advantage of the many chances of self-education which will come to them in their lives. Our ultimate educations are all self-acquired, which brings to mind how important it is to teach all schoolchildren with the view to their after self-education, and to be reminding them continually of the fact that their education is in their own hands, and that it need not be in the way of the secondary schools, the central schools, or any particular school at all. . . .

In regard again to the Committee's special advocacy of more and more adolescents proceeding to the secondary schools, it may be said that this is in accord with the opinion of some of the headmasters of these schools, who are, naturally, believers in their own methods of teaching, and exultant at the success achieved by some of the free-place scholars. They forget that they have been receiving the very best of all the children in the public elementary schools. If the process were reversed and the lower 50 per cent of the elementary school children were admitted to the secondary schools, the worth of the methods and advantages claimed for any such school would be put to a more effective test. This is hardly likely to happen. What is more likely to occur from a crowding-in of children to grammar schools is an over keen competition for jobs accordant with that kind of education, whose limitation of number must give rise to many disappointments. . . .

The arguments for compulsory general advance of the school-leaving age to fifteen are too specious. If it be true that few young persons under fifteen can find occupation, there should at least be liberty to leave school before that age, for those who are wanting to enter occupations, and the evidence of having obtained occupation that is likely to be of some duration might decide it. There is often urgent necessity in poor large families for the children to become wage-earners and, in conjunction with a small show of ability for school learning on the part of the children, the better practice is to allow them to enter simple kinds of work after fourteen years of age. If further school attendance at that age is right for some it is wrong for others. Nothing is likely to be lost to 50 per cent of all the children by limiting the length of their school education, according

to the present usual regulation, to the end of the term in which their
fourteenth birthday occurs.

The Committee in their earnestness to advance the age for compulsory school attendance mention the effect of general unemployment in the country as a reason for holding an additional 450,000
children another year in school, and pretend to a loss in 'intelligence
and character' that is vital to the nation through the want of that
additional year of school attendance. Such an unsound statement
must detract from the value of the Report. In this connection, too,
it may be mentioned that there is a compulsory provision of continuation schools required for children leaving the elementary schools
at fourteen years of age, so that every inducement, even to compulsion, is still offered them for further formal education. This might
well be deemed sufficient for the less able half.

The general argument of the Report in urging compulsory school
attendance of all children to fifteen years of age is discouraging to
young persons in their desire and search for employment. That most
of the children, and their parents, are not desirous of such an additional restraint to their liberty is shown by the withdrawal of a very
large proportion of the children as they arrive at the statutory leaving
age, when the option is open to them to stay another year at school,
because already any child can stay till the age of fifteen who desires
to do so. The suggestion to these children that the kind of work into
which they can enter at this early age, such as delivering goods and
newspapers, is of a derogatory and shameful class, and that they can
do something much better for themselves by remaining longer at
school, is misleading advice, and wanting in moral sense. It would be
much better to endeavour to encourage in them the pride of self-
sustenance, and the recognition that the accomplishment of necessary work, however menial, confers a public benefit by the one who
renders the service, and is entirely praiseworthy and of good account.
There may well be a show of character in it that will stand the young
person in better stead than a trifling degree of formal education got
by further attendance at school.

The threat that a long continuation of school and college offers to
early marriage and settlement is also not a myth but of moment, and
likely to affect the maintenance of national numbers as bred from the
best.

Nothing can be more hindering to the best result possible being obtained in the education of the masses than the idea, too usually held, that it is not a matter of acquisition by the person to be educated so much as a gift by the teacher and, more remotely, by the Government. Many seem to suppose that the Government being agreeable to spend sufficient money, a good and equal education for every child is assured. This fallacy is equalled by the false assumption that if a boy or girl attends a school of renown, or one of exclusive entrance, whether by reason of very high cost, or of social position and amenities, the education acquired will be certain and superior. And the 'equality of opportunity', with people of this idea, lies in the proposition that every child should be able to attend a school just like those above alluded to. Here again we see the worship of the apparatus and the neglect of the personal material. In these times of great public libraries, and all the schools and colleges open for entry by any able child among the poorest, every necessary means for the most extensive general education is supplied, or is likely soon to be so, as the result of the institutions authorized by law, and to a large extent already in being. . . .

Among the many foolish advocacies concerning education is that one that proposes for every child the 'equality of opportunity' provided by proceeding, through the best schools, to what is popularly and awesomely termed 'a college education', and what the proposers vaguely mean is the keeping of the usual residential terms in a constituent college, at Oxford or Cambridge, for example. How utterly spoiling and harmful for the mass of mankind such an experience would be, and how wasteful of time in preventing persons entering into the culture of their life's work, the comprehension of these people does not grasp. The inconsequence of the proposition serves to show how people of ordinary mental ability may be misled, and will seek to mislead others, as the result of a great enthusiasm that is erroneous in its practical bearings and in its neglect of the facts of human life. It may still be said of the moneyed classes that the inferior part of their children get an advantage in school education which they do not deserve. However, their number is not great and competitive life affords much chance for a levelling up and down, especially if you look forward beyond the passing of the first generation. To push forward by artificial means the inferior element of the

elementary schools would be a mistake, and no less would it be a
mistake to interfere radically and artificially with the position
attained through the possession of private money, this last operating
to provide a good education through several generations, and there
are considerable reasons why it should be allowed to do so in spite of
all the envy, jealousy and cupidity that have no corresponding origin
or backing of the virtuous talented effort that led to the accumulation
of the private means.

It is quite bootless to credit one class with having an easier or better
opportunity than another, quite pointless to argue the reasons why it
is so, since that could make no difference to the numbers that must
be respectively employed in mental or physical work. The vast
majority must, in the nature of things, be physical workers, notwith-
standing all the assisting machinery that has, or will be, invented.
Eton, Harrow and the other schools of that kind, are of no good to
them, and even that extra year in the public elementary schools,
proposed by the Consultative Committee with such insistence, would
prove superfluous to the majority of them.

R. H. TAWNEY (1931)

Equality*

The hereditary curse upon English education is its organization
upon lines of social class. 'An elementary school education', remarked recently an experienced educational administrator, 'has
always meant, and still means, a cheap education. An elementary
school textbook means a cheap book, which is carefully adapted in
language and content to a wholly derogatory estimate of the needs
and powers of the children of a certain section of society, who are
supposed not to require or to be capable of the same kind of education as the children of parents who have more money.' The effect

* Reprinted from *Equality* (London, Allen and Unwin, 1931).

of the conditions as to staffing and accommodation still permitted to continue in many primary schools is not merely to cripple the performance of the vital and delicate task on which these schools are engaged. It is to poison their soul. It is to cause, not only their external organization, but their spirit and temper to be smitten by a blight of social inferiority.

Children are apt to think of themselves as their elders show that they think of them. The public school boy is encouraged to regard himself as one of a ruling class, which in politics, administration and business will govern and direct – to acquire, in short, the aristocratic virtues of initiative and self-reliance, as well as frequently the aristocratic vices of arrogance, intellectual laziness and self-satisfaction. The age of spiritual bobbing and curtseying in public education is, happily, over. The elementary schools, with all their defects, have done more than any other institution to straighten the backs of the mass of the population. But, while the theory that the standards permissible in elementary schools ought to be inferior, because they are designed for a class which is inferior, is, if not dead, at any rate dying, the fact of their inferiority is only too alive. If the elementary school boy is no longer taught by his masters that the world has been divided by Providence into the rich, who are the ends of civilization, and the poor, who are its instruments, he is frequently taught a not very different lesson by the character of the surroundings which his countrymen provide for him.

He is taught it by mean, and in some cases even unhealthy, buildings; by the deficiency of playing-fields, school libraries, laboratories, and facilities for practical work; by the shortage of books themselves and the parsimony which holds that less than 2s. a year for each pupil is enough to spend on them. He is taught it by the persistent under-staffing which still permits the existence of 46,000 classes with over forty pupils on the register, and actually over 3,000 classes with more than fifty. He is taught it by his premature plunge into wage-earning employment and the conditions that he meets there. He is taught it by recurrent gusts of educational economy, with their ostentatious insistence that it is his happiness and his welfare which, when the ship is labouring, are the superfluity to be jettisoned. He is taught it by the naïve assurance with which his masters, unenlightened by a century of experience, persist in asserting that they cannot dispense with his immature labour, as though, while their own children continue their education to sixteen or twenty, he and his kind were predestined by Providence to be the cannon-fodder of industry. He is taught it, not least, by the very tenor of the proposals which are applauded as impressive reforms by his well-wishers themselves.

For consider the assumptions implied in the view hitherto held of the scope and purpose of secondary education. When the boys and girls of well-to-do parents attain the great age of thirteen to fourteen, no one asks whether – absurd phrase – they are 'capable of profiting' by further education. They continue their education as a matter of course, not because they are exceptional, but because they are normal, and the question of the 'profit' which they succeed in deriving from it is left, quite rightly, to be answered later. Working-class children have the same needs to be met, and the same powers to be developed. But their opportunities of developing them are rationed, like bread in a famine, under stringent precautions, as though, were secondary education made too accessible, the world would end – as it is possible, indeed, that one sort of world might.

Public opinion is so saturated with the influence of a long tradition of educational inequality, so wedded to the idea that what is obtained by one class without question must be conceded to another only on proof of special capacity, that eminent personages can still sometimes be heard to congratulate the nation on the existence of what they describe as an educational ladder, which has as its effect that less than one child in seven of those leaving the elementary schools wins access, after being strained at eleven through the sieve of a competitive examination, to the secondary education that the children of the rich receive, in most cases, as a matter of course. And now that the Consultative Committee of the Board of Education, by insisting that all children, and not merely a minority, should receive secondary education, has killed one embodiment of that nauseous creed, another, and not less nauseating, embodiment of it appears to be on the verge of starting to live. For, in defiance of the Committee's report, schools are being established in more than one area, which, if post-primary in name, in staffing, equipment and accommodation differ but little from the elementary schools whose place they are designed to take. Not only so, but the recommendation that all children should be retained at school till fifteen, which formed an essential part of the Committee's policy, and the neglect of which for a decade has largely stultified the remainder of their plan, has now been summarily rejected by the Government. 'The small fingers' of children of fourteen, we were told by a speaker in the House of Commons on the Bill of 1926, are indispensable to the survival of the Yorkshire textile industry. The children of the rich, in addition to their other advantages, are apparently blessed by Providence with fingers plumper and more elongated than those bestowed on the wretched brats whose parents happen to be poor. . . .

The goal to be aimed at is simplicity itself. The idea that differences of educational opportunity among children should depend upon differences of wealth among parents is a barbarity. It is as grotesque and repulsive as to suppose that the latter should result, as once they did, in differences of personal security and legal status. The primary school, as the Consultative Committee of the Board of Education asserted in its report on the subject, should be, as in some countries it already is, 'the common school of the whole population, so excellent and so generally esteemed that all parents desire their children to attend it'. It should, in short, be the preparatory school, from which all children, and not merely a fortunate minority, pass on to secondary education, and which, since the second stage would then succeed the first, as a matter of course, when children were ripe for it, would be free from the present pressure to prepare them for a competitive examination affecting their whole future. A special system of schools, reserved for children whose parents have larger bank-accounts than their neighbours, exists in no other country on the same scale as in England. It is at once an educational monstrosity and a grave national misfortune. It is educationally vicious, since to mix with companions from homes of different types is an important part of the education of the young. It is socially disastrous, for it does more than any other single cause, except capitalism itself, to perpetuate the division of the nation into classes of which one is almost unintelligible to the other. All private schools, including those so-called 'public schools', should be required, as a condition of their continuance or establishment, to hold a licence from the Board of Education. Such a licence should be granted to a school only on condition that its governing body is representative, that its endowments are administered in the general interest and that it is equally accessible to all children qualified to profit by it, irrespective of the income or social position of their parents.

J. L. GRAY AND PEARL MOSHINSKY (1938)

Ability and opportunity in English education*

(I) THE MEASUREMENT OF EDUCATIONAL OPPORTUNITY

We are now in a position to attempt an estimate of the total volume of high ability in the school population, of the character of its distribution amongst different social groups and of the extent to which the existing machinery of social selection adjusts educational

TABLE I. *Percentage of pupils in various school populations aged 9·0– 12·6 with high ability*

	IQ		IB[a]	
	130 and over	140 and over	120 and over	130 and over
1 Elementary, 9·0–11·0	21·4	13·3	21·2	13·1
2 Elementary, 11·1–12·6	21·8	11·4	17·6	9·4
3 Central schools	71·7	51·6	65·5	43·5
4 Secondary free pupils	95·3	86·7	93·3	84·2
5 Secondary fee-payers	51·7	37·1	48·7	34·3
6 Private schools	37·0	25·0	35·5	22·7
7 Preparatory schools	61·8	49·6	60·1	47·7
8 Private and preparatory schools (combined)	51·2	39·1	49·5	37·0

* Reprinted from *Political Arithmetic: a symposium of population studies*, ed. Lancelot Hogben (London, Allen and Unwin, 1938).

[a] See note, p. 61 below.

		IQ		IB	
		130 and over	*140 and over*	*120 and over*	*130 and over*
9	All free pupils	25·3	15·9	23·7	14·8
10	All fee-paying pupils	51·5	38·6	49·6	36·6
11	All with opportunities of higher education	67·4	56·1	65·4	53·8
12	All	27·2	17·6	25·5	16·3

opportunity to individual ability. We proceed further to offer some quantitative indices of the prevailing inequality in the assignment of educational opportunities.

Table 1 gave the percentage of children in various school categories who attained or exceeded two high levels of ability. We have now to translate these percentages into actual numbers. In order to do this it is first necessary to determine the total size of these categories, which is done in Table 2.

TABLE 2. *Estimated size of school population in age-group 9·0–12·6*

1	*Free pupils* (present constitution)		
	(*a*) Elementary	2 305 000	
	(*b*) Secondary	41 000	
			2 346 000
2	*Free pupils* (constitution at leaving age)		2 286 000
3	*Fee-paying pupils* (present constitution)		
	(*a*) Secondary	65 000	
	(*b*) Private and preparatory	150 000	
			215 000
4	*Fee-paying pupils* (constitution at leaving age)		275 000
5	*Total school population*		2 561 000
6	*Total population of elementary school origin*		2 377 000
7	*Pupils who have or will have opportunities of higher education :*		
	(*a*) Secondary free	158 000	
	(*b*) Secondary fee-payers	125 000	
	(*c*) Private and preparatory	150 000	
			433 000
8	*Pupils who go or will go to central schools*		252 000

The figures in items 1, 3 and 5 are taken directly from official sources. Items 2 and 4 express the numbers who will be free and fee-paying pupils at the time of leaving school, i.e. after allowance has been made for those elementary school children who, at various ages, will become fee-payers at secondary schools. We estimate them to be 60,000. Item 6 was obtained by adding to the existing elementary school population those secondary school children who have originated in elementary schools. We know the number of secondary free pupils of elementary school origin, and we make the assumption that 50 per cent of the fee-payers within our age-group also come from elementary schools, since this is approximately true for fee-payers of all ages. Item 8 presented greater difficulty. Central schools are not separately distinguished in official returns from other types of public elementary schools. We relied in the first place on figures specially furnished to us by the Education Officer of the LCC. These gave us the total central school population in London in the age-group eleven to twelve. Reference to the total London population of elementary school origin at the same age enables us to estimate that approximately 12·3 per cent of all such children proceed to central schools at that age. It follows, in the absence of any change in the number of central school places, that a similar proportion of the age-group nine to eleven would normally proceed to central schools on reaching the age of admission. Assuming that the same proportion exists for England and Wales, we arrive for children aged nine and over at a figure of 252,000 with opportunities of a central school education. Since, in fact, we have no information concerning the comparative distribution of the elementary school population between central and other types of schools outside London, this estimate must be taken with considerable reserve.

Item 7 is of critical importance in the present discussion and requires very careful treatment. It will be noted that in Table 1 the category entitled 'All with opportunities of higher education' has already appeared.

By higher education we mean education continuing beyond the primary or preparatory stage into the secondary or public school. What number of individuals enjoy a higher education in the sense defined, or may expect to do so when they reach the appropriate age? We assume that all children in private, preparatory and secondary schools fall into this category. Not all necessarily remain at school or go on to the university, but the normal expectation is that such children enjoy at least some educational and social advantages not possessed by those who finish their education in the elementary school. There is no means of estimating the average length of the school life of private and preparatory school pupils, but we do know, in the case of secondary school pupils, that they spend on the average about five years in the secondary school and that the average age of leaving is just under seventeen. We also know that more than 50 per cent remain at school after the age of sixteen. It is common knowledge that attendance at schools of this type, even when incomplete, carries with it a considerable prestige value in the outside world.

The paucity of official information respecting children in private and preparatory schools makes it impossible to determine with any accuracy the total numbers within our age-range of 9·0–12·6. On the assumption that the proportion of such children in this age-group to the estimated total aged five to fourteen is the same as in the case of elementary school children, where the total is known, we arrive at a figure of approximately 150,000.

The calculation of the number of children who will proceed to secondary schools, while resting on official returns, is nevertheless a task of considerable complexity. It is necessary for our purpose to calculate the total numbers who will have the *opportunity* of a higher education. We know the numbers of both free pupils and fee-payers aged 9·0–12·6 who are actually in attendance at secondary schools. We have also to estimate the number of individuals who are not yet at secondary schools, but may expect to proceed there at a later date. Since we do not propose to separate in the final result children receiving a higher education in different types of schools, we need only consider transferences from public elementary schools. Those entering secondary schools from elsewhere are necessarily included in our total of private and preparatory school children.

The obvious method of arriving at such a figure would seem to be to obtain the proportion of children leaving elementary schools for secondary schools at all ages to the total number of elementary school leavers, on the basis of figures for any given year or series of years, and thus the total number in any given age-group. This was in essence the method adopted by Carr-Saunders and Jones in 1927, using figures relating to the years 1922–5. Their procedure is satisfactory as long as there are no great fluctuations in the total number of leavers in successive years. Since 1927, however, the requisite constancy of the number of leavers per annum has not persisted. For example, in the year 1931–2, on which the estimates in this investigation are based, the population in the age-group fourteen to fifteen, which contains the majority of leavers, is unusually small on account of the great decline in the birth-rate that occurred during the war. The figure is 539,000 as compared with 529,000 in the age-group thirteen to fourteen, 741,000 in the age-group twelve to thirteen, and 768,000 in the age-group eleven to twelve. Hence the total number of leavers in the two years subsequent to 1933 would be approximately two-fifths greater than for the year 1931–2. The proportion of leavers who went to secondary schools would be artificially inflated, if account were taken only of years in which the total school population over the age of eleven was unusually small. For these reasons we were compelled to seek an alternative method of obtaining the required information.

It is possible to calculate the *proportion* of all children in elementary schools over the age of nine who will eventually go to secondary schools, on the assumption that the proportion of admissions to secondary schools at each year of age to the total elementary school population at the same age remains constant. With few exceptions, the minimum age of transference from elementary to secondary schools is nine and the maximum fourteen. Hence this method only involves a summation of the proportions admitted at different years of age between nine and fourteen. We have calculated free and fee-paying pupils separately.

(a) *Secondary free pupils*

Let the 1931–2 age-group of children of elementary school origin aged nine to ten be N_{9-10}, the admissions to secondary schools of free pupils from elementary schools at the age of nine to ten be Y_1. Then $P_1 = \dfrac{Y_2}{N_{9-10}}$, where P_1 is the proportion of such admissions to the total age-group of elementary school origin (i.e. including children already gone to secondary schools as free pupils or fee-payers). Similarly, if the admissions for the age-groups ten to eleven, eleven to twelve, twelve to thirteen and thirteen to fourteen be Y_2, Y_3, Y_4 and Y_5 then

$$P_2 = \frac{Y_2}{N_{10-11}}$$

$$P_3 = \frac{Y_3}{N_{11-12}}$$

$$P_4 = \frac{Y_4}{N_{12-13}}$$

$$P_5 = \frac{Y_5}{N_{13-14}}$$

Let P be the proportion of all children aged nine and over who will eventually go to secondary schools as free pupils, then

$$
\begin{aligned}
P &= P_1 + P_2 + P_3 + P_4 + P_5 \\
&= \frac{102}{630,801} + \frac{5,582}{685,857} + \frac{31,532}{728,893} + \frac{7,342}{661,778} + \frac{1,342}{484,394} \\
&= 0.02\% + 0.81\% + 4.33\% + 1.11\% + 0.28\% \\
&= 6.6\%
\end{aligned}
$$

Since the total population of elementary school origin aged 9·0–12·6 is 2,377,000, the number who may hope to obtain free places in secondary schools is approximately 157,000. Since also the great majority of transferences from elementary to secondary schools of free pupils takes place within this age-range, we can provisionally estimate that between 6 and 7 per cent of children starting life in the public elementary school enjoy the opportunity of a higher education, the cost of which is defrayed either wholly or in part by the State or other public authority.

(b) Secondary fee-payers

Similarly, we have calculated the percentage of individuals of elementary school origin who will eventually proceed to secondary schools as fee-payers to be 3·9 per cent and the total number approximately 93,000. The combined percentage relating to free pupils and fee-payers is 10·5 and the total number within our age-group, 251,000.

By this means we obtained the figures for item 7 of Table 2. It remained only to add to the totals of children proceeding to secondary from elementary schools as free or fee-paying pupils those originating in schools of other types. On 31 March 1932 there were about 3 per cent of all free pupils in secondary schools, or 1,230, who had come from private or preparatory schools and approximately 32,000 fee-payers. It was necessary only to take account of such individuals in actual attendance at secondary schools: those who will eventually proceed there are already included in the total of private and preparatory school children.

Table 3 expresses in terms of percentages the relationship between some of the totals given in Table 2.

(II) THE VOLUME AND DISTRIBUTION OF HIGH ABILITY

Table 1 shows the proportion of pupils in various categories of the school population who attain or exceed four different levels of high ability, ranging between a lower limit of IQ 130 and an upper limit of IB 130.[1] While a substantial percentage in both the free and fee-paying groups achieve the selected standards, it will nevertheless be observed that there is a striking discrepancy between the two figures, which confirms the disparity between the mean values already noted. We may repeat that it is not the purpose of this investigation to determine whether this superiority of the fee-paying group is due

---

[1] The authors explain elsewhere in this article:

It was decided to adopt in this investigation, side by side with the more familiar IQ, a device invented by Dr Otis for use with his intelligence scale, namely, the Index of Brightness. IB, as it will henceforth be described, is a measure of the increment or decrement of an individual's score from the normal score of persons of his exact chronological age, the norm being in all cases expressed as 100. For example, if an individual scores 10 points more than the norm for his age, his IB will be 110. Similarly, if he scores 10 points less, his IB will be 90. It follows that the IB of an individual of given chronological age rises with increasing score without limit. Thus the IB makes it possible to compare the intellectual rank of children, even in groups highly selected for ability. Moreover, where the variability of the distribution of the scores at each age is approximately identical, the IB provides a reliable absolute scale on which to assess the intelligence of children of different chronological age.

to nature or nurture. The assumptions we adopt are decidedly conservative in that we do not take into account any possible improvement in the intellectual performance of children of elementary school origin that might result from a diminution of existing economic and cultural inequalities.

Before proceeding to the discussion of the major issues, we venture to draw attention to several points of detail that arise from a study of this table. It will be noted that according to the criterion employed not less than 84 per cent nor more than 95 per cent of all free pupils

TABLE 3. *Comparison of various school populations aged 9·0–12·6 (in percentages)*

1 *As percentage of total school population*	
(a) All free pupils	
(i) Present constitution	91·6
(ii) Constitution at leaving age	89·3
(b) All fee-paying pupils	
(i) Present constitution	8·4
(ii) Constitution at leaving age	10·7
(c) All pupils with opportunities of higher education	16·9
2 *As percentage of all pupils of elementary school origin*	
(a) Pupils of elementary school origin with opportunities of obtaining free places in secondary schools	6·6
(b) Pupils of elementary school origin with opportunities of proceeding to secondary schools as fee-paying pupils	3·9
(c) (a)+(b)	10·5
(d) Pupils who go or will go to central schools	12·3
3 *As percentage of all free pupils*	
(a) All fee-paying pupils	
(i) Present constitution	9·2
(ii) Constitution at leaving age	12·0

in secondary schools possess high ability. This may be held to illustrate the way in which existing scholarship examinations are successful in excluding children of comparatively low ability. As Table 1 shows, it does not mean that they have as their object the selection of all gifted children of elementary school origin. For example, the significantly high proportion of between 43 and 72 per cent of all pupils in central schools possess superior ability. Nevertheless, very few of them may hope to proceed to secondary schools either as free pupils or as fee-payers. Again, of the residual population in the elementary schools, i.e. those who have failed to be selected either for central or secondary schools at the ages at which the overwhelming majority of transfers occur, between 9 and 22 per cent fall within our category of gifted children. In their case also, only an insignificant proportion have any subsequent opportunity of proceeding at a later age to any other kind of school.

Within the fee-paying group itself there are highly significant differences. The superiority of the preparatory school children is in bold contrast with the inferiority of children attending private schools. It will be recalled that in the absence of even approximate official estimates concerning the relative proportion of preparatory and private school children in the country as a whole, we were compelled, in calculating the intellectual indices of the combined group, to assume that the two populations were of equal size. It is obvious that the combined mean and the proportion of high ability for the fee-paying group as a whole would be significantly lower were there any great superiority in the relative size of the private school population. We have argued in a preceding section that this is almost certainly true. In that event the discrepancy between the ability of the two social groups distinguished in this investigation would be less and the inequality of their educational opportunities greater. Thus again our data incline to the side of conservatism.

Table 4 presents the prime data of Table 1, the percentage figures having been converted into actual numbers on the basis of the data set out in Table 2. Table 4 also shows the percentage contribution of each group to the total school population of high ability. Table 5 continues the analysis of the data classified according to the further requirements of this investigation.

The most striking conclusion that emerges from a study of these tables is that there is no shortage of gifted children in the community. Our figures, we may recall, refer only to a restricted age-group. On the assumption that the percentile distribution of I Q and I B would be the same at all ages of school life, it would be possible to estimate the corresponding figures for the entire population of school age. The figures given here themselves suffice to show, when

compared with those in Table 2, a large reservoir of unutilized high
ability. The argument from the discrepancy between the mean
ability and between the relative proportions of gifted children in
schools of different social type is seen to lose much of its practical
significance. It is overwhelmed by the enormously greater actual
numbers of superior children who originate in elementary schools.
We are far from suggesting that the inferiority of the mean intelligence of the children of the relatively poor does not create a problem
which calls for immediate investigation. For the present discussion
the relevant fact is that on their observed performances alone the

TABLE 4. *Estimated totals with high ability in various school categories, aged 9·0–12.6, with percentages of each in terms of total school
population with high ability*

School	IQ			
	130 and over		140 and over	
	No.	%	No.	%
Elementary, 9·0–11·0	279 000	39·2	174 000	37·9
Elementary, 11·1–12·6	190 000	26·7	100 000	21·8
Central	92 000	12·9	66 000	14·4
Secondary free pupils	39 000	5·5	36 000	7·8
Secondary fee-payers	34 000	4·8	24 000	5·2
Private and preparatory	77 000	10·8	59 000	12·9
Total with high ability	711 000	100·0	459 000	100·0

School	IB			
	120 and over		130 and over	
	No.	%	No.	%
Elementary, 9·0–11·0	277 000	42·0	171 000	40·5
Elementary, 11·1–12·6	154 000	23·4	82 000	19·4
Central	84 000	12·7	56 000	13·3
Secondary free pupils	38 000	5·8	35 000	8·3
Secondary fee-payers	32 000	4·8	22 000	5·2
Private and preparatory	74 000	11·2	56 000	13·3
Total with high ability	659 000	100·0	422 000	100·0

TABLE 5. *Estimated totals with high ability in various categories of the school population, aged 9·0–12·6, and percentages of each in terms of total school population with high ability*

	IQ				IB			
	130 and over		140 and over		120 and over		130 and over	
	No.	%	No.	%	No.	%	No.	%
Total with high ability	711 000	100·0	459 000	100·0	659 000	100·0	422 000	100·0
All free pupils	600 000	84·4	376 000	81·9	553 000	83·9	344 900	81·5
All fee-paying pupils	111 000	15·6	83 000	18·1	106 000	16·1	78 000	18·5
All who will leave as free pupils	569 000	80·0	353 000	76·9	523 000	79·4	323 000	76·5
All who will leave as fee-payers	142 000	20·0	106 000	23·1	136 000	20·6	99 000	23·5
All in elementary (including central) schools	561 000	78·9	340 000	74·1	515 000	78·1	309 000	73·2
All in secondary, private and preparatory schools	150 000	21·1	119 000	25·9	144 000	21·9	113 000	26·8
All pupils with opportunities of higher education	293 000	41·2	243 000	52·9	283 000	42·9	232 000	55·0
All pupils without opportunities of higher education	418 000	58·8	216 000	47·1	376 000	57·1	190 000	45·0
All pupils who go or will go to central schools	181 000	25·5	130 000	28·3	165 000	25·0	110 000	26·1

comparatively poor very greatly preponderate in the production of individuals of high ability. That being so, it follows that an educational policy concerned with the training of a sufficient number of children to supply the social demand for highly educated persons will be mainly directed to the provision of adequate facilities for the higher education of children of elementary school origin.

When we compare present free with present fee-paying pupils, we find that the former contain between four and five times as many gifted children as the latter. Similarly, when we consider the status of children at the time of leaving school, we note that there are three or four times as many gifted free pupils as gifted fee-paying pupils. It will not fail to be observed that in the single case of children whose educational future is limited to the central school there are many more superior individuals than in the entire group of fee-paying pupils. Yet practically none of these has the opportunity of entry into the professions and the higher ranks of the business world enjoyed by those who have attended fee-paying schools.

The most unexpected and disturbing result of the analysis in Table 5 is that on the highest criterion of ability 45 per cent and on the lowest 59 per cent of the total number of gifted children in the school population do not enjoy the opportunity of a higher education. None of these belong to the group whose parents are able and willing to pay fees for their children's education. The entire mass of unutilized talent consists of children for whose education the requisite financial provision from public funds is not available.

(III). THE MALADJUSTMENT OF ABILITY AND OPPORTUNITY

In order to obtain a clear picture of the existing disparity with reference to differences of ability and of opportunity, it has been necessary to adopt certain arbitrary levels of ability as a basis for comparison. For example, we noted that an IQ of 130 is the figure reached by approximately 25 per cent of the total school population. If we have regard only to these arbitrary levels, then for the purpose of the present discussion we can speak of maladjustment as occurring (a) when individuals who attain or exceed them do not have the opportunity of higher education, and (b) when individuals who fail to attain them nevertheless receive a higher education. It must be clearly understood that there is no justification for the assertion that only children with intelligence above these levels can *benefit* from higher education. This investigation is in no way concerned with the problem of deciding in what different senses the term 'benefit' may be legitimately employed in the discussion of educational policy. It aims only at bringing into relation objective criteria of educational performance and quantitative indices of educational opportunity.

Table 6 describes the way in which the existing facilities for higher education are distributed between the two social groups and between those individuals who possess high ability and those who do not.

For example, 569,000, or 25 per cent, of all children who will leave as free pupils attain or exceed an I Q of 130. The number of such gifted children who actually enjoy the opportunities of a higher education is only 151,000 or 26·5 per cent, while whose who have the ability but are not afforded the opportunity number 418,000 or 73·5 per cent. Thus the wastage of talent from this source alone is nearly three times the total that is at present utilized, or 16·3 per cent of the total school population. In addition, a maladjustment of

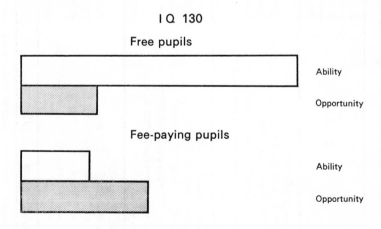

FIGURE I *Comparison of total numbers with ability and numbers who have opportunity of higher education in the two groups of free and fee-paying pupils respectively*

TABLE 6. *Maladjustment of ability and opportunity in higher education (age group 9·0–12·6)*

| | IQ | | | | IB | | | |
| | 130 and over | | 140 and over | | 120 and over | | 130 and over | |
	No.	%[a]	No.	%[a]	No.	%[a]	No.	%[a]
1 Free pupils [2 286 000]								
(a) No. with high ability of	569 000	24·9	353 000	15·4	523 000	22·9	323 000	14·1
(b) No. of (a) *with* opportunity	151 000	6·6	137 000	6·0	147 000	6·4	133 000	5·8
(c) No. of (a) *without* opportunity	418 000	18·3	216 000	9·4	376 000	16·5	190 000	8·3
(d) No. with opportunity but without high ability	7 000	0·3	21 000	0·9	11 000	0·5	25 000	1·1
2 Fee-paying pupils [275 000]								
(a) No. with high ability of	142 000	51·5	106 000	38·5	136 000	49·5	99 000	36·0
(b) No. of (a) *with* opportunity	142 000	51·5	106 000	38·5	136 000	49·5	99 000	36·0
(c) No. of (a) *without* opportunity	—	—	—	—	—	—	—	—
(d) No. with opportunity but without high ability	133 000	48·5	169 000	61·5	139 000	50·5	176 000	64·0
3 All pupils [2 561 000]								
(a) No. with high ability of	711 000	27·8	459 000	17·9	659 000	25·7	422 000	16·5
(b) No. of (a) *with* opportunity	293 000	11·5	243 000	9·5	283 000	11·0	232 000	9·1
(c) No. of (a) *without* opportunity	418 000	16·3	216 000	8·4	376 000	14·7	190 000	7·4
(d) No. with opportunity but without high ability	140 000	5·5	190 000	7·4	150 000	5·9	201 000	7·8
4 Total maladjustment (3c + 3d)	558 000	21·8	406 000	15·9	526 000	20·5	391 000	15·2

[a] The percentages refer to the relation between the figures in the rows and the figures in square brackets in column I.

a different kind takes place when children who fail to attain the selected levels of high ability receive higher education. Seven thousand, or 0·3 per cent, of children of elementary school origin fall into this category. This percentage is not greater than would be expected when individuals are selected mainly as a result of a mass examination. The corresponding maladjustment in the case of fee-paying pupils amounts to no less than 133,000, or 49 per cent, of the entire population of fee-paying pupils. Thus the overwhelming majority of sub-standard children who nevertheless obtain a higher education consists of fee-paying pupils. The final conclusion, taking I Q 130 as our criterion of ability, is that there are 558,000 individuals, or 22 per cent of the entire school population, aged 9·0–12·6, in whose case there is a maladjustment of ability and opportunity of one kind or the other. This total is considerably in excess of the total number who actually enjoy opportunities of higher education (irrespective of ability) and twice as great as the number of such children who also attain our selected levels of high ability. . . .

(IV) SUMMARY

1 Over 10,000 individuals between the ages of nine years and twelve years six months, drawn from public elementary (including central), secondary, private and preparatory schools in the London area, were tested with the Otis Advanced Group Intelligence Test (Form A) and assigned Intelligence Quotients on the basis of the existing American norms.

2 Norms based on the data of the present investigation were used to derive Indices of Brightness for all subjects examined.

3 Correlation coefficients which were obtained for Age and I Q and Age and I B demonstrated the superiority of the latter in the comparison of individuals in populations selected for intelligence.

4 The reliability coefficient for I Q was found to be $r = 0.85 \pm 0.027$ and for I B $r = 0.92 \pm 0.015$.

5 A system of weighting was designed to take account of the selective factors in English education and inequalities in sampling.

6 Mean figures and percentile distributions were calculated for the I Q and I B of various categories of the school population.

7 Estimates are given of the percentages and numbers of individuals of different social and educational status who attain various selected levels of high ability.

8 The proportion of individuals of elementary school origin who are afforded the opportunity of a secondary school education at the expense of the State was found, on the basis of official statistics for 1931–2, to be 6·6 per cent.

9 Similarly, the proportion of such individuals who normally proceed to secondary schools as fee-payers is 3·9 per cent.

10 If we take the level of ability attained by approximately 50 per cent of children who are educated at their parents' expense (IQ 130 or IB 120), then approximately 25 per cent of pupils educated at the expense of the State attain the same level. When account is taken of the unequal size of these two social groups, it is found that the numerical contribution at this level of ability of the last-named group amounts to 80 per cent of the total. Of these only a little more than a quarter have the opportunity of proceeding as free pupils to secondary schools. Individuals at this level of ability, whose education is limited to the central school, alone exceed the numbers of all fee-paying pupils of similar ability. In the whole school population more than 50 per cent of the able pupils are without the opportunity of higher education. While only 3 per 1,000 of free pupils in secondary schools fall below the selected level of ability, the corresponding figure for the entire group of fee-paying pupils (all of whom nevertheless enjoy the opportunity of a higher education) is nearly 50 per cent. In other words, taking children of equally high ability, seven fee-paying pupils will receive a higher education for every one free pupil. Conversely, if we consider children who fall below the selected level of ability, for every one free pupil who is afforded the opportunity of a higher education, there are 162 fee-paying pupils who enjoy the same advantages.

11 Similar calculations have been made, using higher criteria of ability.

12 If, instead of 50 per cent, we assume that only 10 per cent of children educated at their parents' expense are ineligible by virtue of inferior ability for receiving a higher education, then 72 per cent of free pupils are eligible.

13 At a very high level of ability, represented by the attainment

of the uppermost I per 1,000 in the general school population, two-thirds of the total originate in elementary schools, of whom 70 per cent are of wage-earning parentage. Of the entire group of such exceptional individuals, 50 per cent are the children of wage-earners, and 33 per cent of members of the higher social and professional classes.

F. CLARKE (1940)

Education and social change*

THE PRESENT SITUATION

We may begin with a brief catalogue of the institutional forms of educational provision at present functioning in England:

(1) A national system of 'elementary' schools, derived from the nineteenth century and now (a) expanding and specializing itself at both ends, at the lower end by the growth of nursery schools and reintegrated infants schools, and at the upper end by the development of senior schools (eleven-plus to fifteen) under the Hadow reorganization, leaving the junior school (seven to eleven-plus) in between: (b) reinterpreting itself as an institution for the communication of a *basic common culture* rather than as one for the guarantee of *lower-class usefulness*, and finding in the process an urgent need for the prolonging of systematic education well into the years of adolescence.

(2) An extraordinarily complex system of 'secondary' schools (i.e., 'secondary' in the technical administrative sense, which from any purely *educational* point of view is as illogical as it is ill-defined. The Spens Report could not fail to recognize this.)

The diversity here presented is in no sense *educational*. It is

* Reprinted from *Education and Social Change: an English interpretation* (London, Sheldon Press, 1940).

important that this should be understood. For 'secondary' education in England is suffering severely, as the Spens Report again recognizes, from a grave lack of genuine educational diversity. The newer schools, staffed in many cases by men bred in the old tradition, and, often under the influence of governors of the same cultural stock, have tended to follow only too faithfully the model of the ancient schools, 'public' and 'grammar'. In this they have not been discouraged, if not actively encouraged, by their lower-middle-class and upper-working-class *clientèle*. In British colonies, especially in Africa, strong suspicion is revealed of any attempt to adapt secondary education to local needs and conditions as concealing a design to rob aspiring pupils and parents of the hope of achieving 'caste'. The same suspicion was strong until recently even in England, towards attempts to work out special secondary curricula suitable for the education of girls. Now today it is active among the classes of the population whose hopes of achieving status are founded upon the new facilities that were opened up by the Act of 1902. Overwhelmingly the driving force is the desire for *status* rather than for education as such. Within broad limits any kind of curriculum will be accepted so long as the successful study of it achieves this. It is not easy, in view of all the circumstances, to condemn the attitude of the socially aspiring in such a matter. They are not to blame either for a very natural ambition or for accepting the conditions, not determined at all by them, under which alone the ambition can be satisfied.

The result has been a certain failure on the part of the secondary school to seize its full opportunity. Obsessed too often with an idea of 'education for its own sake' which in point of fact derived very largely from the peculiar position of a small leisured class, and a notion of the 'true' content of a liberal education which failed to take note of the extent to which this curriculum was really designed to serve the vocational needs of a ruling class of cultivated amateurs, it has so far not fully grasped its true social purpose. As we might expect, this is less true of the girls' schools than of those for boys, but it is truer than it ought to be for all alike.

It should have been recognized that if the new aspirants were to become members of a ruling class at all it would be a ruling class of quite a new kind, needing a new kind of discipline; that the social origin and conditions of home experience of this great new body of pupils differed widely from those of pupils of the older 'privileged' schools and therefore called for a different educational treatment; and that, in general, the situation called for a determined effort in a society so constituted to transcend a distinction between culture and vocation which was itself an integral and necessary element in an older class inheritance. As for the parents, so long as the all-important issue of the achievement of status was not compromised they would have accepted a curriculum which gave to John or Mary a truly *relevant* education, even though it departed somewhat widely from the traditional curriculum, provided that John and Mary could obtain the School Certificate equally well on either course.

So the problem of *relevant adjustment* still faces us after nearly forty years' experience of the new conditions. Happily the Spens Report reveals a clear grasp of the situation and quite justly apportions to the Board of Education a large share of the blame for the failure. For it was the Board's own Regulations of 1904 which gave official sanction to the view that the new schools were to follow so closely the model of the old.

It is necessary to make this much clear at once in view of the crucial importance of the new 'secondary' schools for the coming order. We can now return to the task of discriminating roughly the various types of 'secondary' school. The differences, as has been noted, are much less educational than they ought to be. They are rather social, historical and administrative. We may thus distinguish:

(*a*) The 'public' schools, falling perhaps into the two groups of the greater and the less, with the boundary line at the lower end sufficiently vague, except in so far as it is marked by membership of the Headmasters' Conference. These schools regard themselves as 'national' in a special and almost exclusive sense and are disposed to regard public service as limited to the ranges – the upper ranges generally – in which they themselves are interested. They are intensely jealous of their private and independent status, and have hitherto been little disposed to assimilate themselves to the State-controlled system which they have tended to regard as being 'for the people' rather than 'national'. Liberal movements towards the breakdown of exclusiveness and a wider conception of the truly national are by no means lacking, but they seem unable to make much headway against the weight of an oppressive inheritance, or against the pressure of the *clientèle* for the social privilege which the schools are regarded as able to guarantee. In their present condition the public schools are much more the tied prisoners of their own history than the stage villains they are sometimes represented to be, bent on slaughtering in its infancy the unwanted child of an upstart democracy.

(*b*) The State-controlled schools. These again fall into various groups. Many are provided and maintained by local authorities. Many others, chiefly old grammar schools rehabilitated, are classed as schools 'aided' by local authorities. Still others remain administratively independent of the local authority and receive grants direct from the Board of Education. But all alike, as sharing in public funds, are required to reserve a certain number of 'special places' for pupils selected at eleven-plus from the elementary schools.

Allowing for certain local and special differences we may regard the members of this group as very much alike educationally, bound together as they are by the strong common tie of the School Certificate, a goal to which the great bulk of their pupils aspire. . . .

(*c*) The 'private' schools. This again is a somewhat motley group. It includes all those schools which regard themselves as 'secondary' (though taking often many pupils not of adolescent age) but are neither 'public' nor State-controlled. A good many of them are inspected and, if satisfactory, 'certified efficient' by the Board; a few are 'freak' schools; of many very little is known.

It is difficult to see how, in a reconstituted order of things, any of these schools can be left altogether free of public supervision.

(*d*) Junior technical schools. These may be included here, though their claim to 'secondary' status is sometimes contested. They take pupils (mainly boys, but some girls) at the age of thirteen-plus and prepare them in a three years' course for a specific trade or group of trades, taking care at the same time of the claims of general culture. Though their number is small – they exist only in large cities – their importance as an educational experiment is increasingly recognized. What they are trying to do is now better understood, being nothing less than that transcending in practice of the vocational-cultural distinction which we now see to be of such urgent importance. The experience gained by these schools provided the Spens Committee with grounds for proposing the further experiment of technical high schools.

(3) Institutions of 'Further' Education. Of these there is a bewildering variety, covering either part-time or full-time courses. They include: technical education, senior and junior; evening institutes, senior and junior; adult education of a more systematic and continuous kind than that given in evening institutes; day continuation schools; art schools; and some other varieties. All of these are in some form or other 'recognized' – that is, they are supported by local education authorities and rank for grant-aid from the Board of Education. Their relation to the full-time 'ordinary' school system varies. Technical courses are closely related, most evening institute courses can hardly be said to be related at all. Much of the provision has come into existence to meet demands of almost endless variety, including not only play-acting and keep-fit classes, but even such interests as pigeon-fancying.

(4) Informal organizations. The term is used to include a very numerous and widely varied body of community activities, not necessarily designed for an expressly educational purpose, not usually aided from public funds or controlled by public authority, but having nevertheless real educational value and importance. These include such organizations as Boy Scouts and Girl Guides, women's institutes, young farmers' clubs, community centres in town and village, BBC listening groups, dramatic societies, ramblers' clubs and many others in rich abundance. Co-ordinating machinery, like that of the National Council of Social Service and the recently created Youth Organization, exists to preserve some unity of direction and to promote mutual help. . . .

One illustration may be given to throw light on what some would call the rich diversity, others the caste structure, of English educational tradition. If by the term 'educational system' is meant a series of school stages or separated avenues by which one may pass to the university, then England has at least *three* rather sharply segregated education systems. These are:

(1) Home governess: preparatory school; public school
(2) Elementary school: State-aided secondary school
(3) Private school or schools.

These are routes entirely separate from one another, touching no-
where until they reach the university. Composites of two of them
are possible, such as:

Private school: State-aided secondary school (common)
Preparatory school: State-aided secondary school (less common)
Elementary school: public school (virtually unknown).

So far as we are aware there are no studies of English social structure and class distinction which have set themselves to estimate
with some precision the real social effects of these diverse routes to
the goal. If their diversity arose, as it is sometimes claimed to arise,
from healthy desire for originality and adventure in educational
effort, this might well be cause for congratulation rather than mis-
giving. But it can hardly be seriously maintained that this is so. The
segregation is surely to be explained on social grounds, and it might
well be argued that the three routes traced above might be expressed
as:

(1) The Free Front Door
(2) The Side Entrance
(3) The Front Door on Conditions.

Criticism of such a state of things is probably misdirected if it fastens
upon the mere fact of the existence of alternative routes. There is
nothing inherently anti-social in such an arrangement taken by
itself. Indeed, it is easy to see that it may hold out positive advantages
not offered by a single 'end-on' system of *grades* such as finds favour
all over North America. English habit would not take kindly to such
a system in any case.

What is open to criticism is the comparative absence of cross
connections between the different routes, the virtual exclusion of the
great mass of pupils in the senior schools from any of them, and the
fact that certain of the routes lead more surely and directly than
others to social advancement and positions of authority, even apart
from any purely *educational* superiority that these more favoured

routes may be able to claim. We can hardly continue to contemplate an England where the mass of the people coming on by one educational path are to be governed for the most part by a minority advancing along a quite separate and more favoured path.

COMMITTEE OF THE SECONDARY SCHOOL EXAMINATIONS COUNCIL (1943)

Curriculum and examinations in secondary schools (Norwood Report)*

WHAT IS SECONDARY EDUCATION?

The term 'secondary', as is well known, is used in at least two senses in England. On the one hand it is used to denote the education given in those schools which fall under the Regulations for Secondary Schools, and hence it arises that, while a secondary school has been defined officially, secondary education as such has received no precise definition. A 'secondary school' is officially defined as 'a day or boarding school offering to each of its scholars up to and beyond the age of sixteen a general education, physical, mental and moral, given through a complete graded course of instruction of wider scope and more advanced degree than that given in elementary schools'. Thus the meaning of 'secondary school' is dependent upon the meaning of 'elementary school', and to ascertain the meaning of 'secondary' and 'elementary' education acquaintance with the schools of both kinds is necessary. This definition excludes senior schools, junior technical, junior commercial and trade schools. On the other hand 'secondary education' is used in a much looser sense to mean any kind of education which follows upon 'primary' education, and therefore has reference to a stage in educational progress

* Reprinted from *Curriculum and Examinations in Secondary Schools* (London, HMSO, 1943).

corresponding to particular years in a child's life rather than to the precise nature of the instruction.

These two senses lead to much confusion of thought and statement. In this report we shall print the word Secondary with a capital initial letter when we wish to refer to existing 'Secondary' schools, as envisaged in the Regulations for Secondary Schools, and we shall print the word 'secondary' without a capital initial when we refer to the stage of education which follows the elementary or primary stage and which is sometimes called 'post-primary'. But we shall endeavour to make clear in other ways also the sense in which we use the word.

We have some sympathy with the hesitation to give a precise definition to the term 'secondary', and indeed to 'primary'. It is easier, and perhaps in the long run more satisfactory, to describe than to define. We have viewed the problem thus: at the primary stage the main preoccupation lies with basic habits, skills and aptitudes of mind, using as data the veriest elements of knowledge which all children should be put into the way of acquiring; such instruction is adapted to the degrees of general ability of the children; attention given to special interests or aptitudes can be only tentative, since these have not yet declared themselves emphatically or constantly enough to justify such attention. In the secondary stage, on the other hand, the attempt is made to provide for such special interests and aptitudes the kind of education most suited to them; they may have begun to indicate themselves at least roughly in the last phases of primary education, or they may not declare themselves in such degree as to deserve attention till a different kind of education is encountered. It is the business of secondary education, first, to provide opportunity for a special cast of mind to manifest itself, if not already manifested in the primary stage, and, secondly, to develop special interests and aptitudes to the full by means of a curriculum and a life best calculated to this end. Thus within secondary education there must be both diagnosis or prognosis and special treatment adapted to the particular case. At what age special abilities most generally declare themselves is clearly a matter of great importance for the structure both of primary and of secondary education; it is considered in its appropriate place.

VARIETY OF CAPACITY

One of the major problems of educational theory and organization has always been, and always will be, to reconcile diversity of human endowment with practical schemes of administration and instruction. Even if it were shown that the differences between individuals are so marked as to call for as many curricula as there are individuals, it would be impossible to carry such a principle into practice; and school organization and class instruction must assume that individuals have enough in common as regards capacities and interests to justify certain rough groupings. Such at any rate has been the point of view which has gradually taken shape from the experience accumulated during the development of secondary education in this country and in France and Germany and indeed in most European countries. The evolution of education has in fact thrown up certain groups, each of which can and must be treated in a way appropriate to itself. Whether such groupings are distinct on strictly psychological grounds, whether they represent types of mind, whether the differences are differences in kind or in degree, these are questions which it is not necessary to pursue. Our point is that rough groupings, whatever may be their ground, have in fact established themselves in general educational experience, and the recognition of such groupings in educational practice has been justified both during the period of education and in the after-careers of the pupils.

For example, English education has in practice recognized the pupil who is interested in learning for its own sake, who can grasp an argument or follow a piece of connected reasoning, who is interested in causes, whether on the level of human volition or in the material world, who cares to know how things came to be as well as how they are, who is sensitive to language as expression of thought, to a proof as a precise demonstration, to a series of experiments justifying a principle: he is interested in the relatedness of related things, in development, in structure, in a coherent body of knowledge. He can take a long view and hold his mind in suspense; this may be revealed in his work or in his attitude to his career. He will have some capacity to enjoy, from an aesthetic point of view, the aptness of a phrase or the neatness of a proof. He may be good with his hands or he may not; he may or may not be a good 'mixer' or a leader or a prominent figure in activities, athletic or other.

Such pupils, educated by the curriculum commonly associated with the grammar school, have entered the learned professions or have taken up higher administrative or business posts. Whether the curriculum was designed to produce men of this kind we need not inquire; but the assumption is now made, and with confidence, that for such callings a certain make-up of aptitudes and capacities is necessary, and such make-up may for educational purposes constitute a particular type of mind.

Again, the history of technical education has demonstrated the importance of recognizing the needs of the pupil whose interests and abilities lie markedly in the field of applied science or applied art. The boy in this group has a strong interest in this direction and often the necessary qualities of mind to carry his interest through to make it his life-work at whatever level of achievement. He often has an uncanny insight into the intricacies of mechanism whereas the subtleties of language construction are too delicate for him. To justify itself to his mind, knowledge must be capable of immediate application, and the knowledge and its application which most appeal to him are concerned with the control of material things. He may have unusual or moderate intelligence: where intelligence is not great, a feeling of purpose and relevance may enable him to make the most of it. He may or may not be good at games or other activities.

The various kinds of technical school were not instituted to satisfy the intellectual needs of an arbitrarily assumed group of children, but to prepare boys and girls for taking up certain crafts – engineering, agriculture and the like. Nevertheless it is usual to think of the engineer or other craftsman as possessing a particular set of interests or aptitudes by virtue of which he becomes a successful engineer or whatever he may become.

Again, there has of late years been recognition, expressed in the framing of curricula and otherwise, of still another grouping of pupils, and another grouping of occupations. The pupil in this group deals more easily with concrete things than with ideas. He may have much ability, but it will be in the realm of facts. He is interested in things as they are; he finds little attraction in the past or in the slow disentanglement of causes or movements. His mind must turn its knowledge or its curiosity to immediate test; and his test is essentially practical. He may see clearly along one line of study or interest and outstrip his generally abler fellows in that line; but he often fails to relate his knowledge or skill to other branches of activity. Because he is interested only in the moment he may be incapable of a long series of connected steps; relevance to present concerns is the only way of awakening interest, abstractions mean little to him. Thus it follows that he must have immediate returns for his effort, and for the same reason his career is often in his mind. His horizon is near and within a limited area his movement is generally slow, though it may be surprisingly rapid in seizing a particular point or in taking up a special line. Again, he may or may not be good with his hands or sensitive to Music or Art.

Within this group fall pupils whose mental make-up does not show at an early stage pronounced leanings in a way comparable with the other groups which we indicated. It is by no means improbable that, as the kind of education suitable for them becomes more clearly marked out and the leaving age is raised, the course of education may become more and more supple and flexible with the result that particular interests and aptitudes may be enabled to declare themselves and be given opportunities for growth. That a development of this kind yet lies to great extent in the future does not preclude us from recognizing the existence of a group whose needs require to be met in as definite a manner as those of other groups.

TYPES OF CURRICULUM

In a wise economy of secondary education pupils of a particular type of mind would receive the training best suited for them and that training would lead them to an occupation where their capacities would be suitably used; that a future occupation is already present to their minds while they are still at school has been suggested, though admittedly the degree to which it is present varies. Thus, to the three main types sketched above there would correspond three main types of curriculum, which we may again attempt to indicate.

First, there would be a curriculum of which the most characteristic feature is that it treats the various fields of knowledge as suitable for

coherent and systematic study for their own sake apart from immediate considerations of occupation, though at a later stage grasp of the
matter and experience of the methods belonging to those fields may
determine the area of choice of employment and may contribute to
success in the employment chosen.

The second type of curriculum would be closely, though not
wholly, directed to the special data and skills associated with a
particular kind of occupation; its outlook and its methods would
always be bounded by a near horizon clearly envisaged. It would thus
be closely related to industry, trades and commerce in all their
diversity.

In the third type of curriculum a balanced training of mind and
body and a correlated approach to humanities, Natural Science and
the arts would provide an equipment varied enough to enable
pupils to take up the work of life: its purpose would not be to prepare
for a particular job or profession and its treatment would make a
direct appeal to interests, which it would awaken by practical
touch with affairs.

Of the first it may be said that it may or may not look forward to
University work; if it does, that is because the Universities are
traditionally concerned with the pursuit of knowledge as such. Of the
second we would say that it may or may not look forward to the
Universities, but that it should increasingly be directed to advanced
studies in so far as the universities extend their orbit in response to
the demands of the technical branches of industry.

PURPOSES COMMON TO VARIOUS TYPES OF CURRICULUM

Hitherto we have treated secondary education as that phase of
education in which differences between pupils receive the consideration due to them. But when the boy with special interest in Languages
or Art has been provided with an education which takes this interest
into account, he still remains a boy. In other words, in spite of
differences all pupils have common needs and a common destiny;
physical and spiritual and moral ideals are of vital concern to all alike,
and secondary education, whatever form it may take, must regard
as its chief aim the satisfaction of all the needs of the child, both as a
human being and as a member of a community. At the earliest

stages there must be much that is common to the various types of secondary education, even as regards curriculum. For it would be a mistake to regard transfer from the primary to the secondary stage as a 'break': rather it is a process, and the transfer must be eased by a curriculum which carries over to some extent from the primary stage, and later takes on a more pronounced colour according to the type of secondary education chosen. Hence it would be reasonable that in the various types of school offering secondary education there should always be resemblances resulting from common purposes, but that in the early stages the resemblances should be stronger.

To sum up, secondary education is the second stage in the growth of the child. Healthy growth implies continuity, and, as we have said, the change from primary education is a process. For this reason all schools offering secondary education will have certain resemblances, but, since the function of the secondary stage is to provide for special interests and aptitudes, the differences between one type of curriculum and another will progressively become more pronounced as the child grows older. If secondary education as a whole is to do justice both to the individual pupil and to the community, each type must strive for the achievement of those aims which it shares with other types, while at the same time providing for the special need of those pupils to whom it offers its particular form of education.

SECONDARY EDUCATION AS IT EXISTS IN FACT

Under the existing organization of secondary education in this country the three kinds of curriculum which we have indicated have in fact been provided in the Secondary Schools, in the various types of Junior Technical Schools and in the Senior Schools; within each type of school and within individual schools various kinds of courses have been offered. In so far as these schools assume, as they do, previously acquired skills and habits exercised upon the elements of knowledge and on that assumption go on to differentiate special aptitudes and interests and to cater for them, the schools are in fact secondary in character, using the term secondary to denote the second stage in education. Secondary education, as it exists in fact, already shows the diversity which we regard as essential to its health. The

Junior Technical Schools, though inadequate in number and equipment, provide varied opportunities; the Senior Schools, though only in an early stage of development, are showing enterprise in meeting the special needs of particular localities. With Junior Technical Schools and with Senior Schools we are not specifically concerned, except in so far as consideration of them is necessary to the building of a single structure of secondary education, and we shall make no attempt to describe them in detail. The Secondary Schools show great variety as regards traditions, the aim and destination of their pupils, the interests and abilities of pupils, organization and curriculum. Inheriting the tradition of the grammar school they have at the same time held to it and deviated from it: indeed they now display a variety which some critics would say has reached the point of confusion in aim and function. That there should be variety we regard as essential; willingness to recognize needs and to make the adaptation necessary to meet them is a sign of vitality in education.

W. LLOYD WARNER, ROBERT J. HAVIGHURST AND MARTIN B. LOEB (1946)

Who shall be educated?*

(I) THE SCHOOL IN THE STATUS SYSTEM

New social responsibilities of education

Equal opportunity to all – that was America's promise. It was on the lips of every preacher and school-teacher. It was taught at every humble fireside. Every business man, industrialist and politician proclaimed it and believed it . . .

It was evident to all that America offered equality of opportunity,

* Reprinted from *Who Shall Be Educated? The challenge of unequal opportunities* (London, Kegan Paul, Trench and Trubner, 1946).

because so many people rose from humble beginnings to high places. As long as upward social mobility is so common that everyone can observe it all the time, people will believe that opportunity is equal and plentiful. If upward social mobility becomes less frequent, if the common man sees fewer people rising in the world, belief in the existence of equality of opportunity fades. In spite of the possible argument that people at the bottom of the social heap are born with less innate ability and therefore cannot expect to rise, the ordinary man is apt to diagnose a lack of social mobility as a lack of opportunity.

The social mobility of nineteenth-century America has been explained by sociologists and historians as due to three causes – cheap land, expanding frontiers and expanding business and industry.

There was plenty of good land to be had at a low price for the labour of clearing, ploughing and planting. Little capital was required – no more than could be saved in a year or two's work or advanced by an ordinary man from his savings. Immigrants, younger sons and disgruntled city workers could always move out to the frontier and be sure of a fair reward for hard work. Those who were foresighted and industrious could count on growing wealthy as the West developed and could be reasonably sure of placing their children at the top of the social pyramid.

Business was usually good, and industry was always growing. Great new industries developed: lumber, meat-packing, flour-milling, steel, oil – then chemicals, electrical products and automobiles – and finally aeroplanes, motion pictures and radio. There was always room at the top in the ever-expanding industry of the country.

During that century education played only a small part in promoting social mobility. The elementary school made people literate, but family, church and community gave young people the character which fortified their native wit and made them push ahead. High school and college provided avenues of mobility for a few who rose thereby into the professions of medicine, law, the ministry and teaching. But this was a narrow pathway compared with the broad highway provided by agriculture, business and industry.

Social mobility continued to be the outstanding feature of American social life on into the twentieth century. Although the frontier had disappeared and the good land was all taken, business and industry continued to grow. The post-war business boom of 1920–30 may have accounted for more upward economic mobility than occurred in any other decade in the country's history.

But by 1930 a change had come over the pattern of social mobility. The preceding few decades had seen marked increases in the number of people in the technical and service professions. Chemists, engineers, teachers increased greatly in numbers. Anyone aspiring to these positions needed general education and special skill. Native wit and perseverance were no longer sufficient. The collapse of business expansion after 1930 put the finishing touches on a picture of social and economic mobility that was entirely different from the nineteenth-century picture.

The people turn to education

A study of high school and college enrolments tells what the American people did when it became clear that education and special skill were needed more and more for social mobility. Before 1890 attendance at high school and college was confined to less than 5 per cent of the youth of the country. These were mainly boys and girls of high social position and economic status who were being educated to take the places of their parents, together with a few lower-status boys and girls who aspired to high status and chose to secure this higher status by entering a profession.

The schools and colleges began to grow rapidly during the period from 1890 to 1910, and they expanded with almost explosive velocity from 1910 to 1930. Within a period of fifty years, the proportion of young people attending high school multiplied tenfold, and the proportion of young people attending collegiate institutions multiplied three- to fourfold.

Still believing that their children should rise and seeing in the secondary school and college the principal avenues of mobility, the people sent their children to secondary school and college. The American people learned what the people of older cultures have learned, that the schools are the social elevators in a hardening social structure. The Chinese have known this and used the schools in this way since the time of Confucius. In Europe the school system represents a social elevator moving from the very bottom of a society to its top and has been used for this purpose for a long time.

At great sacrifice American parents struggle to put their children through high school and college. They want their children to 'have an easier time' than they have had. They hope that their children will secure white-collar jobs. Most American parents believe that the best measure of their success in this life, and a good indication of their deserts in the future life, are to be found in the rise or fall of their children in the social scale.

How the school fits in

The educational system bears these expectations as it operates in our social system. We shall see, now, how it meets these expectations.

The educational system is a sorting and selecting agency

The educational system may be thought of as an enormous complicated machine for sorting and ticketing and routing children through life. Young children are fed in at one end to a moving belt which conveys them past all sorts of inspecting stations. One large group is almost immediately brushed off into a bin labelled 'non-readers', 'first-grade repeaters' or 'opportunity class' where they stay for eight or ten years and are then released through a chute to the outside world to become 'hewers of wood and drawers of water'. The great body of children move ahead on the main belt, losing a few here and there who are 'kept back' for repeated inspection.

At a station labelled 'high school' there are several types of inspection and the main belt divides into smaller belts which diverge slightly from each other. From some of the belts the children, now become youths, are unceremoniously dumped down chutes into the outside world, while the other belts, labelled 'college preparatory', 'commercial', 'vocational', roll steadily on. The young people are inspected not only for brains and learning ability, but also for skin colour, pronunciation, cut of clothes, table manners, parental bank account. Strangely enough they are not inspected for moral integrity, honesty or other qualities which go under the name of 'character'.

At the end of the high school division several of the belts project their human freight into the outside labour market, and the sorting machine is now much smaller, housing a few narrow conveyors labelled 'college', 'professional school', and 'trade school'. The inspectors quickly shunt aside the majority of this small band of young men and women into the labour market, leaving a few indeed who reach the next station, labelled 'bachelor's degree', which is the end of the machine really, though there is a small extension called 'graduate school'.

Whatever figure of speech we use, the school system appears to be a sorting device with various selective principles operating. In addition to the principle of intellectual ability, there are such principles of selection as economic status, social class and social personality. There is little or no selection for moral character.

The Hometown school has already sorted out Tom Brown from Bob Jones. Tom will be promoted regularly and prepared for college. Bob will be dropped as soon as possible. It is not yet clear what will happen to Joe Sienkowitz, but it appears that he will finish high school and because of his talent his teachers may help him to get a scholarship for study of music. There are probably two or three other boys in Tom Brown's class, fully as able as Tom, but without any special artistic talent, who will have to stop their education at the end of high school because their way into college is blocked by lack of money.

We can see how much selection takes place by looking at the figures for the numbers of young people who reach various levels of the educational ladder. Table 1 gives the number of youth out of 1,000

TABLE 1. *The school as a selecting agency*
(Number of people out of every 1,000 who reach a given educational level)

Level	1938	1910
First year high school (age 14)	850	310
Third year high school (age 16)	580	140
Graduation from high school (age 18)	450	93
Entrance to college or a similar educational institution	150	67
Graduation from college (bachelor's degree)	70	23
Master's degree	9	1·5
Doctor of philosophy	1·3	

who were reaching certain rungs of the ladder on two dates a generation apart, 1938 and 1910. The high school is much less selective at present than it was a generation ago. The college has also lost some of its selective quality though it remains a highly selective institution.

Through its function as a sorting agency the educational system is supposed to sift out the people with best brains and ability and to help them rise to the top. Thus the school is not only a system of education, it is also a system of elections. In America this system of elections is not 100 per cent efficient. That is, it does not succeed in selecting all the people with the best brains and ability and helping them to rise in the status system.

Educational opportunity is not equally available to all

There are two senses in which we might say that educational opportunity is equally available to all children. We could speak of equal educational opportunity if all children and young people went to schools of their own choosing as long as they or their parents pleased. In that sense we fall far short of providing equal educational opportunity and we shall probably never attain such a goal.

In a more limited sense we might speak of equality of educational opportunity if all children and young people exceeding a given level of intellectual ability were enabled to attend schools and colleges up to some specified level. This is the only practicable kind of equality of educational opportunity. For example, if all boys and girls with I Qs over 100 were able to attend high school up to the age of eighteen, and if all young people with I Qs over 110 were able to attend college for four years, we could say that equality of educational opportunity existed to a considerable degree.

It is possible to investigate the availability of educational opportunity in this sense in various parts of the country. For example, a study of youth in Pennsylvania was conducted about a decade ago by the State Department of Public Instruction and the American Youth Commission. The socio-economic status and educational history were ascertained for a group of 910 pupils with intelligence quotients of 110 or above. It is generally assumed that pupils with intelligence quotients above 110 are good college material. This group of superior pupils was divided into two subgroups on the basis of socio-economic status. Of the upper socio-economic group 93 per cent graduated from high school and 57 per cent attended college. Of the lower socio-economic group, 72 per cent graduated from high school and 13 per cent attended college. Further study of the data in Table 2 will show even more clearly that the group with below-average socio-economic status had relatively less educational opportunity than the group with above-average socio-economic status, although both groups were about equal in intellectual ability.

TABLE 2. *Relation of intelligence to educational opportunity* (Record of students with intelligence quotients of 110 or above)

Educational advance	Socio-economic status above average		Socio-economic status below average		Total group	
	No.	%	No.	%	No.	%
Dropped school at eighth grade or below	4	0·7	27	7·9	31	3·4
Completed ninth, tenth or eleventh grade but did not graduate from high school	36	6·2	69	20·2	105	11·6
Graduated from high school but did not attend college	206	36·3	202	59·0	408	44·8
Attended college	322	56·8	44	12·9	366	40·2
Total	568	100·0	342	100·0	910	100·0

A similar conclusion must be drawn from a study made by Helen B. Goetsch on 1,023 able students who graduated from Milwaukee high schools in 1937 and 1938. These students all had IQs of 117 or above. The income of their parents is directly related to college attendance, as is shown in Table 3. The higher the parents' income, the greater is the proportion who went to college.

The same general result is found in the data of the National

TABLE 3. *Relation of parental income to full-time college attendance of superior Milwaukee high school graduates*

Parental income $	Percentage in college full-time
8 000+	100·0
5 000–7 999	92·0
3 000–4 999	72·9
2 000–2 999	44·4
1 500–1 999	28·9
1 000–1 499	25·5
500– 999	26·8
under 500	20·4

Health Survey, which was conducted in eighty-three cities in eighteen states during the winter of 1935-6. When boys and girls of ages sixteen to twenty-four are classified by family income, school attendance increases markedly with increase in family income.

(II) STATUS IN THE CLASSROOM

Class and the rating of a child's ability

Outwardly, the school is that institution which sorts out people by achievement, and as the standards of judgement seem to be fairly objective, we might believe that the school is not closely bound to the social structure in which it exists or that, if it is, then the social classes tend to separate out with those with the most intelligence at the top of the school and those with the least at the bottom.

In some elementary schools where there is more than one class-room per grade there is a section system by which students are rated and put together into A section, B section, C section, and more if necessary. In the Old City, we find such a system. Each grade is divided into three sections: A, B, C. This division into sections pervades the whole school system but of necessity it has less formal characteristics in the later years of high school. The junior high school principal says of these sections:

When a child enters school he is put into one of three sections according to what the teacher thinks his ability is. When you have dealt with children much you soon find that you can pretty well separate them into three groups according to ability. Then if a child shows more ability he may be shifted into a higher group or if he fails he may be moved into a lower group.

Some time later when this same principal was asked whether there seemed to be any class distinctions between the sections, he answered:

There is to some extent. You generally find that children from the best families do the best work. That is not always true but usually it is so. The children from the lower class seem to be not as capable as the others. I think it is to some extent inheritance. The others come from people who are capable and educated, and also the environment probably has a great effect. They come to school with a lot of knowledge already that the others lack.

Whatever one may think of this principal's theory in explanation of the correlation between social position and school section, this correlation holds true. There is a strong relationship between social status and rank in school. An analysis of the classes of three years in which the social position of 103 girls was known, shows that

(1) of the ten upper-class girls eight were in section A, one in B and one in C
(2) of the seven upper-middle-class girls, six were in section A and one in B
(3) of the thirty-three girls from lower-middle and indeterminate middle class, twenty-one were in section A, ten in section B and two in section C
(4) of the fifty-three lower-class girls, only six were in section A, twenty-eight in section B and nineteen in section C.

A teacher in junior high school was willing and able to talk more explicitly about these sections than was the principal quoted above. This teacher was asked if there was 'much class feeling in the school' and she said:

Oh, yes, there is a lot of that. We try not to have it as much as we can, but of course we can't help it. Now, for instance, even in the sections we have, it is evident. Sections are supposed to be made up just on the basis of records in school but it isn't and everybody knows it isn't. I know right in my own A section I have children who ought to be in B section, but they are little socialites and so they stay in A. I don't say there are children in B who should be in A but in the A section there are some who shouldn't be there. We have discussed it in faculty meetings but nothing is ever done.

Later on, she said:

Of course, we do some shifting around. There are some border-liners who were shifted up to make the sections more nearly even. But the socialites who aren't keeping up their standard in the A section were never taken into B or C section and they never will. They don't belong there socially. Of course, there are some girls in A section who don't belong there socially, but almost every one of the socialites is in A.

In Old City the ranking of students in their classrooms is clearly influenced by status considerations. . . .

In many school systems intelligence tests are used as a means of sectioning children according to ability. If an intelligence test measures 'real' intelligence, we cannot say that discrimination on status grounds exists in these schools. But the intelligence tests generally used as a basis for grouping children are known to favour urban children with family backgrounds that encourage reading, travel, talking, museum visiting and so on. The problems given and the vocabulary used in these tests are taken pretty largely from urban middle-class life. Accordingly, rural children and lower-class urban children do not do as well on these typical *verbal* intelligence tests as they do on *performance* tests of intelligence and on other tests in which efforts have been made to eliminate the factor of cultural background. And if pupils are grouped according to their showing on the usual verbal tests of intelligence, the upper group will consist mainly of upper- and middle-class children.

Of course, there are exceptions to grouping on the basis of social class. The explanation of these exceptions falls in two parts. In the first place, there is no doubt that ability is frequently rewarded regardless of class. It is true though that the lower-class child must show greater ability to be recognized than does the higher-class child.

Secondly, whenever a lower-class child shows in his behaviour that he or she is quick to learn the middle-class standards of acting, the teacher is more likely to reward that child. Or if the child shows any exceptional talent, the teacher will act encouragingly. What appears to happen is that the teacher, like a speculator, puts her efforts and rewards where she thinks they will bring in the biggest gain. She knows that those who are most likely to succeed, here placed in their order of probability, are those from better-class families, those who have exceptional ability and those who seem to have the stuff to learn the ways of living which make them comparable to children of the better-class families.

As previously pointed out, social mobility depends as much on 'proper behaviour' as on anything else. Children learn proper behaviour as they learn other things by being rewarded for doing the correct thing or by being punished for doing the wrong thing. The teacher does a good deal of rewarding and punishing as she consciously or unconsciously encourages behaviour according to middle-class standards.

Thus we see the school formally dividing its pupils into groups which have as part of their standards the social class position of the family and the class behaviour of the child. Young people from families of a given social position learn to be with one another and to exclude those of lower social status.

MINISTRY OF EDUCATION (1947)

The new secondary education*

Everyone knows that no two children are alike. Schools must be different, too, or the Education Act of 1944 will not achieve success. They must differ in what they teach and how they teach it, just as pupils differ in tastes and abilities. The secondary school system

* Reprinted from *The New Secondary Education* (London, HMSO, 1947).

must consequently offer variety in the curriculum and variety in the approach, suited to the differing aptitudes and abilities and stages of development of the children concerned. Moreover, for many years to come the school life of some children will be longer than that of others. Pupils who hope to go on to the university, for example, will naturally remain at school longer than those who aim at being apprenticed at fifteen or sixteen. Secondary courses for some pupils will thus have to be planned to cover six to seven years, while other pupils will need courses of four or even (until the leaving age is raised to sixteen) of three years. The importance of these factors is recognized in the 1944 Act, which requires secondary schools to be 'sufficient in number, character and equipment to afford for all pupils opportunities of education offering such variety of instruction and training as may be desirable in view of their different ages, abilities and aptitudes, and of the different periods for which they may be expected to remain at school'. Clearly there must be wide variety in the secondary system. The curriculum must be made to fit the child, and not the child the curriculum. The schools must offer individual children who differ widely from one another the kinds of curriculum that will fit them all to live happily and to become useful members of the community.

Experience has shown that the majority of children learn most easily by dealing with concrete things and following a course rooted in their own day-to-day experience. At the age of eleven few of them will have disclosed particular interest and aptitudes well enough marked for them to require any other course. The majority will do best in a school which provides a good all-round education in an atmosphere which enables them to develop freely along their own lines. Such a school will give them a chance to sample a variety of 'subjects' and skills and to pursue those which attract them most. It is for this majority that the secondary *modern* school will cater.

Some children, on the other hand, will have decided at quite an early stage to make their careers in branches of industry or agriculture requiring a special kind of aptitude in science or mathematics. Others may need a course, longer, more exacting, and more specialized than that provided in the modern school, with a particular emphasis on commercial subjects, music or art. All these boys and girls will find their best outlet in the secondary *technical* school.

Finally, there will be a proportion whose ability and aptitude require the kind of course with the emphasis on books and ideas that is provided at a secondary *grammar* school. They are attracted by the abstract approach to learning and should normally be prepared to stay at school long enough to benefit from the 'sixth form' work which is the most characteristic feature of the grammar school.

Both 'books' and 'activities' are essential in all the three types of secondary course; no school can afford to base its work exclusively on one or the other. The person who has no kind of skill with his hands is as imperfectly prepared for life as one who cannot read. The proportions in which these two ways of learning are to be combined should be determined by the capacities and needs of the individual pupil, and the basic principle is that whatever his native ability a child must be guided towards the kind of work in school over which he can acquire some sense of mastery. This means, for instance, that it is of little use to present subject-matter to him which he is unable to appreciate or to press him to labour in an atmosphere of frustration. It will be evident that it is as unfair to the child to expect him to develop through a study of Latin or advanced mathematics, if he shows no sign of attaining any standard in them, as it is to restrict him to a practical or scientific approach if his more characteristic outlet is through the humanities. No organization, indeed, will adequately meet the situation that involves the sacrifice of the best interests of one type of child to those of others. This is a sacrifice our country cannot afford.

Every secondary school, then, of whatever type, must be able to provide for the full development of its pupils, since this is a vital part of the new plan of secondary education for all. The Minister desires to lay down no set guides for organization but to encourage local authorities to plan as best suits their local needs. In some places where conditions are favourable the best way of carrying out the new plan may be to combine two, or three, types of secondary education in one school. Current controversy on this subject has shown the disadvantages, as well as the obvious advantages, in such an organization. Where it is adopted it will be particularly necessary to ensure that the courses provided are sufficiently varied to meet all needs and are of equal status, that transfer from one course to another is facilitated, and that opportunity is given to all children, the less able as well as the abler, to develop fully and to gain some experience of responsibility.

In order to ensure that a school providing secondary education for all the senior children in a given area offers proper scope and opportunity for all its pupils, it will have to be a very large school. It is doubtful whether a school with less than a ten-form or eleven-form entry (that is a total of 1,500 to 1,700 pupils) is capable of offering the necessary variety of suitable courses.

There is much to be said for what is sometimes called the school base or 'campus plan'. In this, a number of schools varying in character and tradition are built on a single site, and make common use of many facilities and amenities, such as playing-fields, swimming-baths and dining-halls. They constitute a kind of federation of schools, each one developing its own individual character, yet each making its contribution to the life of the larger unit.

There is, indeed, no end to the possible varieties of organization; the system must be flexible and experiments of many kinds are to be welcomed. The only proviso that must always be observed is that the real interests of the children must come first.

Whatever type of organization is adopted and however careful and thorough the methods of allocation at eleven may be, there are likely to be some misfits. For a few pupils it may turn out that a wrong choice of secondary course was made at eleven. A few others may develop aptitudes in the first year or two at a secondary school that were dormant and unsuspected earlier. To meet the needs of such pupils all local education authorities must have arrangements which make it possible without difficulty to transfer them at any stage in their secondary school career from one type of secondary education to another. The way must be clear for boys and girls in any type of secondary school to continue their education in such ways as will give them the opportunity to go on to higher studies at a university, a college of further education, or elsewhere.

The distinction between the three main types of secondary education is bound to appear much more definite and rigid on paper than it need be in practice. While the differences of method and approach should be kept clearly in mind, the preceding chapter illustrates the need to avoid exaggerating and stereotyping the differences between types of education that have and must always have a great measure of common ground. Whether education is offered in separate grammar, technical and modern schools, or in schools that combine two or more of these types of course, it must contain as essential ingredients such common features as have been described, it must appeal to the interests of the pupils and it must be related to their ability. It must provide them with the best possible conditions for growing up, for reaching the appropriate stage in the maturing process so that they may leave school as balanced individuals ready socially, emotionally, physically, spiritually and intellectually for the next stage in their lives.

2

Selection under attack 1948-67

2

Selection under attack 1948-67

In *Three Schools or One?* (1948) Lady Simon of Wythenshawe drew on American experience of the 'common secondary school' for her analysis of the problems facing English education. Her book and American writing in the tradition of *Who Shall be Educated?* played an important part in English educational debate. Although the situations and structures were clearly different the underlying class situation was taken to be similar and relevant. Alison Davis's *Social Class Influences upon Learning*, for example, published in the United States in 1948, was concerned primarily with differences in socialization between classes, and the importance of social class in shaping opportunity, behaviour, educational incentives and performance:

> The child's social learning takes place chiefly in the environments of his family and its friends, and of his own play-group. All these groups, we now know, are restricted in the range of their social and cultural participation by social-class barriers. Thus the culture of both the child's family and his play-group become class-typed. This social-class patterning of the child's learning, as exerted through the family, extends from control of the types of food he eats and of the way he eats it to the kinds of sexual, aggressive, and educational training he receives.[1]

The study pursued these and other differences in detail, and discussed their relevance to the education of children from working-class and middle-class, white and black families. From an awareness of this kind of evidence the discussion in Britain of equal opportunity derived some of its impetus in the late 1940s and early 1950s. It derived impetus, however, from other sources also.

[1] Alison Davis, *Social-Class Influences upon Learning* (Cambridge, Mass., 1948), p. 12.

It drew, for example, on the wartime and post-war discussions about democracy and welfare, and the ideal of social justice that underlay the concept of the welfare state. The 1944 Act itself had been in part a product of this social consciousness, but by the end of the 1940s there was a growing sense in radical political and educational circles that educational advance had been too limited. Still coupled with discussions of opportunity were questions of waste and rights. T. H. Marshall pointed out in 1949 that 'recent studies of educational opportunity in the pre-war years have been concerned to reveal the magnitude of social waste quite as much as to protest against the frustration of natural human rights'. The post-war situation had not yet solved either problem, as Marshall's discussion of the 1944 Act went on to show. Quoting the provision in the Act for education according to age, aptitude and ability, he commented: 'Respect for individual rights could hardly be more strongly expressed. Yet I wonder whether it will work out like that in practice.'[2] There was an increasingly expressed view from the end of the 1940s that it was not 'working out like that'.

In the early 1950s criticism of the system of secondary education also drew on two other sources. The first was the work on social mobility conducted under David Glass at the London School of Economics in the Department of Sociological and Demographic Research, and in which Jean Floud and others who were to play a prominent part in this discussion were engaged. The second was the experience of the early comprehensive schools, mainly under the completely comprehensive systems of the Isle of Man and Anglesey, and in the comprehensive schools of London. Robin Pedley began a survey of this experience in 1954 with the statement that 'the field of debate on comprehensive schools is shifting from theory to practice'. Most of the schools, he pointed out, were developing cautiously:

> The first comprehensive schools . . . reflect – as indeed one might expect – the pattern of the society in which they are set; they are content to tread the middle of the road. Tactically, at the moment, this is an advantage: the comprehensive school has to defend itself on a narrow front instead of a broad one. To some the

[2] Marshall, *Sociology at the Crossroads*, pp. 111–12.

observation will bring comfort, to others regret; but that is a matter for debate rather than description, and must be pursued elsewhere.[3]

Pedley's data and observations were, in fact, pursued. The fact that the schools were organizing themselves with caution, streaming, grading, and reproducing some of the educational and social divisions of the tripartite system, was seized on by critics to show that comprehensive schools brought none of the advantages claimed for them. Defenders used such findings to press for new, less middle-of-the-road approaches. Debate was to some extent shifting, as Pedley indicated, from the theory of opportunity to the practice of comprehensive schools.

Among psychologists in the early 1950s some confusion began to emerge, as to how reliable intelligence tests were in measuring 'innate ability' and to the validity of tests, when it was realized that performance in them could be influenced by coaching. Psychologists like P. E. Vernon, whose research had uncovered some of these ambiguities, nevertheless defended testing as the most scientific predictive instrument available. Sociologists and other critics of selection pointed to the wide margins of error involved in their use, and attacked their 'objectivity' and value in predicting future educational performance. Brian Simon's *Intelligence Testing and the Comprehensive School* in 1953 made a sustained attack on the process of selection and the testing on which it relied. Vernon, while defending the overall position, admitted that Simon, 'while chiefly expressing the left-wing egalitarian point of view, does make a strong case against many of the assumptions underlying the use of intelligence tests, and the segregation of different streams of pupils in different secondary schools'.[4]

With this widening field of discussion in the early 1950s, as well as other developments in comprehensive education (most notably the Leicestershire plan from 1957), a new stage in the history of the concept of equal opportunity had clearly been reached. The evidence of inequality, and the class, family and environmental explanations of it, mounted from Floud, Halsey and Martin's *Social Class and*

[3] Pedley, *Comprehensive Schools To-day*, pp. 1, 20.
[4] P. E. Vernon (ed.), *Secondary School Selection: a British Psychological Society Inquiry* (London, 1957), p. 35.

Educational Opportunity in 1956 to studies like Jackson and Marsden's *Education and the Working Class* in 1962 and J. W. B. Douglas's *The Home and the School* in 1964. As Floud, Halsey and Martin pointed out, 'the problem of equality of educational opportunity is now more complicated than when it took the simple form of the need to secure free access to grammar schools on equal intellectual terms.'[5] Elizabeth Fraser's *Home Environment and the School* pointed in 1959 to the fact that 'in spite of general acknowledgement that environmental factors exert considerable influence on a child's school progress, relatively little scientific research has been carried out to determine which aspects of the environment are most influential'.[6] The need for more research was being expressed in almost every article, book or official report in this area of discussion in the late 1950s and 1960s.

The evidence and the argument were carried into other fields, and produced other results. Controversy increased in the Labour Party during the long period in opposition up to 1964, and local pressures from Labour teachers very often moved reluctant Labour authorities into planning for comprehensive schools. The idea of comprehensive schools gained increasing support in the Conservative Party. Official committees used and extended the sociological evidence. The Crowther Report, *15 to 18*, for example, in 1959 looked at parents' occupational background in relation to early leaving, and the Robbins Report on *Higher Education* (1963) discussed and documented at length the influence of social class on access to different stages of education, in relation to the concept of a 'pool of ability' and the expension of the universities. Much of this writing contained a strong element of historical analysis. Floud, Halsey and Martin, for instance, explained the historical processes at work in the areas they investigated; the Crowther and Robbins reports offered useful historical comparisons; Flann Campbell's *Eleven-Plus and All That* (1956) rested a picture of the grammar schools and social change on a detailed historical account of London's scholarship and selection procedures. There was at the same time much descriptive writing. For example, the Newsom Report of 1963, *Half Our Future*,

[5] J. E. Floud (ed.), A. H. Halsey and F. M. Martin, *Social Class and Educational Opportunity* (London, 1956), p. 149. See p. 167 below.
[6] Elizabeth Fraser, *Home Environment and the School* (London, 1959), p. 1.

contained a vivid chapter which described 'Education in the slums'. J. B. Mays the following year published *Growing up in the City: a study of juvenile delinquency in an urban neighbourhood*, with a penetrating picture of 'the scope and effectiveness of existing agencies' in relation to a specific set of social problems. Richard Hoggart in 1957, in *The Uses of Literacy*, included a portrait of the 'scholarship boy', adding a human dimension to the discussion of education and society.

The discussion was also moving in other directions. Little and Westergaard, in an important survey of 'The trend of class differentials in educational opportunity in England and Wales' in 1964, summarized the position at that point:

> Differentials in educational opportunity coincide with many other social differentials. . . . A good deal of recent work has pointed to the important – and almost certainly increasing – role of cultural, rather than crude material, factors in perpetuating educational inequalities: class differences in educational aspirations, occupational orientations, language, intellectual climate, and so on.[7]

Basil Bernstein's work on language was gaining a wide audience in the early 1960s, and was seen to extend the range of analysis of social class and education as it had been previously conducted. Bernstein's contention was that research showed

> a pattern of difficulties which the lower working-class pupil experiences in trying to cope with education as it is given in our schools. This will not hold in precise detail for every pupil, but we can say that the probability of finding such a pattern is greater if the pupil's origin is lower working-class. Such children will experience difficulty in learning to read, in extending their vocabulary, and in learning to use a wide range of formal possibilities for the organisation of verbal meaning; their reading and writing will be slow and will tend to be associated with a concrete, activity-dominated, content; their powers of verbal comprehension will be limited; grammar and syntax will pass them by; the propositions they use will suffer from a large measure of

[7] Alan Little and John Westergaard, 'The trend of social class differentials in educational opportunity in England and Wales', *British Journal of Sociology*, XV (1964), p. 313.

dislocation; their verbal planning function will be restricted; their thinking will tend to be rigid – the number of new relationships available to them will be very limited.

He suggested that in arithmetic such children 'may master the mechanical operations involved in addition, subtraction and multiplication, provided they have also mastered their tables, but they will have some difficulty in division. However, verbal problems based upon these operations may confuse them.' Their 'time-span of attention will be brief . . . They are not interested in following the detailed implications of a concept or object and the matrix of relationships which this involves.'

Bernstein's analysis led him to formulate two 'linguistic forms'. One, a *public* language, 'associated with the lower working-class', had a more rigid syntax and a 'restricted use of formal possibilities for verbal organisation'. With the middle-class *formal* language the 'possibilities for sentence organisation are used to clarify meaning and make it explicit'.[8] Whereas middle-class children had access to both language forms, other children were restricted to the public language. Bernstein concluded that 'a linguistic environment limited to a *public* language is likely to produce (from a formal educational point of view) deleterious effects'.[9] Bernstein's analysis and argument, in the late 1950s and early 1960s, was obviously an important extension of the discussion of the *processes* which underlay the facts of educational inequalities. His work was widely quoted and discussed, and became the basis for extensive further research into the nature and implications of different language codes.[10]

Detailed American studies, in many ways parallel to British ones, were being published in the late 1950s and 1960s by such writers as R. J. Havighurst and Patricia Sexton. Continental researchers were now discussing British experience, and vice versa. Demands for longer common schooling in France, it was realized, were based on

[8] Basil Bernstein, 'Social structure, language and learning', *Educational Research*, III (1961), pp. 164–5.
[9] Basil Bernstein, 'Social class and linguistic development: a theory of social learning', in A. H. Halsey, Jean Floud and C. Arnold Anderson (eds.), *Education, Economy, and Society* (New York, 1961), p. 303.
[10] It was intended to include an example of Bernstein's work from this period in this collection, but this has unfortunately not proved possible. The reader is referred to either of the two papers quoted above.

situations not unlike those in Britain (in France in the 1950s, for example, 85 per cent of children of members of the liberal professions, civil servants and administrators, and 20 per cent of the children of industrial workers, were obtaining secondary education).[11] Extensive analysis of Swedish educational reforms in the 1950s and 1960s, such as those of Torsten Husén, was reaching conclusions similar to those of comprehensive supporters in Britain. 'The educative society', wrote Husén, 'requires an elective school, not a selective school. By elective school I mean a type in which the pupils, by being permitted a phased choice of electives, can gradually focus their studies in a direction to which they are drawn by their abilities and interests.' The educational drawbacks could not 'outweigh the national and individual benefits accruing from a school which caters for everybody'.[12] At the same time attempts were beginning to be made in Britain to analyse in greater detail some other educational and social mechanisms, for example in Brian Jackson's *Streaming: an education system in miniature* (1964). Stephen Wiseman, in *Education and Environment* (1964), produced a wideranging survey of existing research on socio-economic and environmental factors influencing educational attainment. Such research, egalitarian argument and educational change were not without their critics, as the passage from G. H. Bantock indicates.

Two documents point clearly to the changed climate of opinion of the late 1960s. After the election of a Labour government in 1964 the Department of Education and Science issued circular 10/65 on *The Organisation of Secondary Education*. The Labour Party leaders, some of them reversing long-held principles, decided to move towards a fully comprehensive secondary school system, not by parliamentary legislation but by persuasion, and local authorities were 'requested' to submit plans for reorganization if they had not already done so. In some areas much controversy resulted, and resistance was organized; by the time the Labour government was defeated in 1970 the circular had been only partially effective (and the withdrawal of the circular was one of the first acts of the new

[11] W. R. Fraser, *Education and Society in Modern France* (London, 1963), p. 54.
[12] Torsten Husén, 'Social determinants of the comprehensive school', *International Review of Education*, IX (1963), pp. 171-2.

Conservative government in June 1970). The second important document was the Plowden Report on *Children and their Primary Schools* in 1967, based essentially on the principle that 'equality is not enough',[13] and that priority, positive discrimination, in favour of underprivileged areas was necessary. The report directed attention more precisely and firmly to the roots of inequality in the period before secondary education.

By the end of the period covered in this section a substantial change had taken place in the nature and tone of the argument about equality of opportunity. Investigations had become more detailed and moved to new ground; 'secondary education for all' had been replaced as a slogan by the comprehensive school, which had been adopted as government policy; the theory and practice of the comprehensive school had come under scrutiny and attack; international experience was being more widely drawn upon; the facts and mechanisms of educational underprivilege had been demonstrated at many levels, and the data had become common currency in national and local policymaking and planning. The concept of equality of opportunity had been challenged as 'not enough'.

LADY SIMON OF WYTHENSHAWE (1948)

Three schools or one?*

(I) ARE THERE THREE TYPES OF CHILDREN?

The tripartite or unilateral system rests on the assumption that there are roughly three types of children, academic, technical and the 'also rans'. These latter, it is said, need a general education, more practical in its approach and with a generous allowance of handwork.

---

[13] Central Advisory Council for Education, *Children and their Primary Schools* (London, 1967), p. 56. See p. 246 below.
* Reprinted from *Three Schools or One? Secondary education in England, Scotland and the U.S.A.* (London, Frederick Muller, 1948).

Both the Spens Committee and later the Norwood Committee based their recommendations on this assumption, but, whether or not psychologists were ever unanimous in supporting it, educational opinion now is not nearly so sure about its validity as it was ten years ago. In fact the reaction against it is fast gathering speed. There is, of course, a considerable amount of truth in the recognition not only of different abilities in children but of differing amounts of those abilities in each child. Different methods of approach, a variation in the contents of subjects, a different balance of subjects in the curriculum, are generally agreed to be necessary if children are to be given the secondary education that accords with their different abilities and aptitudes. But is it possible – leaving aside for the moment whether it is desirable to separate children so clearly into three types – that by setting up three separate schools the intention of the Act will be fulfilled? Those who support the tripartite system evidently assume that the answer to these questions is in the affirmative. But the West Riding Education Committee recently approached Professor Godfrey Thompson, Sir Cyril Burt, Dr Fleming, and Sir Fred Clarke for help in solving this problem. There was general agreement amongst these authorities that it is not really possible to segregate children according to aptitudes at the age of eleven-plus. We need, they said, more experiment with different kinds of secondary education as well as with methods of selection before we can make such a decision. Professor Thompson said, 'Although I think *some* indication of special aptitudes can be discovered at eleven, I am certain that the indications at that age are so slight and elusive that no great reliance can be placed upon them.' Sir Cyril Burt said that the classification of pupils for literary, scientific, technical and other forms of specialized education is as much a matter of vocational as of educational guidance. The general opinion today seems to be that the only assessment that can be made at eleven-plus is the amount of whatever it is that can be measured by intelligence tests at that age.

Dr Earle, the Principal of Kirkcaldy High School, a multilateral school, and himself an educational psychologist, writes, 'There are not two or three main types, there are many varieties of human ability and character and any reduction in the number of groups or types – even to six or eight or ten – necessarily produces those

misfits for whom progressive adjustment is always necessary.' Dr
Fleming in an article in *The Schoolmaster* says,

> Mention may at this point again be made of the myth as to the
> existence of three types of child corresponding to the administra-
> tive provision of buildings which may house separate schools of
> academic, of technical and of modern type. Recent evidence both
> as to the variability of human growth and the complexity of
> human functioning indicates the inadequacy of such a clear-cut
> division. There are a few children who are interested only in
> ideas, and a few who are interested only in things. There are
> some who are not aware that they are interested at all. There do
> not seem, however, to be enough pupils with such markedly
> twisted functioning to fill even a classroom in any district where
> measurements of interests has been attempted. There is also no
> evidence which would lead one to believe that segregation of such
> pupils when they do appear is any more desirable on educational
> grounds than any other form of artificial segregation of human
> beings. The interest profiles of pupils can be shown to vary as
> widely and to show as great a complexity of pattern as their
> ability profiles.

Against this formidable array of experts we must get Dr Alexander
and the Ministry of Education.

Dr Alexander, who has himself invented tests for practical
ability, says,

> At eleven we can measure academic ability, can we measure
> practical ability? This is a real problem. Group tests do not do it
> at eleven and it is so easy in research work to use group tests and so
> difficult to use individual tests, that most research work has been
> done on group tests. At thirteen group tests show evidence of this
> third factor; under group testing it is not evident at twelve or
> eleven, and therefore it is assumed that it does not mature till
> thirteen. But the fact is, that it does emerge at eleven on individual
> testing, using apparatus independent of words. The question is, is
> such a test used at eleven sufficiently reliable to make an important
> judgement? I can only tell you that the correlation between the
> test results and success at sixteen in a technical diploma is actually

higher than between the verbal tests and success at sixteen in verbal subjects. I will not say it is completely reliable, but is as reliable as what we have been doing for the last fifteen years on the verbal side ...

and again,

> The point is that you can have a record at the age of eleven-plus, which shows the judgement of teachers for the whole range of the child's interests and abilities and you can have an objective measure of academic and practical aptitude; you cannot have any objective measure of personal characteristics, determination or stability or any of these other things, assuming that these are independent factors. . . . There are some children with so much aptitude that they will succeed in a certain kind of school without trying; but there is a very broad borderline, and the problem is to make a considered judgement as to whether, having regard to aptitude and character qualities such as determination, the child will be successful in this school or that.

In a later paper given to the North of England Conference in January 1947, Dr Alexander elaborates this point. He suggests that children could be allocated to an academic course as the result of a combination of intelligence tests and an assessment for a desire to succeed. . . .

The Ministry of Education has, in the recent publication, *The New Secondary Education*, somewhat modified the view it put forward in a previous pamphlet, *The Nation's Schools*, in that it now admits the possibility that bilateral and multilateral schools may be established as well as unilateral schools. But with regard to the problem I am now considering, it says, 'Experience has shown that the majority of children learn most easily by dealing with concrete things and following a course rooted in their day-to-day experience' – namely the modern secondary school; 'some children, on the other hand, will have decided at quite an early stage to make their career in branches of industry or agriculture requiring a special kind of aptitude in science and mathematics' – for these the technical secondary school; 'finally there will be a proportion whose ability and aptitude requires the kind of course with the emphasis on books and ideas, that is provided at the secondary grammar school. They are attracted by the abstract approach to learning and should normally be prepared to stay at school long enough to benefit from the sixth form work.' There seems to be a confusion here between types of ability in the child and the financial ability of the parents. Many children who according to the above analysis should have a grammar school education will, owing to economic circumstances, have to leave school at sixteen. Does the Ministry mean that these children should go to the modern school? If so, it is nonsense to speak as if allocation is on the abilities and aptitudes of the child. Also does the Ministry really think that children decide at eleven-plus if they are going 'to make their career in branches of industry or agriculture' and is it advisable that they should? The Ministry continues, 'Both books and activities are essentials in all three types of school; no school can afford to base its work exclusively on one or the other. . . . *The proportions in which these two ways of learning are to be combined should be determined by the capacities and needs of the individual pupil.*' The italics are mine, but how does this sentence fit in with the tri-partite system? Books figure more, and practical activities less, in the grammar school than in the modern school, but if the proportion is to vary to suit each child, would it not be much easier to do this in a school that provides both books and practical activities? . . .

Apparently, the development of the 'whole child' in the secondary sphere is to be entrusted chiefly to the modern school. It is a pity that the authors of a pamphlet which says so many wise things about secondary education as a whole should have felt compelled to think of it and present it to the public as a matter of three separate and unequal institutions instead as of a 'house with many mansions'.

(II) THE COMPREHENSIVE SCHOOL

This school, according to the Ministry's definition, 'is a school which is intended to cater for all the secondary education of all the children in a given area without an organization in three sides'. That is to say, it is as unselective as the omnibus school, but without its multi-lateralism. The LCC uses this term rather than multilateral to describe its proposed new secondary schools, but in settling their size it appears to have based its calculation on an assumption of the percentage of children who will follow a grammar, technical or modern course, and arrives at the figure of 1,500 to 2,000 pupils. It is probably for this reason that the Ministry, when considering the minimum size for a comprehensive school, says, 'It seems likely that the comprehensive school, if it is to provide the desirable varieties of education to cater for all the senior children in a given area, may settle down to an organization very little different from that of the multilateral school, except that the terms grammar, technical and modern will not be used.' This, however, seems to show a misconception of what the advocates of the comprehensive school propose.

The County of Middlesex also proposes to set up comprehensive high schools and, in a discussion of its development plan, Mr C. T. Giles said that

> such schools could be smaller than those proposed by the LCC, since the Middlesex plan does not assume three distinct streams. The comprehensive school should not be a clumsy amalgamation of the grammar, technical and modern school curriculum, but should provide a new content and organization calculated to overcome the weakness that all types of school had shown in the past.

There is, as yet, no comprehensive school in either England or Scotland – the omnibus schools in the latter country being organized in separate streams with no mixing of children for any subjects. They are found in the USA as a development from the multilateral high school, but the internal organization there, as I pointed out, is combined with a system of electives and credits which, whether or not it is a good system, has never been suggested for this country. It would be quite possible to combine the organization of a comprehensive high school with our system of progressive study throughout school life of subjects combined to make a coherent whole.

The distinction between a comprehensive and a multilateral school lies in the fact that in the former it is proposed that groups of children shall take the place of 'streams'.

In our English grammar and modern schools, we divide the children, on entry, into streams of thirty; A, B, C, if it is a three-stream school, and continuing down the alphabet if it has a large entry. These children usually then learn *all* the subjects of the curriculum together. In the grammar and modern schools the curriculum for each stream is roughly the same in each school. In the boys' grammar school, the A stream will probably take School Certificate in four years, and the B stream in five. The B and C streams may also take easier options in that examination. The assumption underlying the stream organization is that children with similar I Qs will show a similar capacity for learning similar subjects.

In the omnibus schools of Scotland too the streams are kept separate and are based on the I Qs of the children. The children never mix in their work.

If, as the psychologists now tell us, there are not three types of children corresponding to three types of schools, but a variety of types shading into one another at different points, then is the assumption upon which the stream system in the multilateral schools is based sound? . . .

When we have records of children through their primary school life, it will be possible to take into account, at the beginning of their secondary school career, their interests and aptitudes for all subjects, as well as their attainments in English and arithmetic and their intelligence quotients. They could then work with children of like interests and aptitudes for the different subjects.

This system has always been used in certain schools, particularly the public schools, for mathematics and languages. Boys are put in 'sets' with others of similar attainments for that subject, but work at other subjects with their form. Why should not the system be applied to all subjects? If such an organization were possible, children of varying I Qs might be found working together at dramatic performances, art, music, cookery and craft work. I am not denying, what I understand is an established fact, that children with high I Qs are better not only at academic, but at practical work, than children with low I Qs. But that surely depends upon their 'aptitudes'? Some children are more clumsy in using their hands than others, and I doubt if this is related to I Qs. Unless there happens to be a very exceptional teacher, art work in a grammar school is usually, I find, inferior to art work in a modern secondary school, although the I Qs of the former are, of course, higher than those of the latter. In the multilateral school it is claimed that although children of varying abilities do not actually work together, they meet in school assembly, games, prefects meetings, meals, choirs, school plays and other functions. This is certainly an advantage over the unilateral schools, but if they could meet in some of the work of the school, such as projects in history and geography, the advantage of having them all under the same roof would be immensely greater.

A comprehensive high school, besides fulfilling more completely than any other school the ideal of providing secondary education suited to the age, ability and aptitude of each child, might fulfil another function. Alone of the three countries, the USA has come nearest to the ideal of providing a high school 'which is a unifying and enriching agent . . . of its local community'. England, in spite of its broad conception of secondary education derived largely from its public schools, has allowed this same education to be the cause of bitter class division between its people. Scotland has avoided that state of affairs, but its conception of education has been so narrowly academic that division has developed on those lines. The USA, where from a very early period the people fashioned the high school to suit their needs has, in spite of many limitations, developed a common secondary school which reflects and thus perpetuates the American way of life.

Sir Fred Clarke remarked recently that, in England, schools had always been given from above – they had never developed from the people.

This is indeed true; first the churches, then the universities through the grammar schools, have set the aim of our education and influenced its methods. Now at least we have a chance to fashion a common secondary school that will unite instead of dividing the nation, and that will be the expression of the new spirit which must inspire the working of the 1944 Act if it is to come to full fruition.

BRIAN SIMON (1953)

Intelligence testing and the comprehensive school*

INTELLIGENCE TESTING AND SELECTION FOR
SECONDARY EDUCATION

The changing intelligence quotient

Selection for different kinds of secondary schools at the age of
ten can only be justified on the grounds that the child mind has a
single central factor ('innate all-round intellectual ability'), which
determines the ultimate level of his intellectual powers, and which
can be reliably measured at an early age.

Leaving aside, for the moment, the many theoretical problems
involved in this hypothesis, and ignoring also the evident bias of
intelligence tests already described, we may inquire, on the purely
practical plane, whether the scores obtained by children on tests are
reliable measures.

Intelligence tests can only claim to be reliable measures of an
innate quality if children, tested a number of different times over a
period of years, consistently obtain an approximately similar
Intelligence Quotient.

In the 1920s and 1930s, it was widely held that a child's IQ
remained constant as he grew older. This view was not, however,
based on long-term studies of individual children, since, at that time,
no such investigations had been carried through. It was based primarily on the results of testing groups of children two or three times
at fairly short intervals, results which showed that, *on average*, the
IQ remained roughly constant.

For instance, Terman, discussing this question in 1921, wrote,
'speaking roughly, 50 per cent of the IQs found at a later test may be

* Reprinted from *Intelligence Testing and the Comprehensive School* (London,
  Lawrence and Wishart, 1953); reprinted in *Intelligence, Psychology and
  Education : a Marxist critique* (London, Lawrence and Wishart, 1971).

expected to fall within the range between six points up and four points down. . . . It is evident, therefore, that the IQ is sufficiently constant to make it a practical and serviceable basis for mental classification.'

The last part of Terman's statement was repeated, while the qualification in the first sentence was conveniently forgotten. All that Terman in fact claimed was that 'roughly speaking' half the children tested a second time showed a variation of up to about five points. The other half showed an even greater variation, nor does he indicate how large were the individual changes. Clearly this is not convincing evidence for claiming that the individual child's IQ remains constant; nevertheless it was consistently suggested that this was so.

The theory of the constant IQ has, however, recently had to be abandoned as a result of long-term researches undertaken primarily in the USA. These have shown beyond any doubt that children's scores vary from year to year, some steadily increasing, others decreasing, yet others oscillating up and down although usually showing a long-term trend. For a child's IQ to remain the same year after year is entirely exceptional. Further, it has been demonstrated that the longer the time interval between the first and the last test, the greater, in general, is the discrepancy between the scores.

In view of this it can hardly be claimed that the tests are a reliable measuring rod of that supposedly innate and unalterable quality, 'intelligence'. Children's scores on a particular test at the age of ten have significance for that moment in time only. If the same test were given to the same group either a year later or earlier, the scores would almost all be different, some considerably so, and the actual order in which the children were placed would also be very different. Practically, this means that the group of children selected for the grammar schools by a certain test at ten would be different from the group selected at nine or at eleven or twelve, even if a proportion of the children were in each group.

In addition, all kinds of influences may affect the child, and so his score, under the conditions of the actual selection examination; influences which the psychologist would regard as strictly irrelevant. For instance, the child's attitude to the test and his own emotional reaction at the time will, to some extent, determine his success. If he is sick or tired, or suffering from any degree of nervous strain, he

118   BRIAN SIMON

may not do himself justice. He may be unfamiliar with examinations, become overawed and muff his papers. There are half a hundred possible reasons of this kind why a child may do less well than he normally would, or again why some children might do better than usual. It has even been shown that the way the test is supervised, whether strictly or slackly, has a profound effect on the children's scores.

Clearly children cannot be compared to machines giving always a constant output. On the contrary, the way they behave at a particular moment may depend on all kinds of complex and subtle influences. For this reason alone, a group intelligence test score is slender evidence on which to base a final judgement of a child's ultimate intellectual development. Quite apart from this, the tests themselves are very unreliable as guides, partly owing to differences in methods of construction and validation. 'Few experienced persons' writes Professor Vernon 'appear to put much trust in an individual's group test score, not only because of prejudice or conservatism, but also because different group tests are known to yield remarkably discrepant results. . . . A child who is given two or more may obtain IQs differing by as much as thirty or even forty points.' One might add that practically no child will get exactly the same score if given the same test twice. And yet, as Mr Clegg has pointed out, success or failure in the selection examination at ten is often determined by a decimal point on the examination as a whole, an examination dominated by one particular intelligence test, which, of course, puts children in a different order than would be the case if any other intelligence test were used.

Psychologists themselves are, of course, aware of the limitations of group intelligence testing. Thus Vernon concludes that such tests 'are not (very useful) for obtaining trustworthy information about individuals', although they have their uses in the testing of groups, and for large-scale experiments. Sir Cyril Burt, one of the two psychologists who gave oral evidence to the Spens Committee, has himself said: 'No predictions are so confidently offered by the educational or vocational psychologist as those which are based on some such factor as "g" or general intelligence. Yet again and again his forecasts are falsified.' This is the expert's view, yet in selection the results of these tests are treated as if they were trustworthy and normally given great weight; and, of course, as far as parents are concerned, it is the individual child and his future opportunities that matter.

Coaching for intelligence tests

The fact that an individual child's IQ varies from test to test, as well as from day to day and from year to year, is itself an indication that these tests are scarcely satisfactory instruments on which to base not only the practice but also the whole theory of selection. But recently mental testing has suffered a much severer blow than any that have gone before. It has been clearly established that coaching in the 'tricks of the trade' can have a profound effect on children's test results. Late in 1952, Professor Vernon announced that the *average* rise in IQ which was obtained from a limited amount of instruction in the technique of answering test questions was as much as fourteen points. One investigator actually raised the average IQ of a complete class by seventeen points after four hours' work, while with a similar class he obtained an increase of sixteen points after one hour only.

Professor Vernon himself pointed out the significance of this discovery. The typical cut-off point for a pass into a grammar school is supposed to be at an IQ of 115. Normally 17 per cent of an average class of children may be expected to pass this borderline, and so win a place. But if this same class were coached and the average IQ rose fifteen points, exactly half the class would pass the borderline. In other words, 33 per cent of the class who, without coaching, would not have qualified for a grammar school, would do so after coaching.

Coaching for intelligence tests has, of course, been going on for a long time. Parents, not unnaturally, have bought practice test booklets and given their children instruction. In some junior schools the children spend many hours on different kinds of test questions. It has been known that this kind of coaching produced good results, but the implications for testing were so serious that this undoubted fact had been ignored. At a meeting of some 200 Middlesex teachers in 1952, Professor Vernon, in his own words, 'tried to play down the seriousness of coaching'. He continues: 'I was informed from the floor in no uncertain terms how widespread it was in the country.' Consequently, he embarked on the research outlined above. He found that his conclusions paralleled those of other researchers in the 1920s and 1930s; conclusions, incidentally, to which little or no attention was paid until it became impossible to avoid the issue.

It is natural that psychometrists should have tried to ignore the very considerable changes in test scores that result from coaching. Until recently, the *cornerstone* of psychometry has been that intelligence tests measure, at least approximately, the same inherited, unchangeable quality of mind – intelligence; and it is on this assumption and this alone that their use in selection – and indeed selection itself – has been justified to the public. If a local authority can say to a protesting parent: we have scientific evidence that your child simply has not got enough intelligence to profit from a grammar school education, the parent has no alternative but to accept this dictum.

And yet it has been shown beyond any doubt that children can be taught to do intelligence tests, just as they can be taught to do English and arithmetic, chess and crosswords. . . . There is nothing unteachable in the kind of questions or problems set. Teachers and parents, of course, have been aware of this, the number of practice tests on the market is sufficient indication of their wide and general use. . . .

The defects in the practice of intelligence testing, summarized in this chapter, have led to much heart searching among teachers, local authorities, psychologists and indeed among all those concerned with the unhappy business of sorting children out at ten or eleven. Nobody is satisfied with the present methods or procedure, least of all the parents, as the pages of the popular and the local press abundantly testify. In particular, it is the intelligence test that is most sharply criticized. The I Q is under fire.

One county authority, Hertfordshire, announced early in 1953 its intention of cutting 'the knot in which intelligence testers have entangled themselves' by dropping these tests from the selection examination, chiefly for the reasons given above. Other authorities are trying to work out methods of selection that put less emphasis on these scores. Articles in the educational press describing these methods reflect this unease. 'Selection tests for secondary education are now under hot fire, and some of the shots are going home', writes a reviewer of a pamphlet on selection in Wiltshire. 'That there is a widespread dissatisfaction with the present system of selection for grammar schools needs no emphasis.' This, it may be noted, was written by a grammar school headmaster; there is no 'system of selection' for modern schools. When Hertfordshire abolished intelligence tests, the *Schoolmaster*, organ of the National Union of Teachers, published a cartoon of a tank breaking through a wall described 'I Q barrier', and headed the cartoon 'Hertfordshire strikes again'.

But selection cannot be saved simply by abolishing the 'intelligence' test, which has hitherto been the keystone of the whole system. What is the alternative? To hand over selection for grammar schools largely to the grammar school headmasters (as in Hertfordshire and Wiltshire), or to the primary school headmaster (as is apparently proposed in the West Riding), or, alternatively, to include different *kinds* of tests (essay papers, comprehension tests and so on), as various other authorities are doing, does not solve the problem at all. Fundamentally the same kind of decision has to be made by somebody. Children must be sorted out at the early age of ten *according to predictions made about their future intellectual development*. The basic assumptions of intelligence testing must therefore underlie these 'new' methods as well. The only difference will be that these methods, relying as they do to a greater extent on the personal judgement of one or two people, can make no claim to scientific validity at all. They represent an advance, therefore, only in this sense, that with the relegation of intelligence tests into the background, it becomes impossible for anybody to maintain that selection is a scientific procedure. The case against separating children into different groups at the age of ten becomes proportionately more overwhelming.

H. T. HIMMELWEIT (1954)

Social status and secondary education since the 1944 Act: some data for London*

In this chapter, some new data concerning the relationship of social status to secondary school education will be presented. The data were obtained in the Greater London area as part of a more comprehensive inquiry into the influence of social status upon the outlook, attitudes and behaviour of young adolescents. Since the study was carried out in 1951, several years after the Education Act had come into force, the results may serve to throw light upon the way in which 'secondary education for all' has worked out in practice.

Questionnaires and tests, dealing with the boy's relationship to others, with his leisure interests, his vocational aspirations and his attitude to school were administered to over 700 young adolescent boys in grammar and secondary modern schools, the two main types of secondary schools within the State system.

The study was restricted to one age-group; thirteen- to fourteen-year-old boys were chosen because at that age they are already sufficiently close to school-leaving to make questions both about school and about vocational aspirations meaningful to them. It is also the latest age at which secondary modern school boys can be tested as a group and at which one can be certain of obtaining a truly representative cross-section of the grammar school population. To ensure representativeness, all the boys in the third forms were tested.

Each boy was assigned to a given social status group on the basis of his father's occupation, using the Hall-Jones scale of occupational prestige. But because of the limited numbers, a fourfold classification of status was adopted: the middle middle group (comprising in the main Hall-Jones categories 2 and 3); the lower middle group; and the upper and lower manual groups. It must be emphasized that

* Reprinted from *Social Mobility in Britain*, ed. D. V. Glass (London, Routledge and Kegan Paul, 1954).

TABLE I. *Percentage distribution of sample by type of school and social status groups*

Social status of pupils	Grammar school %	No.	Secondary modern school %	No.	Total %	No.
Middle middle	21·7	(72)	5·9	(23)	13·1	(95)
Lower middle	26·5	(88)	13·7	(54)	19·6	(142)
Upper working	37·0	(123)	38·5	(151)	37·8	(274)
Lower working	14·8	(49)	42·0	(165)	29·5	(214)
Total	100·0	(332)	100·0	(393)	100·0	(725)

these divisions are relatively crude and that the groups adopted here are defined exclusively in terms of occupational prestige, thus leaving out of account the other important indices which may affect an individual's position in the social hierarchy. This should be borne in mind in connection with subsequent references in this chapter to 'working class' and 'middle class'; those terms are used as a convenient shorthand description, but they refer to groups defined in terms of occupational prestige and not to 'classes' in the classic sense of the word.

To move upwards in status, a working-class child must not only have the opportunity of attending a grammar school, but also pass its examinations. This chapter will therefore first consider the proportion of sons of manual workers in the sample who go to grammar schools, and then examine their performance and standing at such schools as compared with those of the sons of white-collar workers.

SELECTION FOR GRAMMAR SCHOOL EDUCATION

In order to increase the range of geographic and social variation, the schools covered in this inquiry were chosen from two districts from the centre of London – one a predominantly working-class district in the East End (Schools A), the other a more 'mixed' district in the south-west of London (Schools B) – and from two rather more middle-class suburban districts (Schools C and D). Grammar and modern schools were drawn from the same or equivalent districts to permit a more systematic study of the effect of different school environments upon boys from similar socio-economic background coming from the same neighbourhood. . . .

While we have no figures for these particular schools prior to the Education Act of 1944 from which to draw precise comparisons, there can be little doubt that the number of children from upper-working-class homes in grammar schools has increased considerably. They constitute one-third of both grammar and modern school populations. By contrast, children from lower-working-class homes, despite their numerical superiority in the population as a whole, continue to be seriously under-represented. They constitute only 15 per cent of the grammar school as against 42 per cent of the modern school sample. This under-representation, while most pronounced in the suburban districts, is also evident in the working-class district. . . . The figures show that in recent years the upper working class has become more adequately represented, but, given the social composition of the neighbourhoods served by the grammar schools, the middle class continues to be over-represented. It is unlikely that there are so few children from lower-working-class homes in the grammar schools because parents refused the offer of a grammar school place. What is much more probable is that the performance of the children at the selection examination at the age of eleven-plus was such that only very few came within the top fifth of their age group which would qualify them for entry into the grammar school. It might be argued, in turn, that this occurs because, in the lower working class, the number of boys of the requisite ability is small. But several facts speak against such an interpretation.

In the first place, previous research has shown that, except for the extremes of the occupational ladder, variations in IQ *within* occupational groups are generally greater than those *between* the groups. Very large occupational groups like those to which semi-skilled and unskilled manual workers belong should, therefore, contain a larger absolute number of individuals of the requisite ability than some of the numerically much smaller middle-class occupational groups, despite the higher average intelligence level to be found among the latter.

It is more likely that the children from the lower socio-economic groups do relatively less well on the tests of attainment which make up 66 per cent of the total marks. Some indirect evidence in support of such a view was found in comparing the borderline cases in the two school populations. Although the majority of boys in the grammar school sample had significantly higher IQs than those in the secondary modern school, there were some boys with identical intelligence test results who had nevertheless been assigned to different schools. Sixty-nine modern school boys constituted the sample of 'under-achievers' and eighty-nine grammar school boys the sample of 'over-achievers'. It was found that over- and under-achievement were significantly related to social status; thus 55 per cent of the over-achievers came from the middle-class and only 12 per cent from the lower-working-class homes. In the case of the under-achievers, only 19 per cent came from the non-manual and 39 per cent from the manual groups.

TABLE 2. *Percentage distribution of secondary school sample size of family*

	Working class		Middle class		Total		
	Small family	Large family	Small family	Large family	Small family	Large family	Total
Grammar school	62·9	37·1	67·9	32·1	65·4	34·6	100 (332)
Secondary modern school	36·7	63·3	64·9	35·1	42·2	57·8	100 (393)

Secondly, it was found that in both the upper and lower manual groups, family size and ordinal position within a family were factors influencing a boy's chances of going to a grammar school. These were significantly greater for the boy from a small-size family (one- or two-child famiies) $(p < 0.003)$ and also for the eldest son, irrespective of the number of his siblings. Since no such differences were found in the non-manual groups they require an explanation over and above that of the known negative correlation between IQ and family size.

A child, especially a young child, is likely to do better at school the more encouragement and help he receives from home. It is probable that such help is afforded more readily in small families and that for the first-born more ambitious plans are made, plans in which higher education is a necessary stepping-stone. In the middle class, however, scholastic achievement is of concern to all parents since higher education is valued as the necessary means, not only of getting on, but also of maintaining existing social status. Such differences in parental attitude towards education may well influence a child's attitude to school work and so affect his performance in the examination.

In addition, middle-class homes provide greater opportunities for extra-curricular learning. Davis's studies in the United States suggest that verbal intelligence tests draw upon experiences with which a middle-class child would be more familiar than a working-class child. Since the majority of education authorities used verbal intelligence tests, the results for boys from the lower social groups may represent an underestimate of their effective or at least of their potential intelligence.

None of the facts presented here provides more than a hint as to the reasons for the differential performance of children from the various social classes. Nevertheless, the evidence does suggest that, although the main economic barriers may now have been removed, there are other, less tangible, barriers which affect a boy's chances of getting into a grammar school.

A COMPARISON OF THE ACHIEVEMENTS AND ASPIRATIONS
OF MIDDLE- AND WORKING-CLASS GRAMMAR SCHOOL BOYS

In her analysis of educational mobility prior to 1940, Mrs Floud drew attention to the fact that even among the selected grammar school population, the odds were heavily weighted against children from the lower status categories. Compared with children from the middle class, a disproportionately small number of working-class children obtained the school certificate – the first formal qualification – and an even smaller number proceeded to further education, leading to professional qualifications. Increasingly today, for the vast majority, a rise in social status is dependent upon the attainment of professional qualifications. Mere attendance at a grammar school ensures no more than entry into the lowest grades of clerical occupations, representing only a small step up the social scale for the son of a skilled workman. Moreover, before World War II a considerable number of grammar school pupils took up manual work on leaving school, i.e. they retained, at least initially, their parental social status. In view of the academically orientated curriculum of the grammar school and of the fact that teachers judge the success of their school in terms of the size and activity of their sixth form, this tendency to leave school early connoted a failure of the educational system in this respect. The failure, due to an interplay of economic, historical and psychological factors, lay in not mobilizing to the full those resources of endeavour and ability among the working-class youth which enabled them in the first instance to succeed in the competitive examination at the age of eleven-plus.

To what extent has this picture changed as a result of the Education Act of 1944? There are as yet no statistics available concerning the differential school-leaving record of children from the various social status groups. But in the course of the present inquiry it was possible to study the effect of social status upon scholastic performance and upon attitude to education at an earlier stage, i.e. two to three years after entry into the grammar school. The marked differences in academic attainments and in outlook to school life already shown at that age give little ground for supposing that the 'failure of the grammar school' has become a problem of the past.

ACADEMIC RECORD

There is no examination common to all grammar schools, prior to the school-leaving examination, which would make cross-school comparisons possible. The analysis of the scholastic performance of boys of different social status had, therefore, to be restricted to a comparison of the annual examination results within forms. Such small units make a statistical evaluation of the significance of differences meaningless, but the very consistency of the results leaves little doubt as to the likely outcome had the results of a common examination been available. Within each form, the social background of those who belonged to the five best and the five worst in the class was listed. Eleven such comparisons were made for each of the seven subjects common to the curricula of the four schools. . . . Except for the predominantly working-class grammar school in the East End, a consistently higher percentage of children from middle-class homes was found among the top five and less among the bottom five. . . . The superiority of these children was fairly evenly spread over all subjects in the curriculum. Taking all four schools together, in no subject did the manual group attain the higher position.

Analysis of the data showed that this inequality of examination performance was not accounted for by differences in IQ. To throw some light upon the problem, each form master was asked to indicate the boys who, in his opinion, were the five best and the five worst in the form with regard to a number of characteristics, namely, industriousness, sense of responsibility, interest in school affairs (extra-curricular activities), good behaviour, good manners and popularity with other boys. These characteristics were chosen as being likely to bring out differences in the evaluation of pupils from varying home backgrounds. The results were analysed on the lines of those on academic performance. ... Throughout, without a single exception, middle-class pupils received a higher rating. The consistency of the findings, irrespective of the quality rated, is of interest. True, this may simply reflect the well-known 'halo effect' which so greatly influences ratings of apparently independent characteristics. Nevertheless, the results show that, in the teacher's view, the middle-class boy, taken all round, proves a more satisfactory and rewarding pupil. He appears to be better mannered, more industrious, more mature and even more popular with the other boys than his working-class co-pupil.

In the eyes of the teachers, therefore, the boy with a working-class background is not so well integrated into the school. It is difficult to estimate how far such evaluation is the result of genuine differences in behaviour and outlook on the part of the boys or to what extent it reflects differences in the teacher's attitudes to pupils coming from different social backgrounds. No generalization would be justifiable at this stage. But there is evident need for an investigation into the attitudes of grammar school teachers to the recent educational changes and to the resultant increase in the numbers of working-class boys among their pupils. ...

CENTRAL ADVISORY COUNCIL FOR
EDUCATION (ENGLAND) (1954)

Early leaving*

THE INFLUENCE OF THE HOME

One of the significant findings to which we wish particularly to call
attention concerns the children of semi-skilled and unskilled
workers. Of the 1,621 children in our sample who entered the grammar school from these two classes, 917, or more than half, failed to
get as many as three passes at Ordinary level, and of these 520 left
before the end of their fifth year; 32 per cent and 37 per cent respectively of the failures in these two ways, compared with 21 per cent of
the whole entry, were from these types of homes. Our sample tells us,
therefore, that of approximately 16,000 children who in 1946 entered
grammar schools throughout England from such homes, about 9,000
failed to get three passes at Ordinary level, and of these about 5,000
left before the end of their fifth year.

So many of the unskilled workers' children achieved little that it
will be worth while considering them separately. The first point to
observe is the low rate of entry from the unskilled workers' home.
The number of children from unskilled workers' families who might
have been found in our grammar school sample if the proportion
were the same as in the population as a whole is about 927; the
actual number was 436. This suggests that some 5,000 children from
unskilled workers' homes who might have been expected, if the
yield from unskilled workers' homes were the same as from other
homes, to enter grammar schools in England in 1946 did not qualify
for admission. The second important finding is the high rate of
academic failure among those who did. Of the 436 children admitted
284, or two-thirds, left without as many as three passes at Ordinary
level. Thus, of about 4,360 children from unskilled workers' homes
who entered grammar schools, only about 1,500 obtained the

* Reprinted from *Early Leaving* (London, HMSO, 1954).

benefit that the grammar school is specifically designed to give. At a higher level the wastage was even more marked: on the same calculation only 230, or one in twenty, obtained two Advanced passes or entered for two Advanced subjects. These represent 1·4 per cent of the 17,000 children who took advanced courses, about one-ninth of the proportion in which unskilled workers' children are found in the population as a whole.

The reasons for this phenomenon must be very complex and we do not claim fully to understand them. The factors which we discuss below are the more obvious, but they are clearly incomplete. Throughout our consideration of this problem we felt ourselves, in spite of much public discussion, to be in territory that had so far been little explored; and it is probable that many economic, social and perhaps biological factors have escaped us. We are here in a field where many inhibitory influences are at work, often in an obscure manner. Educational sub-normality in parents may play a part. We do not consider that we could undertake any further study of the problem since this would call for machinery of research beyond our means. It is most important that further research into the problem of the effect of the home background, particularly that of the semi-skilled and unskilled worker, upon a child's education at a grammar school should be undertaken by some body competent to inquire into social problems and able to give the necessary time for a prolonged and thorough investigation.

We are not here concerned simply or even mainly with difference of income. . . . Although in a very broad sense the respective groups of parents' occupations into which our sample is classified represent different ranges of income the correspondence is far from exact. For example, it would not be easy to say how the incomes of parents in the clerical group compare with those of the skilled and semi-skilled workers respectively; and while the parents of professional or managerial standing will on the whole be better off than the members of any other group there will be some among them, such as clergymen and teachers, of whom this is not true. We cannot assume, therefore, that the differences revealed in the performance of children in the several occupational groups are primarily attributable to differences in parental income.

At the same time, we do not underrate the effect of bad living conditions. Unhappy and broken homes, family quarrels and lack of sound home discipline can be found in all walks of life and at all levels of society, and they will always tend to have the gravest effect on school work. So will the physical conditions of the home. A child's chances at a grammar school may be very seriously impaired by bad housing or over-crowding, the absence of suitable space for study, inadequate lighting or heating, lack of quiet, the constant distraction of the wireless or television, or other forms of disturbance. In the 55,000 households shown by the 1951 census as having an average of more than three persons per room the difficulties of a grammar school child may well be overwhelming. The 300,000 households with an average of more than two persons per room are likely to provide a most unsatisfactory background. The 750,000 households with an average of one and a half to two persons per room will also impose undue strain on a grammar school child. This number of over 1 million congested households is likely to be playing an important part in the problem we are studying.

We have not been able to make any inquiry into the conditions under which grammar school children do their homework. A survey which was carried out on Merseyside about six years ago found that conditions varied a good deal between summer and winter. About 4 per cent of the children did without a fire in winter in order to work alone, but in summer nearly a quarter used their bedrooms and 41 per cent, compared with 16 per cent in winter, were able to work alone. Less than half of them could say that they did not hear the wireless at all and one in eight heard it all the time. The survey concluded that in summer 27 per cent and in winter 44 per cent of the children were working under definitely bad conditions.

It is clear then that a grammar school child may be seriously handicapped by physical conditions at home. But the difference between the records of children in the respective occupational groups is too marked and too widely spread to be accounted for mainly by such conditions. Another distinction which we have tried to draw is between children whose mothers are and are not at work; but on this point the schools so often had no information, particularly about children who had left, that the evidence is inconclusive. It does not seem likely, however, that this is a major influence on the age of leaving.

One of the main influences must be sought in the outlook and assumptions of parents and children in various walks of life. Consider first the outlook of parents in professional occupations. Most of them have themselves received a grammar school or similar education, and others have made their way into a position in society in which they find such a background taken for granted. They are all engaged on work for which a fairly high level of education is an obvious advantage and many follow professions to which a specified educational standard is a condition of entry. In the circumstances it is not surprising if they assume that their children will not leave school at fifteen but will stay as much longer as their ability justifies. This assumption is not necessarily due to any conscious sense of the value of education; it may be a mere social convention which has never been questioned. But it is in any case a powerful influence on the parents towards keeping their children at school, and on the children towards staying.

Most of the parents whose occupations are described in our tables as skilled, semi-skilled and unskilled will themselves have left school at fourteen. It does not of course follow that they will lack a sense of the value of education; indeed this sense may be more keenly felt by a man who is conscious of what he has missed than by anyone else. But inevitably the continuance of full-time education to the age of sixteen, seventeen or eighteen cannot be taken for granted by such parents as it is by most parents of professional standing; and if it is not taken for granted by the parents it will not be by the children. Thus children in different social groups may start their grammar school life with different sets of unspoken assumptions about the length of school life. Similarly their fathers' varying occupations cannot fail to influence their first assumptions about their own careers.

But ideas are picked up not only in the home but in the neighbourhood. It is easy to imagine, for instance, that a headmaster may despair of keeping in the sixth form any boy from a particular street, not only because of the poor conditions in the houses but because of the character and atmosphere of the street as a community. There is no doubt of the strength of the pressure on even conscientious parents from neighbours who see no point in education beyond fifteen or sixteen as the case may be; and if the pressure on the parents is strong it is much stronger on the children.

The decision to leave may well be the child's and not the parents'. We tried in all our questionnaires to find out how often it was one rather than the other. From the answers it will be seen that the schools thought the parents responsible twice as often as the children, but one of the strongest impressions received from the other inquiries was of decisions to leave made by the boys and girls themselves; they often answered that their parents did not mind one way or the other and left the decision to them. It does not follow, of course, that in such cases the home influence is negligible; in this context neutrality on the part of parents is likely to tell in favour of leaving, since ephemeral irritations and ambitions may well be uppermost in an adolescent mind. It should be the function of the parents to look further ahead.

It is a common experience in most families, except perhaps where the academic tradition is very strong or the children are at boarding schools, that about the age of fifteen or sixteen children become restless and anxious to assert their independence and their grown-up status. We tried in our inquiries to assess how often the desire for independence was an effective reason for leaving school and we found that the proportion of leavers affected varied from 59 per cent of the national servicemen to 34 per cent of the grammar school sample and 22 per cent of the boys and 38 per cent of the girls who belonged to youth organizations. These variations are not of much significance in themselves as the respective questionnaires were not phrased in strictly comparable terms: but it may be surmised that more than a third of the leavers are influenced at least in part by feelings of this kind. Such feelings may be strong enough to amount to the degree of emotional compulsion which we have recognized as a sufficient reason for leaving school, but more often they can be overcome by sympathetic handling. In this the school may be expected to play an important part, but the main responsibility must be the parents'. Thus a positive attitude towards staying at school, and not a mere absence of opposition, must be looked for among parents if children are to be dissuaded from leaving hastily.

It is worth considering how far the attitude of parents seems to vary towards boys and girls respectively. All the evidence shows that early leaving is commoner among girls than among boys. From the heads' answers it seems that far more boys than girls left for career reasons and rather more because they found school work difficult; more girls than boys left because they found the restraints of school life irksome and because their families could not afford to keep them at school longer, and rather more because their friends were leaving. This suggests that petty irritation with school is commoner among girls than boys and that parents are not prepared to make sacrifices so readily for their daughters as for their sons.

This is not surprising. It is common knowledge that many parents attach more importance to their sons' education than to their daughters'. The idea is not dead that a good education is wasted on a girl because she will get married, and if a choice seems necessary between taking a boy or a girl away from school it is usually the girl who leaves. If the mother dies, falls ill or is overworked, a girl may be brought home to look after the family. Some light is thrown on the respective attitudes of parents in different walks of life by a comparison of the figures shown for boys and for girls in the table below.

Length of school life: boys compared with girls

| Academic categories (grouped to show length of school life) | Father's occupation | | | | | | | | | |
| | Professional and managerial | | Clerical | | Skilled | | Semi-skilled | | Unskilled | |
	Boys %	Girls %	Boys %	Girls %	Boys %	Girls %	Boys %	Girls %	Boys %	Girls %
A and B (sixth form leavers)	46·8	41·1	30·9	27·0	23·3	18·1	12·7	6·7	7·2	6·1
C, D and E (fifth form leavers)	46·0	52·5	61·0	57·5	60·4	59·1	62·6	59·6	55·0	51·4
F ('premature' leavers)	7·1	6·4	8·2	15·5	16·4	22·9	24·7	33·7	37·8	42·5
	100·0	100·0	100·0	100·0	100·0	100·0	100·0	100·0	100·0	100·0

It will be seen that at the sixth form level boys are found in the majority in all groups. Among the earliest leavers there is a marked preponderance of girls everywhere except in the professional and managerial group. This suggests a difference of social convention about the level of education necessary for girls and may indicate the critical stages in the school life of girls with different social back-grounds.

We have decided that it would be wrong to adjust the machinery of selection specifically to allow for home background. We must accordingly face the challenge which this presents. Since we do not fully understand the causes of the problem it is certain that we cannot immediately expect to know the answer. Yet it is illogical to admit 16,000 children to grammar schools from the homes of semi-skilled and unskilled workers and to accept, without strenuous effort to prevent it, that 9,000 will drop out or fail academically. We might indeed go further back and ask whether it is to be accepted without demur that so many children of unskilled workers, who might go to grammar schools, do not do so.

J. E. FLOUD (ED.), A. H. HALSEY
AND F. M. MARTIN (1956)

Social class and educational opportunity*

(I) THE SOCIAL ORIGINS OF BOYS IN GRAMMAR SCHOOLS BEFORE AND AFTER 1944

Sources of information

We have classified the social origins of grammar school pupils according to the occupations followed by their fathers, which is the only evidence available in respect of past generations of children. Admittedly it is an uncertain guide, especially since fathers' occupations are rarely recorded by the schools in sufficient detail to enable them to be classified with any degree of precision. The Registrar-General's classification of occupations for the purposes of the census, for instance, is the outcome of quite detailed information as to the

* Reprinted from *Social Class and Educational Opportunity* (London, Heinemann, 1956).

actual work on which people are engaged, and in the 1951 Census thirteen socio-economic groups are designated. Nothing more was available to us, however, than a brief entry (e.g. the single word 'clerk') in the school admission register, in some cases made forty years ago; our method is therefore rougher and the classification simpler.

We have grouped occupations into five categories under the following headings: professional workers, business owners and managers; clerical workers; foremen, small shopkeepers and other persons in miscellaneous occupations of similar standing; skilled manual workers; unskilled manual workers. To make broader distinctions between the social classes possible, these categories have in some cases, been combined; thus: the Middle-Class (professional workers, business owners, managers); the Lower-Middle-Class (clerical workers, foremen, small shopkeepers, etc.); and the Working Class (skilled and unskilled manual workers). This classification is based on that used by the Government Social Survey.

It was intended to obtain information about the social origins of entrants to the schools for periods when it might be expected that, under the influence of events or of official policy, the social composition of the schools would be changing. Thus, we were interested (for purposes of comparison) in the years before 1900; in the effects of the introduction of free place awards in 1907, of the First World War, and of the regulations introduced in 1933 under which free places became 'special' places, and the fees payable became dependent upon the means of parents. Unfortunately, it proved impossible to gather extensive and reliable information concerning girls' schools, so that our account of the history of the social composition of the grammar school population is confined in both areas to boys. Neither was it possible to study the same periods of years in the two areas. In the case of south-west Hertfordshire the information does not relate to every year in all periods, although in all years for which information was collected a complete census of entrants was taken.

Information as to the occupations of the fathers of boys entering grammar schools after 1944 is much fuller, since it was obtained by direct inquiry of the parents either in writing or by interview in the course of our investigation into other aspects of the children's home background. Our description of the social distribution of places after

1944 has, therefore, a much sounder basis than our description of their distribution before that date.

'The educational ladder'

In 1885 the occupations of the fathers of boys attending the Watford Grammar School were the subject of an inquiry by the Headmaster, who reported to the Governors that there were in the school at that time:

> 33 sons of shopkeepers
> 22 sons of clerks, commercial travellers and managers
> 21 sons of inn and hotel proprietors
> 12 sons of auctioneers, civil engineers, teachers and nonconformist ministers
> 10 sons of farmers and dealers in corn and cattle
> 19 boys with no father living

Thus the school catered almost exclusively for middle- and lower-middle-class boys. The school admission registers show that during the period 1884–1900 about two-thirds of the entrants were sons of clerks and small shopkeepers, and just under one quarter were the sons of professional people, business owners and managers. Only 11 per cent were the sons of skilled manual workers, and it is interesting to note that as many as three-quarters of these paid fees.

The admission of scholars, even in small numbers, inevitably modified the middle-class character of the school and raised doubts in the minds of the responsible authorities. In 1904, however, the Headmaster reported reassuringly to the Governors:

> It will be seen that the number of free scholars from Elementary Schools is eighteen or less than 10 per cent of the whole school, a proportion which presents no element of difficulty or danger. On the other hand they are picked boys, generally of good ability and they have every incentive to industry. The consequence is that they are amongst our most successful boys.

As a result of the introduction in 1907 of the Board of Education scheme for the award of free places in grant-aided secondary schools to children from elementary schools, the proportion of boys from working-class families rose to 15 per cent of the total entry in the years 1904–18. But the principal change in the composition of the entry during these years took the form of a redistribution amongst the middle-class groups themselves. Thus there was a sharp increase in the proportion of sons of business owners, managers and clerical workers mainly at the expense of the sons of foremen and small shop-keepers and, to a much smaller extent, of the sons of professional people. These changes no doubt reflected the changing occupational and residential character of the area.

Although no larger proportion of free places was awarded in the years after the First World War, the expansion of the school resulted in a great increase in the number of free places available. A further rise in the proportion of working-class boys entering the school followed, and during the period 1922–30 such boys made up 19 per cent of the total entry.

After 1931, however, the world economic depression and conse-quent measures of educational retrenchment reversed the upward trend in the fortunes of working-class boys, and the period 1934–8 saw the lower-middle-class group, which had been losing ground since 1900, restored to something like its former strength. The proportion of boys drawn from the working class fell from its former peak of just under 20 per cent in 1922–30 to 16 per cent in 1934–8, while the proportion of boys of lower-middle-class origin rose sharply from 51 per cent to 62 per cent.

As was mentioned above, changes in the occupational structure of Hertfordshire resulted in a decline in the importance of small shop-keepers and an influx of clerical and other black-coated workers into the area. These trends are reflected in the changing contribution of these groups to the boys' grammar school up to 1930. The sharp decline during 1934–8 in the proportion of manual workers' sons, and the rise in the proportion of the sons of clerical workers entering the school, cannot, however, be attributed to these gradual changes in the local occupational structure. In the main they must be attributed to changes in national financial policy following the depression; the effect of these changes was to diminish the proportion of places awarded to the sons of unskilled manual workers.

The educational fortunes of working-class boys revived during the more prosperous years of the Second World War, and an analysis of the social composition of the entry to grammar schools in 1943 shows that the proportion of boys drawn from the families of manual workers had increased from the pre-war figure of 16 per cent to 25 per cent. It is interesting to note, however, that these boys were mainly sons of *skilled* workers, and that although the proportion from the unskilled group showed some improvement, it never surpassed their peak proportion of the total entry – 5 per cent – which had been reached as early as 1922–30. The war also saw a small increase in the proportion of boys drawn from professional and business families. But the lower-middle-class group both declined in strength and underwent an internal redistribution which benefited the sons of foremen and small shopkeepers at the expense of those of clerical and other workers. Both these latter trends in the social composition of the school were to be dramatically accentuated after 1944.

In Middlesbrough, the first significant provision for the entry of children from the elementary to the secondary schools was made in 1888 with the founding of fifteen annual scholarships, financed jointly by the Science and Art Department and a local donor. They were tenable on the science side of the high school and were intended for the 'cleverer boys' attending elementary schools. The scholarships, so the trustees were informed, introduced quite a new class of boys into the school and caused the exodus of a good many others. Ten exhibitioners were sent by the North Riding County Council from 1893 and they too were 'viewed with distrust in many quarters'. The 'number of middle-class boys fell still further', and for several terms following the admission of elementary school boys, 'the school suffered severely in consequence by the withdrawal of boys who were sent to boarding schools'. However, the head-master was able to report that 'the tone of the school (had) not suffered in the least', and although scholarships were restricted to those whose parents' income did not exceed £200, 'they would be drawn from respectable families in which the moral tone would be high and the proper bringing up of the children a matter of anxiety to the parents'. In fact, the quality of the work in the school rose, 'the fee-payers benefited' and middle-class parents were asked to 'reconcile themselves to what was happening' and to recognize the advantage of educating the working classes. But there was an un-favourable side to this otherwise generally satisfactory picture as the headmaster revealed in his annual report for 1896. In the last eight years, he reported, 160 scholars 'whose mental development in many cases is marvellous' had been admitted from elementary schools. 'But', he went on, 'I cannot forbear expressing my deep regret that no suitable careers appear open to these youths. Up to, say, seventeen they receive an education well fitted to modern requirements ... (but) ... we have no means of placing them in business or sending them forward to a university. ....'

As might be expected from a more liberal policy in awarding free places, there was a steady increase in the proportion of working-class boys admitted annually to the secondary schools in Middlesbrough. In 1935 a second boys' grammar school was opened and the award of still more free or special places was accompanied by an attempt, which was largely successful, to see that the entire age-group of eligible children took the preliminary selection tests. There was no decline after 1935 in the proportion of entrants of working-class origin such as took place in south-west Hertfordshire, and the sons of manual workers increased their proportion of the total entry from 38 per cent in 1922–30 to 46 per cent in 1935–8. By this time the sons of *non-manual* workers ... accounted for only a little over half the entry, and only the sons of clerical workers had improved their position. The proportion of boys from professional and business families, and especially the sons of foremen and small shopkeepers, declined steadily throughout the period up to 1938.

The effect which the economic depression and the Special Place Regulations clearly produced on the composition of the entry in south-west Hertfordshire was not so evident in Middlesbrough because of the larger number of places thrown open to competition. This sustained the working-class contribution to the total entry despite a fairly steep fall in the *proportion of awards* to the sons of skilled workers.[1] We can only speculate as to what effect the increase in the proportion of free places might have had under more favourable economic conditions. When the war years brought full employ-

---

[1] It is difficult to account for this decline in the competitive position of skilled workers' children in Middlesbrough, which is in direct contrast to the position in south-west Hertfordshire, where the brunt of the depression was borne by boys from unskilled workers' families. It is possible that the depression in Middlesbrough was felt more keenly by skilled workers in the shipbuilding industry than by unskilled workers mainly employed in the steel industry which was not so badly hit.

ment there was an increase in the proportion of both skilled and unskilled workers' sons entering the grammar schools; the working-class group in the entry as a whole increased from 46 per cent in 1935-8 to 52 per cent in 1939-44. It seems, however, that this was caused by an increase in the proportion of working-class fee-payers as well as by an improvement in the competitive strength of these boys.

'Secondary education for all'

In 1945 fees were abolished in all maintained and aided schools, and in both areas the result has been that an increased proportion of working-class boys have entered the grammar schools. This increase has, of course, been more striking in south-west Hertford-shire than in Middlesbrough, where even before 1944 over half the entry was drawn from the working class.

In Middlesbrough, the balance of the distribution of the total entry of boys to the grammar schools as between the sons of non-manual and of manual workers has moved slightly since 1945 in favour of the latter group. The change has, however, been insignificant.

In south-west Hertfordshire a number of special circumstances were responsible for a series of fluctuations in the composition of the grammar school entry after 1945. Strangely enough, the immediate result of the abolition of fees was a sharp reduction in the intake of working-class boys. This was probably due, however, to the admission of a large number of intending fee-payers from the preparatory department of the school. During the years 1946-9 there appeared to be a 'flight' of middle-class boys from the school; and the opening in 1950 of the new mixed grammar school at Bushey, which admitted many working-class children from the expanding LCC housing estate at Oxhey, lowered still further the representation of the middle class in the total grammar school entry. Since 1950, however, the middle-class group has regained its former strength and now contributes more than 20 per cent of the entry. But the lower-middle-class group of boys from the families of clerical, supervisory and self-employed workers has continued to lose ground, and their proportion has fallen from about two-thirds in pre-war years to a figure nearer one-third in 1950-2. Their place as the largest of the occupational groups has been taken by the sons of manual workers.

It is not surprising that in the many areas of the country which have a social structure and educational history similar to that of south-west Hertfordshire, the frustration of an earnest and ambitious body of parents is widely advertised. Nor is it surprising that the schools themselves are worried by the problems which the new conditions have created. Disquiet today replaces the equanimity, and indeed enthusiasm, with which the nineteenth-century headmasters welcomed their able recruits from the elementary schools and attempted to allay the fears of middle-class parents.

Table I shows the social origins of the boys attending the grammar schools in these two areas during the years of our inquiry. This picture of the position after a decade of 'secondary education for all' illustrates the cumulative effects not only of the distribution of opportunity at the moment of entry to the schools, but of a process of social selection going on within them. Working-class children tend to leave early rather than late, and are under-represented in the upper forms of the schools. The distribution of opportunity and this process of internal selection in the grammar schools will be examined more closely.

TABLE I. *Social origins of boys attending grammar schools, south-west Hertfordshire (1952) and Middlesbrough (1953)*

Father's occupation	South-west Hertfordshire (1952) %	Middlesbrough[a] (1953) %
Professional workers and business owners and managers	21·6	11·6
Clerical workers	16·2	13·3
Foremen, small shopkeepers and other similar grades	21·2	21·2
Skilled manual workers	30·5	25·8
Unskilled manual workers	5·9	16·6
Unclassified	4·6	12·5
Total	100·0	100·0
No.	718	774

[a] Excluding boys attending Roman Catholic grammar schools

TABLE 2. Social origins of boys entering grammar schools. South-west Hertfordshire, 1884–1953

Father's occupation	1884–1900 %	1904–18 %	1922–30 %	1934–8 %	1943 %	1950–3 %
Professional workers and business owners and managers	23·8	31·3	27·6	19·1	23·0	21·0
Clerical workers	16·6	23·8	21·0	32·5	23·8	16·0
Foremen, small shopkeepers and other similar grades	48·4	30·4	30·3	29·0	25·4	19·0
Skilled manual workers	10·8	12·8	14·6	12·8	20·6	34·0
Unskilled manual workers	0·4	1·7	4·7	3·3	4·8	8·0
Unclassified	0·0	0·0	1·8	3·3	2·4	2·0
Total	100·0	100·0	100·0	100·0	100·0	100·0
No.	517	873	694	366	126	639

TABLE 3. *Social origins of boys entering grammar schools,* [a] *Middlesbrough, 1905–53*

Father's occupation	1905–18 %	1922–30 %	1935–8 %	1939–44 %	1948–51 %	1953 %
Professional workers and business owners and managers	29·8	22·8	16·1	13·9	15·4	23·3
Clerical workers	7·8	7·6	15·2	15·7	12·6	7·7
Foremen, small shopkeepers and other similar grades	38·6	30·5	18·6	18·1	18·0	24·4
Skilled manual workers	16·2	27·0	29·5	33·7	31·6	30·8
Unskilled manual workers	6·6	10·5	16·1	18·6	22·4	13·8
Unclassified	1·0	1·6	4·5	—[b]	—	—
Total	100·0	100·0	100·0	100·0	100·0	100·0
(No.)	993	811	575	888	556	148

[a] Excluding those entering Roman Catholic Grammar Schools, of which an account is given separately (see p. 134, below).

[b] In this period the occupations of an unusually large proportion (11 per cent) of fathers could not be classified since they were recorded simply as 'Army'. The numbers have been distributed proportionately among the occupational groups.

(II) SOCIAL CLASS AND CHANCES OF ADMISSION TO GRAMMAR SCHOOLS

'Class chances'

The proportions of the ten to eleven age-group of children in each occupational group selected for admission to grammar schools give what may be called the 'class chances' of a grammar school education.

The following are the figures for boys in 1953 in south-west Hertfordshire and Middlesbrough:[1]

	South-west Hertfordshire %	Middlesbrough %
Professional workers, business owners and managers	59	68
Clerical workers	44	37
Foremen, small shopkeepers, etc.	30	24
Skilled manual workers	18	14
Unskilled manual workers	9	9
All	22	17

As might be expected, there were in both areas considerable disparities in the chances of boys from different social classes. In general, the sons of manual workers had a chance below the average, and the sons of non-manual workers a chance above the average, of being selected for grammar schools. The sons of clerks had four or more times as good a chance as the sons of unskilled manual workers, and two to three times the chance of sons of skilled workers. The difference in chances at the extremes of the occupational scale was still greater. In Middlesbrough the son of a professional or business man had more than seven times the chance of the son of an unskilled worker, and almost five times the chance of a skilled worker's son, while in south-west Hertfordshire he had three times the chance of the skilled worker's and six times that of the unskilled worker's son.

'Class chances' vary from year to year, however. For example, in

[1] In this chapter the Middlesbrough figures include children of Roman Catholic families.

south-west Hertfordshire they have varied for boys over three years as follows:

	1952 %	*1953* %	*1954* %
Professional workers, business owners and managers	40	59	64
Clerical workers	35	44	46
Foremen, small shopkeepers, etc.	21	30	32
Skilled and unskilled manual workers	15	14	12

If the chances of working-class boys diminish over a period of years – i.e., if a smaller proportion of the particular age-group at this social level is admitted to the grammar schools – does this mean that working-class boys of appropriate ability are being excluded? Or have the terms of competition turned against them? Are there proportionately fewer grammar school places available (say, because the numbers in the ten to eleven age-group have increased without a corresponding expansion of the grammar school intake)? Is the competition from middle-class children of higher average IQ more intense than formerly (say, because of a change in the social composition of the age-group or because middle-class parents are turning in increasing numbers away from independent to grammar schools)?

'Class chances' depend on several factors: on the number of grammar school places, on the proportion of them open to competition and the qualifying conditions for competing, and on the size and the social and intellectual composition of the age-group of children from which entrants are drawn. To calculate class chances precisely and relate them to ability, information is needed on all these points – and is rarely available. We were, in fact, able to assemble it accurately only in respect of grant-earning schools and for the single years of our inquiry. As regards other years, although we have collected information about the provision and social distribution of places in grant-aided schools, we know nothing about the social distribution of intelligence; and we can only estimate changes in the size and social composition of the age-group from the information available in census returns from the two areas as to the numbers of children of ten to fourteen and the social composition of the general population. Precise calculations of class chances and their relation to ability cannot, therefore, be made except for the years 1952 in south-west Hertfordshire and 1953 in Middlesbrough. Nevertheless, we decided to make estimates for other years with the aid of a simplified model based on the available data for these years and on the assumption that the size and social and intellectual composition of the age-group are constant. The error to which the calculations based on this assumption give rise, so far as it can be assessed, and the general limitations of the method will be made clear in the course of the following discussion.

'Class chances' and measured intelligence

The broad facts of the social distribution of measured intelligence are well-known. Capacity to score in intelligence tests improves with social level, but the differences within occupational groups are greater than those between them. Thus, the mean I Q of the highest occupational group was greater by 15 to 20 points than that of the

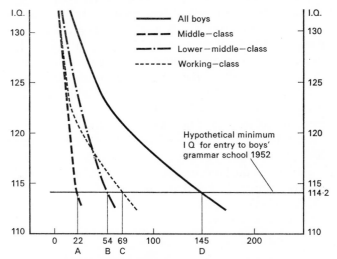

A—Hypothetical middle–class entry to boys' grammar school 1952
B—Hypothetical lower–middle–class entry to boys' grammar school 1952
C—Hypothetical working–class entry to boys' grammar school 1952
D—Total intake to boys' grammar school 1952

FIGURE I *Social distribution of measured intelligence among boys entering secondary schools in south-west Hertfordshire in 1952*

lowest, both in south-west Hertfordshire in 1952 and in Middles-brough in 1953, but the range of IQ within the groups overlapped between them to a considerable extent.

The problem is to assess the relevance of these facts to the ability of children at each social level to compete with others for entry to grammar schools at any given level of provision of places.

The Intelligence Quotients of the boys aged ten to eleven who provide our samples can be plotted cumulatively, as in Figure 1, which relates to south-west Hertfordshire in 1952. A given point on any of the curves then shows on the horizontal scale the number of children in our sample with an IQ equal to, or greater than, that indicated at the corresponding point on the vertical scale. For instance, in south-west Hertfordshire in 1952 at and above the IQ level of 125, there were forty-three boys, ten of whom were lower-middle-class, twenty-six middle-class, and thirteen working-class.

We know that there were 145 places available for boys in 1952. It is possible to deduce what the social composition of a group of 145 entrants would be, were the places awarded solely according to ability as measured by intelligence tests. The point at which a line at the number 145 on the horizontal scale intersects the curve describing the intelligence of the total age-group can be seen in Figure 1 to correspond on the vertical scale to an IQ of 114·2. This is the hypothetical minimum level of ability required to obtain a place in a grammar school in 1952. The distribution of the entry among the three social classes that would have resulted from selection solely on the basis of measured intelligence can then be obtained by reading the values on the horizontal scale of the points at which the appropriate curves meet the line drawn at 114.2 IQ.

Thus the hypothetically 'perfect' or 'expected' social distribution of the 1952 entry is as follows:

	No.	%
Middle-class	22	15
Lower-middle-class	54	37
Working-class	69	48
	145	100

This may be compared with the *actual* distribution of the 1952 entry which was:

	No.	%
Middle-class	22	15
Lower-middle-class	49	34
Working-class	74	51
	145	100

The model has been used to make these calculations for each area in respect, firstly, of the annual intake of boys holding free and special places (Table 5, p. 155), and secondly, of the total annual entry of boys at various periods between 1904 and 1952 (Table 6, p. 156). The degree of error in the assumptions on which it is based as to the size and the social and intellectual composition of the age-group cannot be accurately assessed. The size of the age-group has obviously fluctuated with changes in birth rates and movements of population, but it has certainly not increased at the same rate as the general population. The general population of both areas has increased since 1900; it has trebled in south-west Hertfordshire and increased by some 37 per cent in Middlesbrough. But it has been ageing, and the number of children between the ages of ten to fourteen has increased much less rapidly – by only 63 per cent in south-west Hertfordshire and 14 per cent in Middlesbrough. The social class structure in both areas has remained only roughly constant; on balance, there has probably been some shrinkage in the proportion of manual to non-manual workers, and within the latter group, an increase in the proportion of clerical workers as against small shopkeepers and self-employed workers. These changes in the social composition of the general population would be more marked in the case of the ten to eleven age-group as a result of class differences in birth rates. Nothing is known about the changes in the social distribution of intelligence, but there is no reason *prima facie* to suppose that it has not in fact remained constant as we have assumed.

Nevertheless, though the model is simplified, it does enable us to estimate in approximate terms the part played by the social

distribution of measured intelligence in the long-term decline in
the competitive capacity of working-class children and the extent to
which 'ability' and 'opportunity' are more closely related today than
when J. L. Gray and Miss Moshinsky demonstrated discrepancies
in the 1930s.

Social class and competition for free and special places

Column 8 of Table 5 (p. 155) shows the increase in the annual
provision of free and special places, which, on the assumption that
the age-group is constant in size, is reflected in the fall shown in
column 1 in the minimum IQ necessary to obtain a place in competition. In fact, the age-group increased over the period covered by
the table in both areas, but the increase in the number of free and
special places easily outstripped it, and the decline in the minimum
IQ is not seriously exaggerated in column 1. Graph readings presented in percentage form in columns 2, 4 and 6 show the proportions in which the social classes would have been represented in the
competitive entry at each point of time, had the competition been
open to all and had all competed. The social composition of the age-
group is assumed to be constant. In fact, the proportion of working-
class children in the age-group probably decreased over the period
covered by the table, so that the discrepancy between the expected
and the actual proportions of free places awarded to working-class
boys (columns 6 and 7) is probably slightly underestimated for the
years before 1945. That is to say, the proportion of awards which
working-class children would be expected to win in open competition on the basis of measured intelligence alone was probably lower
than is shown in column 6 for the pre-1945 years, and the terms of
competition before 1945 were probably even more in their favour
than the figures suggest.

The distribution of intelligence is such that had the competition
been open to all, and had all competed, the proportion of the available awards won by working-class boys would have increased with
every increase in the number of places open to competition, whilst
that of awards to middle-class, and later also to lower-middle-class,
boys would have fallen (columns 2, 4 and 6). In fact, columns 3, 5
and 7 show the opposite trend.

Middle-class children who attended private schools were for long excluded from the competition, and right up to 1945 they entered the schools as fee-payers more or less without regard to their ability. Working-class children were to that extent 'protected' in the competition, and won a correspondingly greater proportion of the available free and special places. (It need hardly be pointed out that the effect of their advantage on the general relation of ability to opportunity was far outweighed by the alternatives open to children in other social groups.)

In south-west Hertfordshire working-class boys competed on very favourable terms for a limited number of free places right up to 1945; middle-class boys hardly competed at all. In the 1930s lower-middle-class boys benefited from middle-class abstention, gaining a slightly higher proportion of free or special places than would have been awarded to them solely on grounds of their relative ability. But the greatest gain went to the working-class boys, who, in terms of their relative ability, were consistently over-represented – though to a diminishing extent – in the group of free and special place pupils. In 1945 their position was suddenly and dramatically reversed; this reverse was only temporary however, and was probably the result of the admission, under the special circumstances of the sudden abolition of fees, of a large number of intending fee-payers from the preparatory department of the grammar school. In 1952, the year of our inquiry in the area, the relationship between 'ability' and 'opportunity' was strikingly close in all social classes.

In Middlesbrough working-class children lost the 'protection' of a substantial fee-paying group as early as 1935, and thereafter won a proportion of the large number of free and special places which steadily approached that to which their relative average level of measured intelligence entitled them. The actual contribution of the middle class to the group of holders of free and special places was far below its expected level until the abolition of the small fee-paying group in 1945 forced them into the competition.

Social class and entry to grammar school

We have so far been concerned with opportunity and ability in relation to free or special places before and after 1945. It remains to consider opportunity and ability in relation to *all* places, whether open to competition or not.

The actual distribution of places of all kinds at various periods is shown in Table 6 (p. 156), against the expected distribution for the same periods, which is now calculated on the basis of the total number of grammar school places annually available and not merely of the number open to competition.

Column 1 of Table 6 shows a fall in the minimum IQ required for entry to a grammar school which would follow from the increase shown in column 8 in the number of boys admitted annually, if the assumption were correct that the size of the age-group remained constant. But, in fact, the age-group increased in both areas. In Middlesbrough, the increase of the annual intake to the grammar schools was far greater than that of the age-group, so that the decline in the minimum IQ shown is not seriously exaggerated. In south-west Hertfordshire, however, the growth of the annual intake to the grammar schools did not quite keep pace with that of the age-group. Although the catchment area of the grammar schools of the division has narrowed, compensating to some extent for the stiffening of the competition for places, the minimum IQ may have actually remained at the pre-1918 level, or even have risen slightly rather than fallen as is shown in column 1. This would have the effect of reducing the expected intake of working-class boys shown in column 6, so that the discrepancy between the expected and actual intake of these boys (columns 6 and 7) in the years before 1945 is probably slightly exaggerated.

It is nevertheless clear that although a rough equality of opportunity was established in Middlesbrough as early as the 1920s, in south-west Hertfordshire many able boys of working-class origin were excluded from the grammar schools before 1945. Indeed, it seems likely that for every able boy from a working-class family who was admitted two or three were excluded. The post-war revolution has been a reality in south-west Hertfordshire, establishing the same equality of opportunity there as has existed in Middlesbrough for twenty-five or thirty years. In 1952 virtually the full quota of boys with the necessary minimum intellectual qualification was admitted from every social class to grammar schools.

We may compare our findings with those of J. L. Gray and

P. Moshinsky in their study of a representative sample of London children attending private and preparatory as well as public elementary schools in 1933–4.

They showed that there was a striking positive relationship between the social origins of able children and their chances of obtaining entry to a grammar (then 'secondary') school, or its equivalent in the independent system. Thus, while nearly all the children of the larger business owners and the professional classes who possessed high ability had the opportunity of higher education, the corresponding figure for clerical and commercial employees was 50 per cent, for skilled wage earners 30 per cent and for unskilled wage earners 20 per cent. Conversely, at a lower level of ability, only 1 per cent of the children of unskilled workers had the opportunity of a higher education, compared with nearly 50 per cent of the children of larger business owners and 35 per cent of those of professional workers. Although our data differ in important respects the comparison with earlier findings is worth making and is set out below. For each occupational group the number of children given a grammar school education is expressed as a percentage of the number of children with 'high ability' in that group. A percentage of 100 for each group would indicate that able children, whatever their origins, had free access to grammar schools.

	London (1933–4)	South-west Hertfordshire (1952)	Middles-brough (1953)	
Professional	153·9 ⎫			
Larger business owners	195·3 ⎬	96·4	100·0	Professional workers and business owners and managers
Minor professional	103·8 ⎭			
Small business owners	29·2 ⎫	101·8	113·8	Foremen, small shopkeepers, etc.
Shopkeepers	56·5 ⎭			
Clerical and commercial	68·0	83·7	113·3	Clerical workers
Skilled manual	35·1	98·2	93·2	Skilled manual
Unskilled manual	23·2	83·7	87·2	Unskilled manual

TABLE 4. *Social distribution of measured intelligence among entrants to secondary schools*

SOUTH-WEST HERTFORDSHIRE (1952) Father's occupation	No. of children	Mean IQ	Standard deviation
Professional workers, business owners and managers	98	112·95	11·62
Clerical workers	104	109·15	12·59
Foremen, small shopkeepers, etc.	243	103·70	13·47
Skilled manual workers	583	100·10	12·79
Unskilled manual workers	288	97·15	13·24
Total	1 316	100·97	14·15

MIDDLESBROUGH (1953) Father's occupation	Catholic children			Others		
	No.	Mean IQ	Standard deviation	No.	Mean IQ	Standard deviation
Professional workers, business owners, and managers	11	121·37	8·52	42	115·24	12·0
Clerical workers	(1)	—	—	42	108·23	12·97
Foremen, small shopkeepers, etc.	24	102·92	15·75	98	104·36	13·06
Skilled manual workers	72	98·51	16·63	306	99·05	13·24
Unskilled manual workers	86	98·72	15·09	267	96·50	12·94
Total	194[a]	100·49	16·41	755[a]	100·43	14·09

[a] These numbers represent a 50 per cent sample of the age-group.

TABLE 5. *Expected and actual social distribution of 'free and special' places for boys in grammar schools at various periods*

| Period | Hypothetical minimum IQ | Middle class | | Lower-middle-class | | Working-class | | Annual intake of free or special place holders |
	1	Expected 2 %	Actual 3 %	Expected 4 %	Actual 5 %	Expected 6 %	Actual 7 %	No. 8
A SOUTH-WEST HERTFORDSHIRE								
1904–18	129·5	21	13	50	43	29	44	24
1922–30	127·5	24	4	49	40	27	56	33
1934–8	126·5	24	2	46	50	28	48	37
1943	125·0	23	6	47	44	30	50	43
1945	116·7	16	31	40	44	44	25	113
1952	114·2	15	15	37	34	48	51	145
B MIDDLESBROUGH								
1905–18	129·5	5	12	55	35	40	53	20
1922–30	126·8	15	8	45	27	40	65	40
1935–8	118·5	24	12	28	32	48	56	111
1939–44	117·5	24	11	29	32	47	52	119
1945	116·5	23	14	28	34	49	52	130
1948–51	115·5	21	15	29	31	50	54	139
1953	114·8	24	23	29	32	47	45	148

TABLE 6. *Expected and actual social distribution of places for boys in grammar schools at various periods*

Period	Hypothetical minimum IQ 1	Middle class Expected 2 %	Middle class Actual 3 %	Lower-middle-class Expected 4 %	Lower-middle-class Actual 5 %	Working-class Expected 6 %	Working-class Actual 7 %	Annual intake of boys 8 No.
A SOUTH-WEST HERTFORDSHIRE								
1904–18	117·8	18	31	40	54	42	15	96
1922–30	116·4	15	28	39	52	46	20	116
1934–8	115·9	16	19	38	64	47	17	122
1943	115·6	15	24	38	50	47	26	126
1945	116·7	16	3	40	44	44	25	113
1952	114·2	15	15	37	34	48	51	145
B MIDDLESBROUGH								
1905–18	125·3	4	31	56	46	40	23	52
1922–30	121·5	15	23	45	39	40	38	88
1935–8	115·8	24	17	28	36	48	47	137
1939–44	114·8	24	14	29	34	47	52	148
1945	116·5	23	14	28	34	49	52	130
1948–51	115·5	21	15	29	31	50	54	139
1953	114·8	24	23	29	32	47	45	148

(III) SOCIAL FACTORS IN SELECTION FOR GRAMMAR SCHOOLS

Material prosperity and parents' attitudes

Both in Middlesbrough and in south-west Hertfordshire and at each social level, the parents of successful children were on the whole better educated than those of unsuccessful children. As can be seen from Table 8 (p. 159), the percentage of fathers and mothers who had received selective secondary schooling and some further education was nearly twice as high amongst the successful as amongst the unsuccessful children in south-west Hertfordshire, and three times as high in Middlesbrough; and the same is true in varying degrees at each social level. The mothers of successful working-class children moreover had frequently before marriage followed an occupation 'superior' to that of their husbands.

Not surprisingly, these better educated parents of successful children . . . were to a marked degree more interested in and ambitious for their educational future than were the parents of unsuccessful children. They had a better knowledge of the rather complex procedure employed in allocating children to the different types of secondary school and had more frequently visited the child's primary school to discuss his secondary education with his teachers. They showed a clearer awareness of the long-term importance of selective secondary education and expressed a marked preference for the grammar school. As compared with the parents of unsuccessful children, they favoured a longer school life, preferred further education of the academic type for their children (i.e. at a university rather than a technical college) and looked forward to seeing their children enter non-manual rather than manual occupations.

Thus, the favourable attitudes of their parents to their education distinguished the successful from the unsuccessful children in both areas. But the part played by the material prosperity of their homes was strikingly different. . . . In south-west Hertfordshire at a given social level the children who gained grammar school places were not those whose parents earned the highest incomes, nor did they enjoy superior standards of housing. In Middlesbrough, on the other hand, the successful children at each social level were distinguished by the relative material prosperity of their homes.

TABLE 7. *Social distribution of awards of grammar school places*

	No. of candidates			% suc-cessful (*1*) as % of (*3*) (*4*)
	Suc-cessful (*1*)	Unsuc-cessful (*2*)	All (*3*)	
SOUTH-WEST HERTFORDSHIRE (1952)				
Middle-class				
Professional workers, business owners and managers	53	51	104	51
Lower-middle-class				
Clerical workers	41	66	107	38
Foremen, small shopkeepers, etc.	57	198	255	22
	98	264	362	27
Working-class				
Skilled	107	523	630	17
Unskilled	36	276	312	11
	143	799	942	15
All	294	1 114	1 408	21
MIDDLESBROUGH (1953)[a]				
Middle-class				
Professional workers, business owners and managers	34	16	50	68
Lower-middle-class				
Clerical workers	17	29	46	37
Foremen, small shopkeepers, etc.	33	104	137	24
	50	133	183	27
Working-class				
Skilled	55	346	401	14
Unskilled	34	343	377	9
	89	689	778	12
All	173	838	1 011	17

[a] Including children from Roman Catholic primary schools

Now let us look at the same information about the family environment of the children in our samples from a different point of view
relating the distribution of awards of grammar school places at each
social level in turn to the basic income of the household, housing

TABLE 8. *Education of parents of successful and unsuccessful candidates for grammar school places*

	Father's education				Mother's education			
	Selective secondary		Some further education		Selective secondary		Some further education	
	S[a]	U[a]	S	U	S	U	S	U
	%	%	%	%	%	%	%	%
SOUTH-WEST HERTFORDSHIRE (1952)								
Middle-class	85	36	77	63	83	63	49	26
Lower-middle-class	49	36	44	41	51	32	50	10
Working-class	14	10	32	18	31	14	22	13
All	38	17	45	25	44	20	31	18
MIDDLESBROUGH (1953)								
Middle-class	88	56	85	70	65	50	56	38
Lower-middle-class	40	17	48	28	36	14	28	17
Working-class	8	6	25	12	11	3	12	7
All	33	8	43	15	29	6	25	9

[a] S and U indicate successful and unsuccessful children respectively.

conditions, parents' education and interest in their children's education. In south-west Hertfordshire the rates of success in the competition for places are virtually the same for all families at a given social level, whether their income is rated 'high' or 'low' or whether they occupy a detached, a semi-detached or a terraced house. But in Middlesbrough the more prosperous families at each social level show markedly superior rates. . . . Thus, for instance, of the children of skilled workers, in our Middlesbrough sample, proportionally twice as many were successful among those whose fathers earned a basic income of more than £7 10s. per week and occupied a detached or semi-detached rather than a terraced house as among those from the less prosperous and well-housed families.

There is, however, no such marked difference between the areas in the relation of success to the educational background of parents and their interest in and ambitions for their children's educational future. In both areas . . . at all social levels there was a noticeably higher proportion of awards to those children whose parents had enjoyed a selective secondary education, or some further education, and in the case of working-class children, to those whose mother's occupation before marriage was of superior standing to that of their father. The importance of parents' attitudes was marked in both areas at all social levels. . . . Thus of those children of skilled workers in both areas whose parents had expressed a strong preference for a grammar school for their child's secondary education, or who had shown enough interest in their child's future to discuss it with the headmaster or a class teacher at the primary school, twice as high a proportion were successful as of children at the same social level whose parents took less interest in their education.

Evidently, the general level of material prosperity *in all social classes* in south-west Hertfordshire is high enough to prevent its having any consistent influence on success rates; the education, attitudes and ambitions of parents are left as the only clearly distinguishing characteristics of successful candidates and the only consistent environmental influences on the rate at which children in every social class succeed in obtaining grammar school places. These factors are also important in the case of Middlesbrough children; but the influence of the material environment of homes there cannot be discounted in the same way.

Size of family

Size of family is a factor which in both areas is inversely related to success in the selection examination. It cannot be regarded simply as a feature of the material environment of homes, although it obviously has important economic implications. In the first place, it is a well-established fact that, for whatever reason, children from large families score less well on the average in intelligence tests than children from small families even at the same social level. Moreover, it is noteworthy that the inverse relationship of success to size of family was much less marked for the children of Catholic families in Middlesbrough despite the fact that the fathers of some three-quarters of these large Catholic families were unskilled workers.

However that may be, we find that in south-west Hertfordshire 17 per cent of the children of unskilled workers with families of only one or two children were successful, as compared with 2 per cent of those whose families numbered five or more. In Middlesbrough the corresponding figures for the non-Catholic unskilled workers were 9 per cent and 3 per cent respectively. Among the children of skilled workers in south-west Hertfordshire the proportion of awards to the group drawn from families of only one or two (21 per cent) was almost twice as great as to that drawn from families of three or four (12 per cent). In Middlesbrough the corresponding figures for the children of non-Catholic skilled workers were 19 and 12 per cent respectively, and for children of even larger families of five or more at this social level the proportion of awards was only 5 per cent. . . .

(IV) CONCLUSIONS

In the generation which followed the 1902 Act there was an unprecedented expansion of secondary education in which the grammar schools in south-west Hertfordshire and Middlesbrough played their part. In 1892 there were well-informed complaints of public apathy towards 'intermediate' education, but thirty years later, the situation had been transformed. Every year after the First World War a greater number of parents sent their children to the secondary schools as fee-payers. Competition for the safety and prestige of a black-coated job was growing keener and a secondary education became an indispensable investment to secure a good occupational prospect. The provision of free secondary education was related to the demand for fee-paying places when in 1907 official policy stipulated that a number of free places should be provided annually in schools on the Grant List proportionate to the total number of pupils admitted in the previous year.

Even before the First World War more than one-quarter of the growing total number of places in the grammar schools in both areas were open to competition. As the proportion grew, after the war, the middle-class and lower-middle-class character of the schools was undermined, slowly in south-west Hertfordshire and quite rapidly in Middlesbrough, by the inflow of pupils of working-class origin. To some observers equality of opportunity already appeared to be a reality in the 1920s. Lord Birkenhead went so far as to claim that 'the number of scholarships from the elementary schools (is) not limited, awards being made to all children who show capacity to profit'.

The assumption that the educational ladder was for the exclusive use of the gifted poor became more and more unreal with each increase in the provision of places open to competition, and the expansion of the grammar schools had profound effects upon the social composition of the primary, then called 'elementary', schools. These schools, and through them the competition for free places in grammar schools, were always open to those of the middle and lower middle classes who cared to use them. The small minority of parents who could afford to realize higher aspirations for their children sent them to independent schools, and others used the private schools and the preparatory departments of the grammar schools. But an increasing number sent their children, especially their sons, through the rough and tumble of the elementary schools.

The result was that as the scholarship ladder widened it carried an increasing number of middle-class boys, and the competitive strength of working-class boys declined. After 1933, when economies were introduced to meet the economic depression, a place won in competition meant, more often than not, partial rather than total remission of fees, and the selection examination was opened to children attending private schools as well as public elementary schools. Boys of middle-class origin, and particularly those from

lower-middle-class families of clerks, small business people, trades-
men, etc., took up an increasing share of fee-paying places; they also
improved their competitive strength with every increase in the
number of places open to award. The long-term decline in the
competitive strength of working-class boys was as marked in south-
west Hertfordshire, where the proportion of places open to award
remained virtually constant up to the Second World War, as in
Middlesbrough, where, by 1937, 80 per cent were open to award. The
abolition of fees in 1945 accentuated the decline in both areas.

The effect of these developments on the social composition of the
schools themselves naturally depended upon the proportion of places
open to competition. In south-west Hertfordshire the grammar
school was the undisputed preserve of middle-class, and especially
of lower-middle-class boys who, by 1939, represented two-thirds of
the annual intake. When all places were opened to competition in
1945, these boys suffered severe competition and today constitute
only one-third of the entry. In Middlesbrough working-class boys
formed 40 per cent or more of the annual intake throughout the
decade after 1935, and the abolition of fees has not brought about
any drastic change in the social composition of the schools such as
has taken place in south-west Hertfordshire.

It is obvious that the number of working-class boys entering the
grammar schools each year has been increasing fast, and that there
are more in the schools today than ever before. Nevertheless, the
probability that a working-class boy will get to a grammar school is
not strikingly different from what it was before 1945, and there are
still marked differences in the chances which boys of different social
origins have of obtaining a place. Of those working-class boys who
reached the age of eleven in the years 1931–41 rather less than 10 per
cent entered selective secondary schools. In 1953 the proportion
of working-class boys admitted to grammar schools was 12 per
cent in Middlesbrough and 14 per cent in south-west Hertfordshire.
Thus, approximately one working-class boy in eight was admitted in
Middlesbrough, as compared, for instance, with nearly one in three
of the sons of clerks; and approximately one working-class boy in
seven in south-west Hertfordshire, as compared with nearly one in
two of the sons of clerks.

Our findings as to the social distribution of measured intelligence are closely consistent with those of earlier inquiries, and provide an adequate explanation of these differences. Virtually the full quota of boys with the requisite minimum IQ from every class was admitted to grammar schools and the distribution of opportunity stands today in closer relationship to that of ability (as measured by intelligence tests) than ever before. Yet the problem of inequality of educational opportunity is not thereby disposed of.

We have considered some of the material and cultural differences in the environment of the children who succeed, as distinct from those who do not succeed, in the selection examination for secondary education, and we have shown how the success of children varies with the distribution of these features of the environment even at the same social level. Since measured intelligence is so closely related to the results of the selection procedure our findings are relevant to the problem of the influence of environment on intelligence test scores. But this was not our direct concern, and the features of the environment we have selected for study cannot, of course, be regarded as social determinants of intelligence. Nevertheless, though they touch on less fundamental problems, certain conclusions do emerge concerning the part played by differences of environment in the social distribution of educational opportunity.

In the past, the problem of social waste in education could be seen in comparatively simple terms, for gross material factors overshadowed all others. Poverty caused ill-health and poor attendance; facilities for study could not be provided in slum homes, nor proper instruction given in over-crowded schools; grammar school places were refused by parents who could not afford to forgo adolescent earnings. But the influence on the distribution of educational opportunity of the material environment, in which children live at home and are taught at school before the age of selection, is tending to diminish in importance in face of the general prosperity and the measures of social reform which are characteristic of post-war Britain. Social factors influencing educational selection reveal themselves in more subtle forms today. . . .

Once the grosser material handicaps are eliminated, the size of the family emerges as the most important single index of the favourable or unfavourable influence of home environment on educational is prospects. Very little known as to what determines the size of families at different social levels, but there is no doubt about the existence of a relationship between family size and educational opportunity. This relationship obviously has its economic aspect, even in the Welfare State. It is a well-established fact, however, that children from small families, at all social levels, tend on the average to do better in intelligence tests and therefore also in the selection examination for secondary education. Dr Nisbet has suggested that the child of a large family learns verbal skills less effectively from his peers than does the child of a small family from adults, and that he carries the handicap at least until the age of eleven. But the evidence from Middlesbrough suggests that the educational disadvantages of a large family are far less marked for the children of Catholic parents, and if generally true this would cast doubt on the notion that there is some distinctive quality of educational value in the environment of a small family. . . .

The social waste at the point of selection indicated by Kenneth Lindsay in the 1920s has today been pushed forward *into* the grammar schools where it now occurs at the threshold of the Sixth Form. In both areas, as nationally, there are marked differences, according to their social origins, in the length of school life and opportunity for further education enjoyed by children at the same general level of ability. It is possible that material differences in home background come into their own again here, even in southwest Hertfordshire, underlying and reinforcing differences of attitude to the value of an extended secondary course and further education on the part of parents and children alike.

However, it seems doubtful, on the evidence available to us, whether parents can be held wholly responsible, at least so far as their early intentions are concerned, for the wastage of children from secondary schools before or when they reach the age of sixteen. It is evident that their strength of purpose as well as their capacity to make sacrifices on behalf of their children's education varies from class to class. But there has undoubtedly been a post-war revolution in parents' attitudes towards their children's education, especially at the bottom of the social scale. The frustration of parents whose children are sent to other secondary schools despite their wish that they should attend grammar schools is not confined to the middle classes. The frustrated minorities of skilled and unskilled working-class parents in Middlesbrough and south-west Hertfordshire were proportionately not so very much smaller than in the lower midde class, and in absolute numbers they were, of course, much larger. Moreover, working-class parents who said that they wished their children to attend a grammar school also said, in the great majority of cases, that they were willing to keep them at school at least until the age of sixteen; and a surprisingly large proportion contemplated a leaving age of eighteen or over (one-quarter in Middlesbrough and nearly one-third in south-west Hertfordshire). Admittedly, the proportion of middle-class and lower-middle-class parents contemplating a six or seven year secondary course for their children was larger and it is often argued that it would be expedient to take this into account in making the selection, at least at the borderline of differences in ability. But it would be difficult on ethical and political grounds to justify such an evasion of a problem which should be regarded as an educational challenge to the schools. Each generation of more or less able children allowed to leave school before or immediately after completing the minimum course (or denied admittance because of their suspected intention of doing so) ensures a recurrence of the wastage in the next generation, even allowing for the possibility that in a number of cases parents may regret their own lack of educational qualifications and encourage their children to take opportunities which they themselves missed.

It is tempting to regard the problem as merely one of 'assimilation' into selective secondary schools with a distinctive tradition and rather specific educational aspirations. The secondary grammar schools, despite considerable regional variety in their social composition, are by tradition schools serving the middle classes. Their traditions and ethos tend to be foreign to the boy or girl of working-class origins and the problem of assimilation is a real one. A small and highly selected minority of working-class free-place pupils may be expected to be assimilated – to become in effect socially mobile, accepting school values, making the most of the course by remaining at school at least until the age of sixteen or, in some cases, until a later age and going on to full-time further education. But when, as is now the case, the grammar school is open to a much wider population, assimilation is more difficult and this approach to the problem becomes less and less fruitful.

The precise nature of the hindrances placed by their home background in the way of educating working-class children in grammar schools urgently needs investigating both for its own sake as an immediate problem of educational organization, and for the light it would throw on the problems and possibilities of the comprehensive school. But in the long run, the problem must be viewed as part of the broader question of the interaction of homes and schools generally – of the influence of the home at each social level on the educability of children in schools of particular types and with particular traditions and aims. The problem of equality of educational opportunity is now more complicated than when it took the simple form of the need to secure free access to grammar schools on equal intellectual terms. With the expansion of educational opportunity and the reduction of gross economic handicaps to children's school performance the need arises to understand the optimum conditions for the integration of school and home environment at all social levels in such a way as to minimize the educational disadvantages of both and to turn their educational advantages to full account.

FLANN CAMPBELL (1956)

Eleven-plus and all that*

SCHOLARSHIPS AND METHODS OF SELECTION

The history of scholarships in London goes back many centuries. Originally, many grammar schools were founded with the main (or sometimes even the sole) object of providing a good secondary education for poor, ill-fed, sick, orphaned or otherwise deprived children. Christ's Hospital, for example, the most famous of the charity schools, was founded in 1552 with the aim of taking off the

[1] Reprinted from *Eleven-Plus and All That : the grammar school in a changing society* (London, Watts, 1956).

streets all 'fatherless children and other poor men's children that were not able to keep them'. Charterhouse, another famous early City foundation, debarred in 1613 children 'whose parents have any estate of land', and admitted into the school 'onlie the children of poor men that want means to bring them up'. Merchant Taylors' in its original statutes of 1561 required that 100 out of its 250 scholars be 'poore men's sonnes' paying no fee. When the Rev. Ralph Davenant, rector of St Mary's, Whitechapel, bequeathed money in 1680 for the schools that afterwards bore his name, he specified that it should be spent on '40 poor boys . . . and 30 poor girls in the parish'. Similarly, Mrs Prisca Coborn, who founded a school in Bow in 1701, specified that her legacy should be used to 'teach and instruct the children, male and female, of such poor inhabitants of the said hamlet (St Mary's, Stratford) not being able to give them sufficient learning and education at their own costs and charges . . .' John Roan, a philanthropist of Greenwich, in his will dated 1644 was so far ahead of his time as to provide for maintenance grants as well as fees for pupils in the school he founded. His money was left to 'bring up soe many poore towne-borne children' each of whom should have 'fortie shillings per annum towards their clothing' until they reached the age of fifteen years.

Many other examples could be given of legacies and charitable bequests that had as their prime object the provision of secondary schools for the 'poor, but able' children of London.

But over a long period of time, in many cases, the original aims of the foundations were lost or obscured. Some grammar schools became public schools for the sons (and to a less extent, daughters) of the rich; others were taken over or developed by trusts or City Livery Companies, and took as pupils, with a few rare exceptions, the children of middle-class parents who wished their sons and daughters to have a secondary education but could not afford the high fees of boarding-schools. Alterations in the distribution and size of London's population, the spread of industry and commerce, and changes in social structure and the relation of classes had all created new educational circumstances very different from those envisaged by the original benefactors. Consequently, many anomalies and injustices persisted in the provision of scholarships despite the reforms of the Charity Commissioners between 1850 and 1900.

Towards the end of the century it had become apparent that certain essential conditions must be fulfilled if a scholarship system was to be successful.

The scholarship examination should be centrally controlled and administered over a wide area. It should be held in various centres at the same time, and the regulations should be uniform and as simple as possible. The tests given should be suited to elementary school children, and the value of the scholarships sufficient to make worth while the entry of very poor children. The awards should preferably help towards maintenance as well as school fees. It was particularly important that the public should be fully aware of procedure for entry and conditions of tenure of scholarships. Above all, the scholarships should be sufficient in number to meet the needs of the considerable proportion of intelligent children who were debarred from grammar school education only by their inability to pay fees.

Inadequacy of scholarship system in the 1890s

Not one of these conditions was fully complied with in London in the early 1890s. For example, in 1892 there were less than 1,000 scholarships available in London for about 500,000 children of secondary school age, a mere 'drop in the bucket' as Llewellyn Smith described it. A few years previously a witness at the Cross Commission (1885) had said, 'It would be next to expecting a boy out of a London Board School to take wings as to expect him to advance by his own efforts to the University.'

There were many endowed or other publicly recognized secondary schools that took only a tiny proportion of scholarship entrants, and frequently the latter were so selected as to discriminate against very poor children. Apart from the inadequate number of scholarships, the organization of the awards was so chaotic and the anomalies so numerous that it was impossible to discover any coherent plan or principle in the methods used. . . .

Reform of scholarship system

In view of these deficiencies it was not surprising that there should arise a strong demand for the reform of the scholarship system. . . . The proposals to reorganize the scholarship system were seen as an integral part of the general movement to reform secondary education.

The demand for reform became irresistible when three streams of thought joined together in one powerful tide of opinion. First, there were individuals such as Sidney Webb, or organizations predominantly Socialist in character, such as the Fabian Society and Labour Party, that wanted a fairer deal for working-class children. Secondly, there were educational bodies such as the National Union of Teachers who disliked the inadequacies and disorganization of the old system, and wanted efficiency and order in secondary education. Many school governors and head teachers, concerned with financial difficulties of their schools, were also anxious to see an increased flow of State or locally aided scholars into the schools. Thirdly, there were the more far-sighted politicians and administrators (Morant being a typical example) who were not necessarily sympathetic to progressive political views, but who saw the urgent need to recruit from the widest possible sources talent and ability for the growing professional and commercial occupations.

Junior County Scholarships

The combined influence of these three groups, which often overlapped in their views, grew sufficiently powerful towards the end of the century to force the introduction of the Technical Instruction Act (1891) enabling county councils to incur expenditure on scholarships in secondary schools.

> In the year 1893 the (London County) Council recognized that one of the most pressing wants which had to be met was that of further inducements and facilities for the very poor to keep their children at some secondary or continuation school after leaving the elementary school,

reported the London County Council's Education Officer, continuing, 'the bridge by which the children were to pass from the elementary school to the secondary school was at once erected: it took the form of the establishment of a system of county scholarships.'

This bridge, though weak in relation to the load it was asked to bear, was stronger and broader than anything so far devised by an English local authority; and because in an expanded form it remained for fifty years the main pathway by which poorer children could move from the State elementary into the grammar schools, it is worth considering in some detail. Fundamentally, the new scheme consisted of the award of up to 600 scholarships each year, tenable at certain aided secondary schools in London. They were awarded to children under thirteen years of age, and consisted of free tuition (usually for two years) and maintenance grants of £8 for the first year, and £12 for subsequent years up to fourteen, with possible extension.

As well, there were 100 intermediate scholarships offered at sixteen-plus, and from 20 to 40 scholarships offered at eighteen-plus for study in a university. An upper income limit of £150 per annum was fixed for parents of Junior County Scholarship holders.

In 1904 when the London County Council took over responsibility for secondary education, this scheme was slightly modified, and in 1905 a more ambitious plan was introduced after a vigorous discussion in which Sidney Webb took a leading part. In the latter year there were 2,068 Junior County Scholarships held in about eighty secondary schools in London. This figure, though an improvement on the total of fifteen years previously, still represented less than one in ten of all grammar school pupils.

The revised scheme visualized the annual award of 2,600 Junior County Scholarships with free education up to fourteen-plus, with the possibility of extension for another two years. A maintenance grant of £6, £10 or £15 was payable in certain circumstances. The number of intermediate scholarships was to remain at 100 but maintenance grants were to range from £20 to £35 per annum, and the upper limit for parents' income was raised to £400 per annum. There were also to be 800 probationer scholarships for potential teachers. An important new development (which was abandoned in 1908) was that two-thirds of the Junior County Scholarships were to be allotted to girls, presumably in order to encourage the training of women teachers who were then in great demand because of the expansion of elementary schools.

During the next five years the London County Council consolidated the ground already won, a process that was assisted by the provisions of the 1907 Education Act. This Act made grant aid to secondary schools conditional upon the school offering a fixed proportion (usually one-quarter) of free places.

By 1910 the proportion of scholarship holders had risen to over

one-third in the case of aided and over one-half in the case of
maintained secondary schools, or 7,880 pupils out of a total
attendance of 18,977. . . .

First World War and the Fisher Act, 1918

During and immediately after the First World War the number of
grammar school places in London steadily increased. Many secondary schools, which had previously been independent, accepted State
financial assistance and became recognized as aided grammar schools.
Simultaneously, the number of scholarships increased, though not in
proportion to the total number of new places. By 1920, the attendance at all assisted secondary schools in London was just over 35,000,
of which a little under one-third did not pay fees.

Attendance at London secondary schools in 1919–20

Assisted		Maintained	
Total attendance (*1919*)	Non-fee-payers (*1919*)	Total attendance (*1920*)	Non-fee-payers (*1920*)
35 447	11 041	9 579	4 356

The mood of the immediate post-war period, so far as education
was concerned, was one of optimism and dreams of expansion – soon
to be shattered by the harsh realities of the economic situation. Arising out of the ruins of the War it was hoped to build a land fit for
school children, at least, to live in. The Fisher Act of 1918 promised,
among other things, that there would be an increase of scholarships,
requiring that 'Children and young persons shall not be debarred
from receiving the benefits of any forms of education by which they
are capable of profiting through inability to pay fees.'

The Board of Education also hinted about this time that free
places in secondary schools might be increased from 25 to 40 per
cent if schools were to qualify for grant. As soon as the War was
over the London County Counil began to consider what plans should
be made to increase the number of grammar and central school
places.

The onset of severe trade depression in 1920–1 brought all these
plans to a standstill. Instead of thinking of increasing the number of

free places and cutting fees in secondary schools, the Council sought to economize on educational expenditure. In 1920, for example, the Council decided that:

> Before giving a grant in addition to free education, it was only reasonable to require evidence that the community as well as the student himself would benefit from his admission to the particular type of education required.

It therefore agreed that a maintenance grant would be awarded when the student 'possessed ability above that indicated by mere capacity to profit, showed fitness for the teaching profession and was prepared to undertake to enter upon this work'. The Council also decided that, as well as introducing more stringent scholarship regulations, grammar school fees should be raised wherever possible.

During the mid 1920s the financial position improved somewhat and the number of Junior County Scholarship awards was again increased to nearly 2,000 a year, while the number of supplementary and intermediate awards was also increased. By 1925 the number of non-fee-payers in London secondary schools reached 12,500, and by 1930 nearly 15,000.

Then began in 1931 that world-wide economic crisis that seriously reduced the financial expenditure of all local authorities in Britain. The London County Council reported the pressing need for economy occasioned by the national financial situation, and proposals were made for an immediate cut in the education services. In December 1931, the Council decided to reduce the number of new Junior County Scholarship awards to a maximum of 1,750.[1] Maintenance grants for new scholars were cut by 20 per cent and for old scholars by 10 per cent. The standard of the intermediate examination was raised.

In 1932, on the advice of the Board of Education, it was decided also to raise fees in some grammar schools. This extra charge was confined to schools in wealthier districts because it was feared that if fees were raised in the poorer districts the number of new entrants would quickly decline.

In September 1932, the Board of Education issued new regulations

---

[1] This rule does not seem to have been observed, as the lowest number of Junior County awards after 1931 was 1,888 in 1934.

to the effect that scholarships should only be granted if the parents' financial circumstances justified such aid. A kind of 'means test' was visualized. The main change was that 'free places' were superseded by 'special places'. Broadly speaking, this meant that the old so-called 'free places' would have to be reconsidered or reduced. They were no longer to be regarded as automatically free. The London County Council proposed that those who were getting free places should either continue to have them free or else pay reduced admission fees. Those who were getting free places plus maintenance grants, i.e. full scholarships, should get free places without maintenance. Pupils who were most in need, however, would get the highest scale of grant.

The Education Officer's report for 1933–4 contains a table showing how the 'special place' awards of 1933–4 differed from the 'free place' awards of 1932. In 1932 there were 2,681 'free places' held – 1,021 in maintained, and 1,660 in aided grammar schools. During the following two years the 'special places' were split up as follows:

School	Full fees		Partial fees		Remission of fees		Totals	
	1933	1934	1933	1934	1933	1934	1933	1934
Maintained	34	37	107	131	1 181	1 278	1 322	1 446
Aided	59	48	154	168	1 507	1 662	1 720	1 878
Totals	93	85	261	299	2 688	2 940	3 042	3 324

Analysing these figures it would appear that, out of a total of between 3,000 and 3,400 'special places' held in 1933–4, only about 350 to 400, or one in nine, were compelled to pay full or partial fees as a result of this new regulation. So far as was known no candidate declined a special place because he was requested to pay full or partial fees.[1]

[1] In 1938, 2,550 Junior County Scholarships were awarded at the age of eleven to twelve based on an examination in English and arithmetic with an intelligence test. The maximum value was free tuition at a grammar school with a maximum maintenance allowance of £9 rising to £14 per year at age of fourteen-plus. Sixteen hundred special places were awarded, usually to pupils who had just failed winning a Junior County award, on the basis of examinations in the grammar schools themselves. The maximum value of these was free tuition with no maintenance grant up to the age of fourteen-plus, when £13 per year was paid if annual parental income did not exceed £150, and there was one dependent child. Five

Social and economic factors causing increase of scholarships

But the economic depression passed after a few years, and as financial conditions improved so the Board of Education and the London County Council became willing once more to increase their expenditure on grammar schools. There were other economic and social factors affecting scholarships that proved more decisive in their long-term influence than the temporary fluctuations of the trade cycle. These factors, which had already shown themselves so powerful in their influence upon grammar schools at the beginning of the century, increased in significance as the years went by. Broadly speaking, they were three in number:

1 The demand on democratic grounds, generally expressed in the slogan 'secondary education for all', for wider educational opportunities for working-class children. Individuals such as Professor R. H. Tawney and organizations such as the Labour Party, Workers' Educational Association and National Union of Teachers carried forward the campaign that had been initiated by Sidney Webb, the Fabians and others before the First World War. This campaign reached its peak during the years immediately preceding the 1944 Act when the Council for Educational Advance was set up, comprising the National Union of Teachers, Workers' Educational Association and the Trades Union Congress.

2 The ever-growing need for more trained and qualified 'white-collar' workers compelled the authorities to expand the number of grammar school places. It was realized that if the commercial, administrative and professional occupations were to get the personnel they required then they must recruit from among the most intelligent working-class as well as middle-class children.

3 As the cost of running the grammar schools rose steadily

---

hundred supplementary Junior County awards were made at the age of thirteen-plus on the basis of examination in English, arithmetic, history and geography. About 65 per cent of these were won by pupils already in grammar schools, 20 per cent by pupils in central schools and 15 per cent in modern schools. The value was the same as Junior County awards. A smaller number of Intermediate and Senior County Scholarships were also awarded at the ages of sixteen or eighteen respectively.

because of higher building standards, more expensive equipment and improved pay for teachers, so the governing bodies were faced with the question of either increasing fee-paying income or else accepting more scholarship pupils. But in London especially, where the middle-class fee-paying population was falling gradually because of migration to the suburbs, it was difficult to attract more fee-payers into the grammar schools. Indeed, the problem was to maintain rather than to increase the number of fee-payers. So serious was the decline in fee-paying income in many of the grammar schools situated in the poorer central and East End boroughs that the London County Council decided to allow governors of certain schools to remit up to 75 per cent of fees in what were termed 'hard cases'. Undoubtedly one of the reasons why the 'special place' system was not extended as much as it might have been in 1931–3 was the fear that grammar schools in poor areas would be gravely depleted if the regulations were enforced too strictly.

In the long run the pressures making for the expansion of free secondary education proved stronger than those making for contraction, and gradually the number of scholarships was increased. By 1935 more than half of all the places in aided and maintained London grammar schools were held by scholarship pupils. The expansion in the number of scholarships may be seen in the following tables:

Attendance at London secondary[a] schools

	All secondary schools			Maintained schools		
Year	Total attendance	Non-fee-payers	Non-fee-payers as % of total	Total attendance	Non-fee-payers	Non-fee-payers as % of total
1920	35 447 (1919)	11 041 (1919)	31	9 579	4 356	45·5
1925	42 832	12 548	29	9 587	4 090	43
1930	43 239	14 728	34	10 987	5 128	46·5
1935	43 842	18 818	43	12 139	7 025	58

[a] 'Secondary' refers to schools of the grammar or independent type.

Number of Junior County Scholarships held in London grammar schools

Year	No.	Year	No.	Year	No.
1905	2 068	1916	6 725	1927	7 987
1906	3 929	1917	6 653	1928	8 182
1907	5 646	1918	6 897	1929	8 464
1908	6 876	1919	7 069	1930	8 757
1909	7 869	1920	7 300	1931	9 143
1910	7 675	1921	7 568	1932	9 085
1911	7 524	1922	7 708	1933	9 040
1912	7 378	1923	7 362	1934	8 847
1913	7 307	1924	7 263	1935	9 338
1914	7 291	1925	7 242	1936	9 708
1915	7 047	1926	7 757	1937	10 425

Abolition of fees

During the Second World War the demand for a more democratic secondary school system culminated in the 1944 Education Act, which abolished all fees in aided and maintained grammar schools, and thus represented the triumph of the 'free place' idea.

The fact that the provisions of this Act were so easily adopted is an indication of how widely accepted the scholarship system had become by Members of Parliament and public as well as by teachers and administrators. Criticisms of the working of the free-place system there were in individual cases, but in broad outline the reforms were generally recognized as necessary, and even inevitable. The innovation of earlier decades became the commonplace of the 1940s and 1950s.

The abolition of fees represented a fundamental change in attitude towards secondary education, but at the time the 1944 Act was passed not all its implications were fully understood. In particular, it was not really appreciated how the grammar schools, with their special historical, social and vocational problems, would be affected. For example, would the introduction of the 100 per cent free-place system simplify the question of selection? Would it alter the vocational aims of the grammar schools? How would it affect the different social classes in their efforts to get the secondary education to which they thought they were entitled? Was it to be assumed that the basic principle of scholarships was to enable children of very poor parents to get into the grammar schools? And if so, how far had this aim already been achieved?

To answer these questions (which are, of course, vital to the understanding of the whole idea of secondary education for all) it is necessary to describe how the State-scholarship system affected children of different social classes and to what extent environmental factors have influenced children's chances of winning scholarships.

Scholarships and social status

In the late 1880s, Charles Booth made a survey of the social class of scholarship winners in London grammar schools. His main conclusion was that the few scholarships that then existed were being won, not by the sons and daughters of the very poor, but by the children of the lower middle class, or else by what he called the 'upper fringe of the working class'. Analysing the occupations of parents of 100 free scholars attending three east London secondary schools, he found that 70 could be broadly classified as middle-class and 30 as working-class. In a group of girls' high schools he found that out of fifty-six scholarship winners twenty-nine were middle-class and twenty-seven working-class.

As a result of his investigations, Booth concluded:

> ... the elementary scholars, who as yet have found their way into London Secondary Schools, had been the aristocracy, no less socially than intellectually, of the schools from which they have been drawn ... the social class of the majority of the boys selected by scholarships does not differ very greatly from that of the other pupils of secondary schools ... boys who are successful in the competition for scholarships come from the richer homes, for by the age of eleven or twelve the influence of the home atmosphere has had time to tell to such a degree as to handicap severely the boys from rougher homes where there is little appreciation of education and little opportunity for quiet study.

There seems good reason to believe that instead of the scholarship enabling working men to send their daughters to middle-class schools it rather encourages middle-class men to send their daughters to Board schools in the hope of obtaining a scholarship.

Booth (or more properly Llewellyn Smith, who wrote the chapter on Education in Booth's famous survey of London) was, of course, writing of the period before there was any State or local authority system of scholarships. Nevertheless, later and more comprehensive evidence bears out the point that it was the children of skilled workers, clerks, shopkeepers, and the like who mainly benefited from the new London County Council schemes of 1893 and 1904.

It was not the Council's policy that these more socially privileged children should win most of the scholarships. On the contrary, it was the ablest and most talented children from the poorest homes that the Council hoped to get into the grammar schools. 'In the year 1893 the Council recognized that one of the most pressing wants which had to be met was that of further inducements and facilities for the *very poor* [my italics] to keep their children at some secondary or continuation schools', says an early Council report. Income limits for scholarships were introduced in order that 'access to the scholarship ladder can be made really effective to the clever children of the *poorest homes*' [my italics].

Social class of parents of Junior County Scholars 1904 and 1905

	No.		%	
Social Class	1904	1905	1904	1905
Middle	1	—	0·3	—
Lower middle	83	569	24·7	24·0
Skilled working	176	1 152	52·4	48·5
Unskilled working	63	594	18·7	25·0
Unclassified	13	60	3·9	2·5
Totals	336	2 375	100·0	100·0

That the scholarships did not during the first decade of the century, in fact, mainly reach these 'very poor' children is clear from the Council's own investigations. In 1904 and again in 1905, an analysis was made of the occupations of parents of over 2,500 Junior County Scholarship winners, which showed that less than 25 per cent came from the unskilled and labouring class, about 50 per cent from skilled workers, and the remaining 25 per cent from clerical, commercial and minor professional occupations. The results of this analysis are given in the table above.

The London County Council Education Officer made an income analysis for 1905–6 with the following results:

Incomes of parents of Junior County Scholars selected 1905–6

Income	1905		1906	
	No.	%	No.	%
Less than £160	2 080	87·6	1 667	84·2
£160 to £300	230	9·7	250	12·6
Over £300	65	2·7	64	3·2
Totals	2 375	100	1 981	100

What is surprising about these figures is not that four-fifths of the scholarships went to children of parents who earned less than £3 per week (one would expect that) but that some hundreds went to those in income groups £160 to £300 per year, and several score annually to those in income groups above £300 per year.

Pre-1914 an income of £6 per week put a person definitely into the middle class, and parents with that kind of income could easily have afforded the comparatively low fees payable at the aided London grammar schools. Such fees varied widely from school to school but were seldom above 10 guineas a year.

During the first decade of this century the great majority of industrial workers were getting under £2 per week, and unskilled men were getting in the neighbourhood of 25s. or 30s. a week, or less. It would, therefore, have been more valuable from the point of view of the social historian if the above figures had been broken down to give further details. For example, what proportion of scholarship winners were in the under £100 or under £75 a year class?

Social status of scholarship winners during inter-war period

After the First World War the London County Council made a further analysis of the occupations and incomes of parents of scholarship winners, which showed that the position was much the same as it had been pre-1914. The children of skilled parents were winning most awards, those of the clerical and shopkeeping class were close behind, and children of unskilled and labouring parents were still relatively unsuccessful in their efforts to win scholarships. Indeed, in the immediate post-war period the lower middle class were doing slightly better, and the poorer working class slightly worse than pre-war.

Social class of parents of Junior County Scholarship winners in London 1921 and 1922

Social class	No.	%
Middle	—	—
Lower middle	1 320	42
Skilled working	1 276	41
Unskilled working	515	17
Totals	3 111	100

Allowing for the rise in prices that had occurred during the war, it can be seen from the table below how less than one in five of the successful candidates had parents in the poorly paid category of under £3 a week, but nearly one in three was in the comparatively well-paid group earning over £5 a week.

Income of parents of Junior County Scholarship winners in London 1921 and 1922

Income	No.	%
Under £160	550	18
£160–£250	1 626	52
Over £250	935	30
Totals	3 111	100

Moreover, writing as late as 1926, another critic of the scholarship system could say:

> ... secondary education is outside the reach of the unskilled worker, except for between $2\frac{1}{2}$ and 3 per cent of the total entering secondary schools; this figure has been fairly constant for the last ten years ... the unskilled and lowly paid worker, the farm worker and the casual labourer, are as yet not really touched by the scholarship system. Individuals there undoubtedly are, but the mass remains unaffected.[1]

[1] *Social Progress and Educational Waste*, by Kenneth Lindsay, pp. 21 and 26 (Routledge, 1926).

No further analysis of the social background of scholarship winners appears to have been made by the London County Council since 1922, but judging by the evidence given in previous chapters it would seem that increased numbers of poor working-class children (all of whom, it would be safe to assume, came in by means of scholarship) began to enter the grammar schools in the late 1920s and 1930s.

Scholarships won in different boroughs

There was, however, another related social aspect of the scholarship problem with which the London County Council remained preoccupied for many years, and that was the question why certain boroughs (and elementary schools) in the metropolitan area won proportionately far more scholarships than others. . . .

Analysis of the figures shows that such comparatively prosperous districts as Hampstead and Lewisham have consistently won several times as many Junior County Scholarships per head of population as such poor districts as Southwark and Shoreditch. To take some of the more extreme examples: in 1905 in Dulwich, 8·3 per 1,000 of the children in average attendance at elementary schools won Junior County Scholarships, but for north Lambeth the figure was only 0·5 per 1,000. In 1914, the figure for Lewisham was 5·8, but in Mile End only 0·3 per 1,000; in 1925 it was 8·2 for West Lewisham and 0·4 for south-west Bethnal Green and Finsbury; in 1935 it was 14·0 for Streatham and 1·3 for north Southwark. The inverse relationship between poverty and scholarship successes is brought out even more clearly when different electoral constituencies in the same borough are compared. Thus, the poorer constituency of west Islington consistently won fewer awards than the wealthier constituency of north Islington. Similarly, north St Pancras remained superior intellectually as well as socially to south-west St Pancras. . . .

Council's attitude to problem

One of the earliest references to this problem was by Sidney Webb, who, writing in 1904 said, 'It is often stated that the system of selecting children from London as a whole results unfairly to the children in the poorer districts, and that a proportionate quota of scholarships should be allocated to each district.'

In spite of evidence to the contrary, Webb did not agree that there was an inverse relationship between the poverty of the district and the number of scholarships won. He therefore rejected the idea that a certain number of scholarships should be allocated to each borough on the grounds that it would 'diminish the keenness of the competition, lower the general average of quality, and result in the exclusion of able children in some districts by less able candidates from other districts'.

In 1916 and 1924, the London County Council again returned to the subject, and on the latter occasion the variations in figures between different boroughs had become so striking as to lead the Council to publish a table showing the relationship between scholarship awards and overcrowding in London.

Nine years later Mr Lewis Silkin and other Labour Councillors pressed for further investigations to be made, and asked that something be done to help poorer boroughs to win more scholarships. In the same year the Council's Education Officer presented a Report, which agreed that 'There is no doubt that the proportion of scholarships won by children in certain areas is very much higher than in other areas.' Junior County Scholarship winners in 1928–9 were analysed as follows:

	Average no. in elementary schools	Scholar-ships	Scholarships per 1 000 elementary school-children
Nine electoral areas in outer ring gaining high proportion of scholarships	69 500	986	7·1
Nine electoral areas in inner ring gaining low proportion of scholarships	71 500	220	1·5
County as a whole	540 000	3 818	3·6

184   FLANN CAMPBELL

A further investigation was made in 1929 into certain specially selected primary schools, which showed that twelve 'better-off' primary schools with 8,000 pupils won 102 Junior County Scholarships but that twelve other primary schools 'attended by children of parents with small incomes' (8,500 children) won only eleven scholarships. The Report continues:

> The director of the New Survey of London kindly supplied figures regarding parental incomes of children attending schools in five metropolitan boroughs. These figures, when related to statistics concerning the incomes of parents of scholarship holders, indicated that the children of poor parents are less successful in winning scholarships than the children of better-off parents. This was most clearly evident when the children of parents with incomes of £2 a week or less were compared with children of parents with £5 a week or over.

Experiments made with intelligence tests only aggravated the trend towards richer children winning more scholarships, as is shown by the following figures:

	Poor electoral area	Better-off electoral area
Junior County Scholarships actual gained in 1929	35	74
Scholarships that would have been gained on basis of intelligence tests	26	78

The Report sums up by stating that children from poor areas, poor schools, and poor homes win proportionately fewer scholarships than children from richer areas, richer schools and richer homes. The introduction of an intelligence test would not make much difference.

Having discussed the nature of the problem, the Report then goes on to mention three proposals that were advocated as remedies:

1 More scholarships for 'poor' areas
2 More marks for schools that have won consistently few scholarships

3 Some scholarships to be restricted to children of very poor parents.

The second of these suggestions is favoured most, but the Report adds that, 'It should be realized that all these three proposals would involve the awarding of scholarships to children who, from the examination test used, are less able intellectually than others to whom the scholarships would be awarded.'

In fact, nothing was done about any of these proposals, and the situation continued that the Council awarded scholarships to the metropolitan area as a whole. No attempt was made to restrict awards in any way to particular districts, schools or sections of the community.

BRIAN JACKSON AND DENNIS MARSDEN (1962)

Education and the working class*

No overhaul of the present system (though not be scorned) will go far enough to meet what we take to be the major problem facing state education. That problem, quite bluntly, is how can we open education to the working class?

The fees are gone, but the grammar schools are still closed. In this they are not crudely unjust. Their entry can very properly be justified in terms of measured intelligence. A greater proportion of middle-class children score more highly in measured intelligence tests than do working-class children. But of course what this means is hard to know. We can only talk here of *measured* intelligence – not, what we are after all concerned with, 'intelligence'. Because children do less well in terms of measured intelligence this does not mean they are unintelligent; and certainly it has nothing to say about the

* Reprinted from *Education and the Working Class. Some general themes raised by a study of 88 working-class children in a northern industrial city* (London, Routledge and Kegan Paul, 1962).

possession, or not, of the many other human qualities that make the mature man or woman. The whole discussion, which underlies so much defence of élite education at eleven, is complex and fluid. But some notes might be helpful here. First of all, no one is in a position to state that middle-class children are *inherently* more intelligent than working-class. The argument is open. Of course the case for a strong influence of inherited ability is well argued, and is being continually reshaped and refined as it meets new criticism. But the hypothesis that intelligence is distributed at random between the different social classes, and that any measured difference is due to environment not birth, is quite as strong. 'Environment' can be a delicate matter to define and grasp, and 'money' can count potently at one or two removes. For example, much interesting work has been done showing that when we measure intelligence we are very often, directly or indirectly, measuring verbal dexterity. A. F. Watts restates in the language of our own time what Shakespeare put before us 350 years ago: that language is not merely the reflection or translation of thought – it is the texture of the mind in movement, the process of definition itself. 'We find that we have been thinking only after we have said what we thought' (*Language and Mental Development of Children*). The world of language in which a child is reared very much controls his potentialities. J. N. Nisbett suggests that the low scores at intelligence tests from large (working-class) families are connected with 'an atmosphere of 'verbal restriction'. When we reflect over the working men and women talking and compare them with the voices of their children, then we can see the point even here. Yet it is *difference* rather than 'restriction' which is caught on these pages. There is a quality about the parents' speech that the children do not possess. Basil Bernstein has shown how working-class speech naturally moves into description, and how middle-class speech just as naturally turns towards abstract conceptions – and how this can be measured. There is something brave and exploratory about this difficult and continuing inquiry into social class, intelligence and language. The impulse is admirable, and our new knowledge of 'intelligence' (even when, as largely, it is clearer knowledge of our ignorance) is a triumph of patient research.

The tragedy of intelligence tests, and the organization and

justification of education in terms of them, is a tragedy of users. The tests are, unfortunately, immensely useful to bureaucracy. Thousands of complex human situations are vastly simplified: situations that were better recognized and left as complex. Under the pressure of mass-produced, mass-applied intelligence tests released from central education offices, children and the problems of their education turn into figures which turn into simple tables – mere fodder for the clerks. No one who works as a teacher and knows the difficulty and delicacy of the work can be anything but shocked to witness some kinds of educational bureaucracy in action, and see 'intelligence' becoming a crude administrative weapon utterly untrue to the situation it stems from. Half-grasped and elusive concepts, fashioned by distinguished research workers, are used facilely by those who have no responsibility back to the work. Intelligence testing is of immense use in education, but this is not that use; as those who won such concepts out of the unknown are the first to announce. And glancing at the difference in speech between working-class parent and middle-class child on these pages, one is reminded again of what it is in language that speaks for quality of feeling, for sharpness of mind informed by generosity of response. It is not necessarily that which can be measured easily. It is not size of vocabulary. It is not number of abstract words to number of concrete words. (We hardly measure language under the pressure of genius in this way.) We need to remind ourselves that 'meaning' and that quality of language which arises out of quality of living is to be defined more in terms of rhythm, of association, of the personal play of words out of the thew and sinew of spoken English: more in terms of these than by width of vocabulary.

Yet it is by such things as 'vocabulary' that we divide children up. And it is this which, if we could but reach 100 per cent 'efficiency', would finally define our process of selection at eleven. The test result is far from the full thinking and feeling child, and much more distant still are those same figures when they emerge from the bureaucratic machine. It is worth bringing our literary culture and the culture of our psychologists together like this, in order to point the abuse of both when 'intelligence' tests become built into the administrative machine: a simplifying marvel in the office, but an utter distortion in the schools. It sets thoughts stirring: thoughts about the quality of man or woman that we could ever hope to measure, and the quality of what we may well reject. . . .

The new pupils have brought new 'manners', and the grammar school seems to have responded in two ways. Sometimes with weary hostility at the entrance of the barbarians:

> The grammar school now includes among its pupils a much higher proportion of children from poorer homes. Some of these children come from homes which are barely literate and where a book is an unusual phenomenon. . . . Others have very low standards of cleanliness and appearance: some seem to have had very little training in social behaviour; even table manners may leave much to be desired. Children like these have very little to give to the social or cultural life of the school, the school itself has to provide much which, before the war, would have been regarded as the normal contribution of the home.[1]

At other times it has shown a calm assurance that all will naturally be well and the working class will be grateful for such gifts as they receive. 'The working-class father and mother who left school at fourteen tend to accept all that a Grammar School can offer their children and be thankful.'[2] Both responses are protective stereotypes, either redirecting criticism safely outwards ('bad backgrounds'), or meltingly absorbing it within a bland satisfaction at the *status quo*. Of course there *are* problems of 'background' taken in this narrower way. (Though it is the secondary modern school which is fighting those battles), and many parents and children *are* only too grateful to accept all that the grammar school offers – though absolute gratitude was not the only note we recorded. But the last two quotations (they are characteristic) go some way to showing why grammar schools can act as if there are few problems here, and why every research worker in the field uncovers wastage and frustration on a disheartening scale. The difference between the grammar school attitude and the discovered facts requires such explanation: it is in itself one of the most startling and interesting of the facts.

The working-class child who does win entry to the grammar

[1] A. Davies, *Bulletin of Education*, November 1950 (quoted in *Social Class and Educational Opportunity*, p. 27).
[2] H. Ree, *The Essential Grammar School*, p. 15.

school must accommodate himself to the prevailing middle-class values, or rub up against them. If this survey is any pointer, it seems likely that most of those who remain embedded in working-class family and neighbourhood life leave school before the sixth form. Those who cling to the world of their family and yet survive do so with difficulty and move often into a disturbed adulthood. This does not mean that the quality of their living is less fine than that of their more accommodating and successful class mates. We do not know; but we can scarcely justify a schooling on the grounds that it prepares an early entry into the more troubling dimensions of life. And yet if this conflict between school and neighbourhood at so many tiny, frictional points is perturbing, the situation of the orthodox child is even more so. There is something infinitely pathetic in these former working-class children who lost their roots young, and who now with their rigid middle-class accent preserve 'the stability of all our institutions, temporal and spiritual' by avariciously reading the lives of Top People, or covet the public schools and glancing back at the society from which they came see no more there than 'the dim', or the 'specimens'. Can we wish that our schools offer longer education in exchange for this worship of the conformist spirit? For it seems to us that despite all the formal talk about 'individuals' and 'character', grammar schools are so socially imprisoned that they are most remarkable for the conformity of the minds they train. Highly inbred institutions, they respond with the talismatic words when challenged – and here and there a gifted and *unorthodox* teacher lives out that older language – but is this, in fact, what *happens*? Schools born out of middle-class needs; schools based on social selection, further refined with each year after eleven; schools offering a complex training in approved images of dominance and deference – are these the bases for general 'individualism', for 'democratic living'? Or would not the individual when really present be more likely to be non-conformist (and a candidate for slow expulsion) in the way that some of the working-class children were?
. . .

If then grammar school education is so shaped by restrictive social pressures, if despite our formal legislation grammar schools remain 'closed' to society at large, in subtle but very firm ways which have as much to do with class as with ability – how then shall we break the impasse? On the one hand we have the central culture of our society ('the best that has been thought and known', 'the very culture of the feelings', 'that spontaneity which is the hardest of all') which must be preserved and transmitted; on the other hand we have institutions which do this for the middle class but not for the working-class majority. It seems to us that what we call our central culture and what the teachers call 'middle-class values' are by no means the same thing, and the problem is to disentangle one from the other in schools which are truly 'open'. When the head-teacher says 'I see grammar school education very strongly as a matter of communicating middle-class values to a "new" population', he is surely not saying something akin to Matthew Arnold's classic statement, but something contrary in spirit, provincial and partisan. It is worth quoting Arnold's statement in some fullness:

> Culture looks beyond machinery, culture hates hatred; culture has one great passion, the passion for sweetness and light. It has one even yet greater! – the passion for making them prevail. It is not satisfied till we *all* come to a perfect man; it knows that the sweetness and light of the few must be imperfect until the raw and unkindled masses of humanity are touched with sweetness and light. If I have not shrunk from saying that we must work for sweetness and light, so neither have I shrunk from saying that we must have a broad basis, must have sweetness and light for as many as possible. Again and again I have insisted how those are the happy moments of humanity, how those are the marking epochs of a people's life, how those are the flowering times for literature and art and all the creative power of genius, when there is a *national* glow of life and thought, sensible to beauty, intelligent and alive. Only it must be *real* thought and *real* beauty; *real* sweetness and *real* light. Plenty of people will try to give the masses, as they call them, an intellectual food prepared and adapted in the way they think proper for the actual conditions of the masses. The ordinary popular literature is an example of this way of working on the masses. Plenty of people will try to indoctrinate the masses with the set of ideas and judgements constituting the creed of their own profession or party. Our religious and political organizations give an example of this way of working on the

masses. I condemn neither way; but culture works differently. It does not try to teach down to the level of inferior classes; it does not try to win them for this or that sect of its own, with ready-made judgements and watch-words. It seeks to do away with classes; to make the best that has been thought and known in the world current everywhere; to make all men live in an atmosphere of sweetness and light, where they may use ideas, as it uses them itself, freely – nourished, and not bound by them.

This is the *social idea*; and the men of culture are the true apostles of equality. The great men of culture are those who have had a passion for diffusing, for making prevail, for carrying from one end of society to the other, the best knowledge, the best ideas of their time; who have laboured to divest knowledge of all that was harsh, uncouth, difficult, abstract, professional, exclusive; to humanize it, to make it efficient outside the clique of the cultivated and learned, yet still remaining the *best* knowledge and thought of the time, and a true source, therefore, of sweetness and light.[1]

How are we to reinterpret Arnold's magnificent prose in our own time? Can it be done at all in an education system which remains 'exclusive' and not 'national'? Or to put it another way, can we not begin by accepting the nation, and rooting our schools and colleges in that acceptance, instead of endlessly improving the amenities and efficiencies of an élite system? And is this so impossible; is it at all true, as the head-teachers say, that the working class (three-quarters of the 'nation') bring nothing of their own to meet the cultural inheritance? Are they so 'new', so raw, so blank?

It is not only in education that this line of questions is being posed. Since the war there has been a whole wealth of documentation of the most stringent nature to refreshen our sense of what working-class life can offer, and to sharpen our discriminations in accepting or refusing aspects of it. Two and a half centuries of urban life have established distinct styles of living with very real values of their own, values which are perhaps essential to civilization, and yet which do not flourish that strongly in other reaches of society. Of course working-class life has its limits, its distortions, its raw and ugly patches; and since research has been heavily weighted in favour

[1] M. Arnold, *Culture and Anarchy*, p. 30–1.

H

of abnormality and delinquency we are not short of the record. But as a society are we in any position to neglect our inherited stores of strength, or to obliterate them? ...

The educational system we need is one which accepts and develops the best qualities of working-class living, and brings these to meet our central culture. Such a system must partly be *grown* out of common living, not merely imposed on it. But before this can begin, we must put completely aside any early attempts to select and reject to rear an élite. They will be the richer and the finer for having come up another way. This does not mean that we overlook the unequal abilities of children. But it does mean that, instead of accepting and reinforcing the environmental limitations, we try to share education with an equality that we have not yet attained. Nothing like this is possible in the present system.

We have come to that place where we must firmly accept the life of the majority and where we must be bold and flexible in developing the new forms – the 'open' school which belongs to the neighbourhood, the 'open' university which involves itself in local life rather than dominates or defies it from behind college or red-brick walls. The first practical step is to abandon selection at eleven, and accept the comprehensive principle. An alteration by Parliament is needed to touch off local experiment and flexibility in making new 'forms' within the comprehensive *principle*. No one would wish to see monster comprehensive schools blueprinted up and down the country. They have their place, but there are many other ways, and much still to be discovered. The local variety of English education is, and should remain a strength, within the new principle. Of course this would not solve everything. Social inheritance and deprivation would not be abolished with the abolition of selection and rejection. Social pressures would still be at work, and the middle-class child, for example, would do as well as ever (and one hopes, even better). But a huge amount would be achieved by shared schooling in a 'national' society, and the way to richer progress at last opened.

COMMITTEE ON HIGHER EDUCATION (1963)

Higher education (Robbins Report)*

(1) REPORT

The so-called pool of ability

It is sometimes argued that growth in the number of those able to
benefit from higher education is something that is likely to be limited
in the foreseeable future by biological factors. But we believe that it is
highly misleading to suppose that one can determine an upper limit
to the number of people who could benefit from higher education,
given favourable circumstances. It is, of course, unquestionable that
human beings vary considerably in native capacity for all sorts of
tasks. No one who has taught young people will be disposed to urge
that it is only the difference in educational opportunity that makes the
difference between a Newton or a Leonardo and Poor Tom the Fool.
But while it would be wrong to deny fundamental differences of
nature, it is equally wrong to deny that performance in examinations
or tests – or indeed any measurable ability – is affected by nurture in
the widest sense of that word. Moreover, the belief that there exists
some easy method of ascertaining an intelligence factor unaffected by
education or background is outmoded. Years ago, performance in
'general intelligence tests' was thought to be relatively independent of
earlier experience. It is now known that in fact it is dependent upon
previous experience to a degree sufficiently large to be of great
relevance. And once one passes beyond tests of this kind and
examines for specific knowledge or aptitudes, the influence of education and environment becomes more and more important.

Considerations of this sort are important at all stages of education,
but especially at higher stages. For by then the effects of earlier
education and environment in moulding and modifying fundamental
biological equipment have produced a cumulative effect. It is no

* Reprinted from *Higher Education* (London, HMSO, 1963), Report and
Appendix One.

doubt true that there are born a number of potential 'firsts' whose
qualities are such that they win through whatever their environmental disadvantages, and another, considerably larger, number who,
if trained by the most famous teachers in history, would still fail their
examinations. But in between there is a vast mass whose performance,
both at the entry to higher education and beyond, depends greatly
on how they have lived and been taught beforehand.

Of this we have received ample evidence both from our witnesses
and also from a survey we conducted of a sample of men and women
aged twenty-one in August 1962. One of the purposes of this survey
was to throw light on the factors affecting the achievement of school
children and their entry to higher education. The Crowther Report
had already indicated the close association between a father's level

TABLE I. *Percentage of children born in 1940–1 reaching full-time
higher education: by father's occupation, Great Britain*

		Full-time higher education		No full-time higher education	All children	No. (= 100%)
	Father's occupation	Degree level	Other			
Boys and girls	*Non-manual*					
	Higher professional	33	12	55	100	*15 000*
	Managerial and other professional	11	8	81	100	*87 000*
	Clerical	6	4	90	100	*38 000*
	Manual					
	Skilled	2	2	96	100	*248 000*
	Semi and un-skilled	1	1	98	100	*137 000*
Boys	*Non-manual*	15	4	81	100	*70 000*
	Manual	3	2	95	100	*189 000*
Girls	*Non-manual*	9	10	81	100	*70 000*
	Manual	1	2	97	100	*196 000*

Source: survey of twenty-one year olds

of occupation and the educational achievement of his children at
school. As Table I shows, our survey confirmed that the association
with parental occupation is, if anything, still closer where higher
education is concerned. For example, the proportion of young
people who enter full-time higher education is 45 per cent for those

whose fathers are in the 'higher professional' group, compared with only 4 per cent for those whose fathers are in skilled manual occupations. The underlying reasons for this are complex, but differences of income and of the parents' educational level and attitudes are certainly among them. The link is even more marked for girls than for boys.

Clearly the economic circumstances of the home are very influential: even in families of the same occupational level, the proportion of children reaching full-time higher education is four times as high for children from families with one or two children as from those where five or more children have claims on the family's resources. Thus a continuing growth in family incomes is likely to increase still further the demand for higher education. There is also a very important influence from the educational background of the parents (although this is, of course, related to their social class or occupation). As Table 2 shows, the proportion reaching full-time higher education is eight times as high among children whose fathers continued their own education to the age of eighteen or over as among those whose fathers left school under sixteen. These facts suggest that, just as since the war more children have stayed on

TABLE 2. *Percentage of children born in 1940–1 reaching full-time higher education: by father's age on completing full-time education, Great Britain*

	Full-time higher education		No full-time higher education	All children	No. (= 100%)
	Degree-level	Other			
Father's age on completing full-time education					
18 or over	32	11	57	100	22 000
16 or 17	14	7	79	100	41 000
Under 16	2	3	95	100	491 000

Source: survey of twenty-one year olds

at school for a full secondary education, so in turn more of their children will come to demand higher education during the 1970s. The desire for education will tend to spread as more and more parents have themselves received a fuller education.

This in itself is, of course, no guarantee that the quality of students will be maintained if there is an increased entry. There is, however, impressive evidence that large numbers of able young people do not at present enter higher education. Table 3 gives some of the results of a recent Ministry of Education survey of school leavers which, at our request, was extended to provide information on parental occupation and on performance at the age of eleven. Column 1 shows that, of grammar school leavers with a given measured ability at the age of eleven, the proportion obtaining the qualifications for entry to higher education varies widely according to their social background. Children of manual workers are on average much less successful than children of the same ability in other social groups. This is largely because they leave school earlier. A comparison of columns 1 and 2 of the table shows that the proportion of children

TABLE 3. *Percentage of leavers from maintained grammar schools having two or more passes at Advanced level: by grading in eleven-plus and father's occupation, England and Wales, 1960–1*

Grading in	Father's occupation	*Percentage of leavers of all ages who have 2 or more A levels* (1)	*Percentage of leavers of all ages who leave aged 18 and over* (2)	*Percentage of leavers aged 18 and over who have 2 or more A levels* (3)
Upper third	Professional and managerial	57	55	79
	Clerical	44	39	74
	Skilled manual	38	40	77
	Semi- and unskilled	21	23	81
Middle third	Professional and managerial	33	42	63
	Clerical	18	29	56
	Skilled manual	18	27	59
	Semi- and unskilled	10	15	58
Lower third	Professional and managerial	14	32	43
	Clerical	16	22	58
	Skilled manual	10	18	51
	Semi- and unskilled	4	7	53
Transfer from secondary modern school		15	29	49
All groups at eleven-plus	Professional and managerial	37	46	67
	Clerical	26	32	64
	Skilled manual	22	29	65
	Semi- and unskilled	11	17	56
All children		24	31	65

Source: Statistics of Education, 1961, Supplement to Part 2, Table 13.

of manual workers who stay on to the age when the General Certificate of Education at Advanced level is normally attempted is smaller than the proportion of middle-class children who actually achieve two passes at Advanced level. But as may be seen from column 3 of the table those children who do stay on are on average as successful as children of the same ability in other social groups.

While the reserves of untapped ability may be greatest in the poorer sections of the community, this is not the whole of the story. It is sometimes imagined that the greatest increase in recent years in the numbers achieving good school-leaving qualifications has occurred almost entirely among the children of manual workers. This is not so. The increase has been almost as great among the children of professional parents, where the pool of ability might have been thought more nearly exhausted. In these groups the performance of children of a given measured ability has in fact continually improved. The desire for education, leading to better performance at school, appears to be affecting children of all classes and all abilities alike, and it is reasonable to suppose that this trend will continue.

The quality of primary and secondary education and its organization also affects the proportion of children who emerge as capable of entering higher education. Reductions in the size of classes, and the lengthening of the period of higher education for school teachers, should both tend to increase the number of those who achieve good qualifications at school. It is probable that courses leading to the General Certificate of Education will continue to become more widely accessible. The evidence suggests that the degree to which children experience an academic environment has a major influence on whether they make the best of their talents. . . . In 1960, for example, the proportion of children going into the sixth form varied between areas of differing grammar school provision. Where the provision was liberal, some 12 per cent of children stayed on, compared with only 7 per cent in areas of relatively low provision.

During the later 1950s, when this group of children reached the statutory school-leaving age, there were comparatively few schools, other than grammar schools, that offered academic courses leading to the General Certificate of Education. Since then the number has been continually increasing and the habit of staying on may also be expected to grow.

Finally it should be observed that fears that expansion would lead to a lowering of the average ability of students in higher education have proved unfounded. Recent increases in numbers have not been accompanied by an increase in wastage and the measured ability of students appears to be as high as it ever was.

In short we think there is no risk that within the next twenty years the growth in the proportion of young people with qualifications and aptitudes suitable for entry to higher education will be restrained by a shortage of potential ability. The numbers who are capable of benefiting from higher education are a function not only of heredity but also of a host of other influences varying with standards of educational provision, family incomes and attitudes and the education received by previous generations. If there is to be talk of a pool of ability, it must be of a pool which surpasses the widow's cruse in the Old Testament, in that when more is taken for higher education in one generation more will tend to be available in the next.

(II) APPENDIX ONE

Achievement of grammar school children of given measured ability

Many studies of the distribution of measured ability have brought out the correlation between ability and social class, and it might be held that superior innate intelligence was the only reason why a greater proportion of middle-class children than of manual working-class children reach higher education.[1] But this is not the case. For, when grammar school children are grouped according to their measured intelligence at the age of eleven, as well as their final educational attainment, one finds that among children of a given intelligence a much higher proportion of those from middle-class homes reach higher education than of those from working-class homes. ... For example, the proportion of children with measured intelligence of between 115 and 129 who entered full-time higher education was 34 per cent for middle-class children and only 15 per cent for those from manual working-class homes. The difference is less striking in

[1] For convenience, the terms middle-class and working-class will be used in the following discussion to describe those whose fathers are engaged in non-manual and manual occupations respectively.

TABLE 4. *Highest course of education: by father's occupation. Children born in 1940–1 in Great Britain.*

| | Higher education | | | | Other post-school course or O level | No post-school course nor O level SLC | All children | Weighted sample numbers (=100%) | Unweighted sample numbers |
| | Full-time | | Part-time | A level or SLC | | | | | |
Father's occupation	Degree-level	Other							
Boys Non-manual	14·8	4·1	11·4	7·8	41·3	20·7	100·0	1 674	505
Manual	2·5	1·7	5·5	2·4	45·9	42·1	100·0	4 549	856
Girls Non-manual	9·4	10·6	0·1	8·0	50·6	21·3	100·0	1 818	536
Manual	0·7	1·8	0·7	1·1	30·0	65·7	100·0	5 034	799
Boys and girls Non-manual	12·0	7·5	5·5	7·9	46·1	21·0	100·0	3 492	1 041
Manual	1·5	1·7	3·0	1·7	37·5	54·5	100·0	9 583	1 655

Source: survey of twenty-one year olds

TABLE 5. *Highest course of education: by father's occupation. Children born in 1940–1 in Great Britain.*

Father's occupation	Higher education			A level or SLC	Other post-school course or O level	No post-school course nor O level SLC	All children	Weighted sample numbers (=100%)	Unweighted sample numbers
	Full-time		Part-time						
	Degree-level	Other							
Higher professional	33	12	7	16	25	7	100	376	128
Managerial and other professional	11	8	6	7	48	20	100	2 170	651
Clerical	6	4	3	7	51	29	100	946	262
Skilled manual	2	2	3	2	42	49	100	6 165	1 176
Semi- and unskilled	1	1	2	1	30	65	100	3 418	479
All children	4	3	4	3	40	47	100	15 000	3 008

Source: survey of twenty-one year olds

the case of the most intelligent children, but even here twice as many of the middle-class as of the manual working-class children reach a course of degree level.

Table 6 traces the progress of grammar school children in England and Wales, showing first the proportions achieving at least five O levels, then those reaching two or more A levels, and finally the proportions entering upon courses of degree level. At each stage, the table shows the proportions for children of the same intelligence but from different social backgrounds. In the case of children whose measured ability at eleven was in the category 115–29, the proportions getting at least five O levels are 56 per cent for middle-class and 45 per cent for working-class children; at A level the proportions are 23 per cent and 14 per cent, and on entry to degree level courses

TABLE 6. *Academic achievement of children at maintained grammar schools: by IQ at eleven-plus and father's occupation. Children born in 1940–1 in England and Wales*

IQ	Father's occupation	Degree level course (1)	At least 2 A levels (1)	At least 5 O levels (3)	Weighted sample numbers (=100%)	Un-weighted sample numbers
130 and over	A Non-manual	37	43	73	67	50
	B Manual	18	30	75	60	63
	A divided by B	2·06	1·43	0·97		
115–29	A Non-manual	17	23	56	201	151
	B Manual	8	14	45	403	237
	A divided by B	2·12	1·64	1·24		
100–14	A Non-manual	6	9	37	138	80
	B Manual	2	6	22	236	124
	A divided by B	3·00	1·50	1·68		

Source: survey of twenty-one year olds

17 per cent and 8 per cent. Thus the difference between children of the same potential but different backgrounds widens progressively. This is illustrated by the ratios between the proportions (A divided by B) shown in the table. In the case of children whose intelligence at eleven measured between 115 and 129, a quarter more middle-class than working-class children achieved at least five O levels; two-thirds more reached two A levels and over twice as many eventually

entered full-time courses of degree level. Among the most able children, the differences between social classes were less marked at the stage of O and A levels, but, as has been mentioned, the proportion entering degree level courses is twice as high for middle-class as for working-class children.

This picture of the effects of social class on O and A level attainment is confirmed by a recent Ministry of Education survey of school leavers, which was extended, at the Committee's request, to give information on parental occupation and, for grammar school children, on their position in the intake at eleven-plus. In the eleven-plus

TABLE 7. *GCE achievement of leavers from maintained grammar schools: by grading at eleven-plus and father's occupation. Leavers in 1960–1 in England and Wales*

Eleven-plus grading	Father's occupation	Percentage having at least 2 A levels	Percentage having at least 5 O levels	No. (=100%)
Upper third	A Non-manual	53	87	8 390
	B Manual	35	72	11 240
	A divided by B	*1·53*	*1·21*	
Middle third	A Non-manual	27	65	7 790
	B Manual	16	52	13 430
	A divided by B	*1·68*	*1·25*	
Lower third	A Non-manual	15	50	6 200
	B Manual	8	29	12 960
	A divided by B	*1·83*	*1·70*	
Transfer from secondary modern	A Non-manual	15	54	1 560
	B Manual	17	50	3 270
	A divided by B	*0·92*	*1·07*	
Unknown	A Non-manual	35	68	12 160
	B Manual	19	49	15 040
	A divided by B	*1·83*	*1·40*	
All children	A Non-manual	33	68	36 070
	B Manual	19	49	55 940
	A divided by B	*1·77*	*1·40*	

Source: Statistics of Education, 1961. Supplement, Table 13

assessment, a number of other factors as well as measured ability are taken into account, but, for the purposes of this discussion, the total assessment can be taken as a broad gauge of potential ability at that age. The results of the survey are summarized in Tables 7 and 8. Table 7 shows that working-class children are progressively less successful than children of the same eleven-plus grading in other social groups. For example, among children in the lower third of the

TABLE 8. *A level performance and age of leaving in maintained grammar schools: by grading at eleven-plus and father's occupation. England and Wales 1960–1*

Eleven-plus grading	Father's occupation	Percentage of leavers of all ages who have at least 2 A levels	Percentage of leavers of all ages who leave aged 18 or more	Percentage of leavers aged 18 or more who have at least 2 A levels	No. (=100%)
Upper third	Professional and managerial	57	55	79	5 530
	Clerical	44	39	74	2 760
	Skilled manual	38	40	77	9 150
	Semi- and unskilled	21	23	81	2 090
Middle third	Professional and managerial	33	42	63	4 830
	Clerical	18	29	56	2 960
	Skilled manual	18	27	59	9 550
	Semi- and unskilled	10	15	58	3 880
Lower third	Professional and managerial	14	32	43	3 450
	Clerical	16	22	58	2 750
	Skilled manual	10	18	51	8 940
	Semi- and unskilled	4	7	53	4 020
Transfer from secondary modern		15	29	40	6 380
All groups	Professional and managerial	37	46	67	23 290
	Clerical	26	32	64	12 780
	Skilled manual	22	29	65	40 820
	Semi- and unskilled	11	17	56	15 120
All children		24	31	65	107 220

Source: Statistics of Education, 1961. Supplement, Table 13

eleven-plus intake, 50 per cent of those from middle-class homes obtained five or more O levels, compared with 29 per cent of those from working-class homes. Thus, as the ratio (A divided by B) shows, the proportion for middle-class children was, already at O level, 70 per cent higher than for working-class children. By the stage of A level the difference had widened further, and the proportion for middle-class children was 83 per cent higher than for children from the working class.

These differences at A level arise largely because working-class children tend to leave school earlier. The proportion of working-class children who stay on to the age when A level is normally attempted is smaller than the proportion of middle-class children who actually achieve two passes. But those working-class children who do stay on are on average as successful as their counterparts in other social groups. The position is illustrated in Table 8, in which children are analysed into four social groups. Column 1 of the table shows the proportions achieving A level and column 2 the proportions staying on to eighteen. The proportion of children from skilled working-class families who stay on to eighteen is lower than the proportion of children from professional and managerial families who achieve two or more A levels. Similarly the proportion staying on from semi- and unskilled families is lower than the proportion achieving two or more A levels whose fathers are in clerical occupations. Column 3 shows the A level performance of children staying on to eighteen. Within each ability group at eleven-plus, there is no significant difference in performance between children from the different classes who stay on.

The evidence presented so far may be summarized as follows. The proportion of middle-class children who reach degree level courses is eight times as high as the proportion from working-class homes, and even in grammar schools it is twice as high. As has been shown, the difference in grammar schools is not chiefly due to lower intelligence, but rather to early leaving. However, it is not only in these schools that the wastage of ability is higher among manual working-class children. There is much evidence to show that, both before the age of eleven and in later years, the influence of environment is such that the differences in measured ability between social classes progressively widen as children grow up. . . .

A. H. HALSEY (1963)

Expansion and equality (a review of Robin Pedley's *The Comprehensive School* (Penguin Books, 1963))*

From the beginning of a national system of education for industrial England the slogan of educational reform has been: Equality. On the whole it has failed. Critics, both foreign and domestic, and not least Mr Robin Pedley, tend to see English society as a rigid hierarchy based on a segregated system of education. In the sixties however, a new slogan is emerging: Expand. Sir Geoffrey Crowther raised the banner, progressives of all parties doubled on to the parade ground, and Lord Robbins is expected to lead a dignified march into 'higher education for all'. It is possible that the expansionists will succeed in democratizing English education in general and establishing comprehensive secondary schooling in particular where the egalitarians have failed.

CONFUSION AND SCALE

This is all very confusing. I used to think that the comprehensive school was a major instrument of egalitarian reform in education. Certainly Mr Pedley, the best-known advocate of comprehensive organization, is first and last an egalitarian, though of the English liberal sort (which means that Eton must go but Summerhill and Dartington are all right), and in his latest book he goes well beyond his title, *The Comprehensive School*, to mark the outlines of a complete egalitarian programme of educational reform. But Liberals also now commonly espouse the comprehensive principle and there is a Tory MP who looks forward, admittedly twenty years, to comprehensive universities. Perhaps they are 'all Socialists now'; but then the country with the most thorough-going organization of

* Reprinted from the *Guardian* (25 April 1963).

secondary schools along comprehensive lines is the United States. Clearly the comprehensive idea is not simply socialism in the school room.

The confusion derives partly from the circumstance that your comprehensives are not necessarily my comprehensives. For some the mere sharing of a campus by a modern and a technical school makes a comprehensive school; for others the continuance of a separate grammar school in the same area denies the comprehensive principle; for me no comprehensive school could have streaming by general ability; for Mr Pedley the comprehensive schools' catchment area would coincide with a clearly defined neighbourhood unit. These differences of definition turn on variations in the social, psychological and educational theory of equality. But the essential point is that they are all dwarfed by the immensely larger principle of scale. The extent of comprehensive schooling is a function not of egalitarian sentiment but of the scale of the educational system.

EXPANSIONIST APPROACH

Thus the comprehensive principle tends to become sovereign in any given stage of education only when expansion has taken place in the next. England has comprehensive primary schooling because her secondary education has become universal. Sweden is establishing comprehensive education up to sixteen years because the gymnasia (sixteen-plus) are gradually opening to the majority. America has comprehensive secondary schooling and even the beginnings of comprehensive undergraduate colleges because of a colossal expansion of higher education (47 per cent in full time enrolment by 1970).

We are accustomed to interpret the 1944 Act as the measure which established secondary education for all: it is more instructive to see it as having founded comprehensive primary schooling. It is roughly true to say that the more advanced the industrialism by which a country lives, the more expanded its system of education and the later the stage at which selection for different (i.e. differently rewarded and esteemed) lives and livelihood takes place: the more economically backward the nation the earlier the selection.

The expansionist rather than the egalitarian approach used by Mr Pedley seems to make sense of the failure of the movement for comprehensive secondary schooling in England. Out of nearly 6,000 secondary schools in England and Wales, less than 250 could be labelled comprehensive on any definition. The only wholeheartedly comprehensive region is rural Wales. Outside London and some of the new towns, urban England has scarcely been touched. Even where reorganization has begun the established grammar schools have normally been retained with the result that the comprehensive schools are 'crammed' and their sixth-form development hampered.

Meanwhile, the accumulated experience, small as it is, recommends the comprehensive school as providing a humane and efficient educational environment. The old bogy of excessive size can be put to rest now that the continuing revolution in educational aspirations has penetrated deeply among working-class families. An adequate sixth form can now be supported by a school of less than 1,500 in all but the educationally most primitive districts. Moreover, the 'practical' arguments about the need to use existing schools have been overcome by Mr Pedley's bold Leicestershire plan and other schemes which adapt the comprehensive principle to an 'end-on' arrangement whereby secondary modern schools become junior high schools and grammar schools either senior high schools or sixth-form colleges. If a local authority is determined to do away with selection at eleven-plus and to allow parents and children to select their own opportunities, it can do so through one form of comprehensive organization or another.

TELLING ARGUMENT

But the most telling argument is that the comprehensives give us a more efficient engine than does unreformed tripartitism for the production of qualified young people. On the standard of five or more GCE ordinary level passes the proportion of successful pupils in maintained secondary schools rose from $8\frac{1}{2}$ per cent in 1953 to 10 per cent in 1962. The comprehensive schools do much better than this with a proportion of 14 per cent. Mr Pedley rightly concludes 'that if one keeps open the door of full opportunity, many more children will pass through it'.

Yet even if expansion fosters comprehensive secondary schooling in the sixties and seventies, this will not dispose of the problem of equality. It is not only that the comprehensive school can be fitted perfectly easily into meritocratic education, but no serious breach in the linkage of class to education in England is conceivable while the independent schools remain as they are. Mr Pedley demands two immediate reforms. All independent schools should be required to conform to the corresponding LEA pupil-teacher ratio; and all schools should be required to pay the Burnham scale. The idea is not to abolish independent schools but to prevent them selling material advantages rather than educational variety. No doubt these reforms would bring the middle classes into the State system and with them would come a force for reform greater than either egalitarian sentiment or economic expansionism.

G. H. BANTOCK (1963)

Education in an industrial society*

The self-realization through self-transcendence I proclaim as my aim can only be achieved within a culturally rich social order which encourages the refinements of the self the history of civilization shows man to be capable of. To bring about those social circumstances which best serve such an order helps to ensure conditions most favourable to the quality of our lives. With this in mind, I will reflect on some of the possible social implications of 'equality of opportunity'.

Mrs Floud and her colleagues, no longer satisfied with the equality manifested at eleven, seek a similar one at sixteen; and her analysis of the forces opposing the achievement of her desire – for she seeks explanation in largely environmental terms, being convinced that 'measured intelligence is widely known to be largely an acquired characteristic' – suggests, firstly, that she accepts as the criterion of

* Reprinted from *Education in an Industrial Society* (London, Faber and Faber, 1963).

the ability to go forward the stripped and denuded conception of human personality which is implicit in the notion of such an intelligence, and, secondly, that the inhibiting factors militating against further selection warrant social investigation.

The precise nature of the hindrances placed by their home 'in the way of educating working-class children in grammar schools urgently needs investigating both for its own sake as an immediate problem of educational organization, and for the light it would throw on the problems and possibilities of the comprehensive school'.[1] The truth is, that too many of these children are leaving at fifteen before they have completed their course. The key words are 'urgent' and 'immediate'; the impression of breathlessness implies a consciousness of wastage, an anomaly that needs clearing up; the ordering and sorting machine is not yet working at full efficiency.

Yet, if we ask her and her colleagues why it should, conscious of the small, nagging irreverence of a persisting 'What for?', what end in view has the great sorting and ordering machine, the only discoverable answer which comes from their book is that of 'the loss of qualified man-power to the national economy'. Now, the language of such a statement no longer causes the raising of eyebrows; it has become a commonplace – and that in itself is perhaps an indication of the extent to which we have substituted a technical for an educated

[1] A recent attempt to diagnose the working-class educational malaise has appeared in B. Jackson and D. Marsden's *Education and the Working Class*. This book is methodologically highly suspect; even its impressionistic aim is marred by its emotionally charged repudiation of middle-class values and its largely uncritical acceptance of working-class virtues. Beneath a surface appearance of fairmindedness, it reveals its authors' conviction that the grammar school must be wrong. If the working-class children fit its ethos, this is wrong because 'There is something infinitely pathetic in these former working-class children who lost their roots young, and who now with their rigid middle-class accent preserve "the stability of all our institutions, temporal and spiritual" by avariciously reading the lives of Top People [*sic*], or covet the public schools and glancing back at the society from which they came can see no more there than "the dim" or the "specimens"'. (Note the emotionally tendentious force of 'infinitely', 'avariciously', 'rigid'; this is not untypical of the book as a whole.) If the working-class child doesn't fit into the ethos of the school, this is wrong because it indicates that the school is geared to a false set of values: 'we have come to that place where we must firmly accept the life of the majority', whatever that may mean. It is quite possible to combine an equivocal appreciation of middle-class virtues with a regret that in this book an opportunity for a serious and soberly impersonal assessment has been lost.

language in the way in which we discuss our educational difficulties. Dr McIntosh has recently sought to *channel* the 'pool of ability . . . into the national reservoir' of the highly educated; a newly published survey of Britain's scientific ability speaks of *funnelling* able children into the desired occupations; and *The Times Educational Supplement* recently advocated that we *syphon* 'wasted adult ability into the professions which need it'. I cannot think that the attitude to human beings which is implicit in these quotations is a healthy one; or is my delicacy irrelevant in the face of these demands for educated manpower presented as a dire (though usually unexamined) social need?

The point is, that there is implicit in the demand for more efficient machinery in the selection of the élite, a narrow and illiberal view of the function of the élite – the view, in fact, inherent in these dismal associations of 'educated manpower', with their overtones of a narrowly conceived social functioning and an emotional aura of a pressed and conscripted population, acceptable at best in the face of great and dire external danger of wartime. Such crudities, with their collectivist implications, render all the more palatable, by contrast, the warnings of Mr T. S. Eliot against the emergence of just such an élite as the notion of educated manpower summons up. Mr Eliot has been attacked by Lord James on the grounds of illiberality; and indeed, his views on education do, as Lord James points out, cut right across the assumptions about the desirability of education and its infinite extension which has been part of the almost unquestioned social policy of the last few decades . . . as, indeed, it cuts across most of the more general social assumptions of our time.

Mr Eliot is concerned with defining the conditions under which a high state of culture is likely to exist; he finds them in a hierarchic condition, when the body politic is divided, not on the grounds of 'brains', but on those of 'classes'. His beliefs about the extension of education which has followed the breakdown of classes, with the consequent expansion of opportunity, can be summarized as follows. He considers that the more education is extended, the less it is likely to be prized. Furthermore, for any high state of culture, continuity of experience is essential; hence the need for 'classes', in contrast to élites. For, through classes based on heredity cultural continuity is possible, whereas an élite, as a constantly changing social group chosen solely on account of 'brains', implies a lack of cohesiveness which is likely to be fatal to a high cultural state, in that it will fail to 'foster the hereditary transmission of culture within a culture'. Basically, Mr Eliot believes that a culture cannot ever be fully 'known' in any intellectual sense; that there is much of value which comes simply from having been nursed in a certain environment, when what is 'known' is only known in Keats' sense of being known along the pulse. This, obviously, is not something that a school education can provide. It is not something which can be provided through the study of 'subjects', particularly if for examination purposes; it is something which can be achieved, if at all, through the 'atmosphere' of a school, and then, presumably, only through a boarding school, when it would be hard to decide whether it emerged from school or background.

Any notion of hereditary 'classes' as distinctive elements in the state is likely to be unpalatable and unacceptable today, when the whole notion of class is in almost universal disrepute. At the same time, the growing lack of continuity between the generations, the lack of a settled social 'style' – manifested as an accepted system of manners and morals, the one refining the other – which the influx of men drawn from different social traditions prevents from developing, carries with it penalties both for the health of the body politic and for the mental ease of the invaders. The strains are already apparent in the comments of Miss Stevens' school children; and the lack of an educated 'public', with clearly defined standards and a reasonably settled mode of expectation, is part of the literary and artistic history of our generation. The 'cultural' effects, indeed, of a policy of 'equality of opportunity' in the terms in which this policy is being implemented need more consideration than they receive. For one effect, certainly, is the too rapid assimilation of the culturally impoverished who have high IQs into sections of the community which carry a good deal of social and economic prestige; the rise of the merely clever in these terms to positions of social influence is a culturally doubtful manifestation. Our present concern for science and technology affords social prestige to what, given the necessary 'brains', can be acquired with a fair amount of ease. The sort of conduct implicit in scientific education is one which, given laboratory space and teachers, can be easily imitated by the able, for its demands are always open to inspection via the acquiring of a special vocabulary which may take time to learn but is never in doubt when learnt. This is because the conventions of scientific investigation are wholly transferable in a way in which the conventions of sophisticated social and moral behaviour and intercourse are not.

The general situation can be presented in terms of a conflict between Justice and Sanity, as indeed it has been by Dr F. Musgrove in a recent article.[1] Dr Musgrove sees the current emphasis on social justice as a factor leading to social disruption and individual distress: 'Social justice, suicide and alcoholism maintain their annual increments', strikes the keynote of his indictment. In this process, the grammar school – and, of course, he could have added, the university – plays an important role: 'The grammar school is the agency for collecting local talent, equipping it not only with the requisite technical skills but also the attitudes and role dispositions needed for "success", and redeploying it on a national scale, distributing it throughout the economy and the anonymous avenues, drives and crescents of outer suburbia.' And he points out, rightly, that this is the system which is being exported to other cultures: ('... our concept of social justice has successfully eroded entire African societies').

The article is an important one even if, within the short space at his disposal, Dr Musgrove is forced to dramatize the dangers of the situation in terms of stress disorder, ulcers, thrombosis and the like. Many of the effects on individuals are likely to be subtler – matters of social insecurity, shynesses and aggressivenesses – the minor neuroses. Any form of social organization necessarily exacts a price, of course; a fact which is likely to be apparent to any but the most hardened of environmentalists who dream of social harmony achievable through social engineering. No such possibility as this is likely; and one's evidence for one's belief is human history. What is needed is a calm assessment of the complexities of the situation. There is nothing self-evidently right about our conception of social justice and the way we interpret it today. And, indeed, such a concept of justice could be criticized on the grounds that it generates nearly as much negative jealousy as it brings positive advantage, or that, in any case, justice is a cold virtue.

[1] Cf. *The Times Educational Supplement*, 18 November 1960.

Again, it must be realized that the particular concern which we manifest over the question of selection and opportunity reflects back on the terms in which we conceive the syllabus which we teach in our grammar schools. It makes of it an instrument, not an end in itself; it strengthens the concern for results in assessable terms, through examinations. It reduces knowledge to the level of 'technical knowledge'.[1] The extent to which Miss Stevens indicates that the grammar school rests content with its chains – the examination syllabus – should have been deducible from the nature of the social policy which examinations are expressly designed to support. Furthermore, along with conventional examinations there has arisen a whole industry of mental and attainment testing, much of it resting on dubious philosophical grounds. Such paraphernalia is an essential concomitant of the need to select people; though it must not be forgotten that such selection is an essential concomitant of a proliferating social and economic system which makes the sort of demands that ours does.

This is not, of course, a plea for a denial of chances to the able; what has been said earlier should make that clear. But in the midst of the great sorting process it is as well to bear certain things in mind. In the aggressive drive for talent – and aggressive is the word to apply to certain expositions of the need – it should be remembered that there are other sources of high satisfaction in life for some who, if in terms of ability they appear fitted for a university education, have not the temperament to respond to the demands made on them or to the opportunities afforded. There is the danger too – recognizable to any university teacher as manifest in certain students – that some will carry with them deep cultural resentments, anxious to exploit what the university can give in terms of status and job prestige, but reacting against the ethos of an institution towards which their life experience has made them hostile because of the inadequacies it reveals in themselves.

For, in the last resort this aggressive drive for talent is itself a manifestation of the assertive will which is the concomitant of the scientific and technological state. Under the guise of a concern for individuals, the bullying will asserts itself in a thousand scholastic

[1] I refer to what Professor Oakeshott, in his famous essay on 'Rationalism in politics', terms 'technical knowledge'.

institutions at the behest of a pressure for 'educated manpower'. 'I am not', complained Lawrence once, when his peace of mind had been disturbed by someone who had snatched him away from the scene of peace and sensuous beauty he was contemplating into the 'desert void of politics, principles, right and wrong and so forth' – 'I am not allowed to sit like a dandelion on my own stem.' No one 'cared' more than Lawrence but he knew, intuitively, the dangers of 'caring': 'They care! They simply are eaten up with caring. They are so busy caring about Fascism or Leagues of Nations or whether France is right or whether marriage is threatened, that they never know where they are. They certainly never live on the spot where they are.' There is a wisdom, in a true education, which would see the relevance of this, too, in our present educational dilemmas.

What, then, am I arguing for? Certainly, it must be re-emphasized, no drastic curtailment of opportunity.[1] But, any principle, however good in itself, contains, when pushed to extremes, dangers of offence in the infinitely complex human situation in which we find ourselves; as Conrad observes in *Nostromo*, 'a man haunted by a fixed idea is insane.' The possibility at least exists that the pursuit of the policy of equality of opportunity can become as rigid, as destructive of human well-being and achievement as over-attention to the opposite policy of rigid stratification. For it expresses an impracticable ideal in that, born into an historical situation as we all inevitably are, the conditions under which we develop can never be called equal. 'Social justice', indeed, in the dogmatic way in which its application is sought in the modern world can be destructive of other felicities and harmonies which may be discordant with its peculiar monotonal demands. It is as well to remember that other principles of social organization have produced their high cultures, their enrichments of our human condition. My point, then, is not to deny what of enrichment the principle itself can bring – and it *can* so fructify. Rather, it is to bring to mind, as part of the essential limitation of our kind, that no discoverable principle of human organization can pre-empt, to the exclusion of all others,

---

[1] What I am saying here, indeed, must be read in conjunction with what I have previously said about the need for able children to accept the aloneness which is often their lot in the achievement of their potentialities. It comes down, once more, to individual decisions in individual cases.

in the business of earthly satisfactions and achievements; and that, while not accepting Mr Eliot's diagnosis in its entirety, it is as well to ask whether some explanation of that sort of cultural impoverishment from which we suffer, and which inevitably reacts on the range of choices available for self-realization, is not aggravated in the situation he analyses.

We should bear this in mind when we come to expand our system of higher education – *which we must*. We hear a good deal of what universities can do for their students; we think a good deal less about what a large influx of purely status-minded students will do to the university, or of those who, in the recent words of Mr R. M. Ogilvie, are 'able but lacking in any interest or drive, both in scholastic work and in the conduct of life'. Such students need a sort of teaching and pastoral care which the universities, with their concern for fundamental research, with exploiting, that is, the *nature* of their disciplines, are not altogether well equipped to offer. But, more to the point, is the degradation of effort implied in the necessity of wooing the hostile or indifferent; not because such an effort is not worthwhile, but because it belongs to a milieu other than that of the highest academic body in the kingdom.

Ideally, the solution is to develop other forms of higher education which could be more specifically directed to the educative and pastoral problems posed by the new influx of status seekers; or that would recognize that the sort of purely cognitive education provided in universities is not the only or necessarily the best type of education even for those of good intelligence. In general, the training college performs an admirable educative as well as professional function because it conceives its work in primarily tutorial terms, undisturbed by the demands of research; and in the emotionally under-educated environment implied by the nature of our popular culture – a culture which in certain of its manifestations often attracts the better intellects as well as the poorer ones – the need for 'affective' training through participation in the arts was never more patent. And, of course, such training is never something simply of the emotions – it needs the intelligence as well.

An objection to such proposals comes from those like Professor Richard Hoggart who fear a hierarchical structure and the creation of a second best with the opportunities for snobbery it fosters. The answer surely lies in the need to accept the realities of things – a teaching institution at least can only become what its pupils will allow it to become; and to call an institution a university which, from the character of its intake, has no chance of providing what is essential to the nature of such an institution is merely a distressing form of *bovarysme*. We can't perpetually live in an *Alice in Wonderland* world where all the creatures are to have a prize. And, paradoxically, our society will be the richer for the honesty and clear-sightedness involved. It is by being itself that our university can best serve the community.

J. W. B. DOUGLAS (1964)

The home and the school*

(1) THE HOMES

There is a danger that by concentrating attention on the methods used to select children for secondary education, we may fail to appreciate the importance of other ways in which talent is lost or diverted. A study of the measured ability of children in relation to their admission to grammar or secondary modern schools does not necessarily give the full picture of educational waste. If the standards of grammar school selection are set too high, there will be waste that is no less undesirable because it is spread over the social classes. If a child's ability at eleven gives only a poor prediction of his ability at later ages, there will also be waste. At an even earlier age, waste of talent may occur through the effects of an adverse home environment or through lack of stimulation in early life or at school.

When considering the relation between environment and educational opportunity, I recognize that innate endowment may well be

* Reprinted from *The Home and the School: a study of ability and attainment in the primary school* (London, MacGibbon and Kee, 1964).

the most powerful influence in determining the level of achievement at school. But even if outside factors such as the parents' interest and encouragement, home circumstances, or the quality of teaching, have only a small effect on performance, their combined action may lead to a considerable waste of talent owing to the exclusion from grammar schools of children who, given other homes or other schools, would have succeeded in getting there. There is evidence that extreme poverty of the environment (such as surrounded mill children in North Carolina, or canal boat children in England), leads to a progressive deterioration in academic ability. At the other extreme, some families have a tradition of making the best use of their brains and their lives and this may depend more on methods of upbringing than on inherited traits. In such families the children are stimulated in numerous ways and are kept busy playing games that demand thought, and so from their earliest years acquire a totally different attitude to learning. I am not, of course, talking here only of 'innate' intelligence, but of the ability to succeed in school studies, which requires qualities of will and continuity of effort. Failure to acquire these will lead to a waste of ability that no redistribution of grammar school places or refinements of eleven-plus selection can avoid.

During the eleven years of this survey home circumstances improved greatly. Thirty per cent of middle-class families moved to houses with better amenities than those they started with and only 7 per cent moved to worse. This was largely owing to the purchase of new homes which in general offered more space and better amenities than the houses and flats rented from private landlords when the survey started. Whereas 39 per cent of middle-class families owned their homes in 1946, 58 per cent did so in 1957. During this period overcrowding decreased from 7 per cent to 3 per cent.

There has been an even greater improvement in the housing of manual working-class families, though a large number of them are still living in circumstances that are far from satisfactory. House purchase played only a small part in this improvement, which was largely brought about by the provision of council houses and flats. Nearly twice as many manual working-class families are living on council estates today as at the beginning of the survey and their homes, though sometimes small in size, provide the modern amenities that were often lacking in the privately rented accommodation they left. Forty-six per cent of these families are now living in council houses and 62 per cent have their own kitchen and bathroom as well as running hot water. There is a substantial improvement in the amenities enjoyed by 44 per cent of them and the amount of overcrowding has been halved. This encouraging picture of working-class housing is offset by the fact that 22 per cent still share a bathroom or kitchen and have no running hot water, and 13 per cent have at least two persons to every habitable room in the house.

Not all the families improved their housing conditions; 7 per cent are living in homes that are less well equipped than those they had eleven years ago. The reason is sometimes prolonged unemployment, mainly through illness, and sometimes the break-up of families owing to death, divorce or separation. In these circumstances, families move into cheaper dwellings or to relatives, and such moves usually result in an acute deterioration of amenities and an increase in the number of persons per room.

Moves to council houses provided the most important source of improved living conditions for the manual working classes. How have these moves affected their children's progress at school and their chances in the eleven-plus selection examinations? It has been noted in Middlesbrough that when families moved from the slums to council estates their children's chances of going to grammar schools were increased. These children may have done better at school because their health improved or because they tried harder when they came into an area where education was valued. Alternatively, there may have been more grammar school places available in these new areas and less competition for them.

The allocation of families to council houses is, of course, not done at random and those given the opportunity to rent them tend to be among the educationally least promising families of any in this sample. They come predominantly from the lower manual working classes; they tend to have many children and, according to the health visitors, look after them badly in the sense that many do not accept immunization when it is offered them, and fail to make use of the ante- and post-natal services which are provided. Their children also have a lower measured ability than manual working-class children in general: they show a deterioration in test scores between eight and eleven years, but this is less than the deterioration recorded

THE HOME AND THE SCHOOL

for those who continued to rent their homes from private landlords throughout the whole survey period.

When manual working-class children who live on council estates are compared with all children from this class, we find that they get 10 per cent more places in grammar schools than would be expected from their measured ability, whereas those who live in homes rented from private landlords get 11 per cent fewer. Similar differences are found in all parts of the country. As the following table shows, the advantage enjoyed by the council estate children is particularly marked for the brighter ones.

Level of test score at eleven	Living throughout on council estates % at grammar school	Moving to council estates % at grammar school	Living throughout in private dwellings % at grammar school
61 and over	98·3	88·5	75·0
58–60	51·4	43·9	38·7
55–7	28·9	19·8	15·0
49–54	4·0	5·3	4·7

There is no suggestion from the teachers that the children who lived throughout on council estates, or recently moved to them, work any harder than those living in houses rented from private landlords. Nor is there any reason to believe that parents who live on council estates are more ambitious for their children to succeed at school; those who live in privately rented houses express similar views on school leaving and show no substantial difference in their level of interest in their children's studies. It seems, then, that the greater educational opportunities of the children who live on council estates arise from a more liberal provision of grammar school places, rather than from a direct influence of improved housing on educational progress.

The next question to consider is whether children who are brought up in houses with plenty of living space and good amenities show any benefit in their progress at school or in the results of the secondary selection examinations. The homes are classified by whether or not they are overcrowded, by whether the survey children share their beds or sleep alone, and by whether there is running hot water and a kitchen and bathroom that is not shared with another family. These are, of course, closely related conditions. Children who share their beds usually, but not always, live in overcrowded homes. The best amenities are found in the most modern houses which are usually, but not always, the least crowded. Preliminary tables showed that the sharing of beds, overcrowding and lack of household amenities each influence the performance of children to a similar extent and in the same direction, and so these measures have been combined to describe two types of home; first, those in which not more than one adverse rating on crowding, bed-sharing or lack of amenities was recorded and, second, those in which two or more adverse ratings were recorded.

This simple division of children into those who live in 'satisfactory' and 'unsatisfactory' homes yields groups which in each social class are of different measured ability.

From the studies of mill and canal boat children referred to at the beginning of this chapter, it seemed probable that an impoverished home environment would have a cumulative effect, so that the children exposed to it would become progressively more handicapped in their test performance as they grew older. For the manual working-class children this is indeed so; those whose homes are unsatisfactory make lower scores in the eleven-year tests than in the eight-year tests, losing an average of 0·66 points of score during these three years, whereas those from satisfactory homes improve their score during the same period by an average of 0·04 points.

In the middle classes the position is reversed, that is to say the children from unsatisfactory homes, far from deteriorating in performance between eight and eleven years, make up part of their earlier handicap. In these social classes it seems that overcrowding, the sharing of beds and poor home circumstances have exerted their full effect by eight years, if not earlier, and that their influence is offset by other favourable factors in the homes or in the schools.

The assessment of the environment in which these children grew up is made from a mass of information gathered over eleven years by health visitors, school nurses and teachers. We know, among other things, about the houses in which the children lived, the social background and education of their parents, the views of their mothers on their education, the size of the families they belonged to and the academic record and characteristics of the schools they attended. All these environmental aspects are, of course, overlapping in their effects; parents who are unskilled workers, for example, will often be of low educational attainment, take little interest in their children's school-work, have large families, live in grossly overcrowded homes lacking amenities (unless they are fortunate enough to have a council house) and may well send their children to primary schools which are ill-equipped, with large classes and less than first-rate teaching. It is important, then, that no firm conclusions on the influence of any one aspect of the environment should be reached until all have been considered together. . . .

When children of similar measured ability compete for grammar school places, those from satisfactory homes have an advantage over the rest which, though small, is consistent in each social class, whether the area be one of good or poor provision of grammar school places. (This finding, however, though in the expected direction, does not reach a level of statistical significance in any social class.)

There are many possible explanations for the deterioration observed between eight and eleven years in the test performance of children whose home circumstances are bad. In overcrowded homes they will be deprived of quiet and privacy. When they share their beds they may sleep badly and, through tiredness, be unable to concentrate on their school work. But such explanations do not account for the observed difference between the educational progress of middle- and manual working-class children. If overcrowding, bad sleeping habits, and lack of amenities are associated with deterioration in the test performance of manual working-class children, why are they not equally associated with a deterioration in the progress of middle-class children?

Middle-class parents are likely to provide some privacy for their children even if their homes are unsatisfactory, whereas similarly placed working-class parents fail to do this. But there may be more to it than this. Perhaps it is the type of area rather than the standard of housing that is important. Middle-class children, even if their home circumstances are bad, are likely to mix with other middle-class children who come from families where education is valued. In contrast manual working-class children in similarly substandard homes will often live in poor neighbourhoods where there is little interest in learning, so that both they and their parents may be discouraged by the apathy and disinterest around them.

(II) THE PARENTS

Even in early infancy contacts between children and parents may influence later educational achievement by establishing a wish to learn. 'The child whose memories are associated with resentment cannot be expected to compete successfully with those whose memories are associated with a feeling of what we call personal satisfaction or a sense of achievement.'[1] There is much evidence to show that the care of intelligent and understanding parents in the early years gives background and meaning to what is learned.

In this study we have no direct knowledge of the early influence of parents on their children's attitudes to learning, and can infer this only from what is known of their social origins and education, and of the level of skill they attain in their jobs. When, in an earlier book,[2] the growth and health of these children was described, a social classification was used that was based on their fathers' jobs alone. They were divided into nine 'occupational groups', ranging from the children of professional workers to the children of unskilled labourers. There were wide differences in the amount of illness, and rate of growth, among these nine groups of children, also in the use that their parents made of the medical services. The main distinction lies between the children of the non-manual workers and those of the manual workers. The former have, on the average, relatively little infectious illness in early childhood, they enjoy excellent standards of care at home and their mothers take them regularly to the child welfare centres and in general make good use of the available medical services. They have in other words what may be regarded as a middle-class pattern of upbringing. In contrast, the manual working-class children are more often ill, particularly with respiratory tract infections, and their mothers are seen by the health visitors as giving low standards of care to their children and homes, as

[1] W. R. Russell, *Physiology of Learning* (1957).
[2] J. W. B. Douglas and J. M. Blomfield, *Children under Five* (1958), p. 29.

making relatively little use of the child welfare centres and as often failing to have their children immunized against diphtheria.

It was originally intended to use the same nine occupational groups in this educational study. It soon became clear, however, that these groups were fluctuating and ill-defined. Some of this instability arose from the difficulty of establishing with accuracy the degree of skill used in particular jobs; job descriptions were often imprecise in spite of checking, and sometimes grossly misleading, so that in the light of further information 12 per cent of the original job codings had to be altered. But apart from this, job changes were frequent, and over the eleven years of this survey 43 per cent of families moved out of their original occupational groups, and some passed through several different groups.

This large volume of occupational movement stems in part from the relatively large number of groups into which the families were divided; there were nine groups instead of the five which the Registrar General uses routinely in his analyses of mortality. The greatest amount of change, however, is among the manual workers, who frequently move from semi-skilled to skilled occupations or vice versa; and so even the Registrar General's classification, which is largely based on the criterion of skill, would turn out to be fluctuating and impermanent when applied to a longitudinal study of this kind.

The survey started soon after the war and it might be thought that the greater part of the changes in employment that were recorded would be in the immediately succeeding years and represent an adjustment to peace-time conditions, but this was not so. The amount of change between the nine groups used at the beginning of this study was relatively steady from year to year, at a level of approximately 6 per cent. Some groups, for example professional or salaried workers, become more stable as time passes, recruiting from the younger men and losing mainly through retirement. Others, for example the black-coated wage earners or agricultural workers, show an even greater rate of change at the end of the survey than at the beginning. The main direction of change is upward, but there is a semi-permeable barrier between the non-manual and the manual groups across which, during the whole eleven years, only 5 per cent moved up and 3 per cent down.

Before going further with this discussion of how to classify these

I

families we shall look at the unemployed; these are few in number but important because of the state of poverty in which they live and the signs of deprivation in their children. Unemployment among the fathers was 0·9 per cent in 1950, increasing to 2·9 per cent in 1957. Virtually all prolonged unemployment was a result of mental or physical illness or handicap, and the families were often profoundly affected. They lived in the most unsuitable and overcrowded homes, showed many other signs of poverty and were usually supported by the wages earned by the wives, who worked for long hours away from their homes and children.

Since these fathers were unemployed because they were ill rather than because they were mentally dull there is no reason why their children should do worse in the tests and in the secondary selection examinations than other children coming from similarly deprived homes. There is here no special element of inherited sub-normality to take into account. But in fact they do considerably worse; they make an average score at eight years of 44·38 and, at eleven, of 44·47. These compare with average scores of 46·88 and 46·00 for the children of unskilled labourers at these ages. Seven per cent of the unskilled labourers' children go to grammar schools as compared with only 3 per cent of the children of the unemployed, and the teachers report that the latter are lazy and inattentive in school and that their parents take little interest in their progress. It may be that the key to their backwardness lies in worries and anxieties at home.

Families that move up or down the social scale have the charac-teristics and aspirations of the group they are joining rather than of the one they have left; this holds also for the ability of their chil-dren as measured by our tests and the results of the eleven-plus examinations. Children in families that are moving up have higher measured ability than those they leave behind though rather less than those they join. They also improve their test scores between the ages of eight and eleven years and if this improvement is maintained will soon eliminate their present slight handicap in the group they have joined. The reverse is true for the children in families that have moved down.

It seems, then, that the occupational changes of the eleven years of this survey have reshuffled the families by the social origins and education of the parents and, at second remove, by the intelligence of their children. It is likely that this process will continue in future years, and for this reason alone the father's occupation is an unsatisfactory criterion of social status for our present purpose. . . .

We cannot afford to ignore the background of the mothers when looking at the educational progress of their children; they make an equal contribution with the fathers to inherited ability and possibly a greater one to attitudes to learning. In ambitious working-class households it is not unusual to find that the mother comes from a middle-class family and supplies the drive and incentive for her children to do well at school.

The education of both the parents is known and also the types of family in which they were each brought up. We will now see how far the social background and education of each parent relates to the views expressed by the mothers on their children's education. As our contacts were solely with the mothers it might be expected that the views they expressed would be more closely associated with their own education and origins than with their husbands'. This, however, was not so; the views expressed, for example, by mothers brought up in working-class families and educated at elementary schools, who were married to men with middle-class origins and secondary education, were exactly the same as those expressed by mothers with middle-class origins and secondary education who were married to men brought up in working-class families and educated at elementary schools. Each group wanted their children on the average to leave school at sixteen years and eight months and each showed the same level of interest in their children's school progress. Moreover the level of their aspirations fell exactly between those of the two most contrasting groups; namely parents with entirely middle-class origins and secondary education on the one hand and those with entirely working-class origins and elementary education on the other.

The influence of the mothers' education and social backgrounds is also evident when we look at the average test scores of their children and performance in the secondary selection examinations; this influence is as strong as that of the fathers' education and social backgrounds, but no stronger. We know that for many young children it is the early contacts with their mothers that are likely to have the greatest influence on learning, and at later ages, too, it is often the mother who is more concerned than the father with school problems, and has the closest contact with the teachers. Because of this it seemed that among the survey children the mothers' influence on performance in school and in the tests might transcend the fathers'. That it exerts no more than an equal influence may perhaps be explained by the tendency for people to marry those with similar standards and ambitions. At any rate these observations show that it would be unwise to ignore the social origins and standard of education of the mothers when devising a new social classification.

The families were then grouped in the following way. First, those with a predominantly 'middle-class' background, that is to say one of the parents was brought up in a non-manual worker's family *and* went to a secondary school, and the other had at least one of these characteristics; second, those with a purely working-class background, where both parents came from manual workers' families and received only an elementary school education; third, those who showed some middle-class characteristics but did not fit into the first group.

When these three classes of families are further divided by the nature of the husband's present occupation a clear picture emerges. The children of non-manual workers fall into two main groups which have considerably different average scores in the eight- and eleven-year tests: those whose parents have middle-class origins and secondary school education form a group which, on the average, make high scores whether their fathers are in the professions, in salaried employment, in black-coated work or are self-employed; the remainder, whose parents may be said to deviate in their upbringing and education from the middle-class pattern, make considerably lower average scores. The children from the first group not only make relatively high scores in the eight- and eleven-year tests, but also work hard in class and do conspicuously well in the eleven-plus examinations, getting more grammar school places than would be expected from their measured ability. In contrast, those from the second group, whose parents deviate from the middle-class pattern, are less interested in their work and do relatively less well in the eleven-plus examinations. These differences in the performance of the children are reflected in the interests and aspirations of their parents. For these reasons the non-manual workers are grouped into two classes, the 'upper middle class' and the 'lower middle class'. Upper class and lower class are phrases we dislike, but in practice they give a convenient short description of these two groups. In making this division the employers and the self-employed are treated in the same way as the rest of the non-manual workers.

The manual working-class families also split naturally into two groups. First, those in which one or both parents come from a middle class family, or have been to secondary schools. The great majority of these are skilled workers and we call them the 'upper manual working class'. Second, those in which both parents were brought up in working-class families and had only an elementary school education; these we call the 'lower manual working class'. The latter may be regarded as wholly manual working-class in origin, whereas the upper manual working-class families deviate from this pattern. The lower manual working-class children consistently show a substantial decline in test scores between eight and eleven years, and this is so whether the father is in skilled, semi-skilled or unskilled employment.

This division into four social classes (the upper and lower middle classes and the upper and lower manual working classes) has the great virtue for this study that it provides relatively stable groups that include essentially the same families whether the classification is made on the information available at the beginning of the survey or the end of it. Some assessments of these families are given in the following table. . . .

	Middle-class mothers		Manual working-class mothers	
	Upper %	Lower %	Upper %	Lower %
Highest standards of infant care	53·1	37·0	22·1	15·1
Highest standards of infant management	66·2	49·4	34·5	28·1
Good use of medical services	78·9	67·4	54·2	42·4
High interest in school progress	41·7	21·7	11·4	5·0
Desires grammar school place	73·3	73·3	57·7	48·8
Late school leaving wished	77·6	40·7	21·7	12·9
At least four of the above	81·0	58·0	34·6	19·6

There are considerable differences, as mentioned already, in the average test scores made by children in these four social classes. The upper-middle-class children, at eleven years, make an average score of 56·99; the lower-middle-class 53·88; the upper manual working-class 50·5; the lower manual working-class 47·55. It might be thought that the social class differences in test performance would be greatest in the tests which measured the level of achievement in school subjects, but this is not so. There are similar differences between the social classes in each type of test that was used, and a slight suggestion that the lower manual working-class children are under-achievers and that the upper-middle-class children are over-achievers. The intelligence test used at eleven years was in two parts, one of which was given pictorially (and so did not involve the understanding of words), whereas the other involved seeing similarities between the meanings of words. There is a very slight tendency for the middle-class children to do better in the 'verbal' than in the 'non-verbal' part of this intelligence test, whereas the manual working-class children do worse in the 'verbal' part. This is mentioned because it confirms the findings of some other studies, but standing alone it might well be explained as a chance effect because the differences are so slight.

At eleven years the average test scores made by children in the four social classes differ more widely than they did at eight. The two middle-class groups come closer together and move further away from the manual working classes; this shows itself in intelligence tests as well as in tests of school achievement.

It is well known that when tests are repeated after an interval, children who make low scores tend, on the average, to improve their position, whereas those who make high scores tend to deteriorate. It would therefore be expected that the middle-class children who, on the average, score highly at eight would show a drop in score at eleven, and that the manual working-class children who make low scores at eight would show an improvement; but, as has already been mentioned, the middle-class children improve their scores and the working-class children deteriorate—this holds at each level of ability. By the time he is eleven, the clever manual working-class child has fallen behind the middle-class child of similar ability at eight years, and equally the backward manual working-class child shows less improvement between eight and eleven years than the backward middle-class child. . . .

Social class differences in secondary selection are marked. Fifty-four per cent of upper-middle-class children, but only 11 per cent of lower manual working-class children, go to grammar schools; and not all of the poor achievement of the working-class children is explained by their lower measured ability. If we compare secondary selection within groups of children whose eleven-year test scores are similar, the middle-class children are consistently at an advantage until very high levels of performance are reached. With children in the top 2 per cent of ability, social background is unimportant, but below this it has a considerable influence on their chances of going to grammar schools. As an illustration consider children who score between 55 and 57 in the tests; among them grammar school places are awarded at the age of eleven to 51 per cent from the upper middle classes, 34 per cent from the lower middle, 21 per cent from the upper manual, and 22 per cent from the lower manual working classes.

DEPARTMENT OF EDUCATION AND SCIENCE (1965)

Circular 10/65*

It is the Government's declared objective to end selection at eleven-plus and to eliminate separatism in secondary education. The Government's policy has been endorsed by the House of Commons in a motion passed on 21 January 1965:

That this House, conscious of the need to raise educational standards at all levels, and regretting that the realization of this

* Reprinted from *Circular 10/65: the organization of secondary education* (London, HMSO, 1965).

objective is impeded by the separation of children into different types of secondary schools, notes with approval the efforts of local authorities to reorganize secondary education on comprehensive lines which will preserve all that is valuable in grammar school education for those children who now receive it and make it available to more children; recognizes that the method and timing of such reorganization should vary to meet local needs; and believes that the time is now ripe for a declaration of national policy.

The Secretary of State accordingly requests local education authorities, if they have not already done so, to prepare and submit to him plans for reorganizing secondary education in their areas on comprehensive lines. The purpose of this Circular is to provide some central guidance on the methods by which this can be achieved.

There are a number of ways in which comprehensive education may be organized. While the essential needs of the children do not vary greatly from one area to another, the views of individual authorities, the distribution of population and the nature of existing schools will inevitably dictate different solutions in different areas. It is important that new schemes build on the foundation of present achievements and preserve what is best in existing schools.

Six main forms of comprehensive organization have so far emerged from experience and discussion:

(i) The orthodox comprehensive school with an age range of eleven to eighteen.

(ii) A two-tier system whereby *all* pupils transfer at eleven to a junior[1] comprehensive school and *all* go on at thirteen or fourteen to a senior comprehensive school.

(iii) A two-tier system under which *all* pupils on leaving primary school transfer to a junior comprehensive school, but at the age of thirteen or fourteen *some* pupils move on to a senior school while *the remainder* stay on in the same school. There are two main variations: in one, the comprehensive school which all pupils enter after leaving primary school provides no course terminating in a public examination, and normally keeps pupils only until fifteen; in the other, this school pro-

---

[1] The terms 'junior' and 'senior' refer throughout this Circular to the lower and upper secondary schools in two-tier systems of secondary education.

vides GCE and CSE courses, keeps pupils at least until sixteen, and encourages transfer at the appropriate stage to the sixth form of the senior school.

(iv) A two-tier system in which *all* pupils on leaving primary school transfer to a junior comprehensive school. At the age of thirteen or fourteen *all* pupils have a choice between a senior school catering for those who expect to stay at school well beyond the compulsory age, and a senior school catering for those who do not.

(v) Comprehensive schools with an age range of eleven to sixteen with sixth form colleges for pupils over sixteen.

(vi) A system of middle schools which straddle the primary/secondary age ranges. Under this system pupils transfer from a primary school at the age of eight or nine to a comprehensive school with an age range of eight to twelve or nine to thirteen. From this middle school they move on to a comprehensive school with an age range of twelve or thirteen to eighteen.

The most appropriate system will depend on local circumstances and an authority may well decide to adopt more than one form of organization in the area for which it is responsible. Organizations of types (i), (ii), (v) and (vi) produce schools which are fully comprehensive in character. On the other hand an organization of type (iii) or (iv) is not fully comprehensive in that it involves the separation of children of differing aims and aptitudes into different schools at the age of thirteen or fourteen. Given the limitations imposed by existing buildings such schemes are acceptable as interim solutions, since they secure many of the advantages of comprehensive education and in some areas offer the most satisfactory method of bringing about reorganization at an early date. But they should be regarded only as an interim stage in development towards a fully comprehensive secondary organization. . . .

The Government are aware that the complete elimination of selection and separatism in secondary education will take time to achieve. They do not seek to impose destructive or precipitate change on existing schools; they recognize that the evolution of separate schools into a comprehensive system must be a constructive process requiring

careful planning by local education authorities in consultation
with all those concerned. But the spontaneous and exciting progress
which has been made in this direction by so many authorities in
recent years demonstrates that the objective is not only practicable;
it is also now widely accepted. The Government believe that both
the education service and the general public will welcome the further
impetus which a clear statement of national policy will secure.

TORSTEN HUSÉN AND GUNNAR BOALT (1967)

The case of Sweden*

THE PROBLEM OF DIFFERENTIATION IN SWEDISH EDUCATIONAL REFORM, 1900–60

Towards the close of the nineteenth century it was generally agreed
that schools in Sweden did not meet the demands of the times. New
methods of production and new social classes brought new educational needs to the fore. Industrialization was creating groups of
manufacturers and businessmen with new demands on education.
The number of industrial workers increased rapidly, which meant
that fewer children could be given the elementary education previously in the agrarian society communicated by the home.

Views of the most suitable solution of the problem of school
organization differed widely. One protagonist of the conservative
solution was Fredrik Anderson, who gave his opinion at the Tenth
General Teachers' Conference in 1881, and the following year published a booklet entitled *I hvilken rigtning bör en reform af våra under-
visningsanstalter gå?* ('What direction should a reform of our schools
take?'). Anderson's idea was that every social class should have a
type of school corresponding to its needs. The elementary school was

* Reprinted from *Educational Research and Educational Change: the case of
Sweden* (New York, Wiley, 1967).

meant for 'the working classes and the lower classes of artisans'. The grammar school, i.e. the *gymnasium*, was for the upper class. What was needed was a third school, called 'citizens' school', for the children of skilled artisans, businessmen and farmers. The three types of school should run parallel to each other, and no organizational co-ordination would be required. In 1882, a young elementary school teacher named Fridtjuv Berg published a prize essay in the *Svensk Lärartidning*, the newly established organ of Swedish elementary school teachers, in which he advocated the elementary school as a six-year 'basic school' for all children. Only if the elementary school received children from all social classes would it be able to rise above its status as a school for lower class children. All members of society would then be interested in this school and, in step with the growing political equality, the gap between the different social classes could be bridged. Nature 'has not given mental powers and ability to rule to certain classes and physical strength and contented obedience to others'. Berg gave a series of lectures to the Stockholm Elementary School Teachers' Association, and published them later in a booklet in 1883 under the title *Folkskolan som bottenskola* ('The elementary school as a basic school'). The ideas expressed in this work formed the basis of the debate around the so-called 'linking' between the elementary school and higher schools until the end of the 1940s.

Until 1894, the elementary school (*folkskolan*) and the grammar school (*läroverket*) ran entirely parallel to each other. Students who had completed the six-year elementary schools could not qualify for grammar school studies; those who were to attend the latter school first went to private preparatory schools. In 1894, by a Parliamentary decision it became possible to transfer from the third grade of an A-form elementary school (a school with one teacher for each grade) to a grammar school. The next stage of development was the creation of the junior secondary academic school (*realskola*). The 1904 Education Act divided the grammar school into a six-year *realskola* with a special leaving certificate, and a four-year *gymnasium* (leading to university studies). Thanks largely to the work of Fridtjuv Berg, Parliament established, in 1909, four-year municipal middle schools following on the six-year elementary schools to enable children living in places without *realskola* and *gymnasia* to obtain a higher education than that given by the compulsory school. The municipal

234   TORSTEN HUSÉN AND GUNNAR BOALT

TABLE I. *Distribution according to social status (in per cent) among students in different types of lower secondary schools* (realskola) *and in the 1940 electorate*

Type of school	Social class			Total
	1	*2*	*3*	
Realskola (4- or 5-year), part of a higher secondary school	18	59	23	100
State *realskola*	11	57	32	100
Municipal 'middle' school	7	50	43	100
Electorate 1940	5	37	57	100

Source : S O U 1944: 21, p. 320.

middle schools have had – as the report of the 1940 School Committee shows – a far more representative social recruitment than the six-year (later five-year) *realskola* (cf. Table 1).

The political swing in a radical direction at the end of World War I led to, among other things, the appointment of a Parliamentary Commission with the mandate to propose a school organization in which the whole educational system was to form an integral whole with the six-year elementary school as the common primary school. The Commission's report was submitted in 1922. By and large it was an attempt to realize Berg's basic school idea. . . .

The recommendations of the 1918 School Commission gave rise to a heated debate, and it was impossible to obtain a majority in Parliament in favour of the recommendations. In 1924, therefore, within the Ministry of Education a committee of experts was appointed to revise the recommendations. On the basis of the report of this committee, Parliament accepted, in 1927, a modified proposal relating to school structure usually known as the 'double link'. This meant, in brief, that pupils could transfer from the elementary school to secondary schools (including girl schools) after the fourth or the sixth grade. In the former case the pupils attended a five-year *realskola*, and in the latter a four-year *realskola*.

In 1937, school attendance by Parliamentary decision was made compulsory for seven years in the whole country. Some local education authorities had already established eight-year elementary schools. This meant increased parallelism between the elementary school and the grammar school, and the problem of linking was brought to the fore again. This was one reason for the appointment of the 1940 School Committee, which meant the initiation of the new reform era leading up to the 1962 Education Act on basic education and the 1964 Act on *gymnasium* education. . . .

A School Commission, a parliamentary committee augmented by a council of experts, was appointed in 1946 and submitted its main recommendation in 1948. These recommendations proposed a Solomonic solution: the parallel types of school were simply to be incorporated into one unitary, compulsory school. The first nine years at school would be common to all children and form a 'comprehensive school'. . . .

On the basis of the commission's recommendations and the observations made by the evaluating bodies, a Bill was drafted and submitted to Parliament in 1950, entitled 'Principles governing the development of the Swedish educational system'. One cardinal point in the Bill was the problem of 'uniformity and differentiation'. The Minister of Education began by quoting a declaration made by the 1940 School Committee that 'an organically integrated school system comprising all forms of schools, in which each growing individual, regardless of residence place and of the socio-economic status of the parents . . . will be given, if necessary with public assistance, an education suited to his aptitude'.

The Minister added:

> Work of a reform intended to bridge old social gaps must ensure that the school system for all classes of society appears as a uniform whole, in which lines of study are available to all young Swedish people, and where every growing individual, regardless of his social starting-point in life, can learn how to make the best of his talents. Such an aim is incompatible with any kind of parallel school system. Differentiation into separate schools should, I believe, not be made until it is necessary on account of choice of vocation. . . .

The decision made by Parliament in 1950 anticipated a rather long period of experimental work with the nine-year comprehensive school, under the supervision of a special division of the National Board of Education. . . .

In 1955, Stockholm was divided into two parts in respect of school organization. In one part, called the North Side, transfer could be made up to this year from grade four of the elementary school to a five-year *realskola* or a seven-year girl school. In the other part, called the South Side, transfer was not allowed until after grade six. At the same time, compulsory school attendance was prolonged from eight to nine years in this part of the city. This meant that in the South Side there was actually a six-year basic school from which pupils could be transferred either to a separate three-year *realskola* or a three-year academic line organized within the elementary school. Some local school units in the South Side were on the pilot programme with the nine-year comprehensive school.

This division provided a unique situation for a research project.

THE RELATION BETWEEN SELECTIVITY AND SOCIAL CLASS

A large body of research has shown that students from socio-economic group 3 (consisting for the most part of working-class families) or from certain categories of socio-economic group 2 (for instance, agricultural families) are greatly under-represented in the secondary academic school.[1] In France, for example, until recently only one-eighth of the student population came from working-class homes, who form two-thirds of the nation's families. Similar findings are reported by Dahrendorf (1964) for West Germany. When Premier Khrushchev in 1958 announced the new educational reform in a speech before the Supreme Soviet, he said that 60 per cent of the

TABLE 2. *Male undergraduates by social class*

Social class	1910	1920	1930	1937	1943
1	35	35	37	36	32
2	55	54	51	52	56
3	9	10	11	9	10
Unknown	1	1	1	3	2

[1] The socio-economic grouping employed here is the one developed for the Swedish Election Statistics. The three groups could roughly be labelled 'upper', 'middle' and 'lower' class respectively. 'Social class', 'social group' and 'socio-economic group' are used interchangeably.

enrolment in Moscow's upper level schools was recruited from the intelligentsia and bureaucracy, and only 40 per cent from the homes of manual workers and farmers.

A study of the social class origins of Swedish undergraduates, made by Moberg (1951) disclosed that roughly the same class proportions had existed from 1910 to 1943 (Table 2).

Boalt (1947) investigated recruitment in 1936 to Stockholm academic schools which were based on four years in the elementary school. A similar study pertaining to Stockholm, Gothenburg and Malmö in 1938 was made by the 1940 School Committee. In 1955, the last year when the dual system was operating in Stockholm, the School of Education determined social class affiliation for the pupils of Stockholm's North Side who in that year transferred to a *realskola* from grade four. The results of this comparison are set out in Table 3.

TABLE 3. *Social class distribution of students transferring from grade 4 to a* realskola

Social class	Stockholm 1936	Stockholm 1938	Stockholm 1955
1	25	20	34
2	57	61	46
3	18	19	20

TABLE 4. *Social handicap in selection for higher school and in screening within school. Handicap defined as partial correlation of selection or screening with social factor (after Boalt, 1947)*

Stage	Socio-economic group of parents	Taxed income of parents
Selection/non-selection for *realskola* (secondary academic school)	0·57	0·25
Screening in *realskola*	0·17	0·28
Selection/non-selection for *gymnasium*	0·47	0·45
Screening in *gymnasium*	0·15	0·07

The same picture emerges from both tables: over a long period of economic levelling-out the conditions of recruitment have altered only slightly. It might well be asked: does the observed social bias derive from the selection mechanisms as such, so that pupils from a lower class are handicapped in competitive selection from one level to another? This problem was illuminated in Great Britain by Floud *et al.* (1956). Boalt (1947) has worked out a technique for estimating the degree of social handicap which asserts itself in selection from a lower to higher school type and in screening within a school type. He defined social handicap as the relationship observable between selection (or screening) and social factors, with scholastic ability held constant. His findings are summarized in Table 4.

We may remark that the degree of social handicap tends to be greater when all the factors underlying the concept of 'social class' are taken into account than when economic background alone is considered.

Social class origins were also explored by the above-mentioned committee of the British Ministry of Education which had at the beginning of the 1950s been appointed to investigate failures in the grammar school. Of those pupils in the grammar school who had been selected after their performance in the eleven-plus examination, 37 per cent could be regarded as failures on either of three counts: they had not completed the five years, had not received any certificate or had received a certificate with less than three passes. The pupils were classified with reference to scores on entrance examinations and their social background. Failures are shown in Table 5

TABLE 5. *Failure rate (in per cent) among British grammar school pupils, by social class and entrance qualifications*

Paternal social status	Entrance standing		
	Best third	Middle third	Lowest third
Professional and managerial	10	25	34
Clerical	19	32	42
Semi-skilled	38	58	62
Unskilled	54	62	76

Source: Early Leaving

as percentages. On the basis of equivalent scores in the eleven-plus examinations we can observe that a much higher number of failures occurred among pupils of lower social class. The most striking datum is that failures were about five times more common for students in social class 3 among the *top third of entrance examination scores* than for pupils coming from homes which by and large correspond to social class 1.

A meticulous study has been carried out by Blomqvist (1958), which illustrates the relation between social class and screening during a specific stage of education. He confined himself to one State secondary academic school (Solna). When comparing grade-repeaters with those who had moved on up through the grades in normal order, he found that the home's cultural standard ranked with scholastic ability as a crucial determinant of success in school. . . .

Theory says that a competitive selection shall be made solely on the basis of ability. Among the criteria set up for this purpose are 'intelligence tests', most of which are constructed to measure scholastic ability. Their validity is established by correlating test scores with the testee's school marks. In the Stockholm study, scores achieved in the group intelligence test were drawn upon to divide the pupils into nine ability groups (a stanine scale). The top 4 per cent were put in group 9, the next best 7 per cent in group 8, and so on. Group 5 includes students who cluster round the average, while other groups fall below the average. In Table 6, the number of applicants to higher schools are distributed by social class affiliation among

TABLE 6. *Number of applicants to higher school as percentages of each social class with students distributed among different ability levels (Population derives from North Side of Stockholm in spring term of 1955. Ability levels grouped so that top 4 per cent belong to group 9, the next 7 per cent to group 8, etc.)*

Social class	Ability level on a stanine scale (according to intelligence test)								
	9	8	7	6	5	4	3	2	1
1	87	89	82	82	70	58	47	21	14
2	85	77	74	59	47	36	20	13	7
3	66	72	45	40	24	18	8	7	5

their ability levels. Figures are given as percentages, i.e. they show the proportion of students from different social classes but of the same ability level who applied for admission.

It will be noted that there were fewer applicants at all ability levels from group 3 than from 1 and 2. However, this difference varies with ability level in that pupils of average or sub-average ability from group 1 apply about three times as often for admission, whereas among the 11 per cent who scored highest on the test the number of applications from group 1 pupils slightly exceeds that of the other classes. We thus see that the very intention of applying for admission correlates significantly not only with the student's ability but also with his social background.

TABLE 7. *Number of* rejected *applicants for higher school as a percentage of number of applicants from each social class, with students distributed among ability levels as in Table 6*

Social class	Ability level (according to intelligence test)								
	9	8	7	6	5	4	3	2	1
1	6	20	18	36	52	69	69	(80)	(100)
2	6	23	33	50	60	68	79	(100)	(75)
3	13	30	31	43	57	61	82	(54)	(100)

With the facts shown by Table 6 in mind, we might expect a relatively higher number of rejected applicants from groups 1 and 2 than from 3, since it could be reasonably assumed that the larger number of applicants from the first two classes (and group 1 in particular) would contain more students who were less able and less qualified for school studies. But as Table 7 shows, the number of rejects tends to be larger in group 3, in spite of the much lower incidence of applications. This tendency is more pronounced among the most able students than for those who cluster round the average. We may accordingly say that social handicap is operative not only in building up the level of aspiration, but also when this aspiration is translated into action, i.e. when students from the cultural environments represented in group 3 apply for an academic education.

At this point several objections can be raised: first, an intelligence test does not measure factors relevant for scholastic ability, or at all events measures these only incompletely; second, tests of this kind favour certain groups of pupils. The latter objection is based on the observation that an ability test tends to discriminate against students from a lower social class. This suggests that the tendencies towards

TABLE 8. *Number of* non-*applicants for higher school from different social classes, with students distributed by ability level according to* achievement tests

Social class	Ability level (according to achievement tests)								
	9	8	7	6	5	4	3	2	1
1	9	10	12	26	42	60	56	100	100
2	12	14	25	34	57	80	90	94	97
3	21	26	34	58	79	91	98	99	98

TABLE 9. *Number of* rejected *applicants from different social classes and at different ability levels: scores on achievement tests used as measures of ability*

Social class	Ability level (according to achievement tests)								
	9	8	7	6	5	4	3	2	1
1	—	7	19	53	83	93	(100)	—	—
2	—	9	28	54	85	93	(81)	(75)	(100)
3	2	5	28	52	81	77	(75)	(50)	(100)

social handicap we noted above to selection to a higher school would have been even more pronounced if we had been able to use a more 'culture-free' intelligence test. The second of these two objections may therefore be said to reinforce rather than weaken our conclusions on social handicap. In answer to the first objection, the Stockholm study did not exclusively rely on the intelligence test but could also draw on the results of achievement tests given in mathematics and Swedish. On the basis of scores achieved in eight tests, students were classified at nine ability levels according to the same procedure as above. Lastly, we had access to school marks, which of course comprise an instrument whose use is held to permit the making of a fair selection.

In Table 8 we have set down the proportion of students from each social class, distributed among ability levels as shown by the eight achievement tests, who did *not* apply for admission to a higher school. It should be borne in mind when interpreting the results that standard tests serve the teacher as 'calibrating instruments', whose readings give him an idea of how his class stands in relation to a nationally representative group. Level of marks is adjusted with reference to the outcome of such a comparison. This means that the tests do not affect the marking of the individual pupil in principle, but do so indirectly by virtue of the student's standing in the class.

If we take the 23 per cent of students who scored highest on the tests (ability levels 9, 8, and 7), it will be noted that non-applicants from socio-economic group 3 exceed those from 1 by between two and three times. Thus when achievement tests are used as measures of ability, the resulting picture is just about the same as when ability classification was based on intelligence tests. Here, again, it would be interesting to see which proportions of applicants from different social classes were rejected. Our findings are set down in Table 9.

By contrast with our findings when the intelligence test was employed as a measure of ability, the socio-economic groups do not differ so very much from one another with reference to the number of rejected applicants. Once again a greater number of rejects might have been expected in groups 1 and 2, since a much larger proportion of pupils from them at corresponding ability levels applied for admission. Why then the different outcome when achievement tests replace an intelligence test as measures of ability? Several explanations can be advanced. To begin with, admissions to a higher school were based on marks. Since these show a higher correlation with standard achievement tests than with the intelligence test, it automatically follows that there is greater resemblance between the social classes with regard to rejection of students at a given achievement level, as indicated by the tests. No partiality was shown along social class lines when applications were passed on. Admissions were made on objective grounds, i.e. on the basis of marks earned by students. A small social bias comes in, favouring students from higher and better-educated social strata when it is a question of converting 'innate ability' into scholastic achievements as manifested in marks. We cannot elaborate on how this mechanism has operated in the population under review.

TABLE 10. *Number of applicants to a higher school from different social classes, with students distributed by ability level according to* marks *received in grade 4*

Social class	Ability level (according to marks)					
	9	8	7	6	5	4
1	92	94	88	84	53	32
2	95	92	90	69	35	14
3	89	87	87	51	14	3

Finally, marks received in grade 4 were used as a measure of ability. These marks were the basis for decisions on admission to a higher school. In Table 10 the number of applicants at each level of ability according to total school marks are shown. Here we have included only ability groups 4–9. Pursuant to regulations, admission was not granted to pupils having an aggregate mark lower than 13·5, which on the nine-point scale corresponds to the lower limit for group 5.

Our previous observation, that fewer pupils of comparable ability levels apply for admission from socio-economic group 3 than from the two other classes, is further confirmed by Table 10. Inter-group difference is slight in respect of pupils with high marks, but is significant in regard to students having average or sub-average marks. We find that socio-economic group differences in terms of applications to a higher school are far less when marks are employed as ability measures instead of tests. This is to be expected, since school marks are 'loaded' to a greater extent not only with intellectual ability, but also with social background than is true of intelligence or achievement tests. In other words, the pupil coming from a more privileged environment reaps a bigger 'dividend' in terms of marks from his intellectual qualifications as compared with his less privileged coeval.

CENTRAL ADVISORY COUNCIL FOR
EDUCATION (1967)

Children and their primary schools (Plowden Report)*

In our cities there are whole districts which have been scarcely touched by the advances made in more fortunate places. Yet such conditions have been overcome and striking progress has been achieved where sufficiently determined and comprehensive attack has been made on the problem. In the most deprived areas, one of HM Inspectors reported, 'Some heads approach magnificence, but they cannot do everything. . . . The demands on them as welfare agents are never ending.' Many children with parents in the least skilled jobs do outstandingly well in school. The educational aspirations of parents and the support and encouragement given to children in some of the poorest neighbourhoods are impressive. Over half of the unskilled workers in our National Survey want their children to be given homework to do after school hours; over half want their children to stay at school beyond the minimum leaving age. One-third of them hoped their children would go to a grammar school or one with similar opportunities. The educational aspirations of un-skilled workers for their children have risen year by year. It has been stressed to us that the range of ability in all social classes is so wide that there is a great reservoir of unrealized potential in families de-pendent on the least skilled and lowest paid work. A larger part of the housing programme than ever before is to be devoted to rebuild-ing and renewing obsolete and decaying neighbourhoods. The oppor-tunity must be seized to rebuild the schools as well as the houses, and to see that both schools and houses serve families from every social class. . . . There is a growing awareness in the nation at large, greatly stimulated, we believe, by our predecessors' Reports, of the

* Reprinted from *Children and their Primary Schools* (London, HMSO, 1967).

complex social handicaps afflicting such areas and the need for a more radical assault on their problems. . . .

We propose a nation-wide scheme for helping those schools and neighbourhoods in which children are most severely handicapped. This policy will have an influence over the whole educational system, and it colours all the subsequent recommendations in our Report. It must not be put into practice simply by robbing more fortunate areas of all the opportunities for progress to which they have been looking forward; it can only succeed if a larger share of the nation's resources is devoted to education. . . .

During the Second World War there was a considerable improvement in the living conditions which bear most directly upon children in deprived groups and areas. In spite of this there has not been any appreciable narrowing of the gap between the least well off and the rest of the population. This is most obvious among children, particularly those in large families. . . . Signs of rickets have recently been reported again from the slums of Glasgow; mortality among children during the first year of life has fallen sharply since 1950, but the difference between social classes remains great. Much the same goes for stillbirth rates which, in different social classes 'despite a dramatic wartime fall, were as far apart in 1950 as in 1939'. Meanwhile 'class differentials in perinatal mortality are as resistant to change as those of infant mortality. The results of the (Perinatal Mortality) Survey suggest, indeed, that the gap may be increasing rather than narrowing.' The Milner Holland Committee's study of housing conditions in London covered a period in which this country probably achieved a faster rate of economic growth than it has ever experienced before, and an area in which conditions are generally better and improving faster than elsewhere. But it showed that progress has been most rapid in those parts of the town where conditions were already best. In less fortunate neighbourhoods there has been less improvement and in some respects an appreciable deterioration. Families with low incomes and several young children were among those who suffered most. . . .

Our educational system, originally moulded by the impress of Victorian economic and social requirements, may not yet have been fully adapted to present needs. In the deprived areas with which this chapter is concerned too many children leave school as soon as they are allowed to with no desire to carry their education further and without the knowledge to fit them for a job more intellectually demanding than their father's or their grandfather's. Yet they face a future in which they must expect during their working life to have to change their job, to learn new skills, to adapt themselves to new economic conditions and to form new human relationships. They will suffer, and so will the economy; both needlessly. It should not be assumed that even the ablest children can surmount every handicap. They may suffer as much as any from adverse conditions.

If the schools are to play their part in resolving and forestalling these problems much of the action required must be taken at the secondary and higher stages of the system. But this action cannot be fully effective if it does not touch the primary schools. Recent research has shown how early in the lives of children the selective processes begin to operate. There are primary schools from which scarcely any children ever take a secondary school course which leads them to O level in GCE. Children of good potential ability enter them, but the doors to educational opportunity have already closed against them when their schooling has scarcely begun. Reforming zeal and expenditure directed to later stages of education will be wasted unless early handicaps can be reduced. . . .

Redistribution of resources within local authority areas has been less marked. 'Equality' has an appealing ring, 'discrimination' has not. It is simpler and easier, for example, to defend staff-pupil ratios that are roughly the same in each school than to explain why they should be better in some and to decide which are to be the favoured. Even so, more and more local authorities do discriminate. They look with a more generous eye on schools whose 'social need' is greatest, as reckoned by the free dinner list, by the proportion of children who do not speak English at home, or (which may be an even better guide) by the opinion of experienced teachers and administrators. These schools may be allowed an extra teacher or more non-teaching help, or a slightly bigger ration of 'consumable stocks'.

These are no more than a tentative beginning. The formulae for allocating grants are designed to equalize the financial resources of poorer and wealthier authorities. But equality is not enough. The formulae do not distinguish between the districts within authorities' areas in which children and schools are most severely handicapped.

These districts need more spending on them, and government and local authorities between them must provide the funds. . . .

The many teachers who do so well in face of adversity cannot manage without cost to themselves. They carry the burdens of parents, probation officers and welfare officers on top of their class-room duties. It is time the nation came to their aid. The principle, already accepted, that special need calls for special help, should be given a new cutting edge. We ask for 'positive discrimination' in favour of such schools and the children in them, going well beyond an attempt to equalize resources. Schools in deprived areas should be given priority in many respects. The first step must be to raise the schools with low standards to the national average; the second, quite deliberately to make them better. The justification is that the homes and neighbourhoods from which many of their children come provide little support and stimulus for learning. The schools must supply a compensating environment. The attempts so far made within the educational system to do this have not been sufficiently generous or sustained, because the handicaps imposed by the environment have not been explicitly and sufficiently allowed for. They should be.

3

Next Monday 1968-73

3

Next Monday 1968-73

In his preface to Taylor and Ayres' *Born and Bred Unequal* (1969)
Richard Titmuss referred to the changed 'time-scale of expectations
of effecting change'. Pessimism had grown deeper, 'especially among
the young – because inequality cannot be abolished next Monday'.[1]
A feature of the late 1960s was an increased sense of new and urgent
educational aims to be accomplished by 'next Monday'. There was
a sense that previously defined aims were not being achieved, that
efforts had been misdirected, too limited or too narrowly planned.
From the Plowden Report onwards there was a sense that the specifically 'educational solutions' of the past had been inadequate. The
National Child Development Study of 1972, for example, concluded
that

> the estimated gap in terms of the average reading performance of
> the most and the least advantaged children . . . was over four years.
> Furthermore, the most potent factors were seen to be located in
> the home environment . . . equality of educational opportunity
> cannot be achieved solely by improving our educational insti-
> tutions.[2]

The educational priority area project, reported on by A. H. Halsey
in *Educational Priority* in 1972, consisted of 'action research' in the
four areas involved (Liverpool, Birmingham, Deptford and the
West Riding) to test out the possibilities of new approaches to community schools. Pressure towards comprehensive organization
slackened as a result of the Conservative government's circular
10/70; at the same time, however, Caroline Benn and Brian Simon
were demonstrating that comprehensive school development was

[1] George Taylor and N. Ayres, *Born and Bred Unequal* (London, 1969), p. x.
[2] Ronald Davie, Neville Butler and Harvey Goldstein, *From Birth to Seven*
(London, 1972), p. 190.

only *Half Way There*. They produced the following table to show what progress had been made in the 1960s:[3]

Secondary education 1961–70
Percentage of total pupil population in secondary education, England and Wales
Shaded areas: selective, fee paying or independent sector
Clear areas: non-selective sector

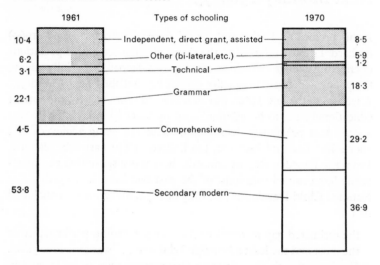

	1961	Types of schooling	1970	
	10·4	Independent, direct grant, assisted		8·5
	6·2	Other (bi-lateral, etc.)		5·9
	3·1	Technical		1·2
	22·1	Grammar		18·3
	4·5	Comprehensive		29·2
	53·8	Secondary modern		36·9

The programme of urban aid to depressed areas, begun by the Labour government in 1968, distributed nearly £25 million in five years for improvements, among other things, in nursery education; the amount spent only revealed how much more was needed. The various attempts at least to reduce inequality by 'next Monday' helped to highlight the nature and magnitude of the obstacles.

We have suggested earlier that the period from 1968 saw three main developments – increasing attention to the family and children's pre-school experience, regional inequalities and theories of knowledge. This is not to say that work on the processes of primary and secondary schooling had come to a halt. In 1967 David Hargreaves, in a book on *Social Relations in a Secondary School*, had explored,

[3] Caroline Benn and Brian Simon, *Half-Way There: report on the British comprehensive school reform* (London, 1970; 1972 edition), p. 86.

among other things, the relationships between school subcultures and streaming, notably between low streams and the 'perception of status deprivation'.[4] Two years later Julienne Ford published *Social Class and the Comprehensive School*, in which she pursued the relationship between the comprehensive ideal and reality, criticizing the limited view of education involved in the notion of equal opportunity:

> ... As Pedley puts it, 'The Englishman of the 1960s does not believe in equality. What he wants is equal opportunity to be unequal'. On closer examination ... even the argument for equality of *opportunity* is seen to be a cover for a yet more limited plea ... we can see the main body of current criticism of the tripartite system of education ... as stemming from the view that selection should be based on the sole criterion of 'ability' ... it should be made clear immediately that this is always an ideological position, a bid to remove an injustice, a statement that discrimination is being made on irrelevant grounds and that this should be replaced by efficient selection on relevant and reasonable criteria.[5]

From this starting point she explored the continued existence – and even exacerbation – of social influences on children's performance and position inside comprehensive schools, mainly as a result of streaming. Out of research of this kind came continued controversy. A research project of the National Foundation for Educational Research declared in 1972 that at four schools studied 'in only one ... do the figures support Ford's findings that streaming/banding in the comprehensive school tends to underline class differentials in educational opportunity, the other three schools give no support to this hypothesis'.[6] The Black Paper opponents of comprehensive schools used findings such as Ford's to buttress their arguments.[7] In an article on 'Labour and inequality' in 1972, Howard Glennerster

---

[4] David H. Hargreaves, *Social Relations in a Secondary School* (London, 1967). See especially chapters on 'relations between streams', 'the delinquent group' and 'two subcultures'.

[5] Ford, *Social Class and the Comprehensive School*, p. 1.

[6] J. M. Ross, W. J. Bunton, P. Evison and T. S. Robertson, *A Critical Appraisal of Comprehensive Education* (Windsor, 1972), p. 46.

[7] See Black Paper Three, *Goodbye Mr Short* (London, [1970]), pp. 6–7.

surveyed inequalities in the educational system and proposed a programme for the allocation of resources in the spirit of positive discrimination.[8] In these and other respects, questions of educability and opportunities in secondary and higher education remained live issues. In many respects these and other debates paralleled debates and uncertainties becoming more explicit in other countries – notably the United States (and described in the last contribution in this section).

Most of the discussion in the earlier periods was, as we have seen, concerned with questions of educational *structures*, social classes, access to secondary education, mechanisms of differential opportunities within the educational and social systems. The increased attention now being given to children's early experience was more concerned with continuing *processes*, in and out of school (as instanced by Halsey's *Educational Priority*, one of the outstanding educational documents of this period). Work on regional differentials also moved attention closer to the precise, intimate relationships between school and environmental influences. The EPA projects were concerned in detail with forms of local underprivilege. Taylor and Ayres were concerned with the impact on education and people of different levels of regional spending on such things as health, housing and children's services, as well as education. Pratt and Allemano investigated the 'equality myth', a statistical exercise to bring home the disparities in educational spending among authorities.[9]

The growing interest in relating educational processes to sociological theory is indicated by the extracts from Earl Hopper and Michael F. D. Young in this section. Work such as the latter's was related to that of Basil Bernstein in connection with 'compensatory education', knowledge and social control. Bernstein's work on language codes in the late 1950s and 1960s had proved both influential and seminal, and resulted in his establishment of a Sociological Research Unit at the London University Institute of Education in 1964. The continuing research into language, socialization and social

[8] Peter Townsend and Nicholas Bosanquet (eds.), *Labour and Inequality* (London, 1972).
[9] John Pratt and Ralph Allemano, 'The equality myth', the *Guardian*, 19 September, 3, 17, 31 October, 14 November 1972.

class was intended to refine Bernstein's concepts and pursue fresh
directions of investigation. There was at the same time increasing
criticism of Bernstein's position. Denis Lawton in 1968, for example,
pointed to inconsistencies or ambiguities in Bernstein's descriptions
of different language codes and use of concepts.[10] Harold Rosen in
1972 criticized Bernstein's confusions, including for example his
failure to look in detail at the class system:

> The working class in his discussion are for the most part the un-
> skilled working class. No further attempt is made at differentiation
> ... As a sociologist, Bernstein is content with the popular term
> 'middle class' to cover the varied strata whose relationship to the
> class system varies widely and whose class position certainly has
> important and different influences on their language. ... But,
> strangest of all in this system, the ruling class do not figure at all.
> When Bernstein talks of social control he is not talking of the
> ways in which one class controls or is controlled by another, but
> only of the ways in which members of the same class control
> each other.[11]

Bernstein defended his work on two important counts. He rejected
the view that his earlier work had been concerned solely with the
family and had neglected the school as an instrument of social
control:

> It has always been very clear to me that the class structure affec-
> ted access to elaborated codes through its influence upon initial
> socialization into the family *and* through its fundamental shaping
> of both the organizational structure and contents of education. I
> was also very sure that there were a variety of ways in which an
> elaborated code could be transmitted.

He rejected also the criticism of changes over time in his use of the
concept of codes in relation to social class. In an important passage
in 1973 he discussed the concept of socio-linguistic codes, the
'exploration of their generating and maintaining social relationships',
and their 'relationship to the wider social structure':

[10] See Denis Lawton, *Social Class, Language and Education* (1968) for 'A
critique of Bernstein's work on language and social class'.

[11] Harold Rosen, *Language and Class: a critical look at the theories of Basil
Bernstein* (Bristol, 1972), p. 6.

K

I have difficulty in understanding, and I have very little sympathy with, complaints that the sociolinguistic thesis of 1958 is in some respects different from the thesis of 1972. Such a critique is based upon a complete misunderstanding of the nature of research. The single most important fact of research is where it *leads*, not where it starts . . .

The basic thesis of his work had been 'that forms of communication may be distinguished in terms of what is rendered implicit and what is rendered explicit'. He had been concerned not with 'differences between social groups at the level of competency', but with performance, that is, the use to which 'basic tacit understanding of the linguistic rule system' was put.[12]

The importance of work by Bernstein and his colleagues at the London Institute in this period lay in its direction of attention to the relationship between language and socialization on the one hand, and the assumptions about them which were reflected in the organization of schools and curricula on the other hand. Discussions such as this were a long way from the description of unequal opportunities as defined in the 1950s and 1960s; they were concerned with refining the theories and concepts which would explain controlling mechanisms in society and education. From such efforts stemmed the interest among some sociologists in looking at problems of the curriculum and processes of communication in schools. The curriculum began to be seen as a means of 'negotiating' with children over views of reality. The interest was in forms of social control – not through educational structures, but through learning and teaching processes. 'Reality', said Berger and Luckman, 'is socially constructed and . . . the sociology of knowledge must analyse the process in which this occurs . . . the sociology of knowledge must concern itself with whatever passes for "knowledge" in a society.'[13] Some sociologists have, from such a starting point, turned to the curriculum as the paramount educational process of communicating what 'passes for

[12] Basil Bernstein, 'A brief account of the theory of codes', in *Social Relationships and Language : some aspects of the work of Basil Bernstein* (Bletchley, 1973), pp. 68-70. This useful publication is block 3 of the Open University second level course in educational studies.

[13] Peter L. Berger and Thomas Luckman, *The Social Construction of Reality* (New York, 1966; London 1967 edition), pp. 13-15.

"knowledge"'. In doing so they have rejected what in previous decades have been accepted as the proper problems of study. David Gorbutt, explaining the new sociology, describes a tendency 'for sociological problems to be taken rather than made'. What sociologists of education have so far taken

> as being the significant problems for the subject are identical to those which are taken to be the official problems of the day. For example, much of the sociology of education is concerned with establishment problems – how to promote equality of educational opportunity, how to run schools efficiently, how to control educational deviants or counteract the effects of the mass media.

As a result of the new sociology, 'the social assumptions underlying compensatory education, meaningful curricula for non-academic school leavers and mathematics for all can become the object of inquiry. We are forced into an often uncomfortable re-examination of the content and underlying assumptions of the curriculum at all levels.'[14] Theoretical weaknesses in the earlier sociological discussion of opportunity are discussed or implied in some of the main contributions to educational discussion in this period. Three collections of papers – Earl Hopper's *Readings in the Theory of Educational Systems* (1971), Michael F. D. Young's *Knowledge and Control* (1971) and Richard Brown's *Knowledge, Education and Cultural Change* (1973) – made similar and often overlapping attempts to draw a new map of the sociology of education. In the main, contributors rejected the framework of discussion we have illustrated in previous sections in favour of new approaches to the analysis of educational processes. Whether sociologists and historians will in general accept the view that concern with the promotion of equal opportunity has been a concern with what Gorbutt calls 'establishment problems' remains to be seen.

Much of the criticism of the equal opportunity movement loses its point, in fact, when one looks at the directions the movement itself has taken, particularly with regard to the concept of positive discrimination. The emergence of experiments with and discussion of the 'community school', for example, is one of the most important

---

[14] David Gorbutt, 'The new sociology of education', *Education for Teaching*, No. 89 (1972), pp. 5, 8.

signs of advance in this period. The account of developments in
this area in Halsey's *Educational Priority*, and reports of community
school projects in a number of EPA and other areas, indicate new
approaches to school-parent-child relationships, a new interpretation
of the relationship between school and community for positive ends.
Eric Midwinter summarizes these relationships:

> The Community School . . . attempts to relate fluently and pro-
> ductively with the ethos, character and values of the community
> it serves. . . . The Community School ventures out into the com-
> munity. The Community School welcomes in the community.
> Ideally, the barriers would collapse completely. . . . Gone would
> be the seclusion of the traditional English school, with children
> drawn in and instructed behind closed doors and high walls. The
> Community School requires a highly socialized format because it
> has a social rather than an academic aim. Its long-term purpose
> is to equip the critical parent, worker, consumer and citizen of
> the next generation, in the hope that that generation might
> respond creatively to the challenge of deprivation. It is an attempt
> to break the poverty cycle, in which deprived parents have bred
> deprived children in deprived situations to become, in turn, the
> deprived parents of deprived children.[15]

It is likely that strategies of positive discrimination along lines such
as these, the policies of regional and local economic and educational
authorities, and the theoretical assumptions underlying educational
processes will be primary objects of attention 'next Monday'.

[15] Eric Midwinter, *Priority Education* (Harmondsworth, 1972), p. 22.

D. F. SWIFT (1968)

Social class and educational adaptation*

The concept of social class has become one of the vital weapons in the armoury of educational analysts. It would be unthinkable, nowadays, to avoid applying it in a book which reviews our present state of research in education. Whatever the educational problem, somewhere the analyst will have to deal with his material in terms of how social class factors influence it. But does this mean that research workers in education have found a sharp new instrument which greatly improves our understanding? In one way, it does; but in another, it does not. Certainly, during the last decade, ideas about social class have played an important part in our ability to *describe* what is going on in the educational system. On the other hand, the concept is neither new nor sharp. The intention behind this paper will be to emphasize the bluntness of the instrument without destroying confidence in the work it has already done.

First of all, then, what has it done? At the very simplest level it has shown that the impact of the system of formal education differs in different strata of societies. Because in social analysis all associations are assumed to be reciprocal, and because it is clearly true, we have to say that the different strata of society also have different kinds of effects upon the functioning of the educational system.

To put these ideas in a proper context, we must start with a model of society in our heads. It is important to realize that we will do this whether we intend to or not; that is, if we ignore a sociological perspective when we are thinking about education, we will be implicitly *assuming* things about how society functions. There will be a model implicitly contained in what we say. Occasionally this may not matter, but when we are dealing with such a social concern as education it is usually dangerous. It is sensible, therefore, to bring these implicit ideas out into the open, so as to ensure that they are as reasonable as we can make them.

* Reprinted from *Educational Research in Britain*, ed. H. J. Butcher (London, University of London Press, 1968).

Let us think of society as a system of interrelated parts. To simplify matters we will think of only its major parts – its institutions.
These institutions are patterns of action and of values which have
grown up in response to major needs of the whole society.

Thus, we have an institution of education consisting of patterns
of action and of values which have produced a set of material arti-
facts – buildings and equipment. The major function of this sub-
system is to transmit the beliefs, habits and skills of thought and
action which exist or are believed to be needed in society. At the
same time, we have certain regularized ways of arranging for the
distribution of power in society, which we call the 'political sphere'.
We have an institution known as 'the family' which attempts to
provide for sexual needs, the procreation of children and their
initiation into society. How far we would wish to go in drawing up
a list of such institutions would depend upon ourselves; but certainly the list would always contain these three basic institutions and
the economy. The crucial point about all of them is that the patterns
of behaviour which earn them their names are, to some extent,
devised deliberately by the members of the society. We make rules
and attempt to enforce them. We insist that one man should have
one vote, one wife, some schooling and only his own money.

In addition to the formal structures, we can also see similar regu-
larities which are not backed by a structure of formal rules, but which
otherwise are similar in that they are reasonably distinct and fundamental patterns of action and values. Perhaps the two most important
ones are religion and stratification. All these great institutions of
society together form a structure which is rather like the skeleton of
a ferro-concrete building. They are the backbone of society.

We now have the basis for a crude model of a functioning society.
It comprises a number of people knowing, doing and valuing. What
they know and do, and how they value what they know and do, is
not just a disordered jumble of unconnected items. It forms interacting patterns which are relatively stable and hence predictable. The
mutual influencing which goes on between these patterns we can call
the 'social process'. We attempt to isolate an aspect of this social
process when we ask questions like, 'Why do dockers' children do
less well at school than the children of doctors?', or 'Why do we
insist upon a school engaging in daily prayers?', or 'What are the

consequences of teaching through note-taking?', or even 'Why does Johnny always play the fool in class?' This paper must deal with the way in which the system of stratification influences the system of education and vice versa. And this is why the instrument of class analysis cannot be called new. Such questions have been asked and sometimes even answered by many great educational thinkers. Plato himself devised a scheme whereby a system of stratification might be wedded to a system of education with what he hoped would be desirable consequences.

However, since the mid fifties a kind of class analysis has been used simply to describe how the stratification and educational characteristics of individuals have tended to coincide. This has been important simply because it showed that factors from a system of stratification were clearly related to aspects of educational consequences which were neither intended nor thought to be desirable (Banks 1958, Floud et al. 1956, Little and Westergaard 1964, Ministry of Education 1954). For example, the Crowther Report (Ministry of Education 1959–60) found that two-thirds of the second highest ability group (out of six – hence reasonably 'able' children) left school at fifteen, and that 80 per cent of them came from manual worker homes. The best descriptive study on these lines was reported by a medical research worker (Douglas 1964), who showed that in a sample of all the children in England children of the upper middle class get three times as many selective (eleven-plus) places as children of the lower manual, twice as many as children of the upper manual and one and a half times as many as 'white-collar' children *when comparing children of equal verbal reasoning ability.*

This, then, is the major contribution to knowledge which has been made through the use of social class as an analytical tool. Chances of receiving and accepting education, however it is defined, are biased according to social class. . . .

Let us return for a moment to the system of stratification in our simple model of society in process. Stratification simply relates to a hierarchy of inequality. It is clear that there exists in our society (many sociologists would say in *all* societies) a series of hierarchies of inequalities. The three obvious hierarchies are those to do with income, prestige and power. (There are also others which relate to, say, height or strength, but these are best dealt with as attributes of

individuals rather than of societies.) While it is true that we can distinguish *analytically* between these three hierarchies in any society, it
is impossible to make a distinction between them in actual life. Power
tends to go with income, which tends to go with prestige, and so on.
A great deal of fairly fruitless effort has been expended in attempting
to find the most important or perhaps even prime mover of the
three elements. For our purposes there is no need to pursue that
debate. The important point is that when a sociologist wishes to
study the stratification system of a particular society, he has to
specify how he will define it. How he does this will depend upon the
kind of analysis he has in mind. Therefore, we must ask ourselves
what relation we want stratification to bear to the education system.

First, we must take a societal view of the process so as to minimize
the danger of analytical myopia – which is an inability to see the wood
because of the trees. We see the whole of society as a process in
which patterns of behaviour and of valuing can be seen to be related
to and to influence each other. This is social structural analysis. We
think of the stratification system (of whatever kind) and the educational system as sub-systems of the wider social system. The ways
in which they influence and adapt to each other are aspects of the
integration of society. As an over-simplified example, we can see that
the present class-chances picture of educational selection indicates the
support which the education system gives the stratification system.

On the other hand – and this is the psycho-dynamic approach – we
have to ask how experience in other sub-systems affects the adaptation *of an individual* to education. In doing this, we can expect to
find that the problems which it sets him will be influenced by the
problems it encounters in adapting to its own environment. Adaptation by an individual to a system is a problem of psycho-dynamics
and a textbook of educational psychology would concentrate upon it.
However, to the extent that such a discipline aims to improve the
practice of education, it is a dangerous thing to do. Taking the education system and its adaptation to society as given involves concentrating upon the problems of adaptation it raises for individuals. But
these very problems may be aspects of its own adaptation to the
wider social structure, and as such may be better solved at that level.
This is not necessarily so, but to assume that it was not so would
deprive the analyst of the chance of ever finding out.

The distinction between the psycho-dynamics of adaptation to education and social structural analysis is not purely academic. It has important consequences for the interpretation of observed data, in that it is an important aspect of the definition of variables. It is also the cause of problems of interpretation which have arisen between psychologically and sociologically oriented researches. In this paper a conceptual framework will be put forward which is suitable to the perspectives of both disciplines.

Basically, the class-chances kind of head-counting has thrown us back upon explicit or implicit social-psychological theories about the adaptation of individuals to social situations. We have looked at data which shows that children of middle-class parents had six times as good a chance of selection at eleven-plus as working-class children (Swift 1965) and added some explanations for it which amount to a fairly unorganized amalgamation of single associations. The class-chances picture came about because potentially clever people have potentially clever children. They teach them to value education, and they teach them ways of behaving which will make them successful at school. Unfortunately, some of these ideas can be contradictory. Parents who force children to work hard will have more successful children than those who do not (Drews and Teahan 1957, Swift 1967). On the other hand, children from democratic (i.e. 'nice') homes also appear to be more successful than those from non-democratic (Clausen and Williams 1963, Elder 1963, Fraser 1959, Griffiths 1959).

The point is that the number of potential single variables is limitless. For example, Orme (1965) found an association between climatic temperature changes during foetal development and subsequent ability. Clearly the associations a research worker finds will always be partly a function of what he chooses to treat as data. However, social class has been shown to matter so often that we must be on to something. But what is it? Clearly, we must see social class as some kind of structuring of human experience which has consequences for the learning of social and cognitive behaviour.

The important questions from a psycho-dynamic point of view must be formulated in the following way. By what means does the structuring of social experience develop cognitive, cathectic and evaluative[1] skills and habits in children? Which aspects of this structuring foster the development of which kinds of skills and habits? Which skills and habits make adapting to the process of formal education easier?

The role of social class analysis in the formulation of questions such as these is fairly obvious. Social classes are social structures according to which experience is organized. Its value in research terms will lie in the extent to which it allows variables to be grouped. The aim of scientific research is to measure all possible stimulus variables efficiently, so as to either control or to randomize them. It only remains, then, to manipulate a single independent variable with a view to observing the consequences upon the dependent one. Ideally this is done by experiment or by statistical manipulation of data. Unfortunately, this state can never be reached in social research. It will always be possible to refine down our analysis of stimuli to the point at which we have discarded sociological or psychological descriptions of them and are concentrating upon physiological ones. These, in turn, could then be refined down into molecular structure analysis, and so on. No sociologist and few psychologists would be prepared to accept that the content of his own discipline can be reduced to that of sub-atomic physics.

Use of the concept social class, therefore, is a categorizing device which will have some value at a particular stage in the analysis of cognitive development, but which may be replaced as our ability to define the stimulus content of social class experience improves. On the other hand, from the point of view of sociological analysis, the concept will never become redundant, since it is related to an aspect of the societal structure. For our purposes, however, we need to think about what is contained in the social class structuring of experience for the individual. To do this we must return to its definition. It is a set of interacting hierarchies of inequality. Principally we said that inequalities of income, power and prestige were the most important.

---

[1] These are three terms used by sociologists to describe how an individual responds to his environment. They see the actor as having to make three kinds of response-channelling definitions. Cognition involves defining what is actually there, cathectic ideas indicate to him whether or not he derives pleasure from it, and evaluative ideas tell him whether he values it as good or bad.

What consequences for the developing child follow from differences in social experience? Perhaps the neatest of the early British studies on this question was carried out by Fraser (1959), who showed that a whole range of environmental factors related with scholastic achievement at age eleven. All these could have been described as consequences of stratification (Swift 1966). By this we mean that differential access to income, prestige and power in society appears to induce styles of life which bear a clear relation to school achievement. The fact that the different social classes have different ways of living is too obvious to have to debate – it is one of the recurring themes in our literature. But these different styles of life are not simply settings within which people function. They are one way of describing *how* people function; that is, we can separate the members of different social strata according to the cognitive, cathectic and evaluative habits and skills they employ. Individually, the habits and skills will be a partial consequence of their social experience. And this will follow from their access to participation in the social process, which is based upon their position in the system of stratification.

Consequently, when we divide a population according to the occupation followed by the head of each family, we are not attempting to measure a single stimulus variable in the way that we might measure an electrical charge being applied to a rat in a maze. A much better analogy to the maze situation could be produced if we had a number of mazes comprising many different kinds of problems and hence different kinds of environments. . . .

The point underlying the theoretical perspective upon stratification is that *when we are concerned with describing the social environment of individuals and relating it to their development*, a social class must be looked upon as a summarizing variable and not an effective influencing factor. As one of the foremost exponents of social class analysis has written:

> social class has proved to be so useful a concept because it refers to more than simply educational level, or occupation, or any of the large number of correlated variables. It is so useful because it captures the reality that the intricate interplay of all these variables creates different basic conditions of life at different levels of the

social order. Members of different social classes, by virtue of enjoying (or suffering) different conditions of life, come to see the world differently – to develop different conceptions of social reality, different aspirations and hopes and fears, different conceptions of the desirable (Kohn 1963, p. 471).

Even this is an over-simplification, because social classes do not exist as discrete entities around which it is possible to draw clear boundaries. They are analytical abstractions from reality. In real life, the boundaries shade into each other and are obscured by the presence of other social abstractions describing other factors. While it is analytically reasonable to think of the sub-culture of a social class, we can equally well distinguish a sub-culture founded upon regional factors or sheer historical accident (Roach and Gursslin 1967). It would be a great mistake to equate, for example, the working-class fisherman sub-culture of Hull with the working-class miner sub-culture of south Wales. Nevertheless, Kahan *et al.* (1966) have produced some recent proof that the simple split between white-collar and manual jobs is a subjectively real one in the British population. . . .

This paper has attempted to develop a perspective, according to which the well-known head-counting association between social class and variations in school achievement may be used as a basis for investigation of the social and psychological processes which go to make up the system of education. The crucial distinction to be made is that between social class analysis as an aspect of societal functioning and the influence of cultural experience upon educational adaptiveness of the child.

Once we begin to concentrate upon the latter kind of question, we must place the social class background of the child in its proper context of other aspects of his culture. For example, the local community and its culture, his religion, his family structure, his peer-group and so on are all important aspects of the total cultural experience which 'produces' him before he goes to school and which influences his responses to the demands of school when he starts going to it. There is a large amount of British and American research which can provide data on the extent to which family background can be said to influence ideas about education and the need to achieve in it. But this is only the superficial aspect of the process of adaptation. We have also to consider how cultural experience provides the individual with the cognitive, cathectic and evaluative habits of thought which are important in the process of education. When we have done this, we will be in a better position to decide whether the explicit and implicit demands of the school system, as they are manifested in consequences upon children, are relevant to our aims for education.

GEORGE TAYLOR AND N. AYRES (1969)

Born and bred unequal*

In the northern region, earnings and personal incomes are low, families tend to be large and unemployment is above average. Since rateable value is low, income available to local authorities is below average despite rate support grant designed to even out local authority income. Opportunities for earning a high income are limited and variety of employment for school leavers is similarly limited. Migration from the region has continued over a long period; the exodus has included the more able, ambitious and highly skilled. In the Tyneside conurbation, in particular, health is below average, housing standards are low, school buildings far from modern.

The majority of children leave school early. The region produces a large number of teachers (many of whom migrate on completion of training) though only a small number of graduates. The combined effect of migration, environmental deficiencies and lack of educational opportunities has resulted in a generation of parents whose level of education is low. Their understanding of the need for change and of the long term advantages of education is inevitably limited.

The major environmental problem of the north-western region, second only to that of the low level of personal and public income, is housing. All three contribute to a high rate of ill health and mortality;

* Reprinted from *Born and Bred Unequal* (London, Longmans, 1969).

in spite of massive migration, unemployment has been persistent
over a long period: families are large: supporting health services are
insufficient. Because a large proportion of schools date back to the
last century, the need for replacement schools is greater here than
anywhere else in the country. The number of children remaining
at school for extended courses is larger than in the northern region
but not noticeably so. Like the northern region, the north-west is a
major producer of teachers though it takes up less than its due share
of university places. Social, educational and environmental inequalities between one area and another within the region are marked. The
outstanding feature of the region is the concentration of every conceivable unfavourable environmental factor in the two large con-
urbations. Although they produce disastrous effects on education,
the problems are not primarily educational nor can they be solved
by educational reform.

The Yorkshire and Humberside region is divided into two distinct
parts which have little in common. To combine them into one region
was imaginative, but the Economic Planning Council lacks the
necessary powers to proceed with the creative planning this combination demands. To the east is an area suitable for development; on
the west is a conurbation of early industrial origin where housing,
schools and environment are of a low standard. Industry, lacking in
variety, has been declining for many years and is likely to decline
still further; unemployment has been avoided only as a result of
migration. General education, except for the most able, has perhaps
never been highly prized; on the other hand, vocational education is
valued and much sought after. Every authority has its technical college working in close co-operation with industry; in the past,
authorities have met the needs of local industry by devoting relatively
more of their resources to vocational education for evening study
and day release than to schools; the region has one of the highest
proportions of young people engaged in full- or part-time courses in
colleges of further education. With this background it is hardly
surprising that children do not remain at school in any great numbers. Earnings of manual workers are low, a moderate standard of
living being achieved only because there is a large proportion of
working mothers – a traditional feature of long standing. There are
few inducements to attract new industry and few opportunities for

varied employment; industry has become stagnant and highly skilled workers have left the area. Workers are slow to change and to appreciate that local manufactures are declining; as parents, they have not yet understood that extended education has replaced apprenticeship in the modern type of industry or that vocational education demands a sound general education. Elected representatives serving on the many local education authorities in the region have similarly failed to realize the place of education in the industrial future of the region.

Perhaps the most remarkable and largely unexpected discovery of this survey relates to the Midlands. In terms of material prosperity, the two Midlands regions are comparable with the south-eastern and southern regions – the alignment known as the London–Birmingham axis. Earnings and personal incomes are high, unemployment is practically unknown, industry is varied and persistently short of labour. Yet in attitude to education, both east and west Midlands compare unfavourably with two of the three northern regions even though they lack the extenuating circumstances of poverty and unfavourable environment experienced in the north. It is true that lack of prosperity and of a favourable environment in the Birmingham conurbation is commensurate with similar factors in the north but, limited in extent, they do not account for the general unwillingness of children in the two regions to take advantage of educational opportunities. Is this a failure on the part of the schools to make children aware of the long term benefits of education or are the schools unable to counteract the attraction of well paid employment?

There is little lack of ability on the part of Midland parents to support children at school beyond the normal leaving age; nor are the children's earnings needed to maintain the family's standard of living. This is especially true of the east Midlands where, with a long record of prosperity, there is little industry or environment deriving from an earlier industrial age. The west Midlands conurbation, however, possesses special features, not to be found in the remainder of the two regions. Towns and industries are declining, migration has taken place and the average level of education among adults is lower than anywhere in the country.

A feature common to both Midland regions has been the persistent shortage of teachers; a shortage that is particularly serious in the conurbation. The regions not only fail to retain children at school (thus losing potential talent) but they also fail to persuade young people to train as teachers or to enter universities. Dependent on recruiting teachers from other regions, schools are chronically understaffed. The Midlands, therefore, do not conform to the general proposition that variation in educational opportunity is related to income per head. The underlying causes of the lack of conformity require further investigation.

East Anglia is one of the few examples in England of a rural and dispersed population where opportunity is restricted by geographical factors. The population is remarkably healthy, reasonably prosperous and environmentally well favoured. Opportunities for school leavers are restricted, the nature of the openings available to young people who have undertaken extended or higher education is outside the experience of most parents. One would suspect that there is much unexploited talent in the region. The proposed development of several centres of population may alter, within a generation, the whole attitude of the region towards education.

The southern regions, comprising just under half the country's population, evince a positive attitude to education deriving, probably, more from a realization of the material advantages it brings than from an appreciation of the social benefits of an educated community. In most parts of the three regions educational and environmental conditions are favourable: well educated and prosperous parents: new schools adequately staffed and equipped: variety of employment: few legacies of the industrial revolution. Consequently the majority of children are able to realize their potentialities, although it is possible that the less able child is no better catered for than elsewhere – in view of the generally higher standards of achievement he may, in fact, be more conscious of failure.

The three regions are not, however, as homogeneous as statistics would suggest. Greater London, for example, is a microcosm of the country as a whole, containing within its area contrasts as great as those between a declining northern town and an expanding one in the south. To the east are boroughs such as Newham, which has sustained a severe decline in population during the last thirty years, where the balance is heavily weighted towards the lower social classes and the environment is unfavourable. To the west are boroughs such as Richmond and Kingston upon Thames, where children not only have good environmental and educational facilities, but also possess the advantages of living in close proximity to the Metropolis – advantages especially important for those with special gifts in such fields as music and the arts.

Outside London, the southern and south-eastern regions are not uniformly prosperous. Hastings has a high unemployment rate with few opportunities for school leavers; relative depression does not appear, however, to affect adversely the desire of the more able to remain at school or their entry to higher education. About its effect on the less able there is no information. County areas in the southern region are predominantly rural and too far from centres of population for further education to be readily available. As in the eastern region, there may well be untapped sources of talent. The booming towns and cities of the south-west – Bath, Bristol, Gloucester – conform to the general picture of the southern regions; the remainder of the region suffers from the drawbacks of remoteness and isolation that reduce parental aspirations and children's expectations. The able seize the opportunities for higher education and subsequent employment elsewhere: the less able have to be content with the education offered by the immediate locality.

Regional inequalities and their effect on educational opportunity have been more fully investigated in France than in any other European country, and French educational reforms have included a serious attempt to lessen the differences arising from geographical location. In a paper submitted to an international conference sponsored by OECD in 1961, Monsieur Jean Ferrez, deputy director of the General Organization and Programming Department (the Government agency in France responsible for this investigation) described the educational plan and the methods of inquiry on which it was based. Among the criteria used was the secondary school attendance rate in the ninety-three departments. Further analysis having revealed that the average rate for departments concealed major differences between areas within a department, a systematic survey was made to define areas of poor attendance and to discover the reasons for variation. The rural factor proved to be decisive in determining whether children continued their education beyond the compulsory stage. Among exceptions to the general findings was the Pas de Calais, a department which, although it is neither rural nor of low density population, had one of the lowest secondary attendance rates. Its distinguishing feature is that it is a mining area, 50 per cent of the working population being engaged in the industry. This is a special case that serves to emphasize the effect of social environment on educational opportunity. In introducing his paper Monsieur Ferrez made the important observation that 'the fact that educational opportunity varies from one region to another so that a child's chances of getting the education he deserves are better or worse, other things being equal, according to where he lives, is one of the proofs that untapped reserves of ability exist'. From the work done in France it is clear that planning for equality on a geographical basis depends upon adequate statistical services, a knowledge of demographic trends and the availability of precise and detailed data relating to units considerably smaller than the region.

In surveying the findings of the conference, Dr A. H. Halsey noted that it was generally agreed that

> the problems of regional inequalities, and especially of educational backwardness of rural areas are a common major obstacle to the mobilization of human resources ... behind the label 'regional inequalities' lies a complex of social, economic and cultural forces which require a comprehensive policy for their amelioration going beyond educational reform to include, as the French plan does, vocational guidance, demographic analysis, regional and community planning and, in short, a wide range of social policy.

The data given in the previous chapters support this summary of the position though the scene in this country differs in important ways from that in most European countries. Although rural areas present problems in the provision of opportunity, the number of children involved is small; England is essentially composed of an urban population, living in or within easy reach of a town. The single most important factor affecting opportunity is the industrial age of a region or an area.

Although statistics in this country are not, in general, compiled on the basis of small units, some do exist in this form as a result of historical accident. The north-western region is unusually well documented because the many towns in the region, dependent on one of the major manufacturing industries of the nineteenth century, were well established as all-purpose local authorities by the beginning of this century. This applies also to the eastern part of the northern region: for the mining areas of Durham and the industrial parts of Cumberland, comparable information cannot, however, be isolated from regional data. Adequate documentation is available for the west Midlands conurbation, largely composed of all-purpose authorities, similar in origin to those in the north-west. Yorkshire is unevenly recorded; statistics are available for a number of comparatively small towns in the conurbation which are, by historical accident, county boroughs. Data for the county area of the West Riding are of limited value; the county area contains not only a considerable rural population but also sizeable industrial communities, mining villages in the south Yorkshire coalfield together with commuter towns such as Harrogate and Ilkley. County statistics describe neither the progress of education in the more favoured areas nor the educational shortcomings of communities adversely affected by dereliction, closed pits and stagnant industry.

There is little information of an educational nature for new towns or for suburban areas in the commuter belts surrounding large centres of population. The recent establishment of new authorities such as Solihull county borough and the outer London boroughs provide useful pointers to the probable nature of education statistics for prosperous suburban areas and to their effect on the statistics of the region in which they are situated. The small number of sizeable centres of population – and hence of local education authorities – in the south-west conceals inequalities; Cornwall contains no education authority other than the county authority. It is, therefore, impossible to assess the effect of sparseness of population, of poor communications and of the absence of a centre for cultural activities on the educational development of the various communities within the county. In the same region, wealthy towns such as Exeter and expanding towns like Bristol, Bath and Gloucester, raise regional averages and render them useless for a valid assessment of the opportunities available to Cornish school children.

A survey of the distribution of educational and environmental inequalities is, therefore, inevitably limited in scope – it must be far less thorough than has proved possible in France. One effect of the probable reorganization of local government into larger administrative units could well be that, from a statistical point of view, areas of unfavourable environment will disappear out of sight, but not out of existence. Unless deliberate action is taken, figures compiled for large units will fail to record local deficiencies, extremes of high and low standards will counterbalance one another within an overall picture based on averages. It is to be hoped that regulations arising out of local government reorganization will include a mandatory requirement that statistics for small units of population shall be made regularly, quickly and publicly available. Only in this way will inequalities be kept before the general public as well as in the forefront of the minds of framers of national and regional policy.

Whatever form local government reorganization takes, it is abundantly clear that administrative units in the three northern regions and in the south-west will remain less wealthy than those in other regions. Internationally, it is recognized that variations in educational opportunity reflect, at least in part, disparities in national income per head. This is no less true of local government units in this country. The league table for inequality follows closely the pattern of local authority and personal incomes per head; in their turn, these are largely related to the industrial age of the locality.

This survey, it is hoped, throws light on the complex nature and the outstanding problems of educational opportunity. Too often educationists, sociologists and politicians tend to think of opportunity in terms of O and A level passes and entry to higher education. In limiting the concept of opportunity to academic ability and in considering solely the wastage of talent, they fail to appreciate the multitude of skills, interests and avocations that exist and are needed in modern society. It is true that to pursue these a sound general education is a prerequisite, but this cannot be measured by any of the currently available yardsticks; the absence of varied vocational education in an area may be a more serious bar to opportunity than the shortcomings of schools and environment. Educational opportunity might best be regarded as the provision of social, environmental and educational conditions that will enable an individual child to realize his potential.

JULIENNE FORD (1969)

Social class and the comprehensive school*

(I) ABILITY AND OPPORTUNITY

Despite the conclusion of Floud, *et al.*, in 1956 that, if measured intelligence was taken as a criterion, then the social class distribution of grammar school places was equitable, Douglas has more recently shown that a problem of social class bias in selection still does exist. The working-class pupil must typically have a slightly higher IQ than the middle-class one in order to stand the same chance of selection for grammar school, simply because working-class areas tend to have smaller proportions of grammar school places than their IQ distributions would justify. It is widely believed that comprehensive reorganization will go some way towards ameliorating this situation, that the extent of 'wastage of talent' or 'uneducated capacity' will be reduced and that, in fact, *'Comprehensive schools will provide greater equality of opportunity for those with equal talent'*.

Now in order to test this and the remaining three hypotheses a sample of pupils in comprehensive and tripartite schools was required. A number of considerations affected the selection of this sample. In the first place, in order for any generalizations to be valid it was necessary to find a comprehensive school which was both typical of the majority of comprehensive schools in England today, and which had been established long enough for the majority of its pupils to have been attending that school for the whole of their secondary education. In addition to these basic criteria it was considered essential that this school be relatively 'uncreamed', drawing almost all the secondary age pupils in the catchment area. For, while the *typical* comprehensive school today *is* creamed of the top levels of ability by neighbouring grammar schools, the theory that we are examining concerns the effects of large scale comprehensive

---

* Reprinted from *Social Class and the Comprehensive School* (London, Routledge and Kegan Paul, 1969).

reorganization. It is therefore desirable to simulate as far as possible the conditions which will obtain when (as seems likely) the whole of the public sector of secondary education is reorganized in this way. In this respect, then, the criterion of typicality was abandoned in order to do justice to the ideals of the comprehensivists who rightly claim that where creaming occurs the basic principle of comprehensivization – a common education for all – is lost.

The problem thus became one of locating a well-established relatively uncreamed comprehensive school of more or less average size which also embraced three characteristics typical of English comprehensives: some system of horizontal organization on the basis of ability groupings (streams), some system of vertical organization unrelated to ability (houses), and co-education. *'Cherry Dale' Comprehensive* was just such a school.

Cherry Dale school stands on a relatively isolated housing estate somewhere in the inner London area. Built to serve the children from the estate, it is certainly a neighbourhood school, for only 1 or 2 per cent from every year's production of eleven year olds 'go away' to school. The neighbourhood, like most neighbourhoods in urban England, does tend to be socially homogeneous – the majority of the children come from backgrounds which can be described as working-class – however a sufficient proportion of middle-class children attend the school to allow comparisons to be made.

Cherry Dale is in its physical appearance typical of modern comprehensives. The buildings are light and colourful, there are sports facilities, a swimming pool, a 'flat' where girls practise domestic science, and all kinds of facilities for scientific, technical and art education. But it is also typical in its academic organization. The school is organized both into academic streams or teaching groups on the basis of ability and into the mixed ability groupings called houses and house-tutor groups. ... It is important at this stage to note that in Cherry Dale, as in most comprehensives, the actual teaching takes place in academic streams. There are, in effect, seven of these teaching groups in each year group, the first two (A_1 and A_2) being 'grammar streams', the next two (B_1 and B_2) covering the upper-middle ability range and the lower streams (C_1 and C_2) being mainly practical in orientation; the final stream (D) is a remedial group.

Having selected a suitable comprehensive school, the problem of choosing tripartite schools for purposes of comparison was precisely delimited. For, in order to control as many confounding variables as possible, it was necessary to find two schools which closely 'matched' Cherry Dale in relevant respects. *'Gammer Wiggins' Grammar School* and *'South Moleberry' Secondary Modern* were therefore selected as suitable coeducational tripartite schools in similar working-class areas of inner London.

The sample comprised the complete fourth years of these three schools: 320 fourteen- to fifteen-year-old boys and girls. Questionnaires were administered to the children in their form groups (or, in the case of Cherry Dale School, their academic streams), in an ordinary classroom during lesson time, and were completed under supervision. In this way the problem of bias from non-response was virtually eliminated, for all the children present returned a questionnaire and it was possible to ensure that practically all of these were completed fully.

The most obvious way of testing the hypothesis on this sample is by analysis of the interaction of social class and measured intelligence as determinants of academic attainment in the three schools. For we know that, under the traditional system of secondary education, the impact of social class on educational attainment is greater than can be explained by the covariation of class and IQ. In other words, under the tripartite system opportunities for those with equal ability (defined as IQ) are not equal and the inequalities are related to social class. If the hypothesis were correct, then we would expect IQ to be a greater determinant, and social class a lesser determinant of educational attainment in comprehensive than in tripartite schools.

Now a number of writers have suggested that, where comprehensive schools employ some system of academic streaming (as most of them do) this may not be the case. Thus, on the basis of a study of about 800 comprehensive schoolchildren, Holly concluded that 'Streaming by ability within the comprehensive school does not seem . . . to result in producing a new élite based on attainment or intelligence quotients: it seems merely to preserve the traditional class basis of educational selection'. Yet the comprehensive enthusiast might well reply that, since no one would maintain that comprehensive schools eliminate class bias in educational attainment completely, the more interesting question is whether such schools are *relatively* more effective in this respect.

Some light can be thrown on this question by examination of the social class and I Q composition of the fourth year streams in the three schools considered here.

Social class was determined by responses to the simple question 'What is your father's job?', accompanied by the verbal instruction 'Imagine that you are explaining to a new friend what your father does, try to give as much information as you can'. The information given was in almost all cases sufficient to enable responses to be classified according to occupational prestige. Of course father's occupation as reported by a child is not the best possible measure of social class. A more precise classification could be produced from an *index* including assessments of income, life styles and the education of both parents as well as occupational prestige. But occupational prestige is certainly the best single *indicator*. For its use is based on the reasonable sociological assumption that, since the work role is such a time-consuming one, it is in terms of this that people evaluate one another. Furthermore, owing to the necessity to control several variables simultaneously in the following analysis, the social class variable has simply been dichotomized. And several studies have shown that the most socially significant and meaningful social class classification is a simple non-manual/manual division.

The sample was also dichotomized according to I Q scores. Since such scores are artificially created to represent comparable deviations from a norm of 100, those children with scores up to and including 100 were classified as of 'low I Q', and those with scores of 101 or more were classified as of 'high I Q'. However, as there were no children in the grammar school with scores of 100 or less, in order to assess the relationship between I Q and streaming in this school, the pupils were dichotomized at the median point. Thus for this group 'low I Q' refers to scores between 101 and 120, while 'high I Q' refers to scores of 121 or more.

Table 1 shows the relationship between social class, I Q and stream for the three schools.

TABLE I. *Social class and IQ composition of streams in the three schools*

| School | Stream | Middle class[b] | | Working class | | No. |
		High IQ[a] %	Low IQ %	High IQ[a] %	Low IQ %	(100 %)
Grammar	A	84	7	7	3	30
	B	60	20	20	0	25
	C	41	26	22	11	27
	D	20	0	47	33	15
Comprehensive	A	33	8	59	0	39
	B	4	9	56	31	46
	C	8	6	29	56	48
	D	0	10	10	79	19
Secondary modern	A	31	7	52	12	29
	B	11	22	44	22	18
	C	0	8	25	67	24

[a] That is 120+ for grammar school or 100+ for comprehensive and secondary modern schools.
[b] That is non-manual paternal occupation.

It can be seen from the table that in all three schools *both* social class and IQ are related to stream. However our interest is primarily in the extent to which the *relative* importance of social class and IQ as determinants of stream differs between the three schools. For this reason Table 2 has been derived from the above figures.

TABLE 2. *'High' IQs only : social class and 'A' stream placement in the three schools*

School	Middle class % placed in 'A' stream	Working class % placed in 'A' stream	p = [ ]
Grammar	46	10	0·01
Comprehensive	68	35	0·01
Secondary modern	82	52	n.s.

[a] 'A' stream compared with all other streams in a 2 × 2 chi-squared test of significance.

Table 2 shows the strength of the relationships between social class and selection for the 'A' stream *when IQ is held constant*. Only children with 'high IQs' are considered and the extent to which social class affects the chances of these children to be placed in the top streams of their schools is analysed. Thus, for example, 46 per cent of the middle-class children in the grammar school with 'high' IQs are placed in the 'A' stream, while only 10 per cent of the working-class children in the same ability range achieve this placement: a difference which is statistically significant. In the comprehensive school the relationship between social class and placement in the 'A' stream is still statistically significant for the 'high' IQ group, however in the secondary modern school, when IQ is controlled in this manner the relationship between stream and social class is reduced to insignificance.

The results of this comparison, then, give no support to the hypothesis. Indeed they tend to confirm the suspicions of Holly and others that selection on the basis of streaming in the comprehensive school, like selection under the tripartite system, tends to underline class differentials in educational opportunity. For in the comprehensive school, as in the grammar school, there appears to be a relationship between social class and 'A' stream placement over and above that which can be explained by the well-known correlation between social class and measured IQ. In other words, at the same ability level the middle-class child stands a greater chance of placement in the 'grammar' streams of a comprehensive school than the working-class child, a situation in one respect not substantially different from that which exists under the tripartite system.

Now it might be objected that to show that a class bias in stream placement exists in the comprehensive school is not necessarily to demonstrate that there are inequalities in educational attainment which relate to social class. For just possibly those children who have been placed in the lower streams of the comprehensive school will achieve the same eventual educational levels as those in the 'A' stream: stream might bear little relationship to level of education reached.

A good index of the extent to which this is the case can be derived by examination of the leaving intentions of the children experiencing the various forms of education. For, if a substantial proportion of those in the lower streams of the comprehensive school intend to stay on at school to follow fifth and sixth form courses, then one could argue that the class bias in streaming has little consequence for actual educational attainment. If, on the other hand, children in the lower streams of the comprehensive school resemble those in the secondary modern in their leaving intentions then clearly streaming has an impact on level of educational attainment and the class bias in streaming is certainly important. In Table 3, therefore, the leaving intentions of children in the three schools are compared.

TABLE 3. *Leaving intentions by school, comprehensive stream and social class*

School	Social class	% leaving in 4th year	% leaving in 5th year	% leaving in 6–8th years	No. (100%)
Grammar	Middle class	0	10	90	68
	Working class	0	28	72	29
Comprehensive	Middle class	0	50	50	16
'A' streams	Working class	0	87	13	23
Comprehensive	Middle class	20	60	20	15
'B–D' streams	Working class	40	56	4	98
Secondary	Middle class	32	47	21	19
modern	Working class	40	52	8	52

It can be seen from the table that streaming within the comprehensive school has a definite impact on leaving intentions, for all of the 'A' stream children intend to stay at least into the fifth form, while 13 per cent of the middle-class and 40 per cent of the working-class children in the lower streams intend leaving in the fourth year and therefore have no hope of sitting for GCE examinations. This is, of course, hardly surprising. For the 'A' streams have been following five-year courses specifically designed to terminate in GCE, and, while many of those in the 'B' and 'C' streams will sit CSE examinations none of those in the 'D' stream are expected to gain any formal qualifications at all. Streaming within a comprehensive school is thus an important determinant of educational attainment and for this reason the class inequalities in stream placement shown in Tables 1 and 2 are important.

Another interesting feature of Table 3 is the comparison of the comprehensive 'A' stream and the grammar school children. For the former represent the highest ability group in the comprehensive, chldren who might well have gone to a grammar school under the tripartite system, yet only 28 per cent of them intend staying into the sixth form. This compares with 85 per cent of grammar school children intending to stay at least one year in the sixth form – a difference which is highly significant ($X^2 = 40\cdot2$, $d.f. = 1$, $p = 0\cdot001$). This differential holds both for the working-class children ($X^2 = 18\cdot09$, $d.f. = 1$, $p = 0\cdot001$), and for the middle class ($X^2 = 14\cdot39$, $d.f. = 1$, $p = 0\cdot001$).

This raises in an acute form the question of 'wastage of ability' which was examined in the *Early Leaving Report*. For the table shows not only that 'home background influences the use which a boy or girl will make of a grammar school education' (18 per cent more middle- than working-class children staying on into the sixth form), but also that this same effect of home background can be observed in the comprehensive 'A' streams. For half the middle-class 'A' stream children in the sample and only 13 per cent of the working-class ones intended to stay beyond the fifth. Indeed it seems from these figures that this 'wastage' is even greater in the comprehensive than in the grammar school.

In order to investigate this alarming possibility it is necessary to compare the leaving intentions of those working-class children who are 'able' enough to profit from sixth form courses under the two systems. For this purpose 'able' children were arbitrarily defined as those with an I Q score of 111 or more – approximately the average level for grammar school pupils. The number of such children in the secondary modern school and comprehensive 'B' to 'D' streams was, of course, too small to be considered.

TABLE 4. *Working-class children with I Q scores of 111 or more : leaving intentions by type of schooling*

	Leaving in 5th year	Staying into sixth form	No.
	%	%	(*100*%)
Grammar School	31	69	23
Comprehensive 'A' stream	84	16	19
($X^2 = 10\cdot98$, $d.f. = 1$, $p = 0\cdot01$)			

The evidence from the three schools, then, far from revealing a greater equality of opportunity for the comprehensive school pupil, shows a persistence of class bias in educational attainment under the comprehensive system. Indeed there is some indication that 'wastage of ability' among bright working-class pupils may be occurring on an even larger scale in Cherry Dale comprehensive school than in Gammer Wiggins grammar school.

For where comprehensive school children are taught in ability groups or streams as nearly all of them are, the 'self-fulfilling prophecy' characteristic of the tripartite system is still very much in evidence. 'Ability' is itself related to social class, but middle-class children get an even larger share of the cake than their ability distribution would justify. The middle-class child is more likely than the working-class child to find himself in the 'grammar' stream at the comprehensive school, even where the two children are similar in ability. And even those working-class children who do succeed in obtaining 'A' stream placement are four times more likely than their middle-class counterparts to 'waste' that opportunity by leaving school without a sixth form education. Thus while, as we have seen . . . there is little evidence on the question of whether comprehensive reorganization of secondary education will promote a greater *development* of talent, there is some serious doubt whether it will decrease inequalities of opportunity for those with equal talent.

In short there is little evidence from this study of three schools that comprehensive education as it is practised at the present will modify the characteristic association between social class and educational attainment. Indeed one could argue that it can hardly be expected to do so. For, as C. Arnold Anderson has said, 'In order for schooling to change a status system schooling must be a variable.' In other words, for the relationship between social class and educational success to be destroyed it would not be sufficient to give every child the *same* chance. Working-class children, disadvantaged by their cultural background and inferior physical environs, would need to be given not the same but superior educational opportunities. Yet in the typical comprehensive school the average working-class child starts off with the same handicaps that would have lengthened the odds against his success under the old system. And the outcome of the race appears to be no less predictable.

(II) TOWARDS UTOPIA?

It has often been noted that while the separate schools of the tripartite system continue to 'feed' different occupational levels one
cannot hope for 'parity of esteem' and, given the political priorities
of most administrations, parity of material conditions is very unlikely. Yet it is perhaps not generally realized that this remains
true under a 'comprehensive' system. For, while the different
academic streams are 'feeding' different occupational rivers, prestige
and resources will be diverted accordingly. And in order to accomplish this selection most precisely the processes of evaluation and
differential training will begin early in secondary school life. For,
even in those few schools where formal streaming does not begin
in the first year, evaluation grading and sorting are going on all the
time. To this extent early selection is not being avoided and the
hoped for consequences of comprehensivization cannot possibly be
achieved.

Now William Taylor has pointed out that the most basic case to
be made out for reform of the tripartite system is not on 'educational'
or 'social' but moral and political grounds. It is, as we have seen . . .
a question of *justice*. For 'we no longer possess a criterion which will
legitimize early selection, allocation and the subsequent differentiation', no criterion is accepted as just. Yet the so-called 'comprehensive' education which is currently replacing tripartite does not
represent an abolition of this unjust selection. Selection, as we have
seen, still occurs within the comprehensive schools yet it is partly
concealed from the public. Under these circumstances discrimination and injustice may well continue unnoticed, for, as Young and
Brandis have pointed out, 'It will become more difficult to determine
how much is spent on whom. At least we know that more is spent
on the grammar school pupil – the accounts will be obscured in the
comprehensive school.' In the comprehensive school selection, allocation and differentiation still occur but are given 'a *prima facie*
rationality which will make it more difficult for the denied to complain. We must accept the point that the educational system can
produce only minimal changes in the world of work and that while
it accepts the task of being a selection agency for occupation, it is
crippled in its wider social functions.'

But, if early selection is an inevitable feature of any educational system which functions to allocate individuals to positions in the occupational structure, and if educational systems have always served as selection agencies for occupation, does not this bring us back to the second interpretation suggested above? Does it not imply that social change cannot be effected through educational reform, for the schools must always remain handmaidens of the occupational structure?

I would like to suggest that this is not necessarily the case. For it *is* possible to conceive of a school system which is freed of the distortions imposed by the selective function. Surely if we are to dream about Utopias (something which the proponents of 'comprehensive' reform have certainly been doing) then we must be much more imaginative. There is no point in tinkering with the type of selection which occurs in the schools, no point in replacing tripartite schools by schools which are no more than 'multilateral'. If we are to produce any change at all we must completely free the schools of their function as selection agencies for occupation.

But *could* a non-selective school system be devised?

RICHARD LYNN (1969)

Comprehensives and equality: the quest for the unattainable*

TRADITIONAL BRITISH EDUCATION

British education has been designed primarily to produce an intellectual élite. This is nothing to be ashamed of. Indeed, such an élite is necessary to keep going the intellectual and cultural tradition of European civilization. When it is finally destroyed, it does not seem

* Reprinted from *Black Paper Two*, ed. C. B. Cox and A. E. Dyson (London, Critical Quarterly Society, 1969).

at all unlikely that the tradition of civilization will be destroyed with
it. No doubt this is the intention of its critics.

There can be little dispute that the British system, now being dis-
mantled, has been exceptionally efficient for the purpose for which it
was designed. For instance, in the first mathematical schools olym-
piad held in 1967, the British schoolboy team came fourth out of the
twelve participating countries. The first three places were taken by
Russia, East Germany and Hungary, which maintain élite schools for
developing their most gifted children. What part in this notable
British achievement was played by boys from comprehensives? None
at all. The British team was selected by taking the best from about
240 schools which participated in the domestic mathematical olym-
piad. The best boys, who were selected for the team, came from
King Edward VI's school, Stafford, Manchester Grammar School,
Winchester and Eton. When the progressives finally have their way
and destroy these schools, it seems unlikely that Britain will be
able to put up any kind of a showing in these international contests.
The cleverest young English children, marking time in their unstreamed comprehensives, simply won't stand a chance.

THE AMERICAN EXPERIENCE

Mathematics is probably the best subject for making international
educational comparisons because the marking is objective and the
syllabus comparatively uniform from one country to another. The
most thorough investigation of achievements in mathematics has been
made recently by Professor T. Husén of the University of Stockholm, who has organized the administration of the same mathematics tests to large numbers of carefully chosen samples of children in
eleven countries. Among those specializing in mathematics at sixth
form level the British came second only to Israel, and here one is
competing against those excellent Jewish genes, as Lord Snow has
pointed out. Husén's results are shown in Table 1.

Let us note the very poor results from the American comprehensives. The low academic standards of American state schools are of
course a matter of common knowledge and have been demonstrated
in other investigations. For instance, Mr D. Pidgeon has published
results of the same arithmetic test given to large random samples of

TABLE I

Country	Mean mathematics score	Country	Mean mathematics score
Israel	36·4	Germany	28·8
England	35·2	Sweden	27·3
Belgium	34·6	Finland	25·3
France	33·4	Australia	21·6
Holland	31·9	United States	13·8
Japan	31·4		

eleven year olds in California and England. Out of a maximum score of 70, the English children scored 29·1 and the Californian children 12·1. This striking difference is statistically highly significant. Some of the details of the investigation may be of interest. For instance, 57 per cent of the English children could correctly divide pounds and ounces by 9, but only 11 per cent of Californian children could accomplish this. Sixty-one per cent of English children know what is half of 9½, but only 15 per cent of Californian children know this.

These dreadful American results must be ascribed to the comprehensive philosophy. This school of thought decries external examinations, which impose a discipline on teachers to ensure that their children pass. Progressive opinion is hotly indignant at teachers having to work to a discipline of this sort. They would rather teachers taught what they felt like without any external test to determine whether or not the children have learnt anything. The American results can also be regarded as a triumph of modern permissive methods in which boring facts like the number of ounces in a pound are no longer thought to matter. Mr Pidgeon, who is himself a supporter of comprehensive schools, attributes the difference between English and American schools partly to the comparative absence of formal teaching in California and partly to the fact that apparently California teachers themselves only know about as much arithmetic as English eleven year olds. The reason for this, according to Pidgeon, is that 'the subject is usually not taught in high school nor is it part of the mathematics syllabus in college'.

L

Such a situation is of course an inevitable development of the comprehensive principle. Since the majority find it hard to grasp the principles of fractions, compound interest and so forth, the simplest thing in unstreamed comprehensives is to drop these taxing subjects and concentrate on projects in which all can join. The standards of American education are surely the clearest indication of the levels to which British education will drop when the comprehensive principle has been long established. The results it produces are clear and indisputable.

It is true that there are some studies which purport to show that the academic results of British comprehensives are comparable to those of grammar schools. But this ignores the fact that Britain is at the present in a state of transition to full comprehensivization. The comprehensives are on their mettle to show that they can do as well as the grammar schools. They are still staffed by teachers who know some arithmetic, unlike their counterparts in California. With full comprehensivization and the destruction of independent schools, the challenge to provide some kind of quality education will disappear. The development of what is called in America 'the blackboard jungle' will drive the best teachers into other professions, so that the quality of teachers will fall. A generation or two ago people of the calibre of Mr Michael Stewart, the foreign secretary, entered the teaching profession, and similarly able people are still teaching in the public, direct grant schools and grammar schools. With complete comprehensivization, we can expect this to cease. Again, the United States shows the pattern of the future. In 1966 only 4 per cent of Harvard graduates entered school teaching (in the private schools?) as against 14 per cent from Cambridge. But Cambridge graduates do not for the most part go into comprehensives. They go into the grammar and public schools and when these are closed down, they will surely work elsewhere rather than in school teaching.

Thus the effect of comprehensivization will be a long term one, as the external disciplines of competition from a quality private sector and from national examinations are removed. The gradual lowering of the quality of staff and the enervating effects of monopoly will take a number of years to work itself out and will show itself progressively as high quality staff retire and are replaced by poorer quality entrants to the profession.

Consider the civilization of the United States: the quality of Peyton Place and Dr Kildare; the ubiquitous cacophony of canned music in supermarkets and restaurants; the horrors of Broadway and Hollywood; the lack of respect for authority and learning; the contemptuous dismissal of intellectuals as 'eggheads'. Is it not probable that these are partly the result of a comprehensive education system which has deliberately sacrificed quality and standards in an attempt to bring about social cohesion – an attempt which the present state of civil disorder in the United States shows to have been an abysmal failure? Those who think that comprehensives will foster love and tolerance between different social classes and groups can hardly be encouraged by present conditions in the United States.

The view may be taken that the United States is not as bad as all that and it may be felt that while academic standards in American comprehensives are unquestionably deplorable, American cultural achievement is at least respectable. Perhaps it may not make too much odds if children are brought up in the blackboard jungle? These wasted years are made up for by the universities; by the natural intelligence and temperament of a minority of children who discover cultural values for themselves; and by the transmission of the cultural tradition through certain upper-middle-class families. There may be some truth in such a view and certainly cultural values have survived and many gifted individuals have managed to discover these values for themselves throughout history with little help from schooling. Bertrand Russell, for example, never went to school and would no doubt have emerged unscathed from a comprehensive. Paradoxically, the destruction of quality education makes the transmission of cultural values through the family more important and thus places a greater handicap on the clever working-class child, the very individual whom comprehensives are meant to help.

But even if the view is taken that American cultural standards have not suffered too greatly from the low quality of their comprehensives, two points may be noted. One is that America has a small number of élite private schools, some of which teach Russian, Chinese, etc., and whose high standards bear comparison with the best English independent schools. Families like the Kennedys do not go to American comprehensives. The other point is that professional standards in America rely heavily on a brain drain educated largely in Europe, especially Britain. Now that Britain has become the poor relation among advanced countries she cannot afford to make up for the deficiencies of a poor educational system by buying professional manpower educated elsewhere, as the Americans do.

THE ROLE OF INTELLIGENCE

With the horrible example of American comprehensives before them, why are the British busily destroying their own excellent system of quality education and replacing it with American-style comprehensives? The answer is that a selective system is alleged to be unfair to the working class. This argument is to a considerable degree specious.

The factual basis of the argument is that working-class children do comparatively poorly in the eleven-plus examination, tend to be placed in the lower streams, have a low chance of entering a university and so forth. All this is true enough. But the next step is to blame this on the educational system. This is of course absurd. There are two principal reasons why working-class children, on average, do worse than middle-class children. One is that they are innately less intelligent (on average) and the other that their families provide a less suitable milieu for scholastic success. Neither of these will be changed to any appreciable degree by abolishing independent and grammar schools.

The progressives rarely even discuss the possibility that there might be class differences in innate intelligence. This is just as well, because once the possibility is raised it becomes obvious that it must be so. We know that intelligence is principally determined by inheritance. Even a psychologist like Mr D. Pidgeon, who as we have seen is a firm advocate of comprehensive schools, writes that 'the evidence is fairly conclusive that children are not born equally gifted intellectually'. The evidence is partly commonsense. Everyone with eyes to see must have noticed that where several children are brought up in the same family they generally differ quite considerably from each other. One is highly intelligent, conscientious, etc., while another is often rather average. Since they are brought up in the same conditions the obvious inference is that they must have been born with different genetic potentialities. More technical evidence comes from twin studies where identical twins separated soon after birth and brought up in different families have always been found closely similar in intelligence, just as they are in eye colour, blood grouping and so on. This again indicates the preponderant influence of heredity, and indeed this is a conclusion on which the great majority of psychologists are agreed.

Now for a good many centuries it has been possible for able people to rise in the social hierarchy. For example, Mr Harold Macmillan's grandfather was born in a croft on the island of Arran, but he made his way to London and by dint of hard work and ability established the family in the upper middle class. The historian Dicey drew attention to the considerable social mobility in Britain at the time of the industrial revolution, but this was not a new feature of English social life to emerge only in the last two centuries. For several hundred years intelligent people have risen from the working class into the middle class and, conversely, unintelligent people have dropped from the middle class into the working class.

The effect of this flexible social system is that the more intelligent genetic strains must have tended to become concentrated in the middle class. Of course this is only a tendency and does not apply to every single middle-class child. Some unintelligent children continue to be born into the middle class and some highly intelligent children into the working class. Nevertheless, on the average innate class differences in intelligence must certainly exist. They can be demonstrated directly by examining the IQs of adopted children. Those born to middle-class parents tend to be more intelligent than those born to working-class parents. Some experts have drawn attention to these facts. For instance, Dr C. O. Carter of the Clinical Genetics Research Unit at the London Institute of Child Health, noting that children of professional fathers have IQs around 120 while those of unskilled workers have IQs around 93, comments that 'these are big differences and in part they are environmentally caused; but in part too they are genetic'. Similarly, Professor Sir Cyril Burt in his criticism of Dr J. W. B. Douglas' findings that middle-class children do well at school, states that the social class of the parents 'might be taken as yielding an approximate estimate for the innate and inheritable ability of the stock from which each child is drawn'.

QUALITY OF THE HOME

After innate intelligence, the second principal factor in school achievement is the quality of the home, consisting of the degree to which parents take an interest in the child's school work, the quality of the parents' intelligence and so forth. This has been demonstrated by Dr J. W. B. Douglas and again in the Plowden Report. Thus the working-class child, especially those from slums, tends to be doubly handicapped both by lower innate intelligence and poorer family conditions. No doubt this is unfair, but those who think that this unfairness can be remedied to any significant extent by turning either the educational system or society itself upside down are living in a dream world. This can be seen readily enough in Russia. Even when the whole social system is destroyed and a good many of the upper middle class shot, it is not long before a new upper middle class emerges whose children take most of the prizes. Thus in Russia today, with a largely comprehensive system (with the addition of a small number of élite schools), it has been found that 82 per cent of the children of professional men go on to higher education, but only 10 per cent of the children of agricultural workers do so.

It may seem harsh to draw attention to these facts and that the progressives are being nicer to pretend that the innate class differences do not exist and that the handicap of a poor family can be overcome by comprehensive schools. I doubt whether this is so. By blinding themselves and others to the truth, the progressives raise false hopes that much more can be done for slum children than is actually possible. No amount of money poured into the 'educational priority areas', enthusiastically espoused in the Plowden Report, is likely to bring any appreciable proportion of slum children up to the standards of university entrance. The same is true of comprehensives and fashionable new methods in teaching. False premises lead to false remedies and ultimately to disappointment. If it is thought desirable to improve the intelligence of the population, money would be much better spent on helping less intelligent people to limit the size of their families. Since many have more children than they wish, this would be a boon both to the families themselves and to the rest of the population. In these egalitarian days such facts may seem harsh, but it is always best to start from the truth.

The suppression of these truths by progressives leads to a whole series of false deductions. One of the most serious is that it is the fault of society that slum dwellers are impoverished and their children do badly in school. To the young red guards, it follows that society is unjust and must be overthrown. They do not realize that slum dwellers are caused principally by low innate intelligence and poor family upbringing, and that the real social challenge is posed by this.

One might have hoped that the progressives would have learnt their lesson from the 1944 Education Act. They used to think that by having intelligence tests for grammar school selection, large numbers of highly intelligent working-class children would pass into the grammar schools and universities. It has turned out that the proportion of working-class children in grammar schools and universities has remained much the same. The same thing will happen when all children are forced into comprehensives. Whatever the system, middle-class children will always tend to do best. The chief effect of universal comprehensivization will simply be to reduce British standards to those in America. Quality education for the able will be destroyed without any appreciable compensating advantages for the working class. . . .

BRITAIN'S CULTURAL TRADITION AND THE FUTURE

Britain has a great cultural tradition of intellectual achievement. Even in the post-war period, Britain has won more Nobel prizes for science and literature per head of population than any other major country. Britain has been enabled to do this partly because of her outstanding educational system which has been so efficiently geared to producing an intellectual élite. This is the system the progressives are now demolishing on the basis of false premises which seriously underestimate genetic class differences and equally seriously over-estimate the value of higher education both for the economy and for all types of temperament. The British grammar and independent schools have been extraordinarily successful in the purpose for which they were designed, the training of an intellectual élite for the maintenance of a cultural tradition. The progressives are destroying this system in a hopeless quest for a degree of equality which can never be attained.

But it is one thing to deplore the destruction of quality education which is now proceeding; it is a more difficult problem to suggest a remedy. The preservation of quality in a democratic age may well be impossible and we should perhaps resign ourselves to the imminence of a new dark age in which the envy, malice and philistinism of the masses, and of intellectuals who identify with them, lead to the destruction of a culture that can never be enjoyed by the majority. Once before, in the concluding years of the Roman Empire, Europe has seen the tyranny of the majority leading to the breakdown of civilization and the survival of the cultural tradition only in isolated outposts.

Those who hope to prevent such a repetition of history are obliged to think in terms of practical politics. Is there anything to hope from the Labour Party? The Conservatives seem resigned to having lost the battle of the eleven-plus, and there are obvious political difficulties in supporting a system which seems to label 80 per cent of the population as inferior. For getting into this position the Conservatives have only themselves to thank for passing the 1944 Butler Education Act, which they should have seen leads to a politically untenable position. Furthermore, the 1944 Act was profoundly alien to conservative philosophy. The idea that state officials should allocate children to different kinds of school, on the basis of the decisions of experts about what kind of occupation they are best fitted for, is part of the philosophy of socialism and the planned society. The conservative tradition is surely one of individual families making such decisions for themselves.

In passing the 1944 Act the Conservatives made a dreadful mistake. But that does not mean that they need capitulate to the comprehensive system. On the contrary, they should now recognize this error and try to re-establish a modified form of the pre-1944 position. The solution is to restore the grammar schools as independent fee-paying institutions with scholarships for intelligent children from poor families. The essential point is that where schools are a state service they are subject to majority control and this inevitably means the destruction of minority values. Only by establishing grammar schools as private institutions independent of the power of the state can minority interests survive.

The practical steps are admittedly difficult. Professors A. Peacock and J. Wiseman and Dr E. G. West have suggested a voucher system which might be possible. As an alternative I suggest that the first step should be to reopen the direct grant school list and encourage state grammar schools threatened with comprehensivization to become direct grant schools. This would of course involve the introduction of fees on a means tested basis. At the same time tax allowances should be given to parents educating their children privately, so that the introduction of fees would be to some degree offset by the tax allowances. With this concession existing direct grant schools might be expanded and new ones founded, so that the pre-1944 position would gradually be restored. Every major city would have at least one independent direct grant school at which able working-class children would be educated, and there would also be a number of fee-paying private schools. In addition there should probably be a system of state loans for any parents who wished to send their children to fee-paying schools. No one could then complain that any family was unable to obtain a grammar school education for its children because of poverty. The responsibility for deciding whether to incur this expense would rest with the individual family and would do something to restore the feeling that people are responsible for their own destinies, which has become so eroded in Britain since 1945. All parents would then have a choice of which school to send their children to, and no child would suffer the stigma of having failed the eleven-plus. This would perhaps be the most politically practical way of ensuring the preservation of quality education in Britain.

MICHAEL F. D. YOUNG (1970)

An approach to the study of curricula as socially organized knowledge*

The almost total neglect by sociologists of how knowledge is selected, organized and assessed in educational institutions (or anywhere else for that matter) hardly needs documenting. Some answers to the question why this has happened, and an attempt to show that this neglect arises more out of a narrow definition of the major schools of sociological thought (in particular, those of Marx, Weber and Durkheim) than out of their inadequacies, may provide a useful context from which to suggest the directions in which such work might develop. This paper explicitly does not set out to offer a general theory of culture, or to be a direct contribution to the sociology of knowledge; it has the more limited aim of trying to suggest ways in which questions may be framed about how knowledge is organized and transmitted in curricula. However, it would be my contention that if such questions became the foci of research in the sociology of education, then we might well see significant advances in the sociology of knowledge in particular, and in sociological theory in general. The paper, then, has four parts:

1 The changing focus of the public debates about education in the last twenty years

2 An examination of the limitations of existing approaches to the sociology of education and the sociology of knowledge in generating either fruitful theories or fruitful research in the field of curricula

3 An outline of some of the possibilities of the Marxist, Weberian and Durkheimian traditions

4 A suggested approach for future work.

* Reprinted from a paper contributed to the 1970 conference of the British Sociological Association, an extended version of which was printed in *Knowledge and Control*, ed. Michael F. D. Young (Collier-Macmillan, London, 1971), and which was printed in *Knowledge, Education and Cultural Change*, ed. Richard Brown (London, Tavistock, 1973).

PUBLIC DEBATES ABOUT EDUCATION

One can only speculate on the explanations, but it is clearly possible to trace three stages in the public debates on education in the last fifteen to twenty years: the foci have been *equality of opportunity* and *wastage of talent, organization* and *selection*, and the *curriculum*. In each case one can distinguish the political, educational, and sociological components. Though both sets of distinctions – between foci and between components – are oversimplified and schematic, they do provide a useful context for the problems posed in this paper; the second set of distinctions refers not to the content of issues, but to the groups involved and the parts they played.

In the first stage, the facts of educational *wastage* were documented by the *Early Leaving* and Crowther Reports (and later by Robbins) and the class nature of the *lack of opportunity* was demonstrated by Floud, Halsey and Martin (1956). Though the sociological research largely complemented the public reports and was tacitly accepted as a basis for an expansionist policy by successive Ministers, it also threw up a new set of questions concerning the social nature of selection, and the organization of secondary education in particular. Thus the second phase of public debate from the mid-sixties focused on the issues of *selection* and *comprehensive reorganization*. That the debate now became an issue of political conflict is an indication that the policies involved, such as the abolition of selective schools, threatened certain significant and powerful interests in society – particularly the staff of career-grammar, direct-grant and public schools, and the parents of the children who expected to go to such schools. The manifest inefficiency and the less well-documented injustice of the eleven-plus made its abolition a convenient political commitment for reformist politicians. This debate was paralleled by an increasing interest by sociologists in all kinds of organizations and the possibility of applying the more general models of 'organization theory' to schools and colleges. It is only in the last two or three years that the focus of debate has moved again from *organization* to *curriculum*, and again one can only speculate on the reasons. Four might be worth exploring; the first three, particularly, in the context of the kinds of project for curriculum reform sponsored by the Schools Council:

1 *Government pressure* for more and better technologists and scientists.

2 *The commitment to raising the school-leaving age* – though many teachers are opposed to this, inevitably it forces them to reconstruct curricula for the large number of pupils who they probably feel are at school a year too long already.

3 *Comprehensive amalgamations* – many grammar schools, with teachers who for years have effectively produced good A level results, are suddenly faced with pupils who do not accept the value of the grammar school curriculum. This poses them with acute problems of finding alternatives.

4 *Student participation* – it is undeniable that, as the demands of students in colleges and universities have moved from the arena of union and leisure activities to matters of discipline and administrative authority and finally to a concern to participate in the planning of the structure and content of courses and their assessment, staff have themselves begun to re-examine the principles underlying their curricula, which have for so long been taken for granted. It is more rather than less likely that this pressure from the students will increase and will extend to the senior forms of schools. Perhaps the most dramatic demonstration of this trend is seen in the Negro students in the USA, who are demanding courses in Black Studies.

Again the public debate has taken place on two levels, the political and the educational – though such a distinction is necessarily an oversimplification.

At the political level the protagonists have been the Marxist Left and the Conservative Right. The Left criticizes contemporary curricula for 'mystifying the students' and 'fragmenting knowledge into compartments', and thus, by denying students the opportunity to understand society as a totality, for acting as effective agents of social control. The Right criticizes progressive teaching methods, unstreaming, and the various curricular innovations in English, history and maths, as well as the expansion of the 'soft' social sciences. In the name of preserving 'our cultural heritage' and providing opportunities for the 'most able' to excel, it seeks to conserve institutional support for the educational tradition it believes in – particularly the public and direct-grant grammar schools. What is significant for the sociology of education is that, in spite of attempts, the politics of the curriculum has remained apart from Westminster. Except for compulsory religious instruction, the headmaster or principal's formal autonomy over the curriculum is not questioned. It is as if by what has been called the 'politics of non-decision-making', by means ot which the range of issues for party political debate is limited, consideration of the curriculum is avoided (except for broad discussions about the 'need' for more scientists). There are sufficient parallels in other contexts to suggest that the avoidance of such discussion is an indication of the interrelation of the existing organization of knowledge and the distribution of power, the consideration of which might not be comfortable in an era of consensus politics.

The context of the 'educationalist's' debate about the curriculum has been different and inevitably less contentious. Examples of issues raised are: early tracking into the sciences or arts; over-specialization and neglect of applied science in the sixth form; as well as the possibility of introducing new knowledge areas such as the social sciences. On another level, what has been labelled the 'tyranny of subjects' typical of much secondary education has been opposed by suggestions for integrated curricula based on 'themes' and 'topics'. Two other features of this debate should be referred to: the stream of working papers and proposals issued by the Schools Council, which we return to again later in the paper, and the critiques put forward by the philosophers of education. Starting from certain *a priori* assumptions about the organization (or forms) of knowledge (Hirst, 1965), the philosophers focus their criticism either on new topic-based syllabi which neglect these 'forms of understanding', or on new curricula for the so-called 'less able' or 'Newsom child', which, they argue, are consciously restricting such children from access to those forms of understanding which in the philosopher's sense are 'education'. The problem with this kind of critique is that it is based on an absolute conception of a set of distinct forms of knowledge which correspond closely to the traditional areas of the academic curriculum, and thus justifies, rather than examines, what are no more than the sociohistorical constructs of a particular time.

In the debate on the curriculum, unlike those on *equality* and *organization*, sociologists, except as political protagonists, have remained silent. We have virtually no theoretical perspectives or research to suggest explorations of how curricula, which are no less social inventions than are political parties or new towns, arise, persist and change, and what the social interests and values involved might be – an analogy with the consensus politics of Westminster is not difficult to see.

LIMITATIONS OF EXISTING APPROACHES

Sociology of education and the curriculum

Having mapped out the context of the debates on the curriculum, let us turn to the sociology of education and consider why its contribution has been so negligible. Sociologists seem to have forgotten, to paraphrase Raymond Williams, that education is not a product like cars or bread, but a selection and organization of the available knowledge at a particular time, which involves conscious or unconscious choices. It would seem that it is or should be the central task of the sociology of education to relate these principles of selection and organization, which underlie curricula, to their institutional setting and to the wider socal structure. I want to suggest that we can account for the failure of sociologists to do this by examining the ideological and methodological assumptions of the sociologists on the one hand, and the institutional context within which the subdiscipline developed on the other. However, perhaps as significant a fact as any in accounting for the limited conception of the sociology of education in Britain has been that, in spite of the interest in the field reported by respondents to Carter's recent survey (1967), *very few* sociologists have been involved in research in education.

Much British sociology in the late fifties, and the sociology of education in particular, drew its ideological perspective from Fabian socialism and its methodology from the demographic tradition of Booth and Rowntree. The resultant studies broadened the notion of poverty from lack of income to lack of education, which was seen as a significant part of working-class life-chances. The stark facts of the persistence of inequalities over decades in spite of the overall expansion of wealth do not need repeating, but what is important is that these studies, and those such as Douglas *et al.* (1968) and Plowden that followed, in their concern for increasing equality of opportunity, focused primarily on the characteristics of the failures, the early leavers and the drop-outs. By using a model of explanation of working-class school failure which justified reformist social policies, they were unable to examine the social nature of the education that the working-class children failed at – for instance, the peculiar content of the grammar school curriculum for the sixteen year old, in which pupils are obliged to do up to ten different subjects which bear little relation either to each other or to anything else. It would not be doing these studies an injustice to say that they developed primarily from a sociological interest in stratification (in the Weberian sense), and in showing how the distribution of life-chances through education can be seen as an aspect of the class structure. It may clarify this point by looking at the implicit model more formally as follows:

Assumptions	Independent variable	Dependent variable
Criteria of educational success – curricula, methods and evaluation	Social characteristics of the success and failure groups	Distribution of success and failure at various stages – stream, eleven-plus, O level, etc.

Though this table illustrates the point in a crude and oversimplified form, it does show that within that framework the content of education is taken as a 'given' and is not subject to sociological inquiry – the 'educational failures' become a sort of 'deviant'. If, however, we reformulate the problem in a similar way to that suggested by Cicourel and Kitsuse (1963) in their discussion of how official statistics on crime are arrived at, and ask what are the processes by which rates of educational success and failure come to be produced, we are led to ask questions about the context and definitions of success. In other words, the methods of assessment, selection and organization of knowledge, and the principles underlying them, become our focus of study. One can see that this kind of reformulation would not have been consistent either with the methods or with the ideology of the studies referred to above. A similar point can be made about studies of schools and colleges as 'organizations'. They have either begun with 'models' from organization theory or compared schools with mental hospitals and prisons as 'people-processing organizations' (e.g.

302 MICHAEL F. D. YOUNG

Hoyle 1965; Brim and Wheeler 1966). In neither case is it recognized
that it is not only people but knowledge that is 'processed' in educational institutions, and that, unless what is 'knowledge' is to be
taken as given, it is the interrelation of the two processes of organization that must form the beginning of such studies.

To turn to the institutional context, it does seem clear that most of
the teaching and published work in the sociology of education has
taken place in colleges, institutes, and departments of education. It is
only very recently that university departments of sociology have
offered main options at either B Sc or M Sc level in this field. Thus
the sociology of education has developed in institutions devoted to
the 'academic' study of education where ten to fifteen years ago it
hardly existed. We can pose the question as to how the new specialists
legitimated their contribution to educational studies and justified
their particular field of expertise – especially when the ex-school subject specialists and the philosophers had defined their area of com-
petence as covering the curriculum and pedagogy. Not surprisingly,
the sociologists mapped out new unexplored areas. They started from
the social context of education, with an emphasis on social class, relations to the economy, the occupational structure and the family,
and moved on to the consideration of schools as organizations and of
pupil subcultures. Through an arbitrary division of labour which had
no theoretical basis, this allowed the expansion of the sociology of
education with the minimum of 'boundary disputes'. Inevitably this
is speculation, but it does suggest an explanation of what appears to
have been a consensus among sociologists and non-sociologists alike
that the curriculum was not a field for sociological research. . . .

A SUGGESTED APPROACH

The previous section has from different points of view suggested that
consideration of the assumptions underlying the selection and organization of knowledge in terms of those in positions of power may be
a fruitful perspective for raising sociological questions about curricula. Drawing on some ideas in Bernstein (1969), we can start by
posing three analytically distinct questions about the organization of
knowledge:

   1 How stratified is the knowledge and by what criteria? This
   question provides us with the dimension of *stratification* of

knowledge and focuses on how far different areas and kinds of knowledge obtain different social evaluations and rewards.

2 How restricted is the area of knowledge expected to be covered by the pupil or student? On this dimension, curricula can vary between specialized and non-specialized.

3 What is the relation between the contents or areas of knowledge? Curricula can vary on this dimension from being open – where boundaries between subjects are blurred and indistinct – to being closed – where boundaries are clearly defined and subjects are insulated from each other.

How related are the knowledge areas?

		Open		Closed	
What is the scope of the knowledge areas?		Narrow (special—ized)	Broad (unspecial—ized)	Narrow	Broad
How stratified are the knowledge areas?	High	1	2	5	6
	Low	3	4	7	8

(Alternatives 1-4 represent 'integrated' types and 5-8 represent 'collection' types in Bernstein's terminology)

FIGURE I *Dimensions of the social organization of knowledge*

In Figure I each dimension, a continuum, is presented as a dichotomy. Bernstein's two ideal-type curricula, the 'integrated' and 'collection' types, are shown to include different subtypes in which the stratification and specialization of knowledge can be high or low.

The expansion of knowledge and the pattern of access to it are paralleled by the increasing differentiation of knowledge. Empirically we could also show that knowledge probably becomes more stratified. However, there is an important analogy here with the functionalist theory of social stratification. Differential social evaluation does not logically follow from increasing differentiation, though empirically it *often does*. The pattern of social evaluation of different knowledge areas must be explained independently, in terms of restricted access to certain kinds of knowledge and the opportunity for those who have access to them to legitimize their higher status and control their availability.

The framework presented focuses on the principles of organization and selection of knowledge and does not directly suggest how these are related to the social structure. The sociological assumption is that the most explicit relation between the dominant institutional order and the organization of knowledge will be on the dimension of stratification: moves, therefore, to 'destratify' (to give equal value to different kinds of knowledge) or to 'restratify' (to legitimize other criteria of evaluation), by posing a threat to the power structure of that 'order', will be resisted. However, movements to make the scope of knowledge in a curriculum less restricted (a decrease in specialization) and the relations between knowledge areas more 'open' will also pose threats to the patterns of social relations implicit in the more restricted/less related forms, and likewise will be resisted. It should, therefore, be possible to account for the persistence of some (or, in the sense defined by the dimension of stratification, the 'essential') characteristics, particularly of academic curricula, and for the changes in others which do not involve the criteria of the evaluation of knowledge, or its scope or relations – or, if they do, do not pose threats to the existing authority structure (for example, the relative ease of introduction of new knowledge areas within departments of general studies in colleges of further education as compared with the resistance to such innovation posed by the tightly knit departmental structure of the grammar school).

I want to suggest, then, that it may be through this idea of the stratification of knowledge that we can point to relations between the pattern of dominant values and the distribution of rewards and power, and the organization of knowledge. Analysis would be necessary both historically and cross-culturally on the societal level and also at different age-levels and in different knowledge areas. Academic curricula in this country involve assumptions that some kinds and areas of knowledge are much more 'worthwhile' than others; and that as soon as possible all knowledge should become specialized, with minimum explicit emphasis on the relations between the subjects specialized in. It may be useful, therefore, to view curricular changes as involving movement along one or more of the dimensions towards a less or more stratified, specialized and insulated organization of knowledge. Further, since we assume that there are some patterns of social relations associated with any curriculum, we may posit that these changes will be resisted in so far as they are perceived to undermine the values, relative power and privileges of the dominant groups involved. Studies relating the career structures of teachers in different knowledge areas and the strategies of the various subject-based associations would seem one way of exploring these suggestions.

In his paper, Bernstein focuses on the two ideal-type curricula already referred to (see Figure 1) and their implications for the various social processes in educational institutions – staff–pupil relations, patterns of authority and forms of evaluation. The complexity of the matter becomes apparent if one moves from this general level to more specific examples. Let us take two examples to illustrate the problems of explaining different curricular changes:

1 The different implications of change in the sciences and in the arts from a collection-type to an integrated-type curriculum
2 The introduction of new subjects into medical and engineering curricula.

1 The characteristic of all science teaching at any level is that, however strong subject loyalties and identification may be (and this is likely to be closely associated with level of teaching), those teaching do share implicitly or explicitly the norms and values of science, and thus chemistry, physics and biology are, at one level, integrated. It is not surprising, therefore, that in an area of the academic curriculum not striking for its innovations, the sixth form, both biological and physical sciences are increasingly taught as fully integrated courses. An indication of the part played by the stratification dimension in knowledge is that the core base of the former is biochemistry and of the latter mathematics: both high-status knowledge fields among scientists. Evidence of the different situation that arises when attempts to integrate appear to reduce the status of knowledge is the failure of the 'general science' movement after World War II. Whereas the physicist and the biologist share an explicit set of values through being scientists, it is doubtful whether being in the 'humanities' has any common meaning for historians, geographers and those teaching English and foreign language. In this case, any movement towards integration involves the construction of new values to replace subject identities. Thus again, it is not surprising

that this side of the academic sixth form curriculum has undergone very little change.

2 One feature affecting both medical and engineering curricula is that those controlling these courses have recently appeared concerned to introduce into them a social science component. In the absence of research one can only speculate about the changing definition of socially relevant knowledge in this broadening of the curriculum. Conceivably, these changes reflect a change in the position of the engineer and the doctor who both find themselves working increasingly in large organizations, isolated from the direct consequences of their work but still subject to public criticism of what they do. The significance of this example is in demonstrating how changes in the social or occupational structure may influence definitions of relevant knowledge and thus curricula.

Both examples illustrate the ways in which the characteristics of curricula are influenced by the values and interests of the controlling group involved.

I would, however, argue that the third dimension, *stratification of knowledge*, may be the most important, for it is by focusing on the relation between social stratification and the stratification of knowledge that we can begin to raise questions about relations between the power structure and curricula; between access to knowledge and the opportunities to legitimize it as 'superior'; and between knowledge and its functions in different kinds of society.

The dimension of stratification refers to the differential status or social value accorded to different areas and kinds of knowledge. Curricula can range from those based on what might be termed a 'caste model', where some knowledge is highly valued and necessary and other knowledge is not valued at all (certain types of religious curriculum would seem the best examples), to those at the other extreme where knowledge is differentiated but no social evaluation is placed on the categories. As previously suggested, the contemporary British education system is characterized by academic curricula based on a selection of knowledge which has high social status. It follows, therefore, that for the teachers (and probably the children) high status is associated with areas of the curriculum that are (*a*) formally assessed, (*b*) taught to the 'ablest' children, and (*c*) taught in homogeneous ability groups. Two other implications follow which would seem to warrant exploration.

First, if pupils do identify high-status knowledge in this way, and assume these features to be the characteristics of 'worthwhile' knowledge, they could well come to disvalue curricular and pedagogic innovations which necessarily involve changing definitions of relevant knowledge and teaching methods.

Second, if the criteria of high-status knowledge are associated with the values of dominant groups in society, one would expect maximum resistance to change of the high status of knowledge associated with academic curricula. This, as I elaborate on later, is supported by evidence from the work of the Schools Council. The Council has accepted the stratification of knowledge and produces most of its recommendations for reform in the low-status knowledge areas. These tend to be associated with curricula which are for younger and less able children and are not linked to the interests of those who are in positions of power in the social structure.

Let us explore a bit further the idea that knowledge is stratified, particularly in the context of its transmission. Two kinds of question are suggested:

1 In any society, by what criteria are different areas of, kinds of, and approaches to knowledge given different social value? These criteria will inevitably have developed in a particular social and historical context but, if isolated, may be useful in accounting for changes and resistances to change in curricula.

2 How can the extent to which knowledge is stratified and the kinds of criterion used be explained in terms of the ways in which educational institutions and the control of access to knowledge are related to the dominant institutional order – whether it be political or economic?

Taking the first question, I want to suggest that it may be useful to conceive of the hierarchy of value and reward on which the organization and transmission of knowledge are based as having four dimensions or aspects:

(i) Abstractness (A), which refers to the level of generality involved.

(ii) Emphasis on literacy (L), which refers to the relative importance of written as opposed to oral, presentation.
(iii) Individualism (I), which refers to the emphasis placed on individual as opposed to group activity and assessment, which is absent from most of the forms of access to knowledge, such as essays, experiments and projects in secondary education.
(iv) Relatedness (R), which refers to the degree to which and the way in which knowledge is related directly to non-school activities.

The assumption is made that, implicitly, areas and kinds of knowledge are ranked on these four dimensions and that academic curricula will be characterized by high-status knowledge which will tend to be abstract (high on A), emphasize writing (high on L), and individual performance (high on I), and have a minimum direct relation to non-school situations (low on R).

One can view these criteria as the specific historical consequences of an education system based on a model of 'bookish' learning for medieval priests, which was extended first to lawyers and doctors, and increasingly has come to dominate all education of older age-groups in industrial societies. However, their use to sociologists may be to highlight the unquestioned characteristics of academic curricula. To elaborate: these dimensions can be seen as social definitions of educational value, and thus they become problematic in the sense that if they persist it is not because knowledge is, in any meaningful way, best made available according to the criteria, but because they are conscious or unconscious cultural choices which accord with the values and beliefs of dominant groups at a particular time. It is therefore in terms of these choices that educational success and failure are defined. One might speculate that it is not that particular skills and competences associated with highly valued occupations 'need' learning contexts defined in this way, but that very different cultural choices or the granting of equal status to sets of cultural choices that reflect variations on these dimensions would involve a massive redistribution of the labels 'educational success' and 'failure', and thus also a parallel redistribution of rewards in terms of wealth, prestige and power.

Two important limitations of this approach must be mentioned. First, the categories are formal and no operational rules are suggested which direct research to analysing questions of substantive content – their use in the analysis of texts, syllabuses, reports, examination questions, marking criteria, and the day-to-day activities of the class-room would lead either to narrower but more substantive categories or to their modification, depending on the nature of the research problem posed. Second, by its emphasis on the social organization and not the social functions of knowledge, this approach does not make explicit that access to certain kinds of knowledge is potential access to the means of changing the criteria of social evaluation of knowledge itself, as well as to the means of preserving these criteria. However, changing the criteria involves social actions, which inevitably are *concrete, corporate* and *related*, and also involves *oral* as well as written communication. Perhaps it is through the disvaluing of social action and the elevation of the value placed on 'knowledge for its own sake' through the separation of knowledge from action that knowledge of social alternatives in our educational system is both restricted and, when available, perceived as knowledge of 'alternatives in theory'.

However, let us illustrate some more specific ways in which this approach might be useful for the sociology of education.

1 If relations between the pattern of domination and the organization of knowledge are as have been suggested, one would expect a reduction in specialization, an increase in inter-subject integration, or a widening of the criteria of social evaluation of knowledge only if there were parallel changes in the pattern of domination. Thus one would expect most curricular 'innovations' to be of two kinds:

(*a*) *Modifications of existing academic curricula which maintain existing social evaluations of knowledge.* Two examples are the new Nuffield O level science syllabuses and the integrated science projects referred to earlier. A significant research problem would be to examine the influence of the Nuffield sponsors – the Science Masters' Association (now the Association for Science Education, an organization which has close links with the universities and traditionally an active membership drawn largely from public, direct-grant, and grammar schools with large science sixths) and the university advisers – which led to the Nuffield Project's being directed, in the first place, to O level (which is taken by about 30 per cent of pupils) rather than to the reform of secondary school science as a whole.

(b) *Innovations which disregard the social evaluations implicit in academic curricula, but only because their availability is restricted to less able pupils.* In becoming the major sponsor for such innovations, the Schools Council can be seen as legitimizing the existing organization of knowledge in two ways. First, the assumptions of the academic curricula are taken for granted, therefore the social evaluations of knowledge embodied in such curricula are by implication being assumed to be agreed upon and, because inviolable, to be in some sense 'absolute'. Second, new courses are created in 'low-status' knowledge areas, and their availability is restricted to those who have 'failed' in terms of academic definitions of knowledge, hence these failures are seen as individual failures, of motivation, ability or circumstances, and not as consequences of the academic system itself. These courses, which explicitly deny pupils access to the kinds of knowledge that are associated with rewards, prestige, and power in our society, are thus given a kind of legitimacy which masks the fact that educational success in terms of them would still be defined as 'failure'.

2 'Knowledge practitioners' will endeavour to 'move up' the status dimensions to legitimize what they define as their rightful exclusiveness in the terms defined by the criteria – some newer A levels and B Ed Part II subjects are cases in point.

Returning to the second question concerning the dimension of stratification (see pp. 320–1 above), we do not know how relations between the economy and the educational system produce different degrees and kinds of stratification of knowledge. One way of approaching this problem would be to compare the kinds of knowledge stratification found in countries like North Korea, where the schools are less separate from the economy and many activities of learning are also activities of production, with the kinds produced by systems like our own where in school nothing is 'for real' even in the workshops.

To sum up, then, an attempt has been made to offer a sociological approach to the organization of knowledge in curricula. The inevitably limited and schematic nature of the outline presented together with the total lack of research by sociologists in the field turns us back to the question posed at the beginning of this paper. Why no sociology of the curriculum? Perhaps we so take for granted the selective consequences of how we organize knowledge that we are unable to conceive of alternatives and thus to accept that academic curricula and the forms of assessment associated with them are sociological inventions to be explained like men's other inventions, mechanical and sociological.

EARL HOPPER (1971)

Educational systems and selected consequences of patterns of mobility and non-mobility in industrial societies: a theoretical discussion*

INTRODUCTION

In 1958 at the IVth World Congress of Sociology, Professor Ralph H. Turner presented a paper on educational systems, which was published subsequently as 'Sponsored and contest mobility and the school system'. His typology of 'contest' and 'sponsorship' educational systems and mobility processes has helped us to understand variations in these phenomena in many societies. In the conclusion to his article, Turner suggested that the structure of a sponsorship educational system would be less likely than that of a contest educational system to increase the probability that the upwardly mobile from the Lowest Social Class would encounter conditions which tend to produce various types of anxiety. In so far as a sponsorship system obtained in England, and a contest system in the United States, upward mobility was hypothesized to be less pathogenic in England than in the United States.

* Reprinted from *Readings in the Theory of Educational Systems*, ed. Earl Hopper (London, Hutchinson, 1971). This also contains the paper on 'sponsored and contest mobility and the school system' by Ralph M. Turner, to which Hopper refers.

In 1966 at the VIth World Congress, I presented a paper on educational systems which was published subsequently as 'A typology for the classification of educational systems'. It was shown in this article that sponsorship and contest systems represented two special cases in an extended typology. The two types of systems do not constitute polarities, at least in terms of this typology, and they are far from being empirically comprehensive. I concluded with the cautious suggestion that one of the ways in which the utility of the expanded typology might be demonstrated would be to take considerations which derived from it in order to revise and reformulate Turner's hypotheses concerning mobility and anxiety in England and the United States. . . .

Turner assumed that four conditions were likely to be pathogenic:

1 a negative discrepancy between a level of normative expectations and a level of achievement
2 competition for desirable occupations
3 interpersonal isolation and loss of interpersonal support
4 working out a personal value system.

Then, with respect to England, he argued that due to the effects of educational sponsorship, of subsequent segregation and systematic allocation of students to their eventual occupations, neither the non-mobile nor the upwardly mobile from the Lowest Social Class would be likely to encounter any of the four pathogenic conditions stipulated above. Implicit in his thesis is the assumption that children in England are not really ambitious until they pass the initial selection examination: if one passes the test, one becomes ambitious; if one fails, one develops a relatively low level of ambition. Those who fail are unlikely to become mobile or to want to become mobile; hence they are unlikely to encounter the pathogenic conditions. Those who pass are encouraged to desire mobility, are given skills and qualifications which enable them to become mobile, and, in general, are guided, insulated and protected; and, hence, they too are unlikely to encounter the pathogenic conditions.

The United States, he argued, presents a different situation. Due to the absence of systematic regulation of aspirations, training and allocation to desirable occupations, both the non-mobile and the mobile from the Lowest Social Class in the United States are more likely to encounter the pathogenic conditions outlined above. Implicit in his thesis is the assumption that a generalized success ideology exists in the United States, and that all members of the society want to be successful despite the fact that both the opportunities for upward mobility and the number of people who are capable of becoming mobile are limited. Consequently, the non-mobile are likely to develop discrepancies between their levels of normative expectations and levels of achievement: and the mobile, despite their relative success, are likely to encounter one or a combination of the other pathogenic conditions. In sum, both the non-mobile and the mobile from the Lowest Social Class in the United States are more likely than their counterparts in England to develop certain types of anxiety as a consequence of their non-mobility or their upward mobility. . . .

Evidence suggests that certain patterns of consecutive experiences are characteristic of particular educational routes. These patterns are influenced and organized through ideologies of legitimization and of implementation of educational selection. Such ideologies are properties of the educational system as a whole. And in order to understand the varieties of both educational and mobility experiences available to a population, it is necessary first to locate the educational system in its societal context, and in this connection to understand the various functions it attempts to perform. Although in its entirety such a topic is beyond the scope of this paper, some aspects of it are among my main concerns.

SELECTED ASPECTS OF SOCIETY AND EDUCATIONAL SYSTEMS

(i) The total selection process as a societal functional problem

All societies, no matter how simple, strive to solve their various functional problems, both universal and organizationally specific. One such problem is the conduct and management of the 'total selection process'. It is comprised of four sub-problems: training, selection, recruitment or allocation, and the regulation of ambition. Although all societies are confronted by these tasks, the social organizations which are concerned primarily with their solution are more readily apparent in societies with a complex system of social stratification, and especially in industrial societies. I am concerned with the attempted solutions of these tasks within Industrial Societies, and in this context I will discuss each component of the total selection process:

1 Training All societies strive to provide their personnel with sufficient kinds and amounts of technical and diffuse skills so that the solution of still other problems can be attempted and, at least in large measure, be met. These skills pertain primarily to the fulfilment of roles associated with adult occupational positions. However, in so far as industrial societies are stratified with respect to status as well as economic and political power, adult occupational roles are embedded within a status hierarchy, and, more precisely, within relatively distinct status groups. Therefore, in addition to the technical and diffuse skills required for adult occupational and economic roles, such societies also strive to provide their personnel with those skills which facilitate their membership of and participation in adult status roles. Of course, these two sets of skills are interrelated: the fulfilment of occupational roles requires both technical and diffuse skills; and, in so far as occupations bestow both economic and status rewards, some technical skills will be required for the fulfilment of status roles, and some diffuse skills for economic ones.

A special case of the provision of skills for the fulfilment of status roles generally is that societies prepare their upwardly mobile members for their mobility experience, i.e. leaving a lower social class and becoming a member of a higher one. Were occupations not such an important source of status positions, such a task would not be so essential. That they do determine the status positions of the vast majority of the population in all industrial societies is beyond dispute. And, to put it bluntly, in all these societies the upwardly mobile are taught through both formal and informal means to speak 'properly', to use the 'correct' accent, to dress 'well', to make friends with the 'right' kinds of people, etc. They are taught to extricate themselves from friendship-networks containing people from their own initial economic and status positions, and to handle the cross-pressures inherent in both conflicting status norms and retentive and rejective normative orientations towards upward mobility (especially as manifest in their relationships with non-mobile kin). It is also important that they learn to exercise authority over those below and to submit in the appropriate manner to authority from those above.

2 Selection All societies select their personnel for more specialized training, but vary with respect to the stringency of their procedures, the degree of specialization, and the phases of the life-cycle in which they do so. For various reasons, all societies also strive to make their selections as effectively and efficiently as possible. They are always constrained by limited resources, the diffuse norms of substantive rationality and the ideologies of implementation. Most important, however, is that the effectiveness and efficiency of the training process depend on the efficiency and effectiveness of a selection process. Indeed, the two are so interdependent as to be almost inseparable.

3 Recruitment and/or allocation All societies structure the process through which their personnel leave the training phases of their life-cycles and enter those phases in which they participate in a labour market and eventually take occupational roles. Such procedures of recruitment and/or allocation are the culmination of the total selection process. However, not everyone is either willing or able to fulfil the most demanding and rewarding occupational roles. Nor are all occupations equally demanding and rewarding. In all societies some people will enter occupations which bestow essentially superordinate economic and status positions, and some will enter those which bestow essentially subordinate ones. Thus, some will be more likely than others to fulfil their expectations of economic and status goals, and to feel contented with their achievements. Similarly, feelings of discontent will also be generated. Such discontent is closely associated with various forms of personal tension and social conflict, both of which are at least to some extent endemic in any society with a clearly stratified distribution of power.

4 Regulation of ambition The most difficult task in a society's total selection process is the regulation of the ambition of its personnel. This takes place at two different phases in the life-cycle. Firstly ambition must be regulated at early and subsequent selection and rejection steps in the training process. Secondly, it must be regulated during the final phases of recruitment to occupational roles. Each should be discussed further:

(1) Effective and efficient training demands effective and efficient selections. Consequently, a society must try to assess the distribution of abilities among its personnel as accurately as possible. But 'ability' is not only an inherited set of qualities. Environmental influences are determinant, there are various kinds of abilities, and people develop them at various rates. Further, all the methods available for the selection of the more able from the less able are exceedingly imperfect, no matter how long their application is delayed. Thus, to make accurate assessments a society must try to encourage its children to develop their abilities, and to display them in whatever is deemed the appropriate manner. This means that all societies must try to raise and maintain at a high level the ambition of a maximum number of people until they have been selected for their eventual occupational roles. Ideally this task must be attempted not only as early as possible, but also at every stage of the selection process. It will involve the management of what objects are cathected as goals, and what amounts of these goals are taken as levels of normative expectations. In effect, all industrial societies must strive to inculcate each of their successive cohorts with the desire to fill the most demanding and rewarding occupations, and to acquire the requisite skills.

(2) To recruit effectively and efficiently a society must try not only to guide its personnel into occupations the demands of which are commensurate with their abilities, but also to encourage the more able to have stronger and higher ambitions than the less able, at least in terms of the 'official' assessments. It must strive to minimize the personal discontents associated with the failure to reach one's level of normative expectations. However, if personal discontents were the only consequence of such discrepancies, most societies would not be concerned. In so far as such feelings are also the foundation of social discontent, it is necessary to regulate them. In brief, in any

stratified society the most powerful groups in various spheres of interest and activities will try to strengthen the established social order and to minimize potential threats to it. Therefore, they will strive to reduce and to maintain at a low level the ambition of those personnel who fill essentially subordinate positions. They will also strive to sponsor and to maintain at a higher level the ambition of those who fill essentially superordinate ones.

In sum, the total selection process is a functional problem which consists of four separate but interdependent component tasks, and with which all societies, and especially highly stratified societies, must strive to cope. However, all societies do not meet this problem with the same degree of effectiveness and efficiency. Some are more successful with one component or combination of them than they are with another. Structural constraints inherent in the complexity of the problem make it difficult to cope equally well with all four. In fact, several structural contradictions are inherent in any attempted solution of the total selection process. This gives rise to a structural dilemma, one which no society can eliminate, yet one with which all societies must cope.

(ii) The structural dilemma inherent in the total selection process

The dilemma is easy to describe: the more effective is a society in raising and maintaining ambition at a high level initially, the more difficult is it to reduce and to suppress ambition at a relatively low level at a later phase. For example, it will usually be necessary to reduce the expectations of adults who as children or as younger men were encouraged to aim high. All the available evidence suggests that such a task is extremely difficult, if not impossible. Thus, the more effective is a society at an early phase of the total selection process in the motivation of its personnel to fill demanding occupations, to acquire the requisite skills and to forgo immediate economic rewards during extensive periods of training, he more is it likely to have to face two problems: the personal discontent and its personal manifestations among those of its personnel who eventually fill essentially subordinate positions and, hence, who fail to meet their ambitions; and the social discontent and its manifestations in social conflict between them and those people who eventually fill essentially superordinate positions, and, hence, who do succeed in their ambitions. In other words, there is an inverse relationship between the likelihood of success in the regulation of ambition at the early stages and the likelihood of success at the later ones.

The social organizations which any society develops to cope with the total selection process will be constrained by the conflicting pressures of this dilemma. Societies vary in the structural mechanisms through which they attempt to cope with it, and in the degree to which they do so successfully. Especially important is that a system of social stratification not only contributes to the severity of the problem (indeed, it tends to define the dimensions), but also helps to resolve it. This is not the place to elaborate the view that stratification is both functional and dysfunctional with respect to the attempted solutions of a large number and variety of societal problems. But a few points are in order concerning the effects of variation in stratification systems on the total selection process.

With respect to the problems under consideration here, it is especially important to determine the degree to which a stratification system is characterized by status rigidity. This can be defined in terms of several aspects of stratification and mobility, but primarily in terms of the status hierarchy and its relationships to the stratification system of which it is a part, as follows:

1 the existence of distinct and mutually exclusive status groups which are arranged hierarchically according to status power
2 the life styles associated with each status group are distinctive and extensive, so that they are difficult to shed as well as to acquire, especially after childhood
3 it is difficult to legitimize a newly acquired economic position by entering with speed the core of the commensurate status group
4 various occupations or sets of them are governed and regulated by certain status groups, with special reference to recruitment and promotion
5 there is great social distance between adjacent status groups, between any one echelon in the hierarchy and any other, and between the core and periphery of status groups in each echelon.

It is impossible to discuss this property of stratification in greater detail here. But it is important to see that a system can be more rigid in some respects than in others. One part of a given system can be more rigid than other parts of the same system. Yet one system can be more or less rigid generally than another. For example, perhaps France is the most rigid Industrial Society in the West, and the United States the least. England would be more rigid than the United States, and perhaps almost as rigid as France. But it is quite possible to find segments of any one of these societies which are either more or less rigid than segments of the others.

The evidence from many industrial societies suggests that the greater the degree of status rigidity, the more is it likely that the lower a person's initial economic and status positions, the less is his

1   ambition to raise them as an adult
2   willingness to acquire the skills requisite for raising them as an adult
3   ability to acquire the requisite skills and to raise these positions.

For the sake of clarity, the converse of this threefold empirical generalization should also be stated. The greater the degree of status rigidity, the more is it likely that the higher a person's initial positions, the greater are his ambition to perpetuate them and possibly to raise them; his willingness to acquire the skills to enable him to do so; and his ability to reach these positions, both in the sense of the acquisition of skill and in the sense of encouragement from, and the lack of interference by, others. These relationships are very complex, but because they are axiomatic for the analysis which follows, at least a brief discussion is necessary.

Much of the variance in talent and ambition which exists prior to initial selections and rejections of personnel can be accounted for by variations in inherited qualities, social class background and its attendant attributes, as well as a number of aspects of family environment. All three factors are interrelated so that children from the lowest social class tend to have less ambition and 'measurable talent' than do the children from higher social classes. The origins of achievement orientations are numerous and multidimensional. Although certain biological and psychological qualities are needed,

M

the ease, frequency and patterns with which they are developed are determined by social experiences. Similarly, the relationship between achievement orientations and mobility orientations is also problematic. However, the evidence suggests that the greater the mobility opportunities, the more likely are people to translate their general achievement orientations into more precise mobility orientations with respect to economic and status positions.

Yet, mobility opportunities alone are not enough. Although they are essential in this respect, equally important is the degree to which people perceive the occupational structures as open to them, and are ready to utilize the means available for occupational achievements. In other words, it is necessary to consider the effects of variations in the degree of status rigidity. For example, the more mobility is visible to members of the lowest social classes, the more likely are they to learn of their opportunities and to act upon them. The greater the proportion of mobility which is accounted for by long range movements, the more is attention drawn to the possibilities of success. The more the acquisition of a new life style depends on the purchase of status symbols, and the less it depends on learning the subtleties of using them, the more obvious will be the rewards for the mobility efforts. The less the most prestigious and economically rewarding occupations (like those of doctor, barrister, corporation president) are maintained as the prerogatives of traditional and tightly knit higher status groups, the more likely are long range mobility and its rapid legitimization to be taken as realistic possible achievements.

To the extent that higher status groups make it difficult for the economically mobile to acquire a legitimate position in the status hierarchy, the currency of their economic achievement is devalued. Thus, when the effort to become upwardly mobile involves leaving a highly supportive status group and family, and is coupled with a low probability of becoming rapidly and easily reintegrated into a new and higher status group, occupational and economic success does not necessarily smell sweet. Moreover, when membership in a status community does not depend primarily on economic accomplishments, money loses its salience as a source of motivation. In other words, although to a potential candidate for upward mobility the greater the difficulty of status legitimization, the greater the value of a new and higher status, it is also the case that he will be less likely to become mobility oriented in the first place. When economic mobility demands occupational mobility, and when the latter removes a person from his original status group and kinship network, even mobility orientations towards economic positions are likely to be less frequent and less intense.

It follows from this discussion that variations in status rigidity will greatly affect the balance, emphasis and elasticity of the dilemma inherent in the total selection process, as outlined above. The greater the degree of status rigidity, the more difficult is it for a society to motivate able people from low initial positions both to fill its most demanding and rewarding occupations and to acquire the requisite skills. . . .

(iii) Educational systems in industrial societies

Although any given society is likely to utilize more than one social organization, some structural arrangements are likely to be more important than others. In Industrial Societies the most important mechanism is the educational system. It becomes responsible, both normatively and actually, for the training, selection, allocation and regulation of personnel with respect to their adult occupational roles, and, hence, their economic and status positions. Thus, it becomes responsible for the task of 'forward placement' in the stratification system. Although this development is by no means inevitable, it is the case in each of the present Industrial Societies, and is rapidly becoming so in most societies now undergoing industrialization processes. This pattern is part of the wider phenomenon of specialization, differentiation, co-ordination and centralization which characterize these societies, largely in response to the emergence of an occupational system which is itself specialized and differentiated both internally and with respect to such institutions as the family and religion. It is therefore understandable that the educational systems of these societies should all be characterized by at least a minimal degree of specialization and differentiation of routes and selection points, and of centralization, standardization and co-ordination of the total selection process.

In industrial societies the functional problem of the total selection process and its attendant dilemma are translated into the terms of reference of their educational systems. With respect to training, the educational system will try to provide their student personnel with the technical and diffuse skills necessary for their subsequent allocation into occupational roles, and for their achievements of various amounts of economic and status rewards. 'Career-training' experiences will be provided with respect to occupational and economic goals, and will involve primarily the development of technical skills. 'Status-training' experiences will be provided with respect to status goals, and will involve primarily the development of diffuse skills. And as a special case of status-training, 'mobility-training' experiences will be provided with respect to the mobility goals of those of its student personnel who are likely to be upwardly mobile from the lower social classes. In fact, more detailed examination of the curricula and extra-curricula activities within educational organizations as well as within classrooms themselves would probably indicate that considerable time and effort are spent on status and mobility training relative to career-training.

The provision of skills, however, is not enough. Because some candidates for 'higher learning' are not sufficiently talented and/or the society has provided a smaller number of places in institutions of 'higher learning' than it has eligible candidates, the educational system must also try to organize the selection of students at various phases of their educational experiences. And this means that the system must also try to organize the regulation of the ambition of its students, especially during the early phases of their formal education.

In this respect, the system is set four tasks:

1 In order to maximize the development and display of academic abilities, the ambition of *all* students must be sponsored and maintained at a high level prior to the initial selections.

2 In order to minimize social conflict and personal discontent the ambition of those students who are rejected initially must then be reduced and maintained at a low level so that it is commensurate with their newly assessed achievement potentials.

3 In order to continue to select effectively and efficiently those who it deems worthy of still further promotion to still higher educational levels, the system must continue to maximize the development and display of academic abilities of those who are

selected initially. Thus, the ambition of all those who are selected initially for advanced training must be sponsored further and maintained at as high a level as possible.

4 And in order to regulate social conflict, personal discontent, and social participation, the ambition of all those who are selected initially but rejected subsequently (at various levels and through various routes) must be reduced and maintained at lower levels so that it is commensurate with their reassessed achievement potentials.

In sum, at every level and through every route within its total selection process, an educational system must strive, on the one hand, to 'warm up' some of its students, and, on the other, to 'cool out' those who are rejected for further training. Those who are warmed up receive further and more specialized training, and those who are cooled out are sent more or less directly into the labour market. Throughout the system, then, a need exists for the simultaneous provision of warming-up and cooling-out experiences.

The dual tasks of warming up and cooling out must be directed, moreover, towards the provision of career-training, status-training and mobility-training experiences. In other words, students must be warmed up and cooled out more or less continuously, successively and correctly with respect to their eventual occupational roles, and, hence, with respect to their eventual economic, status and mobility goals. This means that they must also be warmed up and cooled out more immediately with respect to their contemporary educational goals which stand for each of these long term adult goals.

However, as outlined above, the more successful an educational system is in its warming-up processes at a given phase in the selection process, the more difficult it will be to manage and conduct its cooling-out processes at a subsequent phase. This is not to state that the effective and efficient provision of both sets of experiences is impossible, but to stress that the likelihood of success with one is inversely related to the likelihood of success with the other. Continual tension and conflict are likely to surround any system's attempts to resolve this structural dilemma. It is a contradiction which is likely to generate pressures for structural change, both within the educational system and in the relationships of the system to other institutions. But no matter what the substance and the direction of the structural changes which might occur, the essential nature of the dilemma remains constant, as do the pressures for further change.

Which horn of the dilemma is presented by a society as the longer and the sharper will greatly affect the basic structure of its educational system. This horn represents the demands which the society makes on its educational system over and above the relatively small request for the provision of skills of various kinds and amounts. Thus, a key to the understanding of the basic structure of any educational system is how it attempts to solve its assignment; that is, how it copes with the dilemma implicated by the structure of its warming-up and cooling-out processes. And this, in turn, is a key to the understanding of the personal and interpersonal consequences of various patterns of mobility and of non-mobility.

RONALD DAVIE, NEVILLE BUTLER
AND HARVEY GOLDSTEIN (1972)

From birth to seven*

(I) PARENTS' EDUCATION AND SOCIAL ORIGINS

Commonsense suggests that a positive attitude to school will probably be encouraged by those parents who themselves had a good education. On the other hand, commonsense also suggests that some of the parents who are most anxious and even enthusiastic about their children's education will be those who regret having missed a better education themselves and want to ensure that their children take

* Reprinted from *From Birth to Seven: the second report of the National Child Development Study* (London, Longmans, 1972).

advantage of every opportunity. To what extent, then, is school performance related to parents' education?

When the children were seven, information was obtained from the mothers about whether the fathers had stayed on at school beyond the minimum school-leaving age. The same question was asked about the mothers themselves in the original perinatal inquiry. The criterion is a relatively crude one and the group who stayed on at school will include those who went on to a university as well as those who left school after a year or two beyond the minimum age. Among those who left at the minimum age will be some whose jobs involved a considerable amount of training (e.g. in accountancy) and some who re-entered the educational system for retraining, further or higher education. In general terms, however, the parents who stayed on at school will have received more formal education than those who left.

In order to make an analysis more meaningful, it was confined to those children who were living with both natural parents. In all there were 64 per cent of the children both of whose parents had left school at the minimum age. This varied from a mere 12 per cent in social class I to as many as 87 per cent in social class V.

There was an interesting difference between the picture for fathers and mothers in the social class groups. Amongst the middle-class families, the fathers had more often stayed on at school than their wives, whereas in the working-class families the position was reversed. This may well have arisen because in the working-class groups the mothers more often stayed to take brief commercial courses, whereas those fathers who had further training would have left school to serve an apprenticeship. In middle-class groups a boy's formal education is (or was?) often considered to be of more importance than a girl's.

Information was also obtained about the occupations of both the maternal and paternal grandfathers, which were classified according to whether they were manual or non-manual. Most of the parents whose own background was middle-class will have continued with their formal education, whereas a minority of those with a working-class background will have done so. Parental education will therefore be in part a reflection of social origins.

An analysis was carried out to evaluate the effect of parental education and social origins upon their children's reading and arithmetic attainments and social adjustment in school. It was designed to estimate the effects of these two factors when allowance was made for social class, family size and the sex of the children.

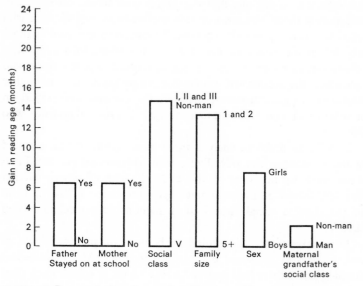

FIGURE I *Parental education and children's reading attainment*[1]

The results for reading attainment (Figure I) indicate that both the mother's education and the father's are of considerable importance. The effect of each is equivalent to approximately six months' gain in reading age in the context of this analysis. In contrast the father's social origins have no effect when allowance is made for the other factors. It is interesting, however, that the effect of the mother's social origins, although quite small, is still present. All these effects are small, of course, in relation to the effects of the *present* social class of the family, and its size.

[1] There was no effect of the paternal grandfather's occupation upon the children' reading attainment.

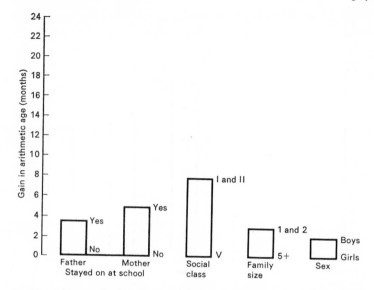

FIGURE 2 *Parental education and children's arithmetic attainment*[1]

In arithmetic (Figure 2) neither parents' social origins show any effect but their educational background is still an important factor. This shows a greater effect than family size, although present social class still stands out as the most potent predictor.

Again for social adjustment (Figure 3), the parents' social origins are in general of little or no consequence. Parental education shows some residual effect, but this is quite small in comparison with social class, sex and family size.

Perhaps the most surprising finding is that, when allowance is made for other relevant factors, the parents' social origins are of little or no importance in predicting their children's school attainments – at least in reading and arithmetic. Does this mean that we are living in an age when 'equality of opportunity' is more than a catchphrase and when the social origins of parents are largely irrelevant to their children's educational achievement? On the basis of other evidence it is perhaps more likely to mean that our society was (or is?) so static socially that the parents' present social class and their

---

[1] There was no effect of either the paternal or maternal grandfather's occupation upon the arithmetic attainment.

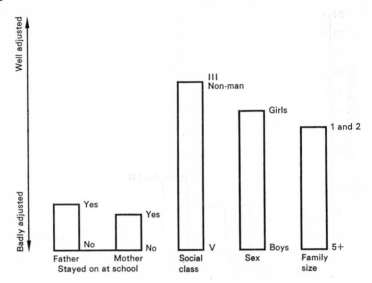

FIGURE 3 *Parental education and children's social adjustment in school*[1]

education can virtually be *equated* with their social origins, so that a knowledge of their social origins is superfluous in predicting their children's achievement. (For example see Floud, Halsey and Martin (1956).)

However, it is clear from the analysis that parents' *education* has an important positive effect on their children's development even when allowance is made for other factors. This finding poses a number of intriguing questions. Can it be attributed to the education itself and the attitudes which this engenders? Educationalists no doubt would like to think so. Or is the explanation that parents who stay on at school are more intelligent – at least in an academic framework – and that the relevant genes are passed on to their offspring? Perhaps parents who stayed on at school already had certain attitudes, for example towards school and, more generally, towards academic pursuits and towards authority, which predispose them to stay on. In this case the relevance of the extended education would be that it identifies parents with certain attitudes, which are acquired

[1] There was no effect of either the paternal or maternal grandfather's occupation upon the social adjustment score.

by their children, who are then better placed to take advantage of schooling in their first two years or so.

(II) SOCIAL CLASS DIFFERENCES IN ATTAINMENT AND ABILITY

There has been a great deal of discussion in recent years about the relationship between social class and school attainments. This has tended to centre upon the issue of social inequality which, it has been alleged, is reinforced by our educational system.

For example, Douglas's (1964) results indicate that during the years of primary schooling the gap in attainment between children from different occupational groups widens. Although this finding has been subjected to criticism on statistical grounds (e.g. Carter, 1964), there seems little doubt that the phenomenon is a real one. Douglas's later work (Douglas, Ross and Simpson, 1968) suggests that this process is continued in the secondary school.

However, in the discussions and controversies which have followed these and other findings, relatively little thought has been given to the role of the primary school. Attention has tended to centre upon the eleven-plus examination and the selective secondary education which follows. In particular, the laudable attempts to provide equal educational opportunity for all children have perhaps overlooked the very marked inequalities which exist even before children transfer to junior school. This is partly because very few studies have been concerned with attainments in infant schools or departments, and even fewer have related these attainments to social class. . . .

It is not difficult to see why there should be some relationship between a father's occupation and his children's progress at school. First, heredity is likely to play a part. The relative contributions of heredity and environment to children's abilities and attainments is a difficult question and psychologists, sociologists, geneticists and others will no doubt continue to debate it until we know a great deal more about brain function. However, that heredity plays some part in perhaps setting limits to the rate of intellectual development or to its ultimate peak can hardly be doubted. Since, in general, parents in a competitive society who have risen to occupations demanding a high level of skill will show a higher level of general intelligence than those in less skilled occupations, it would follow that there will be corresponding differences in their children.

Over and above this, environmental influences will shape a child's abilities and influence his capacity or readiness to learn. A great deal – if not the major part – of learning takes place outside of school and much of this is accomplished even before the child enters school. The vocabulary and concepts used by those around him are vital in providing a framework within which his own intellectual growth can take place. If this framework is bare or impoverished, his own development is likely to be slow; a rich framework of words and ideas will provide the food for more rapid growth. More advanced or abstract thought processes are usually clothed in more elaborate and highly structured language (Bernstein, 1961). A home conducive to learning is one where there is a feeling for the spoken and written word as a tool for conveying precise meaning; and where children are stimulated to question the world around them and receive explanations appropriate to their age.

There are two senses in which a child from such a home comes to school ready to learn. He is intellectually ready in that his language and concepts are already well structured, so that the school is building upon established foundations. But he is also psychologically ready to acquire new skills. For example, he has learned that reading provides pleasure and he wants to be a part of the literate community as soon as possible. His whole attitude to school is conditioned by his parents' high regard for education.

This kind of home is certainly not a monopoly of professional or other non-manual workers. However, it is more frequently found amongst occupational groups which possess a high level of education and skill. Thus, in examining social class differences, we are examining the effects both of environment and of heredity upon children's abilities and attainments. . . .

There is clearly a strong association between social class and reading and arithmetic attainment at seven years of age. The chances of an unskilled manual worker's child (social class V) being a poor reader are six times greater than those of a professional worker's child (social class I). If the criterion of poor reading is made more stringent, the disparity is much larger. Thus, the chances of a social class V child being a *non*-reader are fifteen times greater than those of a social class I child.

A second point which emerges is that the gradient from social class I through to social class V is not regular. There are little or no differences between the results for social class II and social class III (non-manual) children but very considerable differences between the results of these groups and those for social class III (manual) children.

The results for the abilities assessed by teachers' rating and for the copying designs test show the same general pattern with increasing proportions of children with poor ability accompanying lower social class. Again, the gradient of proportions through the social classes is not regular.

It is difficult to draw firm conclusions about the relative differences in the proportions in the social class groups since these are dependent upon the abilities being assessed, the measures used and the stringency of the criteria adopted. However, there appears to be a substantial division between the children from non-manual, or middle-class, homes on the one hand, and those from manual, or working-class, homes on the other. This suggests that whatever the factors are which social class indirectly measures, they are fairly sharply differentiated as between middle-class and working-class homes, at least as far as their effect on attainment or ability is concerned. The results also suggest that there is a meaningful division within the middle-class group between social class I children and the others. In the working-class group, the social class V children appear to be at a particular disadvantage in respect of poor ability or attainment in school.

Of course, these speculations do not throw light directly on the reasons for the differences. Some of the results might suggest that environmental factors are relevant. For example, the proportions of parents who discussed their children with the schools followed the same social class pattern as for the children's abilities and attainments. However, hereditary factors cannot be entirely ignored.

(III) SOCIAL CLASS AND THE NEED FOR SPECIAL
EDUCATIONAL TREATMENT

The teachers were asked whether the children were receiving any
help within the school because of educational or mental backwardness, 'apart from anything which the teacher may be able to do in the
normal way'; and, if No, they were asked whether the children would
benefit from such help. Five per cent of the children were receiving
help and a further 8 per cent were not but would have benefited. The
size of this last figure, as was pointed out in the first report, indicates
an urgent need to re-examine the provision of special educational
treatment in infant schools.

A further question asked of the teachers was whether the children
'would benefit *now* from attendance at a special school'. Some 2 per
cent of children fell into this category. The teachers were not asked
to choose between special schooling and special educational treatment
within the normal school, so that virtually all of the children who
would have benefited from special schooling were also said to be in
need of help in the normal school.

The results presented in Figure 4 show the proportions in the social
classes. The proportion of children in social class V who, it was reported, would have benefited from attendance at a special school was
forty-five times larger than the corresponding proportion in social
class I.

There are two major implications which can be drawn from these
and the earlier findings. First, whatever is being measured when
social class is used as a variable, it is clearly a very useful predictor. It
can be estimated from the above results, for example, that in an
infant school of 200 children, where 100 come from unskilled
working-class homes and the balance from skilled and semi-skilled
working-class homes, some forty children in all are likely to need
special educational help within the school on account of backwardness.

Some feel, however, that in preventive terms such remedial action
is an attempt to shut the stable door when the horse is at least part-
way out. But in the absence of any definitive evidence on the respective contributions of heredity and environment to the social class

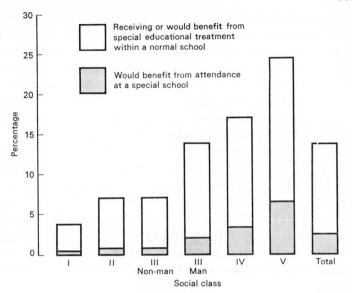

FIGURE 4 *Percentage of children needing special educational treatment by social class*

differences, are we justified in assuming that we can prevent these disparities? Surely the answer is that we have no choice. In the absence of contrary evidence it must be assumed that some form of compensatory education or experience will go some way towards reducing the imbalance. Existing knowledge of child development and learning indicates that the earlier we start the better. . . .

Recent experience in the United States has indicated that compensatory experience cannot be provided as readily as one might think. Hopefully, ongoing research both in the United States and in Britain will suggest some leads which will have implications both for nursery and primary education.

(IV) REGIONAL AND NATIONAL DIFFERENCES IN ATTAINMENT AND ABILITY

The marked social class differences in attainment and ability might lead us to expect that in so far as children from one region were more advanced educationally or more able than children from another region this would be a reflection of the same kind of influences. Therefore we would look for a parallel between the social class distribution for the regions on the one hand and the children's educational performance on the other. For example, if the southeast corner of England has a higher than average proportion of non-manual or middle-class workers one might expect children from this region to have a higher than average reading score.

However, although the results for the regions do show some overall tendencies of this kind, there are many instances where the regional findings run counter to that expected from the social class structure of the groups. These are of interest for a number of reasons. First, they may reflect genetic factors which are not associated with social class. Secondly, they may throw light upon attitudes in parents and/or children which are relevant to education. Thirdly, they may highlight or prompt an examination of differences in educational practice.

In this context the teachers' ratings of abilities or attainments are of limited value. When an individual teacher is asked whether a child has a 'good background of general knowledge' or, in reading, has 'above average ability' and 'comprehends well what he reads', comparisons with other children are usually either implied or specifically requested. The teachers in the study were asked to rate the individual child 'in relation to all children of this age (i.e. not just his present class or school)' but there are obvious limits to the extent to which the teachers could do this. Most of them would not have teaching experience in more than one or two regions so the standards by which they judged the individual child would tend to be influenced to some extent by the prevailing standards in their area or region. The ratings would therefore reduce any regional differences. For this reason, our investigation here is confined to the results from three tests: the Southgate reading test, the arithmetic test and the copying designs test.

The copying designs test was included amongst the small battery of tests given to the children principally in order to identify those with perceptual or perceptual/motor difficulties. However, all the items in the test are used in intelligence tests and it measures one

FIGURE 5 *Percentage of children with 'good' copying designs scores by region and country*

facet of general ability. Furthermore, it is an aspect of ability which is less likely than most to be affected by environmental influences such as different kinds of schooling, or by parental or community attitudes within our society. Thus one would not expect regional differences other than those which could be predicted from the social class differences between the regions. This expectation appears to be confirmed by the results (Figure 5). The proportion of children

N

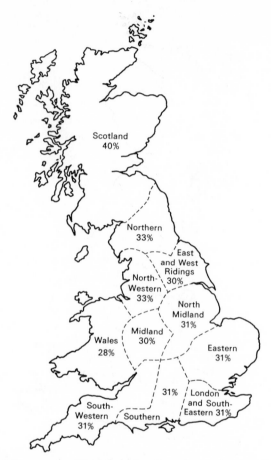

FIGURE 6 *Percentage of 'good' readers by region and country*

with good copying designs scores (≥ 9) tended to be highest in those regions with the highest proportion of middle-class parents: London and the south-east, and the eastern and the southern regions. It was lowest in Scotland, which also has the lowest proportion of middle-class parents.

However, in reading attainment, the most striking feature to emerge from the results (Figure 6) is that the proportion of good readers (Southgate reading test score 29–30) in Scotland is markedly higher than in any other region of Britain. This difference is even more marked for poor readers (score 0–20). For example, for every eighteen poor readers in Scotland there were, proportionately, twenty-nine poor readers in England and thirty in Wales.

The reading test used was essentially a test of word recognition rather than comprehension. However, the superiority in reading of the Scottish children is also evidenced by the fact that the proportion of children in Scotland who had progressed beyond their basic reading scheme was 10 per cent higher than that in England and 12 per cent higher than that in Wales.

What is the explanation of these findings? It does not appear that it is directly related to the general educational approach in Scottish schools since, as we shall see, the Scottish children's arithmetic attainment is lower than that of children in many other regions. Three possible explanations suggest themselves. First, Scottish teachers may place more emphasis on the attainment of fluent reading by the age of seven years than do their English or Welsh colleagues; and their educational programme would be geared to this end. Secondly, the approach to the teaching of reading in Scottish schools may be more effective. Thirdly, some features of the environment in Scottish homes may increase the motivation of children to read or advance their readiness to do so.

There is no evidence in the study which might throw light on the first possibility. However, it does appear that the method of teaching reading in Scottish schools shows a difference in emphasis from that prevailing in England and Wales. In Scotland a systematic phonetic – or phonic – approach is adopted much earlier than in England or Wales. . . . It seems possible that this is at least part of the explanation. It is true that Welsh schools also introduce phonics much earlier than English schools but without apparent advantage. On the other hand, a small proportion of Welsh children at the age of seven would still be having some difficulty with the English language, so that the Welsh children may not have done themselves justice on the test, although some of the teachers translated the test into Welsh to overcome this problem.

Is there any evidence from the interview with parents or elsewhere that factors in the home might be important in this context? One of the questions which was asked of the parents was whether they read to their child. The results show that Scottish parents, both mothers and fathers, more often read to their children than parents in England or Wales. It is interesting to note that this is the case, despite the fact that the Scottish children were already as a group reading fluently. Clearly, then, the Scottish parents were not just reading to their children as a substitute for the children themselves reading, otherwise one might have seen a smaller proportion of Scottish parents reading to their children at this age. This finding supports what must at present be regarded as hearsay evidence that there is in general in Scotland a higher regard for literacy than in England.

The results from the arithmetic test (Figure 7) show a different picture. Here the Scottish children's results are on a par with children from England, when allowance is made for social class. Perhaps the most striking result is the showing of the Welsh children, whose results are better than English or Scottish, particularly if allowance is made for social class differences. This cannot be explained in terms of an early start with formal written arithmetic because the Scottish teachers make an earlier start than those from any other region without any corresponding advantage for the pupils as revealed in this test.

Do the Welsh teachers place more emphasis upon arithmetic skills than their colleagues elsewhere? Or are there relevant factors in the home environment which can account for the findings? At present, these questions must remain unanswered but in an increasingly technological society the answers may have important implications.

The results from the copying designs test indicated that where an ability is likely to be affected by general environmental influences, regional differences will tend to mirror social class differences. The fact that regional differences in educational attainment do not follow this pattern must lead us to look for other explanations. Since the study was not specifically designed to investigate this aspect, our evidence must remain of a somewhat tentative and indirect nature. If the reasons for the differences lie in the kind of emphasis introduced in the classroom, are gains in one direction offset by losses in another? To the extent that differences are a function of community or parental attitudes, it is important to isolate and study these attitudes so

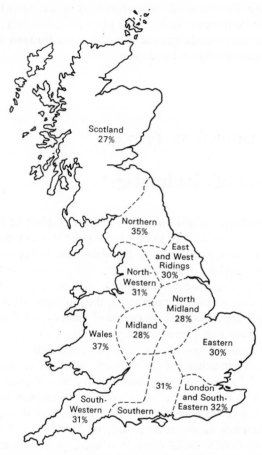

FIGURE 7 *Percentage of children with 'good' arithmetic ability by region and country*

that parents can be made aware of their relevance to children's attainments. Finally, further study may indicate that certain teaching methods are more effective than others.

However, we must remind ourselves again that the children were only seven years old at the time the tests were given. Future follow-ups might reveal changing patterns of regional or national differences. We may find that regional precocity in attainment is ephemeral or else is achieved at the expense of some other facet of development. Even if this should be the case, it may be a price we would be prepared to pay. Given this knowledge, the choice is ours. Without the knowledge, we proceed by trial and error.

DAVID DONNISON (1972)

A pattern of disadvantage*

It has often been pointed out before that the children of poorer and less skilled parents are apt to be handicapped in many ways. It has been pointed out, too, that these handicaps should not be exaggerated: many children from poorer families do very well indeed; meanwhile physical, mental and educational handicaps are also found in middle-class families. Nevertheless, the problems we shall discuss are so often combined and concentrated among poorer people that we must stress these correlations yet again. To consider them as separate handicaps, unrelated to each other and to the deeply rooted inequalities of an urban industrial society, would be to close our eyes to essential features of these problems and the solutions they require. The study, which was not designed to unearth evidence of class differences but only to describe the progress of 16,000 children, shows that those whose parents hold unskilled manual jobs – the Registrar-General's social class V – were, proportionately, more likely than others to:

  be born abnormally early or late
  be abnormally light or short
  have squints, stammers or difficulty in co-ordinating their movements
  be bed wetters or nail biters
  have suppurating ears

* Reprinted from *A Pattern of Disadvantage : a commentary on From Birth to Seven* ed. David Donnison (Windsor, National Foundation for Educational Research, 1972).

come from broken homes
have less well-educated parents.

Society has tried to remedy these handicaps in many ways, yet these children are:

less likely to be immunized or vaccinated
less likely to attend clinics or visit the dentist
less likely to have had physiotherapy
more likely to have parents who are reluctant to consult teachers
more likely to have homes which are overcrowded or lack normal
amenities such as hot water and baths.

Not surprisingly, perhaps, these children are more likely to:

be aggressive and destructive
reject adult standards
be maladjusted
speak unintelligibly and have poor oral ability
have poor general knowledge
be poor readers or poor at arithmetic
be classed as not specially creative
do less well generally at school
or die.

A. H. HALSEY (1972)

Educational priority*

POLITICAL ENDS AND EDUCATIONAL MEANS

To find a strategy for educational roads to equality! That has been a central theme of educational discussion from the beginning of the twentieth century. It has produced a prolific sociology of education

* Reprinted from *Educational Priority* ed. A. H. Halsey (London, HMSO, 1972).

over the last generation in which the centrality of educational systems
to the structure and the functioning of industrial societies has become a commonplace. In the 1950s education in these societies was
seen as having a crucial role for economic growth and change. More
recently the emphasis has shifted to the part played by formal educational organizations in defining what is and what is not knowledge,
and as selective agencies allocating individuals to social positions,
moulding their social personalities and their definitions of the world
around them. But the underlying question is whether, and if so under
what circumstances, education can change society.

The answer, whatever its form, has been controversial in two
apparently different ways. Debate has turned on the *desirability* of
using educational means for political ends. But also, and much more
fruitfully, it has turned on the feasibility of different educational
means towards agreed ends. Thus 'keeping education out of politics'
can be a crude evasion of the incontrovertible fact that, in a modern
or modernizing society, educational arrangements are an important
determinant of the life and livelihood of individuals: education is a
social distributor of life chances. In its more subtle forms, however,
this political or moral stance may be a protest against narrow
definitions of the social consequences of educational reform. As
such it belongs neither to the political right not to the political left.
It is of course associated with such writers as T. S. Eliot, Professor
Bantock and the authors of the Black Papers, but there are equally
important radical criticisms of narrowness in the sociological imagination; for example reform in the direction of meritocracy may fail
to take account of those ramified consequences which Professor
Bernstein has referred to as 'the individualization of failure' and there
is a good deal of current writing from an interactionist or phenom-
enological point of view which insists on the importance of education
as structuring reality for those exposed to it in broader terms than that
associated with a definition of schooling as the agency through
which individuals are allocated to the labour force.

The problem of the entanglement of analysis with value assumptions is intrinsic to sociological study. To get it straight we must first
distinguish the 'scientific' from the 'value' problem: to ask separately
what is possible and thereby, with the issues and alternatives sharply
defined, to decide on preferences and priorities. In this way the

challenge to social science becomes clear and the task for the socio-logist is, literally, to inform the political debate. Of course the distinction between sociology and politics is much less easy than a naïve positivism would presuppose. It is necessary at every step to try to make explicit what are the implicit assumptions of political aims and the value premises of sociological analysis. There is no final or ready-made procedure for either of these tasks. We have only imperfect aids beyond the injunction to constant vigilance.

One aid of particular relevance to our problem in this book can be taken from John Goldthorpe's discussion of futurology.[1] Gold-thorpe distinguishes between futurology as *prediction* and futurology as *design*. Conventional futurology is essentially extrapolation to the future of trends from the recent past. It therefore tends to carry with it the value assumptions of the *status quo* and is in that sense conservative. That is why the book covers of this literature (*USA 2000*) are, as Raymond Aron has remarked, so much more exciting than the pages. The future is only the present, usually writ slightly larger. Futurology as *design* is quite another matter, and not only because it is inherently more radical in its political possibilities. It is scientifically much more challenging in that it directly requires the social scientist to state clearly what he knows or does not know about the possibility of moving from the present state to a postula-ted, presumably desired, future state.

Political aims and programmes in general and the aim of educa-tional equality in particular, together with the various programmes for its attainment, lend themselves fairly readily to translation into futurology as design. The translation can be used to define the critical and constructive role of the social scientist, in this case with relation to the problems of educational reform through political and administrative action. And action-research, as we understand it, is an experimental or quasi-experimental version of futurology as design. Ends are stated together with means to their achievement. In this case the ends are greater social equality of educational opportu-nity and attainment and the means are Plowden's positive discrim-ination for educational priority areas. Ends and means are modified

---

[1] Goldthorpe, 'Theories of industrial society: reflections on the recrudescence of historicism and the future of futurology', *European Journal of Sociology*, XII (1972), pp. 263–88.

and explicated in a programme of action and the relation between them is analysed by research monitoring of the action programme.

A second and related aid to understanding the social science task is the Popperian distinction between holistic and piecemeal reform. The general arguments against holism cannot be rehearsed here. What is relevant however is not a debate over the dichotomy but over the appropriate scale of the piecemeal. It is not so much a question of whether education can change society; it is a question of the level of ambitiousness of social engineering which may be required to change an undesired state of affairs. The Plowden analysis of low educational standards in EPAs points to causes outside the school in the neighbourhood structure of life and therefore calls for a widely based programme of social reform alongside positive discrimination in education. Within this framework Plowden postulates that 'what these deprived areas need most are perfectly normal, good primary schools'. There is in other words a belief here in educational cures for educational evils. Some of the early American compensatory education programmes seem to have gone much further and approached the belief that poverty can be completely abolished through educational reform. Others take an opposing and more radical view of the changes necessary to ameliorate either poverty in general or educational poverty in particular. K. Coates and R. Silburn have expressed this view in a recent comment on the Plowden ideas.

... the schools themselves could become, to a degree, centres of social regeneration: growth points of a new social consciousness among the poor, which might at last bring poverty under attack from its sufferers, no less than from the all-too-small battalions of liberal welfare workers and social administrators.

Obviously many of these are sensible aims. Yet it is important at the same time to state baldly what these aims could *not* achieve. Education, in itself, will not solve the problem of poverty. The social structure that generates poverty generates its own shabby education system to serve it; and while it is useful to attack the symptom, the disease itself will continually find new manifestations if it is not understood and remedied. The solution to poverty involves, of course, the redistribution of effective social power. Self-confidence, no less than material welfare, is a crucial lack of the poor, and both can only be won by effective joint action. More contentiously, it seems to us that educational provision alone cannot solve even the problem of educational poverty, if only because in this sphere there are *no* purely educational problems.[1]

Our own view in undertaking the EPA action-research was cautiously open-minded on the capacity of the educational system to reform itself, dubious about an educational approach to the abolition of poverty, but at least as optimistic as Plowden about the primary school and pre-schooling as points of entry for action-research aimed at inducing changes in the relation between school and community.

In principle action-research can approach the holistic end of the continuum. In practice it usually operates at the other extreme though often with implicit holistic expectations of the kind reflected in the early euphoria and rhetoric of the American Headstart programme. Perhaps it is mainly the confused contradiction between astronomical ends and minuscule means that underlies the asperity of such criticisms as Bernstein's 'education cannot compensate for society'. We have to know what is sociologically and politically possible. In part the answer to both questions turns on the willingness and power of a society to define education imperiously in relation to the other social organizations which carry educative or culturally transmitting functions, especially the family but also classes, neighbourhoods, ethnic groups and local communities. This depends again in part on economic and technical means. Obviously the feasibility of education as the dominant means to a particular social design is eased by wealth and growth, but the crucial factor here is political – the political structure and the will of political leadership.

Perhaps the importance of the economic and technical base for educational development is exaggerated. There are conspicuous variations in the level of educational development between countries of similar income and wealth *per capita*. And the remarkably durable success of classical China in using her educational system to create and maintain a ruling administrative class of mandarins was, it should be remembered, the invention of a pre-industrial society. Perhaps also the serviceability of education as an agent of social

[1] K. Coates and R. Silburn, 'Education in poverty' in David Rubinstein and Colin Stoneman (eds.), *Education for Democracy* (Penguin Education Special, 1970).

selection and distribution is exaggerated until one examines the evidence: for example it was shown in the Robbins Report that two-thirds of *middle-class* children with I Qs of 130+ who were born in 1940–1 did not go on to a university education. Nevertheless it still remains a crucial question as to how seriously a society determines to realize the values in which the use of the educational system as a means is involved. That is the crux of the problem of educational inequality and the ultimate determinant of whether or not Plowden's positive discrimination will bring about its intended effects.

What then, are the sought ends in the politics of education in modern Britain? The dominant slogans are combinations of efficiency and equality. Efficiency for modernity. Equality for efficiency and justice. But both the meaning of these combined ends and the means postulated as adequate to their attainment remain dubious and confused. Thus the combination of equality of educational opportunity with the goal of national efficiency has led to policies designed to create and maintain a meritocracy – a principle which by no means commands universal acceptance.

However the essential fact of twentieth-century educational history is that egalitarian policies have failed. This must be the starting point for understanding the significance of our studies and to reach it we must review past principles and policies. There appears to us to have been a developing theoretical and practical debate in three stages about the way education can be used as a means towards the political and social end of equality.

In the first phase, from the beginning of the century to the end of the 1950s, the definition of policy was liberal – equality of opportunity. It meant equality of access to the more advanced stages of education for all children irrespective of their sex or social origin in classes, religious and ethnic groups or regions. It therefore expressed itself in such measures as building the scholarship ladder, abolishing grammar school fees, doing away with a system of separate secondary education for the minority and elementary education for the majority and substituting a system of common schooling with secondary schools 'end-on' to primary schools. In the later years of this phase it also meant expansion of higher education.

The logical end of the first phase, when equality of opportunity is combined with national efficiency, is meritocracy. In its most advanced educational expression this essentially liberal principle is to be found in the Preface to the Newsom Report written by the then Minister for Education, Sir Edward (later Lord) Boyle: 'The essential point is that all children should have an equal opportunity of acquiring intelligence, and of developing their talents and abilities to the full.' But the inexactitudes of psychometrics, the capriciousness of late developers, the survival of the private market in education along with the continuous renewal of non-educational avenues to higher social positions – all these factors together have prevented the emergence of an educationally based meritocracy.

The liberal notion of equality of opportunity dominated discussion at least until the 1950s. But it was never unchallenged by those who wrote in the tradition of R. H. Tawney and it was effectively lampooned in Michael Young's *Rise of the Meritocracy*. Writers like Tawney and Raymond Williams always sought for an educational system which would be egalitarian in the much broader sense of providing a common culture irrespective of the more or less inescapable function of selection for different occupational destinies. There is a broad distinction of political and social aims here which, in the end, come to the most fundamental issue of the purposes of education in an urban industrial society and about which judgements are explicitly or implicitly made in any action-research programme of the type we have undertaken. One way of putting the distinction is that the liberal goal of efficient equality of opportunity is too restrictive: we have also to consider liberty and fraternity. Properly conceived the community school . . . reflects the attribution of value to these other two great abstractions of the modern trilogy of political aims.

All this is to say nothing about the problems of feasibility of either narrowly or broadly conceived egalitarian aims. Tawney took it for granted that the processes of parliamentary democracy, serviced by the British type of civil administration, would be adequate as means to these ends. There is less confidence now and much more questioning as to what it might mean politically to achieve what Coates and Silburn have referred to as 'the redistribution of effective social power'. Questioning of this kind comes from many sources, but not least from recognition of the failures of past policies directed towards a greater equality of educational opportunity.

The essential judgement must be that the 'liberal' policies failed even in their own terms. For example, when, in a large number of the richer countries during the 1950s, a considerable expansion of educational facilities was envisaged, it was more or less assumed that, by making more facilities available, there would be a marked change in the social composition of student bodies and in the flow of people from the less favoured classes into the secondary schools and higher educational institutions. This has certainly not happened to the degree expected. While expansion of education was accompanied by some increase in both the absolute numbers and the proportions from poor families who reached the higher levels and the more prestigious types of education, nevertheless progress towards greater equality of educational opportunity as traditionally defined has been disappointing. It is now plain that the problem is more difficult than had been supposed and needs, in fact, to be posed in new terms.

Too much has been claimed for the power of educational systems as instruments for the wholesale reform of societies which are characteristically hierarchical in their distribution of chances in life as between races, classes, the sexes and as between metropolitan/suburban and provincial/rural populations. The typical history of educational expansion in the 1950s and 1960s can be represented by a graph of inequality of attainment between the above-mentioned social categories which has shifted markedly upwards without changing its slope. In other words relative chances did not alter materially despite expansion. No doubt, the higher norms of educational attainment contributed something towards raising the quality of life in urban industrial society – that, at least, is the faith of the educationist. But in terms of relative chances of income, status and welfare at birth, the impact of the educational system on the life of children remained heavily determined by their family and class origins. From the same point of view, what appears to have happened was a general adjustment of the occupational structure such that entry to it was in process of continuous upward redefinition in terms of educational qualifications. The traditional social pattern of selection remained remarkably stable. The school is only one influence among others, and, in relation to the phenomenon of social stratification, probably a fairly minor one. Attitudes towards schooling, and actual performance in school, reflect children's general social milieu and family background, and, probably most important of all, the expectations, built in by constraining custom, of their teachers. School reform helps but the improvement of teacher/pupil ratios, the building of new schools and even the provision of a wider variety of curricula have at best a limited effect as counterweights.

Moreover there has been a tendency to treat education as the waste paper basket of social policy – a repository for dealing with social problems where solutions are uncertain or where there is disinclination to wrestle with them seriously. Such problems are prone to be dubbed 'educational' and turned over to the schools to solve. But it was now increasingly plain that the schools cannot accomplish important social reforms such as the democratization of opportunity unless social reforms accompany the educational effort. And it also became more evident that the schools are hampered in achieving even their more traditional and strictly 'educational' purposes when, in societies changing rapidly in their technologies and in the aspirations of their populations, a comparable effort to make the required change in social structures and political organization is lacking.

In summary, it may be said that liberal policies failed basically on an inadequate theory of learning. They failed to notice that the major determinants of educational attainment were not schoolmasters but social situations, not curriculum but motivation, not formal access to the school but support in the family and the community.

So the second phase began with its new emphasis on a theory of non-educational determination of education. In consequence of the experience of the first phase in trying to bring about greater equality of educational opportunity, there had to be a change in the meaning assigned to the phase. Its earlier meaning was equality of access to education: in the second phase its meaning gradually became equality of achievement. In this new interpretation a society affords equality of educational opportunity if the proportion of people from different social, economic or ethnic categories at all levels and in all types of education are more or less the same as the proportion of these people in the population at large. In other words the goal should not be the liberal one of equality of access but equality of outcome for the median member of each identifiable non-educationally defined group, i.e. the *average* woman or negro or proletarian or rural dweller should have the same level of educational attainment as the

350   A. H. HALSEY

average male, white, white-collar, suburbanite. If not there has been injustice.

This important social-cum-educational principle, with its radical implications for both social and educational policies, was graphically illustrated in the findings of the American Coleman Report[1] where educational attainments were compared as between northerners and southerners of white and non-white race. The graph below shows that schooling between ages six and eighteen (grades 1–12 in American schools) is associated with a divergence of the mean attainment of four categories of children who are not directly defined in educational terms. The radical goal of educational equality of opportunity would, if realized, produce converging as opposed to diverging lines.

The Plowden Report belongs to this phase in the development of our understanding of the egalitarian issues in education and relates them to the social setting of the school.

With Plowden the close relationship of social deprivation, in neighbourhood and home, and educational attainment was well-founded in research. Equally valid is the corollary that, if social con-

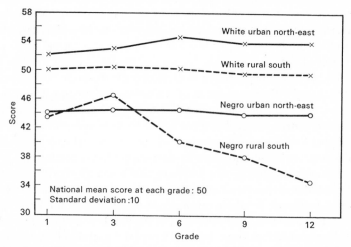

FIGURE 1 *Patterns of achievement in verbal skills at various grade levels by race and region*

[1] James S. Coleman *et al.*, *Equality of Educational Opportunity* (US Government Printing Office, Washington DC, 1966).

ditions and parental interest could be improved, achievement might be expected to rise. One or two examples must suffice. J. W. B. Douglas in 1964 set the attainment scores of a large sample of upper primary children against a number of social factors. From this survey certain extreme cases might be extrapolated. At eleven years of age and with 50 as the average mark, lower manual working-class children in unsatisfactory housing were scoring on average 46·66 as against the 56·91 of upper-middle-class children in satisfactory accommodation; as between the same groups divided by low and high levels of parental interest the scores were 46·32 and 59·26; polarized by 'very disturbed' and 'undisturbed' assessments, the two groups averaged 44·49 and 57·53; while the seventh child of the lower bracket of parents obtained 42·19 over against the 59·87 of the first child in the higher social category. Eleven per cent of the lower manual group and 54·3 per cent of the upper middle group obtained grammar school places. Only 4·8 per cent of the children in a poorly assessed lower-working-class school as opposed to 53·22 per cent of those in a highly assessed upper-middle-class school obtained places in grammar schools. Just below the cut-off point for selection, 1·4 per cent only of the 'lower manual' children and as many as 42·9 per cent of 'upper middle' children were in grammar, technical or independent schools.

These admittedly are deliberately extracted extremes, but the EPA projects were planned to consider one of these extremes. A very disturbed child of unskilled parents, who showed no interest in his schooling and who lived in unsatisfactory accommodation was, for example, no rarity in Liverpool 7. In 1967, the Ministry of Social Security reported that 7 per cent of families were at or below the poverty line. Either figure would include a large number of the study area's population; indeed, in 1968, the Merseyside Child Poverty Action Group found that one in three in Liverpool 8 were living in poverty as defined by the Ministry of Social Security, while, in 1971, the Child Poverty Action Group claimed that one in every six children in the nation was on or below the poverty line.

Professor Wiseman argued convincingly that '"home" variables have, pro rata, twice the weight of "neighbourhood" and "school" variables put together' when correlated with educational attainment.[1]

[1] S. Wiseman, 'The Manchester survey', appendix 9, *Plowden Report*, ii.

o

His research indicated that it was parental attitudes rather than social levels which were more important in the home. Again, the National Child Development Study showed that parents in the highest occupational grouping were much readier to initiate school contacts than those in the lowest grouping, and there was a similar social gap in terms of adjustment to school.[2] A recent examination of truancy suggests that gross absenteeism is solidly linked with unsatisfactory home life and uninterested parents.[3]

We are not here, it must be added, embracing the view that the pre-Plowden literature had over-emphasized the part played by class in determining educational performance. On the contrary we agree with the sociological critique of the Plowden Report by B. Bernstein and B. Davies, in which they expressed the view that, by its concentration on child centredness, Plowden had underestimated class distinctions. As these writers argue, 'evidence suggests a strong relationship between social class and the extent of the mother's preparation of her child for school' and that 'one would wish to guard against an argument that avoided including attitudes as a dimension of class differences'.

GODFREY HODGSON (1973)

Inequality: do schools make a difference?*

Since the days of Horace Mann and John Dewey – indeed since the days of Thomas Jefferson, that child of the enlightenment – education – has occupied a special place in the optimistic vision of American progressives, and of many American conservatives, for that matter. As the historian David Potter pointed out in *People of Plenty*, the American Left, encouraged by the opportunities of an unexhausted

[2] 1st Report of the National Child Development Study (1958 Cohort), April 1966, appendix 10, *Plowden Report*, ii, *Research and Surveys*, 1967.
[3] M. J. Tyerman, *Truancy*, University of London Press, 1968.
* Reprinted from the *Atlantic Monthly* (March 1973).

continent and by the experience of economic success, has always differed sharply from the European Left in that it has generally assumed that social problems could be resolved out of incremental growth; that is, that the life of the have-nots could be made tolerable without taking anything from the haves.

Education has always seemed one of the most acceptable ways of using the national wealth to provide opportunity for the poor without offending the comfortable. As a tool of reform, education had the advantage that it appealed to the ideology of conservatives, to that ethic of self-improvement which stretches back down the American tradition through Horatio Alger and McGuffey's *Readers* to Benjamin Franklin himself. This was particularly true in the age of the Great Migration. The public school systems of New York and other cities with large immigrant populations really did provide a measure of equality of opportunity to the immigrant poor. By the time the New Deal coalition was formed (and educators of one sort and another were to be a significant part of that coalition), these assumptions about education were deeply rooted. And they were powerfully reinforced, and virtually certified with the authority of social science, by the Supreme Court's 1954 desegregation decision in *Brown v The School Board of Topeka*.

When, in the late 1930s and the 1940s, the National Association for the Advancement of Coloured People, its lawyers, and its allies began to go to court to lay siege to segregation, they deliberately, and wisely, chose education as the field of attack. This was not accidental: they well knew that education was so firmly associated with equality in the public mind that it would be an easier point of attack than, say, public accommodations or housing.

In *Brown*, the N A A C P's lawyers deployed social science evidence in support of their contention that segregated education was inherently unequal, citing especially work done by psychologists Kenneth and Mamie Clark with black children and black and white dolls. The Clarks' conclusions were that segregation inflicts psychological harm.

The historical accident of the circumstances in which school segregation came to be overthrown by the Supreme Court contributed to the currency of what turned out to be a shaky assumption. The great majority of American liberals, and this included large numbers of judges, Democratic politicians and educators, came to suppose that there was incontrovertible evidence in the findings of social science to prove, not just that segregated education was unequal, but that if you wanted to achieve equality, education could do it for you.

Then a contemporary development put education right at the centre of the political stage. President Johnson's 'Great Society' was to be achieved without alienating the power structure and, above all, the Congress. Education was an important part of the Great Society strategy from the start, but as other approaches to reducing poverty and racial inequality, notably 'community action', ran into political opposition, they fell apart, and so the proportional emphasis on educational programmes in the Great Society scheme grew. In the end the Johnson Administration, heavily committed to reducing inequality, was almost equally committed to education as one of the principal ways to do it.

Each of the events and historical developments sketched here increased the shock effect of the Coleman report – once its conclusions were understood. A handful of social scientists had indeed hinted, before Coleman, that the effect of schools on equality of opportunity might have been exaggerated. But such work had simply made no dent in the almost universal assumption to the contrary.

James Coleman, Professor of social relations at Johns Hopkins, himself has confessed he does not know exactly why Congress, in section 402 of the Civil Rights Act of 1964, ordered the Commissioner of Education to conduct a survey 'concerning the lack of availability of equal educational opportunities for individuals by reason of race, colour, religion or national origin'. The most likely reason is that Congress thought it was setting out to document the obvious in order to arm the Administration with a public relations bludgeon to overcome opposition. Certainly James Coleman took it for granted that his survey would find gross differences in the quality of the schools that black and white children went to. 'The study will show', he predicted in an interview more than half-way through the job, 'the difference in the quality of schools that the average Negro child and the average white child are exposed to. You know yourself that the difference is going to be striking.'

He was exactly wrong. Coleman was staggered – in the word of one of his associates – to find the *lack* of difference. When the results were in, from about 600,000 children and 60,000 teachers in roughly 4,000 schools, when they had been collected and collated and computed, and sifted with regression analysis and all the other refinements of statistical science, they were astonishing. A writer in *Science* called them 'a spear pointed at the heart of the cherished American belief that equality of educational opportunity will increase the equality of educational achievements'.

What did the figures say? Christopher Jencks (Associate Professor at the Harvard Graduate School of Education) later picked out four major points:

1 Most black and white Americans attended different schools.
2 Despite popular impressions to the contrary, the physical facilities, the formal curricula, and most of the measurable characteristics of teachers in black and white schools were quite similar.
3 Despite popular impressions to the contrary, measured differences in schools' physical facilities, formal curricula and teacher characteristics had very little effect on either black or white students' performance on standardized tests.
4 The one school characteristic that showed a consistent relationship to test performance was the one characteristic to which poor black children were denied access: classmates from affluent homes.

Here is how James Coleman himself summed up the 737 pages of his report (not to mention the additional 548 pages of statistical explanation):

Children were tested at the beginning of grades 1, 3, 6, 9 and 12. Achievement of the average American Indian, Mexican American, Puerto Rican, and Negro (in this descending order) was much lower than the average white or Oriental American, at all grade levels ... the differences are large to begin with, and they are even larger at higher grades. Two points, then, are clear: these minority children have a serious educational deficiency at the start of school, which is obviously not a result of school; and they have an even more serious deficiency at the end of school, which is obviously in part a result of school.

Coleman added that the survey showed that most of the variation in student achievement lay within the same school, and very little of it was between schools. Family background – whatever that might mean – must, he concluded, account for far more of the variation in achievement than differences between schools. Moreover, such differences as *could* be attributed to the schools seemed to result more from the social environment (Jencks's 'affluent classmates', and also teachers) than from the quality of the school itself.

This was the most crucial point. For if quality were measured, as it had tended to be measured by administrators and educational reformers alike, in material terms, then the quality of the school, on Coleman's data, counted for virtually nothing.

When other things were equal, the report said, factors such as the amount of money spent per pupil, or the number of books in the library, or physical facilities such as gymnasiums or cafeterias or laboratories, or even differences in the curriculum, seemed to make no appreciable difference to the children's level of achievement. Nothing could have more flatly contradicted the assumptions on which the administration in Washington, and urban school boards across the country, were pouring money into compensatory education programmes.

As we shall see, the report exploded with immense force underground, sending seismic shocks through the academic and bureaucratic worlds of education. But on the surface the shock was not at first apparent. There were two main reasons for this. The first was that the report was, after all, long, tough, dry and technical. It had been written in five months in order to comply with a congressional deadline, and it therefore made no attempt to point a moral or adorn a tale; it was essentially a mass of data.

The Office of Education, which realized all too clearly how explosive the report was, did not exactly trumpet the news to the world. The report was released, by a hallowed bureaucratic stratagem, on the eve of 4 July 1966. Few reporters care to spend that holiday gutting 737 pages of regression analysis and standard deviations. And to head off those few who might have been tempted to make the effort if they guessed that there was a good story at the end of it, the Office of Education put out a summary report which can only be described as misleading. 'Nationally', it said, to take one example

'Negroes have fewer of some of the facilities that seem most related to academic achievement.' That was true. But it was not the significant truth. The point was that the gap was far smaller than anyone expected it to be.

A few attempts were made to discredit the survey. But the Coleman findings were in greater danger of being ignored than of being controverted when, at the beginning of the academic year in the fall of 1966, Pat Moynihan began to apply his talents to make sure that the report should not be ignored. He and Professor Thomas Pettigrew of the Harvard School of Education organized a seminar on the Equality of Educational Opportunity Report (SEEOR). The seminar met every week at the Harvard Faculty Club, and by the end more than eighty people had taken part.

'When I was at the School of Education ten years ago,' Jencks says, 'almost nobody who was literate was interested in education. The educational sociologists and psychologists, the educational economists, they were all pretty near the bottom of the heap. Suddenly that's changed.' People started coming up to Moynihan in Harvard Yard and asking if they could take part: statisticians, economists, pediatricians. Education had become fashionable.

If schools, as Seymour Martin Lipset paraphrased Coleman, 'make no difference', what could explain the inequalities of achievement in school and afterwards? One school of thought was ready and waiting in the wings with an answer. In the winter of 1969, the following words appeared in an article in the *Harvard Educational Review*:

> There is an increasing realization among students of the psychology of the disadvantaged that the discrepancy in their average performance cannot be completely or directly attributed to discrimination or inequalities in education. It seems not unreasonable, in view of the fact that intelligence variation has a large genetic component, to hypothesize that genetic factors may play a part in this picture.

The author was Professor Arthur Jensen, not a Harvard man, but an educational psychologist from Berkeley with a national reputation. He had jabbed his finger at the rawest, most sensitive spot in the entire system of liberal thinking about education and equality in

America. For after more than a generation of widespread I Q testing, it is an experimental finding, beloved of racists and profoundly disconcerting to liberals, that while the average white I Q is 100 the average black I Q is 85. Racists have seen in this statistical finding confirmation of a theory of innate biological inferiority. Conservatives have seen in it an argument against heavy expenditure on education, and against efforts to desegregate. And liberals have retorted that the lower average performance of blacks is due either to cultural bias in the tests used or to unfavourable environmental factors which require redoubled efforts on the part of social policy makers.

Jensen marched straight into the fiercest of this cross fire. He argued two propositions in particular in his article: that research findings suggest that heredity explains more of the differences in I Q between individuals than does environment, and that heredity accounts for the differences between the average I Qs of groups as well as between those of individuals.

The article was scholarly in tone. In form it was largely a recital of research data. And it was tentative in its conclusion that perhaps more of the differential between blacks' and whites' average I Qs was due to heredity than to environment. That did not stop it from causing a most formidable rumpus. It became a ninety days' wonder in the press and the news magazines. It was discussed at a Cabinet meeting. And Students for a Democratic Society rampaged around the Berkeley campus chanting 'Fight racism! Fire Jensen!'

Two years later, a long article in *The Atlantic* by Professor Richard Herrnstein on the history and implications of I Q provoked a reaction which showed that the sensitivity of the issue had by no means subsided. Herrnstein touched only gingerly on the racial issue. 'Although there are scraps of evidence for a genetic component in the black-white difference,' he wrote, 'the overwhelming case is for believing that American blacks have been at an environmental disadvantage . . . a neutral commentator (a rarity these days) would have to say that the case is simply not settled, given our present stage of knowledge.'

Neutral commentators certainly proved rare among those who wrote in to the editor; Arthur Jensen wrote to say that Herrnstein's essay was 'the most accurately informative psychological article I have ever read in the popular press'; while a professor from the University of Connecticut said: 'This is not new, Hitler's propagandists

used the same tactics in the thirties while his metal workers put the
the finishing touches on the gas ovens.'

If Herrnstein, understandably enough, tiptoed cautiously around
the outskirts of the black-white IQ argument, he charged boldly
enough into another part of the field. The closer society came to its
ideal of unimpeded upward social mobility, the closer he predicted
it would come to 'meritocracy', a visionary state of society described
by the British sociologist Michael Young. A new upper class composed of the descendants of the most successful competitors with the
highest IQs would defend its own advantage far more skilfully and
successfully than did the old aristocracies. Herrnstein did not welcome this trend: he merely argued that it might be inevitable. 'Our
society may be sorting itself willy-nilly into inherited castes,' he concluded gloomily.

If differences in the quality of schools, as measured by money,
facilities and curricula do not explain inequality, because the differences between the schools attended by children of different racial
groups are simply not that great in those respects, then what does?
Genetic differentials in IQ, perhaps, says Jensen. Nonsense, says a
majority of the educational community: the explanation is more likely
to be integration – or rather the lack of it.

The Coleman report gave only three pages to the effects of desegregation, and Tom Pettigrew did not think that was enough. At
Jim Coleman's explicit insistence, the data bank of the survey was to
be made generally available for the cost of the computer tapes. Pettigrew persuaded the Civil Rights Commission to take advantage of
this and to reanalyse the data to see what light it cast on the effects
of desegregation. David Cohen and Pettigrew were the main authors
of the resulting survey, which came out in 1967 as *Racial Isolation in
the Public Schools* and gave the impression that the Coleman data
supported desegregation. This was true up to a point. Coleman had
concluded that desegregation did have an effect. But his report
also showed that social class had a greater effect. Pettigrew is not
much troubled by this, because of the close connection between
race and social class in the United States. 'Two-thirds of the whites
are middle class', he says, 'and two-thirds of the blacks are working
class.'

Pettigrew also draws a sharp distinction between desegregation and integration. By integration he means an atmosphere of genuine acceptance and friendly respect across racial lines, and he believes that mere desegregation will not help blacks to do better in school until this kind of atmosphere is achieved. He is impressed by the work of Professor Irwin Katz, who has found that black children do best in truly integrated situations, moderately well in all-black situations, and worst of all in 'inter-racial situations characterized by stress and threat'.

Pettigrew believes, in other words, that integration, as opposed to mere desegregation, will be needed to bring black children's achievement up to equality with whites'. And he argues that no one can say that integration has not worked, for the simple reason that it has not been tried.

The Civil Rights Commission's report on racial isolation did recommend that the federal government set a national standard that no black children should go to a school that was more than 50 per cent black. In practical terms, that meant bussing. And, in fact, Pettigrew argues that some bussing will be needed to achieve desegregation – and thus to produce the physical circumstances in which integration as he understands it can take place. He has been actively involved as a witness in several desegregation suits in which he has advocated bussing.

It is, therefore, as Pettigrew himself wryly remarks, an irony that he should have suggested to one of his junior colleagues at the Harvard School of Education that he do a study on bussing. The colleague's name was David Armor, and Pettigrew's idea was that it would be interesting to take a look at Project Metco, a scheme for bussing children out of Roxbury, the main Boston ghetto, into nearby white suburban schools.

That was in 1969. Three years later, a paper by David Armor called 'The evidence on bussing' was published in *The Public Interest*. Armor said he had concentrated on the question of whether 'induced integration' – that is, bussing – 'enhances black achievement, self-esteem, race relations, and opportunities for higher education'. In a word, Armor maintained that it did not.

The article used data not only from Project Metco but from reports of four other northern programmes for induced integration: in White Plains, New York; Ann Arbor, Michigan; Riverside, California; and New Haven and Hartford, Connecticut. And on the basis of this data, Armor maintained that 'the available evidence . . . indicates that bussing is *not* an effective policy instrument for raising the achievement of blacks or for increasing interracial harmony'.

As for race relations, Armor found the bussed students not only more militant but actually more hostile to integration than the study's 'control group', which was not bussed. Militancy, as measured, for example, by sympathy with the Black Panthers, seemed to be particularly rife among those children who had high aspirations (such as going to college) but were getting C grades or below in competitive suburban high schools.

But Armor did not limit himself to reporting the results of his own Metco study and the other four studies. His article was a sweeping, slashing attack on the whole tradition of liberal social science.

It was not likely that such an attack would go unanswered and, in fact, the response was both swift and severe. Pettigrew and three colleagues fired back a critique which called Armor's article 'a distorted and incomplete review'. To back up their charge, they argued that the studies Armor had cited as '*the* evidence on bussing' were highly selective. Armor had not discussed seven other studies which they said met his own methodological criteria – from New York, Buffalo, Rochester, Newark, Philadelphia, Sacramento and North Carolina – surveys which had reported positive achievement results for bussed blacks. The integrationists also found what they claimed were disastrous weaknesses in Armor's own Metco study.

'We respect Dr Armor's right to publish his views against mandatory bussing,' they said, 'But we challenge his claim that those views are based on scientific evidence.'

If the tone of the public controversy sounds rough, it was positively courtly compared to the atmosphere inside William James Hall, the new Harvard high-rise where Pettigrew and Armor had their offices, two doors apart. . . .

To an unbiased eye ('a rarity these days', as Richard Herrnstein might say), Armor's paper has been rather seriously impugned. It does not follow that his central thesis is entirely discredited. Even Pettigrew was quoted, at the height of the row, as saying that 'nobody is claiming that integration has been a raving success'. 'That's not what they were saying before', says Moynihan. And Christopher Jencks, who can hardly be accused of conservative prejudice, has summed up the evidence in the most cautious and equivocal way. Blacks, he says, might do much better in 'truly integrated schools, whatever they may be'.

Jencks himself thinks that desegregation is probably necessary, simply in order to meet the constitutional requirements of the Fourteenth Amendment, in virtually every urban school district in the country. He does, however, have personal reservations about mandatory bussing, on libertarian grounds. That is not to say that he has any tenderness toward segregation. On the contrary, he rejects it as absolutely as any of the integrationists. The difference is that Jencks does not think that segregation explains nearly as much of existing inequality as the integrationists think it does.

But with Armor's paper and its reception, we are getting ahead of the story. The Coleman report came out in 1966. It was not until 1972 that two major books appeared, each an attempt to reassess the whole question of the relationship between education and equality in the United States in the light of the Coleman data. Each was collaborative.

The first of these two books was the Random House collection of papers arising out of the SEEOR seminar, which was published as *On Equality of Educational Opportunity*, with Frederick Mosteller (professor of mathematical statistics at Harvard) and Daniel Patrick Moynihan as co-editors. Most of the leading participants in the debate contributed chapters.

Later in the year, Christopher Jencks and seven of his colleagues (two of whom, Marshall Smith and David Cohen, had also contributed to the Mosteller-Moynihan volume) published an only slightly less massive book: *Inequality: a reassessment of the effect of family and schooling in America*. This work displays considerably more intellectual cohesion than the Mosteller-Moynihan book, presumably because Jencks actually wrote his group's text himself from start to finish and according to the preface, it 'embodies his prejudices and obsessions, and these are not shared by all the authors'. But again, though the book draws upon data from dozens of other large and small-scale surveys, the data from the Coleman survey are the bedrock and foundation.

The enormous body of analysis and reinterpretation in these two books represents the completion of the first stage of the reaction to Coleman. A hasty shorthand for Coleman's central discovery is: 'schools make no difference.' Here Professor Pettigrew draws an important distinction. 'Never once was it said that schools make no difference. The belief that Coleman hit was the belief that you could make a difference with money.' However that may be, the nub of the discovery that has set off the whole prolonged, disturbing, confusing, sometimes bitter debate can be expressed as a simple syllogism:

The 'quality' of the schools attended by black and white children in the United States was more nearly equal than anyone supposed; the gap between the achievement of black and white children got wider not narrower over twelve years at school; therefore there was no reason to suppose that increasing the flow of resources into the schools would affect the outcome in terms of achieving, let alone eliminating inequality.

Among the social scientists, the central ground of debate about the meaning of those findings now lies between Jencks and Moynihan. It is a strange debate, for the two protagonists have much in common, even if one does have New Left loyalties, and the other served in Nixon's White House and now as Nixon's Ambassador to India. Both use the same data. Indeed, the spectacle of social scientists reaching into the same data bank for ammunition to fire at each other is sometimes reminiscent of war between two legs of the same octopus. Both agree on many of the implications of the data, and on many of the conclusions to be drawn from them.

Perhaps the very heart of their disagreement, after all, comes down to a matter of temperament. Pat Moynihan looked at the Coleman data and made the very reasonable inference that, if the differences in quality between the schools attended by different groups of children in the United States were so much smaller than everyone had expected to find them, then the United States had come much closer to realizing the goal of equality of educational opportunity than most people realized. He then chose to relate this to the general question of social optimism versus social pessimism. At the time of the Coleman report's publication, 'a certain atmosphere of "cultural despair"' was gathering in the nation,' they wrote, 'and has since been more in evidence. Some would say more in order. We simply disagree with such despair.'

One of the specific recommendations of the Mosteller-Moynihan essay is optimism. The electorate should maintain the pressure on government and school boards, the essay urges, 'with an attitude that optimistically expects gains, but, knowing their rarity, appreciates them when they occur'. Yet on examination this is a strange use of the word optimism. For optimism normally connotes an attitude toward the future. But the emotion that is being evoked here has more to do with the past: it is not optimism so much as pride.

In an article in the autumn 1972 issue of *The Public Interest*, Moynihan spells out what he means. The argument is characteristically simple, forceful and provocative.

Proposition 1: 'The most striking aspect of educational expenditure is how large it has become.' It has now reached $1,000 per pupil per annum, and it has been rising at 9·7 per cent annually for the last ten years, while the gap has risen 6·8 per cent.

Proposition 2 (the Coleman point): maybe not much learning takes place in a school without teachers or a roof. But 'after a point school expenditure does not seem to have any notable influence on school achievement.'

There are, Moynihan concedes, considerable regional, class, racial and ethnic variations in achievement, and he would like to see them disappear. 'But it is simply not clear that school expenditure is the heart of the matter.'

This is where the production function, or what is more familiar to laymen as the law of diminishing returns, comes in, according to Moynihan. The liberal faith held that expenditure of resources on education would produce not merely a greater equality in scholastic achievement, but greater equality in society. On the contrary, says Moynihan, additional expenditure on education (and indeed on certain other social policies) is likely to produce greater *inequality*, at least of income.

'Any increase in school expenditure', Moynihan wrote in *The Public Interest*, 'will in the first instance accrue to teachers, who receive about 68 per cent of the operating expenditure of elementary and secondary schools. That these are estimable and deserving persons none should doubt' – Brutus is an honourable man – 'but neither should there be any illusion that they are deprived. Increasing educational expenditures will have the short-run effect of income inequality.'

As a matter of statistical fact, that may be literally true. But it is a peculiar argument nonetheless, for several reasons. For teachers are not, relatively, a highly paid group.

It is worth noting that this position fits oddly with an exhortation to optimism. There is indeed nothing sinful about taking satisfaction in past progress; but when this attitude is combined with scepticism about the benefits to be expected from future public expenditure, it is usually called not optimistic but conservative.

Like Moynihan, Christopher Jencks is concerned with equality, not only in the schools but also in the world after school. The essence, and the originality, of his thinking lie in the use he makes of two crucial, though in themselves unoriginal, distinctions.

The first distinction is between equality of opportunity and equality of condition. Most Americans say they are in favour of equality. But what most of them mean by this is equality of opportunity. What we have learned from the Coleman report, says Jencks, and from the fate of the reforms of the 1960s, is that contrary to the conventional wisdom, you cannot have equality of opportunity without a good deal of equality of condition – now and not in the hereafter.

This is where the second of Jencks's distinctions comes in. Where the Coleman survey, and most of the work published in the Mosteller-Moynihan volume, looked at the degree of equality between *groups*, Jencks is more interested in inequality between individuals.

It is cause for shock, he says in the preface to his book, 'that white workers earn 50 per cent more than black workers'. But it is a good deal more shocking 'that the best-paid fifth of all white workers earn 600 per cent more than the worst-paid fifth. From this point of view, racial inequality looks almost insignificant' by comparison with economic inequality.

If Moynihan's instinct is to emphasize the real progress that has been made toward reducing inequality in America, Jencks stresses how much inequality remains, not only in educational opportunity, in learning skills and in educational credentials but also in job status, in job satisfaction and in income.

The trouble is, he points out – and here I am summarizing an argument which is based, step by step, on mountains of statistical data – that whatever measure you take – income, socio-economic status or education – there is plenty of inequality among Americans. But the same people by no means always come out at the same point on each measure. In the social scientists' terms, these different kinds of inequality do not correlate very closely. It follows that school reform is not likely to effect much greater equality outside the school. The 'factory model', which assumes that the school's outcome is the direct product of its inputs, must be abandoned, says Jencks. For him, a school is in reality more like a family than a factory.

This idea underlies a surprising strand in Jencks's thought. If there is not direct correlation between expenditure on schools and effects on society – for example, in producing greater equality between racial groups – some would draw the lesson that it is not worth spending more than a (possibly quite high) minimum on schools. No, says Jencks, spend more money; not because of the benefits it will bring in some sociological hereafter but simply because people spend something close to a fifth of their life in school, and it is better that they spend that time in a pleasant and comfortable environment.

'There is no evidence', Jencks writes, 'that building a school playground will affect the students' chances of learning to read, getting into college, or earning $50,000 a year when they are 50. Building a playground may, however, have a considerable effect on the students' chances of having a good time during recess when they are eight.'

Fourteen words from the end of his book Jencks unfurls a word which startles many of his readers. 'If we want to move beyond this tradition, we will have to establish political control over the economic institutions that shape our society. That is what other countries usually call socialism. Anything less will end in the same disappointment as the reforms of the 1960s.'

The post-Coleman challenge to the case for spending money on education is beginning to echo through the halls of Congress, ominously for the supporters of federal aid to education.

Education lobbyists claim that the 'Jencks report' has been freely cited by the Nixon Administration's Office of Management and Budget on Capitol Hill in justification of the cuts in the fiscal 1974 budget. And even in some of the more conservative governors' offices, one lobbyist for elementary and secondary education told me, there is a widespread feeling that 'Coleman and Jencks' have the effect of giving education a low priority.

Money is one issue; integration is another. Even though a majority of the social scientists who have spoken up remains integrationist, there is no mistaking the chill which the Armor paper, supported as it has been to some extent by various influential figures in the intellectual community, has sent down the spines of the integrationists. . . .

What can be said, at the end of the first stage of the reception of the Coleman doctrine is that – whether you believe with Daniel Patrick Moynihan that liberal education policies of the past few generations have succeeded so well that they have run into diminishing returns, or with Christopher Jencks, that they have proved disappointing – those policies, and the intellectual assumptions on which they were built are in bad trouble. They have lost support in the ranks of the social scientists who provided the United States from Roosevelt to Johnson with a major part of its operating ideology.

Index